DOING

BUSINESS

WITH THE

DICTATORS

DOING

BUSINESS

WITH THE

DICTATORS

A POLITICAL HISTORY
OF UNITED FRUIT
IN GUATEMALA
1899–1944

PAUL J. DOSAL

A Scholarly Resources Inc. Imprint
Wilmington, Delaware

The paper used in this publication meets the minimum requirements of the American National Standard for permanence of paper for printed library materials, Z39.48, 1984.

©1993 by Scholarly Resources Inc.
First published in 1993
Printed and bound in the United States of America

Scholarly Resources Inc.
104 Greenhill Avenue
Wilmington, DE 19805-1897

Library of Congress Cataloging-in-Publication Data

Dosal, Paul J. (Paul Jaime), 1960–
    Doing business with the dictators : a political history of United Fruit
in Guatemala, 1899–1944 / by Paul J. Dosal.
        p.   cm. — (Latin American silhouettes)
    Includes bibliographical references and index.
    ISBN 0-8420-2475-1
    1. Banana trade—Guatemala—History. 2. United Fruit Company—
Guatemala—History. 3. Banana trade—Guatemala—Political activity.
4. Guatemala—Politics and government—1821–. I. Title. II. Series.
HD9259.B3G834   1993
338.7'634772'097281—dc20   93-10118
                                                                  CIP

I dedicate this book to Mom, Dad, and Abuela Eva

About the Author

Paul J. Dosal has been an assistant professor of Latin American history at the University of Massachusetts, Amherst, since 1987. In 1982 he received a bachelor's degree in international politics from St. Andrew's College in North Carolina. He did his graduate work at Tulane University under the direction of Dr. Ralph Lee Woodward, Jr., earning a master's in Latin American studies in 1984 and a doctorate in history in 1987. His articles have appeared in the *Hispanic American Historical Review*, the *Canadian Journal of Latin American and Caribbean Studies*, and *Inter-American Economic Affairs*.

Contents

Acknowledgments

When I initiated research on this project, I had no intention of writing a book about the United Fruit Company. I was only going to revise my dissertation on the industrial development of Guatemala by adding some information about the building of railroads. Research on railroads led me directly into an investigation of United Fruit, and, as I pursued that topic, I realized that we know surprisingly little about the company's history prior to the Guatemalan Revolution (1944–1954). While in Thailand, Amy Yeostros convinced me to postpone my original research plan and write a history of United Fruit in Guatemala.

It took me another two years to write the manuscript. The debts I have incurred along the way are not financial, for this project has been completed on my own time with my own money. Nevertheless, I owe a number of people for their kind assistance. My parents have supported me throughout my college career, and, for their love and inspiration, I dedicate this book to them. Michael, Duane, and Darlene have been more than siblings, while John, Ross, Mike, and Valerie have been more than friends. Amy, my dearest companion over the last four years, would not care for a sentimental acknowledgment and deserves more than that anyway. In ways often unrelated to my professional career, my friends and family supported my work and travel, even as it took me farther away from home.

I have had the benefit of exceptional teaching and counseling from some of the finest scholars in the field. My dissertation director, Lee Woodward, laid the ideological and methodological framework for the study of modern Central America. Tom Schoonover and Lawrence Clayton encouraged me to continue my work on United Fruit. David McCreery, Jim Handy, Julio Pinto Soria, and Richard Greenleaf answered queries related to my project. Richmond Brown and Mark Cioc commented on early drafts of some chapters. Todd Little, a friend and colleague, worked for a time as my research assistant, as did my friend Kelly Graves. I also must thank the staff at the Department of Justice for the expeditious processing of my Freedom of Information Act requests for the company files related to the antitrust suit filed against United Fruit in 1954. Those documents, previously unexamined by historians, form the foundation for this history of United Fruit.

I would like to acknowledge the friendly counseling of some of my colleagues at the University of Massachusetts, including Jane Rausch, Carmen Diana Deere, Pauline Collins, Milton Cantor, Gerald McFarland, Dick Minear, Yvonne Haddad, Ron Story, and Bruce Laurie. I am honored to be a part of their distinguished department, and I thank them for their help. The comic relief provided by friends in Northampton, particularly the Sheehans crowd of Mark Hernández, Bob Cook, Sandy Christoforidis, Jim Figlar, Matt Crocker, Julie Foulkes, and Ann Shuh, made the completion of this manuscript bearable. Finally, I would like to thank the editors and reviewers at Scholarly Resources who have shown remarkable tolerance in guiding a young scholar through the publishing process.

Figures and Maps

1

Introduction

In 1951, Sam "the Banana Man" Zemurray, president of the United Fruit Company (UFCO), reflected on the history of the business that he personified. Over the course of one-half century, he had risen from a poor, uneducated Russian immigrant to a respected and feared businessman worth an estimated $30 million. Between 1899 and 1929, as president of the Cuyamel Fruit Company, United's most successful competitor, he sponsored rebellions, hired mercenaries, bribed politicians, defied Guatemalan, Honduran, and American laws, and almost single-handedly provoked a war between Honduras and Guatemala. United terminated the rivalry by purchasing Cuyamel in 1929, but it did not silence Zemurray, who returned four years later to take over UFCO. From 1933 to 1951 he was the driving force behind the largest banana company in the world. In that position, Zemurray had the time and luxury to contemplate his past, and his increasing contributions to numerous charities, including a $1-million donation to Tulane University's Middle American Research Institute, suggested an uneasiness about his own role in a sordid history. Just before he retired from the business, Zemurray expressed some remorse: "All we cared about were dividends. I feel guilty about some of the things we did."[1]

Zemurray repented too late for the Guatemalan revolutionaries. Within three years of his confession, President Jacobo Arbenz expropriated four fifths of the company's Tiquisate and Bananera plantations and offered $1,185,000 as compensation for properties that UFCO valued at $19,350,000.[2] The Arbencistas defended their actions on the grounds that United Fruit had acquired a monopoly on the banana business through illegal and unethical associations with the dictators who had governed Guatemala since 1898. While United had encountered some minor difficulties with the government before, no previous president had even demanded the return of land; indeed, it had grown accustomed to governments that gave land away. To eliminate an inconvenient president, UFCO collaborated with the counterrevolutionary movement organized by the Central Intelligence Agency.[3]

While the history of United Fruit during the revolutionary decade (1944–1954) is fairly well known, the forty-five years preceding the revolution remain relatively obscure. The importance of the company to Guatemalan political and economic life is beyond doubt. When the revolution began, United owned 566,000 acres of land and employed fifteen thousand people, making it the country's largest private landowner and the biggest employer. Through its subsidiary, the International Railways of Central America (IRCA), UFCO also operated 690 miles of the country's 719-mile railroad network and employed another five thousand people. By U.S. standards, United was not a huge corporation, but, by Central American standards, it was a "colossus," according to Piero Gleijeses.[4]

The most important private enterprise in the history of Guatemala and Central America has not received the scholarly attention it deserves. While there are hundreds of books, articles, and pamphlets about United Fruit, the literature is excessively polemical and anecdotal, dominated by company-supported apologias, journalistic critiques, and politically inspired attacks by Caribbean nationalists.[5] Systematic historical analysis of United Fruit, based on primary documents, has just begun. Valuable contributions have recently been made by scholars who have explored alternative sources or uncovered some corporate records, but the definitive history of United Fruit in Latin America remains to be written.[6]

Hence, most of the allegations against United, and the sins that Zemurray acknowledged, have not been examined against a solid documentary foundation. The unsubstantiated consensus is that United Fruit acquired its wealth and power in Guatemala through illicit activities. Even Ronald Schneider, a political scientist generally sympathetic to American enterprise, has acknowledged that United Fruit "bribed politicians, pressured governments and intimidated opponents to gain extremely favorable concessions."[7] From the opposite end of the political spectrum, historian Jim Handy argues that the "unholy trinity" of the United Fruit Company, International Railways of Central America, and the United Fruit Steamship Company collaborated with corrupt dictators to create a system that strangled the Guatemalan economy.[8]

Doing Business with the Dictators surveys the formative years of United Fruit in Guatemala, when its agents extracted the liberal concessions that allowed it to monopolize the railroad network and the banana business. The banana business in Guatemala and elsewhere involved delicate and discreet political negotiations between representatives of American enterprise and the domestic political elite. United's success in Guatemala is partly the consequence of its ability to forge productive alliances with two corrupt and repressive dictators, Manuel Estrada Cabrera (1898–1920) and Jorge Ubico (1931–1944). While United did not create either dictatorship, it profited from the absence of democratic institutions. During the democratic interlude of the 1920s, United faced serious challenges from an independent legislature, a nationalistic press, and a politically activated labor force, all of which advocated either the modification or nullification of United's contracts. In the dictatorships that preceded and followed a decade of relative democracy, the absence of political liberties facilitated United's acquisition of concessions that included either long-term tax exemptions or reductions, large blocks of land, and freedom from government regulation. United Fruit discovered that it was much more profitable to do business with a dictator than with a democratic president.

By doing business with dictators, United grew into *el pulpo* (the octopus), a vast enterprise with tentacles extending far beyond the coastal plantations from which it extracted bananas. The key to understanding the extent of United's influence lies in the relations between it and IRCA, a nominally independent firm. From 1904 to 1936, UFCO held only a small amount of IRCA stock, but it subordinated the railroad through interlocking directorates and traffic agreements. In 1936, United Fruit purchased a 42.6 percent interest in the railroad, enough to give it managerial command. While United denied that it ever controlled the railroad, the New York Supreme Court, in upholding a $4.5-million judgment in favor of minority IRCA stockholders who had been wrongfully denied dividends as a result of the railroad's "unconscionable" freight rates, concluded that United's control of IRCA, even prior to 1936, was "completely effectual."[9]

While control of the railroad network allowed United to stifle or eliminate competition in the banana business, it also had a tremendous impact on the entire economy. A distinguishing feature of Guatemala's economic history is the extent to which United dominated the country's economic infrastructure. For forty years, UFCO monopolized the country's railroad network, controlled the wharves at Puerto Barrios and San José, dominated shipping, and operated the telegraph systems. The tragedy of the country's political history is that its leaders authorized the company's operations, ignored viable alternatives, and virtually abdicated regulatory power over the infrastructure on which the country's two leading exports, coffee and bananas, depended. The U.S. government also bears responsibility for United Fruit's enterprises, for it encouraged the Guatemalan government to adopt policies favorable to American enterprise and supported the company during contractual negotiations, despite serious reservations about its monopoly power within the departments of State and Justice.

United Fruit created, with the assistance of the Guatemalan and American governments, a monopoly that was detrimental to the economic interests of consumers in both countries. Ironically, while the Eisenhower administration objected to Arbenz's nationalization of United's properties, it validated his contention that UFCO restrained competition when the Department of Justice (DOJ) filed an antitrust suit against the company on July 2, 1954, just five days after Arbenz resigned. The suit was settled by a 1958 consent decree that compelled United to divest of some subsidiary corporations, including IRCA and the Compañía Agrícola de Guatemala (the Tiquisate division).[10]

Map 1. United Fruit's Guatemalan Empire, 1930s

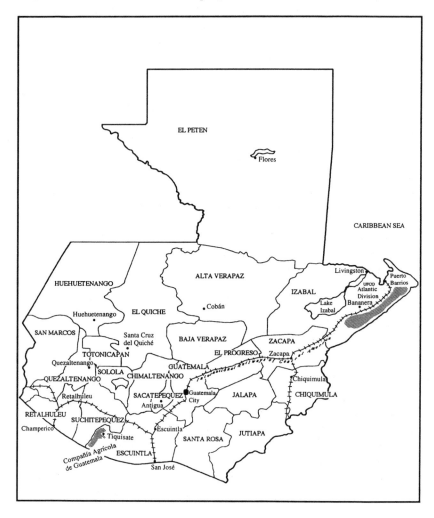

The antitrust suit began the process of dismantling a firm that was created in 1899 to monopolize the banana business. The company united the two largest banana firms in the United States, Andrew Preston's Boston Fruit Company and Minor C. Keith's Tropical Trading and Transport Company. Boston Fruit, operating in Atlantic coast ports from Charleston to Boston, supplied 35 percent of the U.S. market from its plantations in Cuba, the Dominican Republic, and Jamaica. Keith's enterprises, importing through Gulf Coast ports from New Orleans to Tampa, supplied 40 percent of the market from Costa Rican and Colombian sources. In 1899 these two giants, with noncompetitive sources of supply and fields of distribution, consolidated their interests to form the United Fruit Company.[11]

In the first year of operation, United imported 69 percent of all stems that arrived at U.S. ports, and this figure does not even include the business done by companies in which it had acquired a controlling interest. Despite denials by company officials and their apologists, UFCO entered the corporate world as a monopoly and behaved like one for the next half century. Based on a review of company documents still unavailable to independent researchers, the Department of Justice concluded: "The purpose and effect of the unification of the businesses of the Boston Fruit Company and Minor C. Keith and their subsidiaries was to restrain actual or potential competition and to monopolize the banana industry. As a result of the combination of these two dominant members of the industry, United became a vertically integrated enterprise operating throughout the American tropics and the United States wherever any phase of the banana business was conducted."[12]

Monopoly, as interpreted by the Department of Justice, may exist without the elimination of all competitors. United Fruit was never the only banana firm, but it was always in a position to determine the amount of competition it would tolerate. "Immediately upon its formation," according to the DOJ, "United adopted and pursued a consistent policy of absorbing or excluding competitors in all phases of the industry." By 1906 it had acquired a controlling interest in fifteen of the eighteen other firms engaged in the banana business.[13]

On April 22, 1908, the Senate Committee on Interstate Commerce held a hearing to determine if United's acquisitions and business practices violated federal antitrust laws.[14] UFCO defended itself there and in the Supreme Court, where Herbert McConnell charged that United had taken control of his banana company for the purpose of suppressing competition and regulating the price and quantity of bananas imported into the United States. Although the Court rejected the appeal on the grounds that it lacked jurisdiction, its conclusion that UFCO monopolized the banana trade made Keith and Preston more circumspect in the management of their banana empire.[15]

As antitrust sentiment developed in the executive and judicial branches of government, United Fruit recognized that it would have to tolerate a degree of competition. Between the congressional hearing and September 1911, United sold its interests in the Hubbard-Zemurray Steamship Company (predecessor of Cuyamel), Atlantic Fruit, and the Vaccaro Brothers (later Standard Fruit), all of which were engaged in the Central American banana business. Nevertheless, United's share of the U.S. market dropped below 50 percent only once between 1910 and 1951. No competitor accounted for more than 20 percent of the market until the 1950s, suggesting that United Fruit's management wanted to maintain a 50 to 60 percent share of the market.[16]

At the peak of its power in 1950, United cultivated 138,910 acres (although it owned or leased three million acres, representing 85 percent of the tropical land suitable for banana cultivation), operated fifteen hundred miles of railroad, and owned or chartered thirty-six ships. Its closest competitor, Standard Fruit, cultivated only 17,455 acres and chartered ten ships. As it always dominated the cultivation, transportation, shipping, and marketing of bananas, United could select a price and adhere to it, while its competitors adjusted prices in response to market fluctuations. If and when a competitor tried to increase its market share, United could lower its prices until the challenger withdrew. When all other means failed, United could always buy the rival, as it did when it acquired Cuyamel in 1929. United's successful manipulation of the banana market earned it $825,000,000 between 1900 and 1951, during which time it never suffered a net loss. United Fruit earned an average of 12.5 percent on its net worth per year, increasing from $12.5 million in 1900 to $319,530,803 in 1951.[17]

While the stockholders appreciated the high annual dividends, United's apparent wealth made it a target for Caribbean nationalists who lamented the loss of $825 million that could have been reinvested and redistributed in their countries. Unfortunately for Guatemalans, their own political leaders suppressed efforts to obtain a larger share of the banana profits. Estrada Cabrera and Ubico, once they had constructed their dictatorial regimes, simply ignored public demand for tighter regulation and a greater share of the banana business. In the 1920s, when democracy breathed life into the country's political institutions, a strong opposition forced the company to accept substantial compromises, including the first tax on banana exports and a profit-sharing clause.

In Guatemala and throughout the region, United preferred to deal with military governments because it was easier to extract favorable contracts from a dictator than from a democratically checked and balanced government. Guatemala's political elites, having adopted the creed of order and progress in the late nineteenth century, shared United's authoritarian political inclinations. Dictatorial regimes provided a secure environment in which both parties could discreetly offer or solicit favors in pursuit of their private interests. While the dictator faced no formal opposition to his policies, political factors still compelled him to wrest advantages from foreign companies. During the era of Juan Vicente Gómez (1908–1935) in Venezuela, for example, the dictator had personal financial ties to the foreign oil companies, but to secure a broader revenue base and establish his nationalistic credentials, Gómez imposed increasingly higher taxes on the industry.[18] Unfortunately, Guatemalan dictators were more committed to their own wealth and power than to the country's progress, but United Fruit's concessions, which affected the location, extent, and pace of development work, were still the product of bargaining that took placed behind the closed doors of the executive branch.[19]

Preston, Keith, and Zemurray did not export prepackaged units to the tropics; Guatemala's Liberal caudillos imported the product and assembled it in accordance with their needs and priorities. Factions of the local elite welcomed United's investment, collaborated with it, and in the process endowed the fruit company with Guatemalan characteristics. Each United Fruit division assumed a distinct character because unique configurations of political, economic, social, and geographic conditions shaped its development. Rather than the victims of American imperialism, the caudillos were active conspirators with it, for they regularly influenced United's investment and production patterns by rejecting or modifying concessions, amending local labor laws, raising taxes, or playing United off potential competitors.

United Fruit was not imposed on Guatemala by a covert conspiracy launched from Boston; it was truly a multinational corporation, the product of political struggles between Guatemalan dictators and American businessmen. United undoubtedly possessed the stronger hand when negotiating with the Guatemalans; it could threaten to withhold or withdraw its investments in the event that the government refused to sanction the privileges it requested. While it could easily increase production in one division to offset decreases elsewhere, the abandonment of productive plantations represented a serious loss of time and money that United hoped to avoid. Once United invested millions of dollars in plantations, railroads, and wharves, it was understandably reluctant to withdraw until it recovered its investment. United's lobbyists therefore cultivated close relations with the political establishment, offering the bribes and entertainment that local politicians demanded in return for their ongoing support of the banana industry.

Guatemala's authoritarian presidents granted United many favors, but they did not approve every concession it solicited without modifications. Although the State Department usually supported United during its contract negotiations, it did not dispatch the marines every time an unruly caudillo refused to authorize the terms United solicited. Prominent *finqueros* (coffee planters) often demanded more effective state control of the port and railroads that United operated, but they did not control the state any more than Washington or Boston. The Guatemalan state often operated independently of the *finqueros*, United, and the State Department. The string of caudillos who ruled Guatemala from 1871 to 1944 maintained a degree of personal autonomy that they occasionally used in defense of national interests, particularly during the late nineteenth century. To their discredit, too many of them recognized their relative independence as an opportunity to accumulate personal wealth and consolidate their political power rather than as a chance to promote the country's economic development.

From a corrupt and repressive government, United acquired and exploited concessions that sanctioned its monopolistic practices in the rail and banana industries. In 1912, IRCA established a highly prejudicial tariff schedule designed to divert Guatemalan coffee shipments away from the traditional Pacific ports to Puerto Barrios, where United's steamers dominated shipping. *Finqueros* petitioned the government for the elimination of the discriminatory rates, but the government lacked jurisdiction because Estrada Cabrera had surrendered all regulatory authority over the line. Consequently, Guatemalan commerce shifted dramatically from the Pacific to the Caribbean Coast, much to the delight of IRCA and UFCO. In the 1930s, IRCA adopted tariffs that discriminated against goods originating in the United States and refused to modify them despite State Department complaints that the rates obstructed its efforts to increase American exports to Guatemala. As a result of this conflict, Sumner Welles, architect of Franklin Roosevelt's Good Neighbor policy, was the first prominent American diplomat to question the "propriety of an American corporation, possessing a monopoly of essential transportation facilities in a foreign country, and operating in virtually complete independence of the authorities of either the American or Guatemalan governments, taking unto itself the function of arbitrarily directing the course of Guatemalan foreign trade."[20]

United Fruit's command of the economic infrastructure distinguished the Guatemalan division from the typical enclave that it established in other countries. An enclave is an extractive enterprise with few links to the host economy, a definition that does not apply to United Fruit's Guatemalan operations because its influence stretched across the country on IRCA's railroad tracks.[21] In its other divisions, United carved out coastal plantations isolated from the rest of the country, sunk a wharf into the Caribbean Sea, and laid only enough railroad track to transport bananas to its port. United was generally reluctant to extend its lines deeper into the country for fear of broadening the range of issues over which it could come into conflict with local political authorities. In Guatemala, Minor Keith accepted the government's invitation to consolidate his banana line with all other railroads, a decision his successors in United Fruit came to regret.

Keith also attempted to establish a transoceanic railroad monopoly in Honduras, but the government refused to submit to the terms he demanded. Partly because United did not control the transportation network, Honduras offered ample room for competition in the banana business. United shared the banana business with Standard and Cuyamel until 1929, when UFCO merged with Cuyamel, and each firm built and operated only the rail and port facilities required to service the plantations. Unlike in Guatemala, where United cultivated and purchased without any serious competition before the late 1940s, three North American banana firms cut the northern coast into four distinct enclaves.[22]

United Fruit's Costa Rican division resembled the Guatemalan system, given that it dominated the banana business and controlled rail and port facilities on the Caribbean coast. However, United never monopolized either banana production or a transoceanic railroad; it dominated banana marketing, not cultivation. It deliberately delegated production tasks to private planters in order to minimize its risks, to the extent that UFCO produced only 25 percent of the bananas it exported in 1926. Since United had enough power to eliminate competition from rival purchasers, as evident in its quick suppression of Atlantic Fruit's bid for some of the independent banana business in 1912, it monopolized the marketing of bananas until it abandoned the Caribbean coast in 1940. Yet the most significant difference between Guatemala and Costa Rica is that political factors deterred Keith from extending his railroad across the country. The Costa Rican government owned and operated a profitable railroad linking San José to Puntarenas on the Pacific, and the competition between the two lines minimized United's impact on the country's coffee exports.[23]

In Nicaragua and El Salvador, United Fruit and the banana industry played a minor role. United owned extensive tracts of undeveloped land in Nicaragua, but it confined its activities to occasional purchases from private planters along the coast. Standard, Cuyamel, and Atlantic also bought from independents, with Standard accounting for 50 percent of Nicaragua's exports in the 1920s. Although the banana industry never developed in El Salvador, United bid for the country's lucrative coffee traffic by extending the IRCA line to the Salvadoran border in 1929. While some of the coffee traffic was subsequently diverted to Puerto Barrios, the British-owned Salvador Railway Company, which had carried most of the coffee traffic over its lines to the port of Acajutla since 1899, remained competitive.[24]

The Panamanian and Colombian banana industries, initiated by Keith in the late nineteenth century, displayed the characteristics of an enclave. In the Bocas del Toro division of Panama, United controlled all aspects of the production and commercialization of bananas, but, since it built a railroad extending only from Almirante Bay to the Talamanca Valley in southern Costa Rica, it was easier to get to the division from Boston than from Panama City.[25] United confined its Colombian activities to the Caribbean coast and refused to extend its railroad beyond the Santa Marta banana district because it did not want other agricultural products clogging the line or the docks. It occasionally faced competition from foreign and independent Colombian planters, who accounted for 60 percent of production in the late 1920s.[26]

When the banana boom hit Ecuador in the late 1940s, United Fruit was not in a position to dominate the business, even though it was one of the first companies to initiate banana cultivation in the 1930s. Government policies supported infrastructural development and financed independent farmers, thereby limiting the possibility that any firm could establish a monopoly on the marketing or cultivation of bananas. United did not operate a railroad or port, and its plantation, while one of the most productive in Ecuador, accounted for only 2 percent of Ecuador's total banana production. United was one of five major exporters that purchased its fruit from independent planters.[27]

The history of the Jamaican banana industry also shows how government policy could protect local planters and check United's influence. While United is largely responsible for turning Jamaica into the world's leading banana producer by 1900, its relatively small plantations (thirteen thousand acres actually cultivated) coexisted with independent Jamaican planters, who had some opportunities to market their fruit with either Atlantic or Standard Fruit before they formed their own cooperative in 1929. With government support the cooperative established its own shipping line and foreign distribution system. After failing to put the cooperative out of business by raising the prices it offered to independent planters, United terminated the rivalry by forging a cartel agreement with it and Standard in 1936.[28]

The political conditions and institutions that influenced the development of the banana business in Guatemala explain why United Fruit consolidated a banana and railroad monopoly different from its other divisions. The Guatemalan government was so receptive to United Fruit's demands that when the spread of sigatoka disease on the Caribbean coast of Central America forced UFCO to develop new plantations on the Pacific coast, the company selected Guatemala as the site of its first completely mechanized division.[29] Yet the Liberals who came to power in 1871 pursued a nationalistic development program that, if successful, would have prevented United from monopolizing either the railroad or banana industry. UFCO built its Guatemalan enterprises on foundations laid during the late nineteenth century, when three Liberal governments explored alternative development paths. An acute political and economic crisis at the turn of the century bankrupted the government, terminated work on a national railroad, and left the Guatemalans vulnerable to foreign capitalists. These conditions created the opportunity for Keith to acquire all the railroads previously built and consolidate them into one company dominated by United Fruit. The origins of this firm and the means by which UFCO dominated it are discussed in Chapter 4.

Even after Keith acquired the concessions and properties on which UFCO built its empire, neither the banana business nor Guatemala's development followed a predetermined path. The same dictator who sanctioned

Keith's enterprises also obstructed his efforts to establish a national bank and extend his railroad to El Salvador. At several points before 1944 the company and the government could have been diverted along alternative development paths. Challenges to United Fruit's hegemony came from Cuyamel, nationalistic elites, UFCO employees, and European competitors, but United maintained and eventually expanded its enterprises by collaborating with the authoritarian and corrupt presidents who governed during the 1920s.

With the establishment of the Ubico dictatorship in 1931, United silenced its critics and developed a new plantation network on the Pacific coast. (The means by which it expanded to the Pacific and suppressed competition from independent Guatemalan planters are analyzed in Chapter 10.) By the 1930s the octopus was at the pinnacle of its power under Zemurray's leadership. Owning 566,000 acres on both coasts and controlling the railroad network and two of the country's three ports under concessions that gave it administrative autonomy, its monopolistic practices precipitated a conflict with the State Department.

Were it not for World War II and the Cold War, Washington would have cut United Fruit down to size in the 1930s. Because of a long history of costly litigation with its competitors and the U.S. government, company officials are still sensitive about their past and refuse to open the company archives (located at United Brands headquarters in Cincinnati) to independent researchers. Ironically, many UFCO documents have been made part of the public record because of its constant involvement in political and legal disputes, both here and abroad. Although the company tried to maintain a policy of not requesting diplomatic intervention, in the event of a dispute with the Guatemalan government, UFCO officials expected the U.S. government to support them. To defend their cases, company representatives voluntarily submitted lengthy reports on their history, operations, and objectives. Several reels of microfilm deal with the Zacapa dispute, which engaged Keith and three Guatemalan governments from 1912 to 1925. When United Fruit sought and received a lease on the Motagua riverbanks, the company precipitated a military confrontation with Honduras. The documentary legacy is staggering: twenty-six reels of microfilm revealing the company's objectives, competition with Cuyamel, and relationships between the companies and the governments of Honduras and Guatemala.

Scholars have generally used Department of State records to reconstruct the history of political relations between the United States and other countries. The political records, however, constitute only a fraction of the total documentation. The department maintained separate files on military affairs, finances, labor, agriculture, industry, railroads, shipping, and electrical power. American diplomats gathered surprisingly insightful data on these and other subjects, from corrupt practices to the distribution of wealth and power.

The files of the DOJ contain even more useful information about United Fruit and IRCA. In the process of investigating and prosecuting the company, the DOJ accumulated a valuable United Fruit archive holding documents normally found only in the corporate records. Under the Freedom of Information Act, I have obtained access to some minutes of meetings of the board of directors, correspondence between Boston and the division headquarters, and records of competition with and acquisition of rival companies, banana sales, traffic agreements, and market conditions. The suit filed by the minority stockholders against IRCA and UFCO in 1949 also contributed to the development of the small United Fruit archive at the Department of Justice. That case went to the New York Supreme Court with six thousand documentary exhibits, many of which the department subpoenaed. Forming the most valuable part of the documentation concerning relations between UFCO and IRCA, these records detail how United Fruit used the railway to deal with hostile competition, particularly the independent planters who tried to obtain a share of the Guatemalan banana business in the late 1930s.

Because they reflect only the DOJ's concern with enforcing the antitrust laws and the interest of minority stockholders in recovering monetary damages for the preferential treatment that IRCA afforded UFCO, these documents have their limitations. By court order, many of the records covering United Fruit's acquisitions prior to 1920 have been sealed from public view. Hence, they are not as complete as the historian would like, but they provide heretofore unavailable access into the mind of a massive corporation.

In addition to these untapped resources, the Archivo General de Centro América contains uncataloged documents of various Guatemalan ministries scattered chronologically between 1871 and the 1930s. Although difficult to access, thirty-eight *legajos* of Ministerio de Fomento (Ministry of Development) documents related to railroad development provided information about concessions, competition between railroads, and basic data about the companies. Guatemalan newspapers provided vital information on the Puerto Barrios strike of 1923 and the opposition to United Fruit's contracts in the 1920s.

Doing Business with the Dictators examines relations between the country's largest private enterprise and the government through contract negotiations, the boundary conflict with Honduras, the Puerto Barrios strike of 1923, and United's efforts to stifle or eliminate competition. The revolutionaries who tried to dismantle United's monopoly rightfully associated this American firm with the string of dictators who had promoted United's private interests as they repressed Guatemala's democratic aspirations. Because it was good for business to collaborate with dictators, United remained silent about or contributed to the suppression of civil liberties while it created one of the most productive divisions in its kingdom. One should not acquit the company by condemning the dictators who served it; while poverty, corruption, and repression existed long before Keith and Preston founded United Fruit, the American managers of this multinational enterprise showed little respect for either democracy or the free market during the forty-five years under study.

Notes

1. John Kobler, "Sam the Banana Man," *Life* 30:8 (February 19, 1951): 84; Stephen J. Whitfield, "Strange Fruit: The Career of Samuel Zemurray," *American Jewish History* 73 (March 1984): 319.

2. Piero Gleijeses, *Shattered Hope: The Guatemalan Revolution and the United States, 1944–1954* (Princeton: Princeton University Press, 1991), 164.

3. Richard H. Immerman, *The CIA in Guatemala: The Foreign Policy of Intervention* (Austin: University of Texas Press, 1982); Stephen Schlesinger and Stephen Kinzer, *Bitter Fruit: The Untold Story of the American Coup in Guatemala* (New York: Doubleday, 1982).

4. Gleijeses, *Shattered Hope*, 87–89.

5. The exceptional works in this genre include Charles Morrow Wilson, *Empire in Green and Gold: The Story of the American Banana Trade* (1947, reprint, New York: Greenwood Publishers, 1968); Charles David Kepner and Jay Soothill, *The Banana Empire: A Case Study of Economic Imperialism* (1935, reprint, New York: Russell & Russell, 1963); Stacy May and Galo Plaza, *The United Fruit Company in Latin America* (New York: National Planning Association, 1958); Thomas P. McCann, *An American Company: The Tragedy of United Fruit* (New York: Crown Publishers, 1976).

6. Outstanding examples of the recent historiographical trends include Jeffrey Casey Gaspar, *Limón: 1880–1940; un estudio de la industria bananera en Costa Rica* (San José: Editorial Costa Rica, 1979); Oscar Zanetti, ed., *United Fruit Company: un caso del dominio imperialista en Cuba* (Habana: Editorial de Ciencias Sociales, 1976); Catherine LeGrand, "Colombian Transformations: Peasants and the Wage Labourers in the Santa Marta Banana Zone," *Journal of Peasant Studies* 11:4 (1984): 178–200; Philippe Bourgois, *Ethnicity at Work: Divided Labor on a Central American Banana Plantation* (Baltimore: Johns Hopkins University Press, 1989); Aviva Chomsky, "Plantation Society, Land and Labor on Costa Rica's Atlantic coast, 1870–1940" (Ph.D. diss., University of California, Berkeley, 1990).

7. Ronald Schneider, *Communism in Guatemala, 1944–1954* (New York: Praeger, 1959), 48.

8. Jim Handy, *Gift of the Devil: A History of Guatemala* (Boston: South End Press, 1984), 81.

9. Ripley v. International Railways of Central America, 188 N.Y.S. 2d 62.

10. "United Fruit Sued by U.S. as a Trust," *New York Times*, July 3, 1954; "Anti-Trust Suit Faced by UFC," *Times Picayune* (New Orleans), July 3, 1954.

11. Girard B. Ruddick, "A Study in Monopoly: The United Fruit Company," (M.A. thesis, Duke University, 1929), 15; Watt Stewart, *Keith and Costa Rica: A Biographical Study of Minor C. Keith* (Albuquerque: University of New Mexico Press, 1964), 144–49; Kepner and Soothill, *Banana Empire*, 43–49; Wilson, *Empire in Green and Gold*, 105.

12. Memorandum, Milton A. Kallis to Victor H. Kramer and W. Perry Epes, "Banana Investigation," December 20, 1952, U.S. Department of Justice, Antitrust Division, *United States v. United Fruit Co.*, Civil No. 4560, File 60-166-56, 3–4 (hereafter cited as DOJ, followed by file number).

13. Ibid.

14. Senate Committee on Interstate Commerce, *Hearing before a Subcommittee of the Committee on Interstate Commerce, United States Senate . . . on Resolution S. No. 139, Submitted by Mr. Johnston, Directing the Department of Commerce and Labor to Make an Investigation into the Character and Operation of the United Fruit Company*, 60th Cong., 1st sess., 1908.

15. Ruddick, "A Study in Monopoly," 97; Kepner and Soothill, *Banana Empire*, 53–63.

16. Kallis to Kramer and Epes, December 20, 1952, DOJ, File 60-166-56, 7, 30.

17. Ibid., 15, 22, 39–42.

18. B. S. McBeth, *Juan Vicente Gómez and the Oil Companies in Venezuela, 1908-1935* (Cambridge: Cambridge University Press, 1983), 21–69.

19. For some brief examples of United's bargaining tactics in Costa Rica and Panama see Bourgois, *Ethnicity at Work*, 17–23.

20. Undersecretary of State [Sumner Welles] to Whitney Shepardson, president of International Railways of Central America [May 1938], U.S. Department of State, Record Group 59, Records of the Department of State Relating to the Internal Affairs of Guatemala, 1910–1929, 814.773/40 (post-1910 State Department records hereafter cited as SD, followed by decimal file number).

21. Fernando Henrique Cardoso and Enzo Falleto, *Dependency and Development in Latin America*, trans. Marjory Mattingly Urquidi (Berkeley: University of California Press, 1979), xix.

22. Vilma Laínez and Victor Meza, "El enclave bananero en la historia de Honduras," *Anuario de Estudios Centroamericanos* 1 (1974): 187–225; Kepner and Soothill, *Banana Empire*, 141.

23. Chomsky, "Plantation Society," 86–109; Thomas Schoonover, *The United States in Central America, 1860-1911: Episodes of Social Imperialism and Imperial Rivalry in the World System* (Durham, NC: Duke University Press, 1991), 5; Kepner and Soothill, *Banana Empire*, 64–70, 170–78.

24. Victor Bulmer-Thomas, *The Political Economy of Central America since 1920* (Cambridge: Cambridge University Press, 1987), 34; Delmer G. Ross, "The Construction of the Railroads of Central America" (Ph.D. diss., University of California, Santa Barbara, 1970), 308–15.

25. Bourgois, *Ethnicity at Work*, 23–25; Richard Allan LaBarge, "A Study of United Fruit Company Operations in Isthmian America, 1946–1956" (Ph.D. diss., Duke University, 1960), 39–42.

26. LeGrand, "Colombian Transformations," 178–83; Roberto Herrera Soto and Rafael Romero Castañeda, *La zona bananera del Magdalena* (Bogotá: Instituto Caro y Cuervo, 1979), 7–11.

27. May and Plaza, *United Fruit Company*, 169–70; James J. Parsons, "Bananas in Ecuador: A New Chapter in the History of Tropical Agriculture," *Economic Geography* 33 (1957): 213–15; Rubén Moreno S., *Ecuador, economía y política en el último siglo* (Quito: Facultad de Ciencias Económicas, 1984), 57.

28. Peter Davies, *Fyffes and the Banana: A Centenary History, 1898–1988* (London: The Athlone Press, 1990), 147–49; Theodore Sealy, *Jamaica's Banana Industry: A History of the Banana Industry with Particular Reference to the Part*

Played by the Jamaica Banana Producers Association, Ltd. (Kingston: The Association, 1984), 76–86.

    29. Wilson, *Empire in Green and Gold*, 279.

2

The Liberals Lay
the Foundations

United Fruit built its Guatemalan empire on foundations laid during the first phase of the Liberal reform, when Generals Justo Rufino Barrios (1873–1885), Manuel Lisandro Barillas (1885–1891), and José María Reyna Barrios (1892–1897) pursued a modernization program that served the interests of the coffee planters. The Liberals believed that the expansion of the coffee economy would provide them the capital they needed to create a modern diversified economy. To this ambitious end, they seized communal lands, reimposed forced labor systems, confiscated church properties, and promoted infrastructural development.[1]

The modernization projects, particularly railroad construction, required vast amounts of capital and technology, both of which Guatemalans were either unable or unwilling to provide. As a result, the Liberals financed railroad construction using a combination of state, local, and foreign capital. American capital built the Central Railroad (Guatemala City to San José); Guatemalan *finqueros* owned the Occidental Railroad (Retalhuleu to Champerico); and the state financed and directed construction on the Northern Railway (Guatemala City to Puerto Barrios). The failure of the state to complete the Northern Railway created the conditions in which Minor Keith acquired it, the Central, and the Occidental, and placed them at the service of the United Fruit Company.

United built its Guatemalan enterprises on tracks laid by other companies. The three development options that the Liberals pursued demonstrate their original intention to maintain competitive conditions in the railroad business. As the concessions under which the Central operated gave it the right to build or acquire railroads throughout the country, the potential for railroad monopoly existed long before Keith arrived in Guatemala. Collis P. Huntington, the American owner of the Central, tried to use this provision to take possession of the Northern Railway, which would have given him a transoceanic railroad. The caudillos resisted Huntington's monopolistic ambitions because they intended to keep the Northern under national control. At one point the state even tried to nationalize the Central.

A faction of the oligarchy was determined to keep the coffee economy and the economic infrastructure that served it under Guatemalan control. As United Fruit's agents discovered, the venality of the caudillos often undermined their nationalistic ambitions. In 1897 construction on the Northern Railway stopped at El Rancho, a village sixty miles from Guatemala City, and the stage was set for United's entrance. In the process of building the Northern, a wharf at Puerto Barrios, and promoting the banana business of the Caribbean coast, the state bankrupted itself. Keith and UFCO succeeded because the development program launched in 1871 failed.

When the Liberals came to power, Guatemala had not one mile of railroad track, and its main port at San José was just a wooden wharf jutting out into the Pacific surf. Because coffee is a bulk commodity subject to spoilage, the expansion of the coffee industry required the construction of railroads and the improvement of harbors. The first two attempts to build a railroad from Guatemala City to San José failed, evidently due to the poor reputation of the contractors and their inability to raise sufficient capital, an effort complicated by Guatemala's failure to make payments on its English debt.[2] Five years after the Liberal revolution began, Guatemala had not laid one steel rail.

To finance railroad construction the government would have either to settle the English debt or offer attractive terms to American investors. As in many other Latin American republics, the government promoted railroad development through a concessionary policy that included long-term tax exemptions, subsidies, and land grants. Domestic capitalists were reluctant to invest in railroads but quite insistent that they be built. Where and when private initiative was lacking, the state authorized concessions that minimized the risk to either foreign or domestic investors and provided some guarantees that a railroad could be built and operated profitably.[3]

After the second railroad project collapsed, Barrios summoned Henry F. W. Nanne, the general manager of Keith's Costa Rican Railway. By this time, Guillermo, as he came to be called, had settled into his career as a public works contractor known more for his political connections than for his business acumen. He came to Costa Rica via California, married the daughter of the vice president, and supervised the construction of the San José water works for President Juan Rafael Mora, who was deposed in 1859 shortly after he had acquired heroic status by driving William Walker out of Nicaragua. One year later, Mora and Nanne were captured in a rebellion at Puntarenas and condemned to death. While Mora was executed, Nanne's sentence was commuted to imprisonment at a Caribbean jail, where he evidently decided to pursue more remunerative and less dangerous challenges.[4]

His opportunity came in 1871 when Henry Meiggs Keith appointed him the superintendent of the Costa Rican Railway. Henry had recently arrived with his brother Minor to assume command of a railroad enterprise initiated by their famous uncle, Henry Meiggs, whose reputation rested on impressive engineering feats in Chile and Peru. Meiggs had obtained the concession from dictator Tomás Guardia with a bribe of £100,000, then transferred it to his ambitious nephews. Henry Keith left Nanne in charge of the construction while he handled the political and financial affairs of the railroad, a job he performed so poorly that the government rescinded the concession in 1875. His brother Minor, however, had earned enough money and expertise in various business operations in and around Limón to obtain his own railroad contract in 1875.[5]

In his four years as superintendent, Nanne constructed nearly fifty miles of railroad and gained valuable experience dealing with the political and social side of doing business in Central America. Much to the enjoyment of the Costa Rican elite, Nanne celebrated the arrival of the first locomotive in Alajuela with a grand ball in the city hall. He learned that the success of a railroad partly depended on one's ability to entertain the politicians who approved, rejected, or regulated railroad concessions. The political agent, like Nanne, had to negotiate terms in the volatile political process before any of the engineers and work crews could begin their difficult tasks. Nanne honed his political skills as the Costa Rican superintendent, but he scored his first independent success as a railroad promoter in Guatemala when he signed the Nanne-Herrera contract of 1877. The concession authorized construction of a railroad from San José to Escuintla, guaranteed a 12 percent annual return on the projected investment of $1.2 million, established Nanne's exclusive right to railway transportation between San José and Escuintla for twenty-five years, and gave him preferential rights of construction on all future railroad projects. If Nanne chose to exercise his preferential rights, he could monopolize Guatemalan railways for ninety-nine years, after which time the state would assume ownership of the lines.[6]

A 250,000-peso loan from the government allowed Nanne to initiate preliminary work in August 1877, but the project would fail if he did not attract foreign investment. While the British financed most of Latin America's early railroad projects, they were reluctant to invest in Guatemala as long as the government refused to recognize the English debt, a financial debacle inherited from the early days of the Central American republic. As a result, Nanne failed to attract British investors and turned to American capitalists. He organized the Guatemala Central Railroad Company in California with his partner Louis Schlesinger, a Guatemalan citizen of German descent, and transferred his concession to it. Although the company had an authorized capital of $1 million, Nanne and Schlesinger put up only $28,000 of their

Map 2. Railroad Construction, 1871–1897

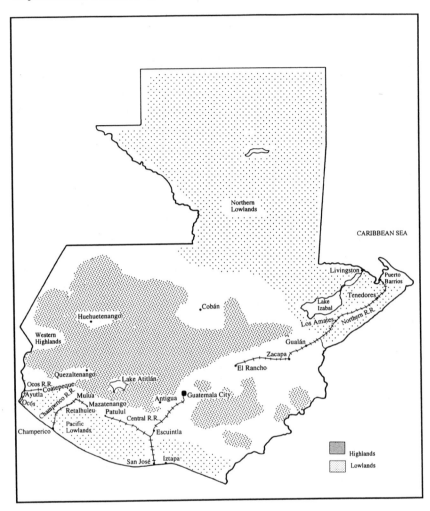

own money. While at the time the concession may have been, as Delmer G. Ross claims, a "good bargain" for the Guatemalan government, it contained the seeds of a conflict between the monopolistic interests of foreign capital and a state committed to a nationalistic development program.[7]

On July 19, 1880, General Barrios celebrated his birthday by officially inaugurating the country's first railroad. For completing the line three months ahead of schedule, the government rewarded Nanne with the rights to extend the railroad from Escuintla to Guatemala City. Once again, Nanne swung a deal whereby he used capital put up by Guatemalans to build a line he or his company would own for ninety-nine years. The 1880 concession included an annual subsidy of 125,000 pesos for twenty-five years, with 500,000 pesos paid to the entrepreneurs in advance; a grant of 150,000 acres of land; and preferential rights to construct the Northern Railway on the same terms offered to any other contractor.[8] If Nanne exercised these preferential rights, he could monopolize rail traffic across Guatemala. He claimed that these clauses were included in the concession because the country's first railroad "was naturally surrounded by exceptional difficulties and of very doubtful pecuniary results."[9]

The 1877 and 1880 concessions contained clauses that American capitalists found very attractive. Essentially, Nanne was given the right to monopolize Guatemalan railroads, and the government guaranteed him a 12 percent annual return on his investment. If and when he extended the line to Guatemala City, he expected the railroad to yield about $500,000 per year, provided that it would come under the management of someone more experienced in business administration than himself. Nanne was a railroad promoter with an interest in power and politics, not a chief executive officer. In 1884, Charles F. Crocker, a director of the firm that acquired Nanne's railroad, complained that "Mr. Nanne is not a practical railroad man, nor for that matter, even a practical business man, and he is getting us into more or less trouble down there constantly, by raising issues between the company and the government, and by splurging around as one in authority."[10]

Nanne had enough business sense to realize the value of the concessions that he had acquired through politics, an arena more appropriately suited to his talents. In 1881 he visited New York and offered to sell his property and concessions to General Daniel Butterfield, who has been described as both a "civil war hero" and a "fraud."[11] On September 29, Butterfield, acting on behalf of unnamed New York associates, tentatively agreed to purchase the Central and the rights to build the line from Escuintla to Guatemala City, and to consolidate both railroads under a new U.S. corporation. On December 13, 1881, following an inspection of the Guatemalan properties, Butterfield purchased 5,150 of the 10,000 shares in the Guatemala Central for $400,000 and one half of Nanne's 1880 concession that authorized construction of a forty-eight-mile line from Escuintla to Guatemala City.[12]

At the same time, Butterfield gave a share of the enterprise to the caudillo, who reportedly held a share in every profitable Guatemalan enterprise.[13] During the negotiations, friends of Barrios intimated that "the influences of the government there against the company in getting workmen and various other ways made it evident that something had to be done," according to Butterfield's lawyers. These same persons confidentially suggested that the goodwill of their chief executive could be purchased by a discreet payment. Butterfield played along with the rules of the game and reserved 8 percent of his company's shares (valued at $80,000) for Barrios and his partners.[14]

Butterfield's unnamed associates turned out to be powerful American railroad men who had a reputation for corrupt dealings with the U.S. government. In May 1882 he formed a new corporation with Huntington, Crocker, and Leland Stanford, three of the four "Pacific Associates" who built the western half of the first U.S. transcontinental railroad. Huntington and associates controlled the Central Pacific and Southern Pacific railroads, in addition to steamships, ports, and, allegedly, scores of politicians. By the 1890s, Huntington owned enough railroad track to connect the poles of the earth.[15] Butterfield transferred his shares in the Central to the Central American Pacific Railway and Transportation Company, a firm in which Huntington controlled 51 percent of the stock and his associates held a minority interest.[16] The main purpose of this new company was to complete the line from Escuintla to Guatemala City and consolidate it with the Central.

After the Pacific Associates took over Nanne's railroad, Crocker demanded to know why 8 percent of the enterprise was reserved for corrupt Guatemalan officials. Butterfield explained the reasons for which he concluded a sub rosa understanding and pointed out that Barrios would not likely cause problems for a company in which he held stock. Crocker recognized the value of maintaining cordial relations with the executive and withdrew his objections to the arrangements.[17] The venal precedent set by Barrios ultimately undermined the Liberal development program.

At the time, few people questioned the wisdom of the policies that had lured Huntington to Guatemala. If he could build a railroad across the United States, there was no doubt about his ability to finance a forty-eight-mile track up a fairly steep grade on the Pacific coast. Under Nanne's skilled supervision, the railroad was completed in time for Barrios to ride it into Guatemala City on September 15, 1884, the anniversary of the nation's independence. Upon arrival in the capital he delivered an emotional and patriotic speech about the country's economic progress. But while Barrios could take pride in the extension of the railroad to the capital, American capitalists financed, built, and owned it. In 1885, Huntington merged the

Central and the Central American Pacific Railway into the Guatemala Central Railroad Company of California.[18]

Given the resources that Huntington commanded and the concessions under which he operated, there was every reason to believe that he would soon monopolize rail transit across Guatemala. Yet Barrios and a faction of the ruling elite opposed foreign control of the nation's infrastructure. In 1881, shortly after the completion of the first line from San José to Escuintla, the Sociedad Económica (Economic Society) presented a plan to organize a Guatemalan company to complete the line to the capital. Although that project failed, the elite remained interested in building and operating its own lines. In 1886, while criticizing the Central's irregular schedule and poor safety record, *finqueros* castigated the foreign monopoly and lamented the policies that had allowed its creation.[19] The strength of nationalistic sentiments among the ruling elite made it imperative for Barrios and his two successors to deal cautiously with foreign investors; while they needed foreign capital and technology, they hoped that control of the economic infrastructure would remain in Guatemalan hands, either private or public.

The same general who gave away monopolistic privileges to foreign capitalists promoted his country's economic independence through the Northern Railway, a line designed to give Guatemalans a Caribbean exit from the two U.S. companies that dominated Pacific coast commerce. The Central monopolized rail transportation between Guatemala City and San José, and the Pacific Mail Steamship Company dominated shipping between California and the Panama Railroad. As the only line calling at the Pacific ports of Mexico and Central America, the Pacific Mail extracted high prices for the poor services it offered to Guatemalan shippers. In the absence of competitive steamship lines and an outlet on the Caribbean, *finqueros* had no choice but to accept the economically and geographically unattractive necessity of sending their coffee south on the Central Railroad, loading it on Pacific Mail steamships, transshipping it across the Panama Railroad, and reloading it in the Caribbean for shipment to North American and European markets. A direct line to the Caribbean would save shippers precious time and money.[20]

The construction of the Northern Railway therefore came to symbolize Guatemala's drive for economic independence, since the line would liberate the country from two foreign monopolies. Yet it meant much more than that, for Barrios and the Liberals believed that the Northern would facilitate the transformation of their "backward" country into a modern industrial civilization. Aside from giving Guatemala convenient access to the Atlantic world, it would also promote agricultural development, attract industrious immigrants, lure foreign investments, and gain Liberals the international respect they desperately sought. To the Liberals the Northern represented the pivotal joint in the entire development program.[21]

The Central Railroad stood directly in the path of Guatemala's economic independence. Possessing preferential construction rights on all railroads, it could legally claim the rights to build the Northern and merge it with the Central and would certainly oppose the construction of any line that diverted traffic away from it, as the Northern would do once completed by the state. Still, the Central could build railroads only on the same terms offered to any other contractor; if it did not find the terms attractive, it could decline to exercise its rights, as Nanne wisely did in 1880 when a local contractor failed to fulfill its obligations to build the first portions of the Northern Railway.[22]

The failure of the first effort did not deter Barrios. Recognizing that the railroad would eventually need enough freight to make it profitable, he promoted the economic development of the region by declaring Livingston (on Lake Izabal) a free port and facilitating the acquisition of public lands, thereby laying the foundations of the banana industry in the department of Izabal. Guatemalan, West Indian, and American planters initiated the business in the 1870s, and bananas became a valuable export commodity by the mid-1880s.[23]

On August 4, 1883, Barrios established a system of obligatory subscription to the Northern Railway. Every Guatemalan who earned 8 pesos or more per month had to purchase at least one share (valued at 40 pesos) in the railroad, and some wealthy individuals, including Barrios, voluntarily purchased large blocks of stock. As the law established a board of directors to manage the company, it demonstrated the caudillo's determination to keep ownership and management under national control. With financing secured from local subscriptions, the government contracted with two American firms in 1884 to build the line from the coast to Guatemala City. Although the concessions included subsidies and large land grants, the American companies acted solely as subcontractors; the government retained ownership of the entire line. Believing that the Central could make a reasonable profit, Nanne invoked his contractual rights and offered to build the Northern Railway on the same terms granted to the two American firms. Government officials side-stepped Nanne's efforts to submit a counterproposal, using what Nanne called "sophisticated evasions."[24]

The Northern Railway project died with Barrios in April 1885, due to diminishing government revenues that came with a decline in coffee exports in the mid-1880s. The American firms built only sixteen miles before the government ran out of money and workers fled. Barrios's successor, General Barillas, liquidated all affairs of the railroad and used the funds that had been raised for other purposes. Barillas still intended to complete the railroad as a national enterprise and refused to yield to the monopolistic designs of the American capitalists. It would be difficult to dislodge them from the railroad, however, because they operated a profitable line under two legitimate concessions. In the first full year of operation, the Central reported profits of $111,917.[25] The profitability of the line only strengthened Guatemalan interest in dispossessing them of it.

To a certain extent the hostility demonstrated by General Barillas toward the Central reflected the degree to which German and conservative interests influenced his government. Barillas inherited a government that had expended scarce financial resources trying to reunite the isthmus while a recession in the coffee market sapped the treasury of export revenues. To restore financial stability, Barillas turned the internal and external debt over to a syndicate of local and foreign capitalists affiliated with German firms. He also mended relations with Conservative landowners and the church, all of which may account for some of the anti-American attitudes that characterized the Barillas administration.[26]

Competition between American and German interests reached a critical stage during the Barillas administration. American investment was basically confined to the Central, while German-owned fincas (coffee plantations) produced about one third of the coffee crop, and German merchant houses financed the operations of a considerable number of other firms.[27] Guatemala and Germany concluded a reciprocity treaty in 1887 that removed all tariff barriers between the two countries and disrupted American efforts to promote U.S. trade and investment in the region. In 1889, U.S. Consul General James R. Hosmer warned the State Department of the pervasive German influence: "The Teutonic element of the foreign population of Guatemala is a financial and commercial absorbent of an Octopus nature, which threatens to grasp in its tentacles, and to swallow up all that is worth having among the possibilities of enterprise and development throughout this Republic."[28]

The real octopus did not invest in Guatemala until 1904. In the 1880s, with the Germans showing as much interest in Guatemala as the Americans (if not more), the Liberals had the means and the confidence to resist those Americans who considered the country reserved for U.S. trade and investment. In reality, the Germans, British, and Americans divided trade and investment opportunities among themselves. Between 1880 and 1900, German and American trade with Guatemala increased at the expense of Great Britain. By 1898, 33 percent of Guatemala's imports came from the United States, with Great Britain and Germany supplying roughly 21 percent. Since most coffee went to Germany, however, that country received the greatest share of Guatemalan exports.[29] The diversity in trading partners partially offset the disadvantages inherent in relying exclusively on one export crop and did not give any of the foreign powers significant advantages over the others.

Consequently, when the Central complained about the government's violation of its contractual rights, American diplomatic pressure on the government was usually ineffectual. The absence of effective diplomatic support made it imperative for American investors to maintain cordial relations with the government by whatever means worked. Partly for that reason, Butterfield had given Barrios 8 percent of the Central, and his company was rewarded with favorable government treatment. To maintain cordial relations with the Barillas government, Nanne offered $300,000 in fully paid stock for the goodwill of the executive branch, a gift that the caudillo accepted on July 10, 1885, without disclosing how he would distribute it.[30]

The $300,000 failed to change the Liberal's policy on the Northern Railway, however, for a month later Barillas turned the construction project over to Martin Roberts, a foreign capitalist not linked to the Central. Although the Roberts contract gave Nanne sixty days to exercise preferential construction rights, he protested the concession on the grounds that it should not have been signed prior to his decision. American minister Henry C. Hall supported Nanne's claims that his contractual rights had been violated and subsequently warned U.S. investors to stay away from the project because there was "not the slightest guarantee that these obligations [in the Roberts contract] will be held to be any more sacred than those which have already been, practically, repudiated."[31]

In response to the Central's complaints, Barillas suspended subsidy payments to the Central in the fall of 1885. Nanne refused to deliver the $300,000 in stock until the government recognized its obligations and resumed the payments; Barillas declined to do either until he received the stock. On November 4 the government threatened to cancel the Central's concessions if the company did not deliver the certificates by November 14. The Ministry of Development justified its threat on the shaky premise that the government had not formally inspected and approved the line from Escuintla to Guatemala City, although no clause in the 1880 contract had provided for any such inspection and Barrios's official inauguration of the line in 1884 suggested that the government had approved the line and opened it for business. Since the government insisted on an official inspection, Nanne conceded the point and promised to make any and all repairs deemed necessary.[32]

The threat of forfeiture passed, Nanne held onto his stocks, and the government withheld subsidy payments for another year. Some illegitimate interests may have influenced the government's actions, but it is also clear that it had little respect for, and perhaps intended to renegotiate, the concessions of 1877 and 1880. It called for the company to replace all wooden bridges with steel and iron bridges and maintained the threat of cancellation because, in the absence of any regulatory mechanisms, it was the only way to secure the company's compliance.[33] In May 1886 the Ministry of Development defended its rigid construction standards by reminding Nanne of the extraordinary privileges that his company had received, particularly 150,000 acres of land and a ninety-nine year tax exemption.

The conflict continued until September 1887, when the government agreed to forego the $300,000 in gold coin in exchange for a reduced annual subsidy. Nanne promised to replace all wooden bridges with iron ones and to drop all claims against the government, which formally acknowledged the Central's fulfillment of the two previous railroad contracts.[34] The Guatemalan legislature approved the settlement in April 1888, and Nanne considered the case closed.

The conflict heated up less than one year later. Still at issue was the monopolistic intent of a foreign company and the nationalistic designs of the Guatemalan state. Despite the conflict between the Central and the government, the railroad's profits averaged approximately $224,000 per year between 1885 and 1890. Profits might have soared even higher than that, however, if the Central could have extended its line to the Caribbean coast, but the Liberals prevented the Americans from reaching this objective until Minor Keith arrived at the turn of the century. In February 1889 the government hired a French syndicate to build the Northern without giving Nanne the opportunity to exercise his option.[35]

Nanne issued his normal protests that the contract violated his company's rights, and American diplomats supported him. Consul General Hosmer viewed the French contract as a significant setback to the Pan-American movement then being promoted by Secretary of State James G. Blaine. He warned the Guatemalans that the concession was detrimental to American-Guatemalan relations because it gave the French the opportunity to monopolize railway transport from ocean to ocean. The prospect of an American monopoly on the same line elicited no protests from the State Department, but Hosmer considered the concession as proof that the Guatemalans treated American interests "with contemptuous indifference, if not absolute scorn." The Guatemalans responded that they had simply engaged the construction services of a French consortium for forty years, after which they would assume ownership of the line.[36]

In fact, the Guatemalans were attempting to do much more than that. Guatemalan *finqueros* had been critical of the Central's poor services and monopolistic pretensions since its completion in 1880. Barillas reflected and promoted the nationalistic interests of the landowning elite and used the French syndicate to build the Northern and eliminate the Central. The French syndicate, directed by Henri Louis Felix Cottu, offered Guatemalans the opportunity of liberating themselves from their dependence on the Central and the Pacific Mail.[37] In the summer of 1889, Cottu, the government, and the Central Railroad signed a series of agreements by which the Guatemalan government would nationalize the Central Railroad.

On August 6, 1889, Huntington sold the Central to Cottu for $3.75 million. The contract gave Cottu until October 31 to make a 20 percent down payment, and on September 8, he signed a contract in which he agreed to raise a $21-million loan to finance the construction of the Northern Railway, by Cottu or a company organized by him. In a separate accord, Cottu agreed to transfer the Central, which he would own by the end of 1889, to the government. "By the single stroke of the pen of Monsieur Henri Cottu," as Nanne explained these three complicated transactions, the government would nationalize the Central Railroad and construct the Northern Railway.[38]

While this nationalization proposal represents an early effort to establish state control over a railroad, it is not unusual in Latin American history. State and local private capital played a more prominent role in railway construction than Latin Americanists generally recognize. Between 1837 and 1861 the initiative for railroad construction in Cuba, Mexico, Chile, Peru, Brazil, and Argentina came from local capitalists. In the province of Buenos Aires, 54 percent of operational mileage in 1898 belonged to a state-owned, locally financed company. During the liberal dictatorship of Porfirio Díaz, the Mexican federal government granted railroad concessions to state, foreign, and local ventures before it nationalized two thirds of the railroad network between 1907 and 1910.[39]

Because Guatemala, like other Latin American countries, lacked capital but not entrepreneurs, it solicited foreign financing for a railroad that it would own and operate. When Cottu exercised his option and made the down payment on October 24, 1889, Barillas was on the verge of consummating the national development project. The caudillos and the French could not dislodge the Americans so easily. Cottu still had to convince French bankers to loan Guatemala $21 million in order to carry out the transaction. Some Parisian financiers had expressed an interest in the deal, but they backed out of the project, and Cottu returned to Guatemala in the spring of 1890 to renegotiate. All parties, including Huntington, wanted to complete the transaction, and therefore Barillas authorized a new contract with Cottu in 1890. Even with the revisions and extensions, Cottu could not generate sufficient European capital, and the contracts expired in 1891.[40]

In the presidential elections of 1891, with coffee prices rising and the state's financial position improving, the Liberals held onto their dreams of completing the Northern Railway. General José María Reyna Barrios, nephew of Justo Rufino, won a fairly free election, and Barillas arranged a peaceful transfer of power. American diplomats considered Reyna Barrios favorably disposed toward the United States because the intervention of an American minister three years earlier had convinced Barillas to exile rather than execute Reyna Barrios for conspiracy. When Reyna Barrios left for San Francisco with his Lousiana-born wife, the American minister, Lansing Mizner, predicted that the United States could count upon him "as our friend" if he ever became president.[41]

Nevertheless, Reyna Barrios proceeded with plans to complete the Northern Railway project as originally conceived by his uncle. Although he inherited only sixteen miles of poorly laid and deteriorating track, the economic outlook in the early 1890s seemed to indicate that his government could raise or borrow the capital necessary to finance the project. On May 10, 1892, the government authorized the emission of one hundred thousand bonds worth 100 pesos each, some of which would be forced on civilians and military personnel. The decree also created a new directory general of the Northern Railway to supervise construction.[42] Over the next five years, construction crews worked at a feverish pace to bring the line to Guatemala City.

Rather than continue the fight against a government that rarely respected its contractual obligations, Huntington gave it the opportunity to realize its ambitions. In June 1893 the government and the Central drafted a modus vivendi in which the government accepted the construction of the San José to Guatemala City railroad as "finished business" and reaffirmed the rights and obligations contained in the Central's 1877 and 1880 contracts. Although the agreement explicitly confirmed the company's preferential construction rights on all railways, the provision had little practical meaning, given that the government had already resumed work on the Northern. Reyna Barrios was determined to keep the Central on the Pacific side of the country, and Huntington was willing to pursue the opportunities still available in the rich coffee districts. On October 24, 1893, the government authorized construction of a line from Santa María to Patulul, and on September 15, 1897, the Central opened this thirty-two-mile line.[43]

The drive to Patulul brought the Central into direct competition with the smaller and weaker Compañía Anónima del Ferrocarril Occidental (Occidental Railroad), a Guatemalan firm operating a twenty-eight-mile line from Champerico to Retalhuleu. In June 1889 a group of *finqueros* from the Quezaltenango region purchased the railroad from the American firm that built it, apparently with the assistance of President Barillas, who may have coerced the Americans into selling by deliberately neglecting the government's financial obligations to the company. In any case, a contract of December 11, 1895, authorized the Occidental to extend its line southwestward to Mazatenango, a point to which the Central would eventually want to extend its lines. The owners of the Occidental could not possibly match the capital reserves of the Central, which had virtually unlimited access to capital through Huntington and cleared more than $200,000 per year. Nanne's predictable protests about the violations of the Central's contracts only irritated the government, and the Occidental's ambitious *finqueros* pushed forward. When the company opened this line on March 15, 1899, only thirty miles separated the Occidental from the Central.[44]

Thus, railroad construction was pushed forward in the 1890s by foreign, state, and local capital. A fourth syndicate, formed by German *finqueros* in the Verapaz region, obtained a concession to build a twenty-eight-mile line from Pancajché in 1892. Their interests in railroad construction, however, were limited to a line that would expedite coffee shipments from their plantations to Lake Izabal. Following the inauguration of the Verapaz Railroad in 1898, the Germans showed little enthusiasm for competing with the Central or financing the Northern.[45]

The state and the Guatemalan capitalists behind the Occidental, in contrast, challenged the Central on two fronts and gradually exhausted Huntington's interest in Guatemala. By far the most serious challenge to Huntington came from the state. In 1892 the directors of the Northern Railway hired American engineer Silvanus Miller to complete the line to Guatemala City. Miller divided the route into six sections and methodically built five of the six sections on schedule. In each of the five contracts, he signed as a subcontractor with the government, which maintained ownership and supervised construction. By September 1895, Miller had completed section three, a short but difficult twenty-mile span that included a bridge over the Motagua River. He also constructed a two hundred-foot wharf at Puerto Barrios, with two sets of rails running out to an iron-roofed building at its end. As the wharf was twice destroyed by fire in the 1890s, service at the docks was irregular and generally inadequate, but Miller completed eighty miles of track from Puerto Barrios to Gualán by 1895.[46]

Once the line reached Guatemala City, only seventy-one miles of the Central Railroad and the wharf at San José stood between Reyna Barrios and a state-owned, transoceanic railroad. If the Central did not bend to his wishes, he would have to get around it. In April 1895 the government proposed to do just that by building a short railroad spur from Obero (just north of San José) to Iztapa, an old port that the government planned to convert into a deep-water anchorage. With the railroad spur and a new port, the government-owned Northern Railway could bypass the wharf at San José, which the Central purchased from a Guatemalan firm in 1895. Nanne was given the opportunity to exercise his preferential rights on this branch, but he naturally refused because there was no reason to divert freight from a wharf controlled by his company. Nanne claimed that this project violated the spirit of the 1877 and 1880 contracts, which gave his company the right to control the principal Pacific port, be it San José or Iztapa.[47]

By deliberately ignoring or violating the Central's contracts, Reyna Barrios evidently hoped to convince Huntington to sell the line to his government at a discounted price. On September 4, 1895, after he learned that Huntington had initiated negotiations with British capitalists for the sale of the Central, the caudillo decreed that no railroad could be transferred to another company without his express consent. In the event of sale, he declared that the government possessed preferential rights of purchase. Since this decree contradicted the Central's contracts, which established unlimited rights of transfer, Huntington proceeded with the sale of the line to J. Henry Schroder and Company of London. By contract of September 27 this firm agreed to purchase all the railroad lines, properties, and con-cessions of the Central Railroad, including the wharf at San José, for £1.44 million. In any case, Schroder evidently knew something about conducting business in Guatemala because it inserted a clause in the pur-chase contract that allowed either party to rescind the agreement on account of war, blockade, or financial difficulty.[48]

The clause also gave Schroder the option of rescinding the agreement in the event that the caudillo's terms were "unduly expensive." Expenses, as Schroder's lawyers understood the term, meant "all out of pocket payments that it may be necessary or advisable to make in connection with or in expediting the registration of the new company in Guatemala." "In other words," the lawyers continued, "the word 'expenses' is intended to cover anything that may have to be paid to the Government and officials for their services and for expedition."[49] Given that Schroder was attempting to pur-chase a railroad that the American minister called "the most remunerative piece of railroad in the world, of its length," the price was bound to be high.[50] Evidently, the out-of-pocket expenses demanded by Reyna Barrios led Schroder to rescind the agreement.

At about the same time that Schroder negotiated for the purchase of the Central, it also extended financing to the Northern Railway. With govern-ment expenditures exceeding income from taxes and the sale of bonds, the government was compelled to take out a £658,500 short-term loan with Schwartz and Company, a Guatemala City merchant house founded by Isidore Schwartz, a German-American resident in Guatemala. Schwartz was affiliated with Müller and Thomsen of Hamburg, Germany, and Schroder. Since the loan was secured by a mortgage on the entire Northern Railway, either the German or British syndicate would take possession of the transoceanic line in the likely event that Guatemala defaulted. The Ameri-can minister asked the secretary of state if he should take action to prevent the transfer of the line to the Europeans.[51]

Given that Schroder subsequently financed Keith's railroad project in Guatemala, it is likely that he, rather than British or German investors, would have gained control of the Northern in the event of a default. In any case, the ambitions of Reyna Barrios continued to exceed his government's ability to pay, as he initiated negotiations for the purchase of the Central in 1896, designating Schwartz as his official negotiator. On June 5, Schwartz signed a contract by which Guatemala would purchase all the railroads, concessions, and properties held by the Central, including the 167,000 acres granted to the company in 1880, for $6 million. In anticipation of financial difficulties, he included a clause in the contract whereby it could be rescinded by either party in the event of war, rebellion, blockade, or finan-cial difficulty. Cooler heads prevailed, and the government rescinded the agreement on July 18, citing financial difficulties that made the transaction undesirable.[52]

Had the government proceeded with the purchase, a financial disaster would have surely followed. When Brazilian coffee saturated the international market in 1897 and prices and government revenues fell sharply, Guatemala entered its most serious economic crisis since 1871. Reyna Barrios was still determined to complete the Northern Railway and borrowed another $1.5 million from five local banks in 1897, but it was too late. Work on the railroad came to a halt just after Miller completed the thirty-three miles of section five, from Zacapa to El Rancho. He died in late December 1897, and the construction effort died with him.[53]

The crisis effectively ended the Liberals' hopes of building and owning a railroad linking the capital city to Puerto Barrios. They had spent nearly two decades and $8 million on the line, and the most significant consequence of their efforts was a huge debt and a currency deflated by wild deficit spending.[54] The collapse of coffee prices sapped the caudillos of their willingness and their ability to resist the monopolistic aspirations of American capitalists. Minor Keith knew how to exploit their weaknesses.

The debts incurred during the 1890s made it difficult if not impossible for the state to raise any additional capital, either at home or abroad. The project was nonetheless attractive to foreign investors because the Northern Railway could be operated from Puerto Barrios to El Rancho, and banana plantations in the Motagua River valley were already providing some of the freight it needed to operate profitably. Independent planters had been cultivating bananas in Guatemala for three decades prior to the arrival of United Fruit. The foundations of the banana business were laid during the dictatorship of Justo Rufino Barrios when small farmers, many of them blacks of foreign origin, cultivated bananas as a sideline and sold their fruit to shippers such as the Macheca brothers, who began calling on that coast in the 1880s.[55]

More aggressive efforts by Barrios's successors contributed to an expansion of the banana business. The Barillas administration promoted banana cultivation by making lands available for thirty to thirty-five cents per acre. A number of entrepreneurs, including some American citizens, took advantage of the offer and invested in Guatemalan bananas, recognizing that a well-managed plantation could yield profits of between $75 to $100 per acre per year. Banana exports reached 117,514 bunches in 1887, and Hosmer reported that the banana crop "just now excites much care and attention."[56]

As work on the Northern Railway progressed, the prospects for the banana industry grew even brighter. In Miller's contract for the construction of section three between Los Amates and Gualán, one clause instructed Miller to clear fifty feet on both sides of the railroad and plant "useful" trees as the line was constructed.[57] Miller and the Guatemalans did not have to be told by Keith that the railroad and bananas would have to develop simultaneously. Unfortunately for Guatemalans, the economic crisis put railroad and banana development on hold. If the Northern Railway project had been successful, the future course of Guatemala's political and economic development would have been radically different. It is no coincidence that Keith took a personal interest in Guatemala only after the project failed. As the economic crisis deepened, the chances of the Guatemalans completing the railroad and promoting banana cultivation diminished. The failure of the Northern Railway signaled the defeat of the national development program and drove the next dictator into the arms of Keith and United Fruit.

Notes

1. On the Liberal revolution see Thomas Herrick, *Desarrollo económico y político de Guatemala durante el período de Justo Rufino Barrios (1871–1885)*, trans. Rafael Piedra-Santa Arandi (Guatemala: Editorial Universitaria Centroamericana, 1974); Jorge Mario García Laguardia, *La reforma liberal en Guatemala: vida política y orden constitucional* (Guatemala: Editorial Universitaria, Universidad de San Carlos de Guatemala, 1985); and David McCreery, "An Odious Feudalism: Mandamiento Labor and Commercial Agriculture in Guatemala, 1858–1920," *Latin American Perspectives* 13:1 (1986): 99–117.

2. J. Fred Rippy, "Relations of the United States and Guatemala during the Epoch of Justo Rufino Barrios," *Hispanic American Historical Review* 22:4 (1942): 596–99; David McCreery, *Development and State in Reforma Guatemala, 1871–1885* (Athens: Ohio University Center for International Studies, 1983), 31–32; Henry Franklin Jackson, "The Technological Development of Central America, 1823–1913" (Ph.D. diss., University of Chicago, 1948), 180–81.

3. Colin M. Lewis, "The Financing of Railway Development in Latin America, 1850–1914," *Ibero-Amerikanisches Archiv* 9:3–4 (1983): 260.

4. James R. Hosmer, "Guatemala Central Railroad," U.S. Department of State, Bureau of Foreign and Domestic Commerce, *Consular Reports*, vol. 26, no. 94 (June 1888): 414; Delmer G. Ross, "The Construction of the Interoceanic Railroad of Guatemala," *The Americas* 33:3 (January 1977): 434–35.

5. Stewart, *Keith and Costa Rica*, 1–33.

6. Ross, "Construction of the Interoceanic Railroad," 435.

7. Jackson, "Technological Development," 181–82; "Original Assignment, G. Nanne to G.C.R.R. Co.," November 2, 1878, JL 1, Box 1, Folder 8, Pacific Improvement Company Records, Stanford University Libraries, Department of Special Collections and University Archives, Stanford, California (hereafter cited as PICO records); Ross, "Construction of the Interoceanic Railroad," 436-37.

8. Ross, "Construction of the Interoceanic Railroad," 436–37; "Concession of the Government of Guatemala to Louis Schlesinger and Guillermo Nanne," July 13, 1880, JL 1, Box 1, Folder 8, PICO records.

9. Hosmer to State, April 26, 1889, enclosure no. 1, Henry F. W. Nanne to Hosmer, April 20, 1889, U.S. Department of State, Despatches from U.S. Ministers to Central America, 1824–1906 (hereafter cited as Diplomatic despatches).

10. Charles F. Crocker to J. E. Gates, August 14, 1884, JL 1, Box 2, Folder 11, PICO records.

11. Ross, "Construction of the Interoceanic Railroad," 438; McCreery, *Development and State*, 90.

12. "Memorandum of Agreement between General Daniel Butterfield and Guillermo Nanne," September 29, 1881, JL 1, Box 1, Folder 8, PICO records; "Agreement of Sale, G.C.R.R. Shares and Concession, Schlesinger to General Butterfield," December 13, 1881, JL 1, Box 1, Folder 8, PICO records.

13. Handy, *Gift of the Devil*, 63.

14. W. C. Nicoll (representing General Butterfield) to J. E. Gates (treasurer, Central American Pacific Railway and Transportation Company), May 19, 1884, JL 1, Box 2, Folder 11, PICO records.

15. Oscar Lewis, *The Big Four: The Story of Huntington, Stanford, Hopkins, and Crocker, and of the Building of the Central Pacific* (1938, reprint, New York: Alfred A. Knopf, 1966), 276; Matthew Josephson, *The Robber Barons* (1934, reprint, New York: Harcourt Brace Jovanovich, 1962), 216–30.

16. "Memorandum of Agreement between Collis P. Huntington and Daniel Butterfield," and "Supplemental agreement between Huntington and Butterfield," May 19, 1882, JL 1, Box 1, Folder 8, PICO records.

17. Nicoll to Gates, May 19, 1884, JL 1, Box 2, Folder 11, PICO records.

18. H. Remsen Whitehouse, "Railroads and American Interests in Guatemala," *Consular Reports*, vol. 14, no. 47 (November 1884): 330–31; Chester Lloyd Jones, *Guatemala, Past and Present* (1940, reprint, New York: Russell & Russell, 1966), 251; "Plan of Consolidation, Guatemala Central Railroad, 1885," JL 1, Box 2, Folder 9, PICO records. The line was later transferred to the Pacific Improvement Company, a wholly owned subsidiary of the Southern Pacific, in which Huntington was the major stockholder.

19. Wayne Foster Anderson, "The Development of Export Transportation in Liberal Guatemala, 1871–1920" (Ph.D. diss., Tulane University, 1985), 187–88.

20. Anderson, "Development of Export Transporation," 232, 272; Pierce M. B. Young, "Pacific Mail Steamship Contracts," *Consular Reports*, vol. 47, no. 173 (February 1895): 299; McCreery, *Development and State*, 32.

21 Anderson, "Development of Export Transportation," 316. For more on the railroad project see David McCreery, "Developmental Aspects of the Construction of the Guatemala Northern Railroad: The First Attempt, 1879 to 1885" (M.A. thesis, Tulane University, 1969).

22. Ross, "Construction of the Interoceanic Railroad," 441; Hosmer to State, April 26, 1889, enclosure no. 1, Nanne to Salvador Barrutia (minister of development), April 20, 1889, Diplomatic despatches.

23. McCreery, *Development and State*, 57; Rippy, "Relations of the United States and Guatemala," 603–4.

24. Hosmer to State, April 26, 1889, enclosure no. 1, Nanne to Barrutia, April 20, 1889, Diplomatic despatches; McCreery, *Development and State*, 70–82.

25. Henry C. Hall to State, July 22, 1885, Diplomatic despatches; Samuel Kimberly, "Trade and Commerce of Guatemala," *Consular Reports*, vol. 36, no. 130 (July 1891): 377.

26. Hall to State, July 22, 1885, Diplomatic despatches; Fernando González Dávison, *El régimen liberal en Guatemala (1871–1944)* (Guatemala: Editorial Universitaria, Universidad de San Carlos de Guatemala, 1987), 28–29.

27. Regina Wagner, "Actividades empresariales de los alemanes en Guatemala, 1850–1920," *Mesoamérica* 13 (June 1987): 102. On the role of the Germans see also Julio Castellano Cambranes, *El Imperialismo Alemán en Guatemala: el*

Tratado de Comercio de 1887 (Guatemala: Universidad de San Carlos, Instituto de Investigaciones Económicas y Sociales, 1977); and Guillermo Náñez Falcón, "Erwin Paul Dieseldorff, German Entrepreneur in the Alta Verapaz of Guatemala, 1889–1937" (Ph.D. diss., Tulane University, 1970).

28. Hosmer to State, April 10, 1889, Diplomatic despatches.

29. U.S. Department of State, *Review of the World's Commerce, 1899*, 113; "Commercial Movement of Guatemala in 1895," *Consular Reports*, vol. 55, no. 204 (September 1897): 141; "Imports into Guatemala," ibid., vol. 59, no. 221 (February 1899): 309.

30. Hall to State, November 11, 1885, enclosed letter of Nanne and A. J. Finlay to Hall, October 6, 1885, Diplomatic despatches. Because the stock transfer was specified in a public contract, the state, rather than General Barillas personally, may have assumed partial ownership of the Central Railroad.

31. Hall to State, November 20, 1885, Diplomatic despatches.

32. Ibid., November 11, 1885, enclosed letters of Señor [Antonio de] Aguirre (minister of development) to Nanne, November 4, 1885, and Nanne to Aguirre, November 7, 1885, Diplomatic despatches.

33. Hall to State, July 24, 1886, enclosed translation of Señor Rafael Salazar to Nanne, May 25, 1886, Diplomatic despatches.

34. Hall to State, September 17, 1887; Hall to State, April 3, 1888; Hosmer to State, May 1, 1888; Lansing Mizner to State, December 31, 1889, enclosure no. 1, Petition and Affidavit of William Nanne, December 19, 1889, Diplomatic despatches.

35. Kimberly, "Trade and Commerce of Guatemala," *Consular Reports*, vol. 36, no. 130 (July 1891): 377; Mizner to State, December 31, 1889; Diplomatic despatches.

36. Hosmer to State, April 22, 1889, and April 26, 1889, Diplomatic despatches.

37. Anderson, "Development of Export Transportation," 335.

38. "Memorandum of Agreement between C. P. Huntington and Henry Louis Felix Cottu," JL 1, Box 2, Folder 9, PICO records; Mizner to State, December 31, 1889, enclosure No. 1, Petition and Affidavit of William Nanne, December 19, 1889, Diplomatic despatches.

39. Lewis, "Financing of Railway Development," 257–72; John Coatsworth, *Growth Against Development: The Economic Impact of Railroads in Porfirian Mexico* (DeKalb: Northern Illinois University Press, 1981), 43–46. On the Mexicanization of the railways see John H. McNeely, *The Railways of Mexico: A Study in Nationalization* (El Paso: Texas Western College, Southwestern Studies, Monograph no. 5, 1964).

40. Mizner to State, April 30, 1890; Kimberly to State, April 13, 1891, Diplomatic despatches; Jackson, "Technological Development," 194; Anderson, "Development of Export Transportation," 335.

41. Mizner to State, February 24, 1889, Diplomatic despatches.

42. Ross, "Construction of the Interoceanic Railroad," 445–50.

43. Pierce M. B. Young to State, October 16, 1895, enclosed letter of Nanne to Young, October 12, 1895, Diplomatic despatches; J. W. Kendrick, *A Report upon International Railways of Central America, Located in the Republics of Guatemala and Salvador* (Chicago, N.p.: 1921), 20–21.

44. Kendrick, *A Report upon International Railways*, 21; Jackson, "Technological Development," 191–92.

45. Wagner, "Actividades empresariales de los alemanes," 111–14.

46. Ross, "Construction of the Interoceanic Railroad," 447–48; Anderson, "Development of Export Transportation," 358–64.

47. Young to State, December 4, 1895, Diplomatic despatches; Anderson, "Development of Export Transportation," 89–95.

48. Young to State, October 16, 1895, Diplomatic despatches; "Guatemala Central Railroad Company, C. P. Huntington to Messrs. J. Henry Schroder & Co., Agreement for Sale and Purchase of Railways and Property," September 27, 1895, JL 1, Box 2, Folder 9, PICO records.

49. Stetson, Tracy, Jennings & Russell to Charles H. Tweed, September 25, 1895, JL 1, Box 2, Folder 11, PICO records.

50. Young to State, December 4, 1895, Diplomatic despatches.

51. Donald L. Kemmerer and Bruce R. Dalgaard, "Inflation, Intrigue, and Monetary Reform in Guatemala, 1919–1926," *The Historian* 46:1 (1983): 27; Ross, "Construction of the Interoceanic Railroad," 448; Young to State, December 4, 1895, Diplomatic despatches.

52. José María Reyna Barrios to C. P. Huntington, May 2, 1896, JL 1, Box 2, Folder 11, PICO records; "Agreement between the Guatemala Central Railroad Company and the Republic of Guatemala," June 5, 1896, JL 1, Box 2, Folder 9, PICO records.

53. Sanford A. Mosk, "The Coffee Economy of Guatemala, 1850–1918: Development and Signs of Instability," *Inter-American Economic Affairs* 4 (1955): 15–16; Mary Catherine Rendon, "Manuel Estrada Cabrera: Guatemalan President, 1898–1920" (Ph.D. diss., Oxford University, 1987), 49–51; Ross, "Construction of the Interoceanic Railroad," 450.

54. Alfonso Bauer Paiz, *Como opera el capital yanqui en Centroamérica: el caso de Guatemala* (México: Editora Ibero-Mexicana, 1956), 154–55.

55. McCreery, *Development and State*, 57–60.

56. Hosmer, "Guatemala," *Consular Reports*, vol. 27, no. 97 (September 1888): 421.

57. Ross, "Construction of the Interoceanic Railroad," 447.

3
An Empire Is Born

Manuel Estrada Cabrera walked into the cabinet room on the evening of February 8, 1898, confident that he had the constitution and at least one military officer supporting him. General Reyna Barrios had been assassinated earlier that evening, leaving him, as the first designate, the constitutional successor. He anticipated the opposition of politicians closer to the former president than himself, since he had recently been pushed out of the inner circle. Estrada Cabrera decided to force his way back in. When he barged into the cabinet meeting, the ministers had already decided to appoint an interim president other than him. "That cannot be. It is unconstitutional. As first designate, I must be the interim president. Make another decree," Estrada Cabrera ordered from behind the barrel of a gun. The officials wisely yielded and made him the president, an office he held for the next twenty-two years.[1]

Estrada Cabrera built a brutal dictatorship by purging the army, eliminating political rivals, and terrorizing the entire population through a network of spies and assassins who did not discriminate between commoner and elite. Even foreign diplomats and former presidents were fair game for his assassins. One American minister to Guatemala was recalled from his post after discreet investigations showed that he was being slowly poisoned on the president's direct orders. In 1907 an assassin stabbed to death former President Barillas in Mexico City.[2]

Through such brutal methods, Estrada Cabrera established a political system in which he alone made and executed public policy. The means by which he acquired and maintained power have not been studied adequately, but contemporary observers have remarked about the extraordinary power that this man and his favorites held. The British consul reported that "the property and liberties of every individual are in the hands of half-a-dozen highly disreputable individuals."[3] A special emissary of President Woodrow Wilson reported in 1914 that every officer of the government, from the lowliest bureaucrat to the highest official, was absolutely subservient to the president. According to one American minister, Estrada Cabrera never used the formal machinery of government because the president's "private word was the real law."[4]

Corruption was rampant, and it began at the top. According to Dana G. Munro, a historian and diplomat who was once assigned to Guatemala, Estrada Cabrera became a very wealthy man by using "the power of the government to enrich himself at the expense of private individuals." Documents confiscated after the dictator's overthrow proved how he had extorted money from foreign entrepreneurs and wealthy nationals. With bureaucratic salaries set so low that the government seemed to encourage graft, the chief of the secret police amassed his fortune by selling stolen jewelry and confiscated property.[5]

This corrupt and authoritarian political system offered an "ideal investment climate" to United Fruit. "Guatemala was chosen as the site for the company's earliest development activities at the turn of the century," one UFCO official later explained, "because a good portion of the country contained prime banana land and also because at the time we entered Central America, Guatemala's government was the region's weakest, most corrupt and most pliable."[6]

While Estrada Cabrera was neither the first nor the last corrupt president of Guatemala, his predecessors refused to yield control of the country's economic infrastructure to foreign capitalists even as they accepted bribes from American businessmen. Huntington, who operated a line across the continental United States, could not gain control of a 273-mile line across Guatemala. As the value of coffee exports and government revenues declined after the 1897 economic crisis, the ability of the Liberals to complete their development program as originally conceived diminished. Few options remained. Nevertheless, only a dictator could have authorized the terms of the 1904 concession by which Guatemala surrendered the Northern Railway to Minor Keith. Had it been necessary for Estrada Cabrera to engage in meaningful consultation with the cabinet, legislature, or judiciary, United Fruit may not have acquired the concessions that deprived the country of its economic sovereignty.

Estrada Cabrera's venality, coupled with the economic crisis in which he came to power, allowed UFCO, IRCA, and General Electric to acquire four pivotal economic sectors: bananas, railroads, ports, and electricity. A reflection of his subservience to American enterprise is the sharp increase in the value of U.S. investment from $6 million in 1897 to over $40 million in 1920.[7] These investments deepened the nation's economic dependency and contributed to the dictator's personal wealth. When he approved the sale of the German-owned electrical plant to General Electric, for example, he received $40,000.[8] At best, Estrada Cabrera confused his good fortune and personal needs with that of the country he allegedly served. At worst, he betrayed Guatemala.

Estrada Cabrera's betrayal should be understood within, but not excused by, the context of a severe depression that hit Guatemala in 1897 and lasted for at least ten years. The collapse of the international coffee market virtually eliminated the option of building the Northern Railway with Guatemalan capital and operating it as a state enterprise. Circumstances far beyond his control gave foreign capitalists distinct advantages when they negotiated with the caudillo, who needed them much more than they needed him.

At a cost of $8 million the government had pushed the Northern Railway to El Rancho, just sixty miles short of Guatemala's economic independence. The economic crisis made it difficult to maintain the railroad, let alone complete section six. With his most successful engineer dead and his government's revenues rapidly declining, the dictator tried to rationalize his way into selling the Northern Railway to the highest foreign bidder. An article in a Quezaltenango paper gave an official justification for a new policy. Pointing out that Guatemalans did not need to own the line as much as they needed to use it, the article asked the government to relieve the nation of a heavy burden: "Would it not be preferable to sell the Northern Railroad than to impose economies and taxes on the people which become more impossible every day?"[9] In March 1898, Estrada Cabrera extracted authority from the legislature to sell, lease, or do whatever was necessary to complete the railroad as quickly as possible. The government still entertained hopes of keeping the line under state control, but he was already contemplating its outright sale to foreign investors. The U.S. consul predicted that "a valuable concession can be had, and the completed road purchased for less than half its original cost."[10]

Government efforts to maintain service on the five sections built in the 1890s failed. From April to September 1898, two Americans operated the section from El Rancho to Puerto Barrios, but when the government subsidies disappeared, Estrada Cabrera forced the two men to relinquish the contract. Soon thereafter the government leased the railroad to another American citizen who kept freight cars rolling from El Rancho to Puerto Barrios until his death in 1900.[11]

Without rail connection to Guatemala City, however, the Northern Railway could not gain access to the coffee freight that would make it profitable. The banana plantations of the coastal region would never produce sufficient freight, making it imperative for any railroad, public or private, to tap into the coffee of the western highlands. Until United Fruit entered Guatemala most of that coffee went out of Pacific ports over the Central Railroad, owned by American capital, or the Occidental Railroad, owned by Guatemalan *finqueros*. Both of these would resist efforts of the Northern Railway to divert the coffee trade to its line and Puerto Barrios, unless they had a vested interest in that railroad.

Since Huntington owned the Central Railroad and had preferential rights of construction on all railroads, the government encouraged him to submit a bid for the line. In March 1899 he was reportedly negotiating with Estrada Cabrera for the purchase of the Northern Railway, Puerto Barrios, and the Occidental Railroad. By joining all these properties with his railroad, the *New York Times* reported that "Mr. Huntington would control the transportation problem in Guatemala."[12]

Estrada Cabrera did not have to accept the first bid because French and German syndicates submitted competitive proposals. Huntington's most serious rival, however, was the United Fruit Company, which Keith and Preston had just formed. In April 1899, UFCO acquired a foothold in Honduras and Guatemala by purchasing the properties of Salvatore Oteri and Michael Macheca. Since the 1880s, Oteri and Macheca had shipped bananas from the Caribbean coast of Central America to New Orleans and Mobile. Shortly after the acquisition of the two steamship lines, Keith submitted a bid to complete and operate the Northern Railway.[13]

Extensive flooding in July 1900 washed out most of the bridges and put the railroad out of service for at least two months. The natural disaster forced Estrada Cabrera to accelerate the negotiations and accept one of the bids before the track became utterly worthless. The dictator became obsessed with the line, and the American minister reported in August 1900 that: "I can state positively that he [Estrada Cabrera] is thinking more now about the completion of the Northern Railway, between Puerto Barrios and this city [Guatemala] than he is about anything else."[14]

Huntington's death in the same month took the Central Railroad out of the competition and opened the door for Keith. In the summer of 1900 he surveyed the existing line, formed the Central American Improvement Company (CAICO), and negotiated with Estrada Cabrera for the rights to complete the last sixty miles of the line and operate the entire railroad for ten years. Keith initially solicited a contract that did not include any government subsidies, but he asked for a land grant of five hundred thousand acres on which he would plant banana trees to provide freight for the railway. These contract negotiations represent United's first venture into Guatemala, as Keith, founder and largest shareholder in United, served as the president of CAICO. Although few historians have identified Keith with the project, W. Godfrey Hunter, the American minister to Guatemala, reported in September 1900 that "the Central American Improvement Co. is practically the United Fruit Company, which now runs steamers from New Orleans to most of the Central American ports on the Atlantic side."[15]

On August 31 the minister of development signed a contract with CAICO, and the legislature gave its assent on December 7. Although Keith received a land grant of only fifty-seven thousand acres, the government had already exempted bananas from all export taxes the previous September. The contract obligated CAICO to repair the existing line and to extend it to Guatemala City within thirty-three months. The government authorized the firm to operate the line for ten years, during which time the company would retain all profits. When the contract expired, the government could purchase the Northern Railway for the cost of extending the railroad from El Rancho to Guatemala City (estimated at $4 million), but the company would retain title to the banana lands it had received.[16]

Estrada Cabrera gambled with Guatemala's economic destiny. The government had never ceded even temporary control of the Northern Railway to any private company. Ever since Justo Rufino Barrios had initiated the line, the Liberals had intended to own and operate it. They had contracted with foreign firms to build and operate portions of the line, but the Liberals considered it too valuable to place in foreign hands. If the country did not climb out of the economic depression, the government would not be able to purchase the line, and UFCO would control Guatemala's economic lifeline. To Estrada Cabrera what mattered was not who owned it or on what terms but that the company completed it.

One should not underestimate the Liberal's confidence in and admiration for the multimillion dollar enterprise. They welcomed United's investment in their development project, and the elite celebrated the ratification of the CAICO contract with an enthusiasm that had not been seen in years. The American minister described the festivities of December 7: "Fireworks were set off, the President was serenaded and universal joy was shown that at last, after all these years of delay, disappointment and fruitless negotiation, there is a definite prospect of a railroad across Guatemala from ocean to ocean in three years."[17]

American observers regarded the concession as a long-overdue victory for U.S. enterprise. In the competition for commercial and investment opportunities in Guatemala, the Yankees had not won a significant engagement since 1880, when Guillermo Nanne signed a contract for the completion of a line from Escuintla to Guatemala City. Moreover, CAICO secured this concession despite competitive bids from French, English, and German syndicates. Minister Hunter transmitted news of this "victory" to the *New York Times*, which reported it under the front-page heading "Americans Win in Guatemala." To Hunter the victory meant that the entire Northern Railway would become the absolute property of United Fruit after ten years because the government would be unable to exercise its option.[18]

United Fruit followed up this victory with a seemingly insignificant mail contract. A three-year contract, signed on January 19, 1901, authorized UFCO to transport the government's correspondence, cargo, and selected personnel between the Caribbean coast and New Orleans. For this service the government would pay UFCO 30,000 pesos per year and exempt UFCO steamers from all taxes. United did not sign this contract solely for the privilege of carrying Guatemala's mail. It already provided weekly service between New Orleans and Puerto Barrios, and this mail contract authorized the company to purchase bananas at set prices. At the time, UFCO did not own or cultivate any Guatemalan land, but a number of independent planters had been producing bananas in the region since the 1880s. Having acquired its only competitors—the Oteri and Macheca steamship lines— UFCO was now in a position to dominate the banana trade of the northern coast, and it would not pay any taxes for that privilege.[19]

In the spring of 1901, United inaugurated semiweekly steamship service from New Orleans to Puerto Barrios and began constructing cart roads to feed into the Northern Railway. Although United Fruit terminated the mail contract in October 1901 because the government had never paid the full subvention, it still maintained weekly service to New Orleans and continued to carry the government's mail in return for tax exemptions.[20]

Meanwhile, CAICO encountered serious labor problems and financial difficulties after Keith turned the project over to some associates. By January 1903 the section between El Rancho and Puerto Barrios was back in operation, but in April the new president of CAICO, James McNaught, asked the government to extend the deadline for completing the line. The project had been stalled by chronic labor shortages. The government supplied hundreds of drafted Indian laborers, and the company supplemented this work force with blacks from Jamaica and the southern United States, but CAICO lacked the funds to pay them. McNaught received the extension he requested, but July floods compounded his problems, and the government threatened to cancel the concession in July. In early August floods damaged the railroad again, workers fled to the hills, and the government refused to supply any more workers until the company's financial situation improved.[21]

As Keith desperately wanted the projected railroad incorporated into his own grand Central American railroad network, he assumed personal command and reorganized the venture. On September 4, 1903, he reached an agreement with his associates in the Central American Improvement Company whereby he assumed CAICO's debts and properties, and the company forfeited the railroad contract.[22] Then, he asked Percival Farquhar to negotiate directly with President Estrada Cabrera for a new and broader concession to complete the Northern Railway. Farquhar had gained a reputation as a skilled and intimidating international negotiator in 1898 when he outmaneuvered six other competitors, including William Van Horne, chairman of the Canadian Pacific Railroad, for a concession to electrify Havana's street railway. Although his opponents charged him with bribery and even attempted kidnapping, Van Horne came to respect Farquhar and invited him to join his own firm, Cuba Company. As an assistant to Van Horne, Farquhar directed the railroad's affairs in eastern Cuba, and in that capacity he ran into competition with Keith, as United owned land and railway rights in that region as well. Since Keith also owned stock in Van Horne's Cuba

Company, he recognized the value of collaboration and he, Van Horne, and Farquhar joined forces to complete Guatemala's Northern Railway.[23]

Keith and Van Horne evidently recognized that Farquhar's tough and abrasive negotiating tactics were appropriate for discussions with the dictator of Guatemala. After Keith presented his plans to Farquhar in New York, the latter set out for Guatemala in the fall of 1903. Farquhar knew of the difficulties that dictator Estrada Cabrera could create in the negotiations by either censoring or prohibiting all communications by cable, and therefore he had to work within the original parameters set by Keith. Unlike previous supplicants, Farquhar deliberately kept American diplomats out of the talks. According to U.S. minister Leslie Combs, Farquhar wanted to conduct the negotiations on "purely business lines" because the legation had been involved in too many previous railroad disputes. Combs knew only that the negotiations were being delayed by Farquhar's demand that no future taxes would be levied on anything but coffee and by the insistence of the government that the contractors renounce the right to request diplomatic or military intervention.[24]

For two months Farquhar explained the advantages of contracting with Keith and Van Horne, the two finest railroad builders in the tropics. He argued that railroads and bananas had to develop simultaneously and, for that reason, that the concession must include a large grant of land suitable for banana cultivation. Estrada Cabrera had hoped that either Spanish or German investors would submit a competitive bid, but his attempt to play the Europeans off their American rivals brought him no advantages, for Keith alone was undeterred by Guatemala's unstable political and economic conditions. If the dictator had hoped to receive a competitive bid from the Central, he was disappointed. Because of the depressed coffee market, the Central had been losing up to $250,000 annually for several years.[25] As a result, General Thomas Hubbard, Huntington's successor, did not submit a bid on the Northern Railway, even though the Central still had preferential rights of construction on all Guatemalan railroads.

Farquhar undoubtedly knew that Estrada Cabrera had no other serious suitors, so the dictator's *mañana* tactics exhausted his patience. One afternoon he warned the president that he would leave the next day if the contract was not approved. The next morning reports of Farquhar's imminent departure reached the president from one of his many spies. An emissary from the presidential palace rushed over to the hotel and convinced Farquhar to remain until noon. By then the dictator had invited him to the palace, where Farquhar was shown the contract for which he had waited two months.[26]

On January 12, 1904, Farquhar, representing Keith and Van Horne, signed a contract for the completion of the Northern Railway.[27] The Guatemalans had completed five of the six sections of the projected route, although floods had knocked the bridges out of service. The contract assigned Keith the task of building the last sixty-mile section from El Rancho to Guatemala City and repairing the other five sections. If the line were completed and in operation within three and one-half years, Keith and associates would take possession of the entire Northern Railway for ninety-nine years. Keith also received the right to select 168,000 acres of prime banana land from a tract known as Los Andes in the Motagua River valley. The contract specifically excluded all bananas from any export duties or local taxes for a period of thirty-five years. In addition, Keith would acquire the docks of Puerto Barrios and all of the property, rolling stock, buildings, telegraph lines, stations, and tanks already built or acquired by Guatemala. A reasonable estimate of the total value of the railroad facilities ceded to Keith in this concession is over $8 million; the value of the 168,000 acres could have been as much as $50 million. As if that were not enough, the government guaranteed the company an annual income of 5 percent on the estimated investment ($4.5 million) for fifteen years.[28]

The contract also authorized Keith to build and acquire railroads throughout the country, a provision that he utilized to its fullest. The Guatemalans would not have any legal authority to regulate the company's affairs because Estrada Cabrera renounced the right of the government to intervene in its management. The government could not inspect the books, regulate freight rates, or tax the company, and banana exports would not be subject to duty. In effect, the concession gave Keith and associates a valuable railroad and the rights to develop banana plantations free of any interference or taxes.[29] On the basis of this incredible concession, United Fruit built its railroad and banana empire.

In Miguel Angel Asturias's *The Green Pope* a fictitious Yankee railroad builder, George Maker Thompson, explains the terms of a railroad contract bearing a remarkable similarity to the one obtained by the real green pope, Minor Keith. One of Thompson's associates could not understand how any president of a sovereign country could voluntarily cede part of the national patrimony to a private, foreign enterprise:

"You leave us open-mouthed, Thompson. The person who signed that contract must have been drunk."

"No, staggering a bit, but not drunk," Thompson replied.[30]

Desperate yes, drunk no. El Señor Presidente wanted the line built, and it would not have been out of character for him to give the Northern Railway away. Days after Farquhar signed the contract, he attended a dinner at the German legation where several prominent guests denounced the dictator's graft, brutality, and arbitrariness before he stood to defend Estrada Cabrera's patriotism and integrity. While Farquhar may not have impressed his dinner companions, his biographer claims that Estrada Cabrera "was pleased that Farquhar, in the face of roars of laughter insisted that no bribes were requested or promised."[31]

If Estrada Cabrera did not demand a cut of the business at this point, it was because he did not want to scare off good money. Circumstantial evidence, however, suggests that some out-of-pocket expenses were involved in the negotiations. Generals Butterfield and Barrios established a precedent in 1881 when the former gave the latter $80,000 worth of stock in the Central Railroad. Bribery and extortion greased Guatemala's bureaucratic wheels. In a loan agreement that Keith took out in 1905 there is a suspicious reference to Edward D. Adams of New York City. A representative of Schwartz and Company of Guatemala, Adams received 1,350 shares or $135,000 par value of stock "for the assistance and services he has agreed to give and perform for or in connection with the Railway Company."[32]

Schwartz and Company was then under the control of Adolfo Stahl, a personal favorite and confidant of Estrada Cabrera and Isidore Schwartz's partner since the mid-1890s. After the latter's death in 1903, Stahl retained the firm's name and expanded his political and financial power as the leader of a group of businessmen called the American syndicate.[33] He was the official fiscal representative of the government and controlled the Banco de Guatemala, one of several banks that issued the national currency and financed the government's operations. Beginning in 1903–04, Stahl issued short-term loans of $3 to $5 million at 20 percent interest, secured against anticipated revenues from the export tax on coffee. While this financial scheme profited him, his associates, and Estrada Cabrera, it debilitated the currency and earned him a terrible reputation in Guatemala and within the State Department.[34]

Keith would grow to despise the influence that Stahl had over Guatemalan finances, but he apparently worked with Schwartz to obtain the railroad that he so desperately wanted. Quite likely the shares that Adams received were distributed to high-ranking government officials and the syndicate. The only conclusive evidence of Keith's illicit deals with Estrada Cabrera was discovered in April 1920 when rebel troops ransacked the dictator's personal residence and uncovered the letter from Keith to Estrada Cabrera in which he had submitted five hundred shares of the railroad company.[35]

It was a small price to pay for an empire that now included Hubbard, president of the Guatemala Central Railroad, which was no longer in a position to compete with Keith's Northern Railway. A sharp decline in coffee exports had rendered the line much less valuable than it once had been. Prior to Keith's arrival, Hubbard had even offered to sell it to the government, which naturally refused for want of money. Hubbard believed competition from Keith would ruin his company, so he looked favorably on a consolidation of interests. On June 8, 1904, Keith, Van Horne, and Hubbard incorporated the Guatemala Railway Company under the laws of New Jersey, with a total authorized capital of $40 million divided into four hundred thousand shares valued at $100 each.[36] For five hundred shares valued at $50,000, Estrada Cabrera surrendered a line worth nearly $8 million and control of his country's economic infrastructure.

The full amount of the money he made through United Fruit was considerably more than the value of the stocks he received. Estrada Cabrera recognized that his salary could be regularly and substantially augmented by doing business with the banana trust, since land values and commerce and government revenues would surely increase after United Fruit completed the railroad and planted bananas. Therefore, he acquired at least two plantations of his own and had other properties registered in the names of friends and associates.[37] As dictator, he could gain access to the business easily enough, but staying in operation would be problematic if he did not have an understanding with United Fruit, since it controlled the railroad, the port, and the steamers that called at the port. Hence, Estrada Cabrera had to market his fruit through United Fruit. This arrangement allowed for innumerable and untraceable bribes: UFCO could pay him more than market price for his bananas or discount the freight charges. At a public auction in 1924, UFCO agent Joaquin Hecht bought Estrada Cabrera's Plantation San Joaquin for $55,000.[38]

Estrada Cabrera profited from a concession that formed the basis of United Fruit's empire. For twenty-five years, Guatemalans had struggled to complete the Northern Railway with their own money and to manage it as a national enterprise. In the 1904 concession the dictator essentially terminated the Liberal development project; rather than promoting the country's economic independence, the Northern Railway became the foundation of an American banana enclave on the Caribbean coast and a transoceanic railroad monopoly.[39] Repeated and costly failures undoubtedly frustrated the caudillo and may have led to a hasty decision, but all previous contracts, including the one signed with Keith's Central American Improvement Company, at least gave the government the option of purchasing the completed line after ten years. Under the terms of the 1904 concession, Estrada Cabrera surrendered the Northern Railway on the uncertain proposition that the government might buy it back after the ninety-nine-year contract expired.

During the life of the contract, however, the government could not tax the company's profits or regulate its affairs. The profits and management of the enterprise rested exclusively with Keith, Van Horne, and Hubbard. Although they founded the Guatemala Railway Company as individuals, they all acted on behalf of UFCO. Before Keith undertook the construction of the railroad, he made arrangements with United for extensive banana cultivation. At Farquhar's insistence, Estrada Cabrera included a grant of 168,000 acres to Keith in the 1904 concession. Of these 168,000 acres he gave 50,000 to UFCO, ostensibly as an inducement to plant fruit. The land cession formed part of a larger deal between the nominally independent

Guatemala Railway Company and United Fruit. In return for the land, UFCO agreed to plant at least 5,000 acres with bananas by January 1, 1908. In September 1904, UFCO's board of directors approved the arrangements and authorized the company's first banana plantings in Guatemala.[40] United cultivated its first bananas in the Motagua River valley, which would become the heart of Guatemala's banana industry.

United Fruit entered the banana business in Guatemala on terms denied to the independents who had operated there since the 1880s. Aside from the free land the railroad offered UFCO preferential freight rates. A traffic agreement of September 15, 1904, gave United a competitive advantage over all other actual or potential competitors in the banana business and essentially subordinated the railroad to the fruit company. The contract obligated the railroad to haul all bananas delivered to it at the times and places UFCO specified. Trains carrying United's bananas would be given the right of way and precedence over all other trains and traffic. These bananas would be transported at the rate of ten cents American gold per bunch of firsts (bunches bearing nine or more hands or clusters of bananas). Bananas shipped by any company other than United Fruit would be charged twenty cents per bunch. In the event that UFCO shipped more than two million bunches per year, the rate would drop another two cents; if it shipped over three million it would be charged only seven cents per bunch. In addition to these privileges the Railway Company agreed not to encourage any other banana business, either directly or indirectly, for the ten-year duration of the contract.[41]

This agreement, extended and amended by supplemental agreements of 1913, 1915, 1930, and 1933, provided United Fruit with a devastatingly effective means of eliminating and preventing competition in the banana business. Throughout the Caribbean, United implemented a policy of owning or controlling at least the major portion of rail and port facilities in order to prevent independents from having greater access to the market. While UFCO did not own the rail and port facilities in Guatemala, it controlled them through the IRCA from 1904 to 1936, when United Fruit acquired a controlling stock interest in the railroad. The Department of Justice concluded that, through interlocking directorates and the 1904 traffic agreement, United had dominated the railroad since Keith incorporated it under the laws of New Jersey in 1904.[42]

One must note that the original traffic agreement was signed by Andrew Preston, president of United Fruit, and Keith, president of the Guatemala Railways, who also happened to be vice president of UFCO. Keith nominally acted independently of United Fruit, but how could he act independently of a company he served as vice president? The scope of the privileges he acquired in the 1904 contract, including the land grant and a tax exemption for bananas, suggests that he personally spearheaded a campaign previously conceived in a Boston boardroom. Indeed, according to

Bradley Palmer, secretary and legal counsel to Keith and United Fruit, Keith was the active manager of UFCO's interests in Central America.[43] He had his own business interests when he went into and came out of the merger with the Boston Fruit Company in 1899, but he would carry with him the title of vice president and founder of United Fruit until his death in 1928.

Keith was always more interested in railroads than bananas, however, and the 1904 concession gave him the opportunity to complete one section of what he hoped would become part of a Central American railroad network. He had only a few years to complete the line, and there was no assurance that he would prevail where so many others had failed. Keith still had to raise the money, recruit laborers, fight yellow fever, and deal with Guatemalan politicians, but he initiated the project with United Fruit's millions behind him and his most cherished dream just a few steps in front of him. Several people would obstruct his ambitious projects, but nobody ever detained him for long.

Keith had eliminated his only serious competitor by forging a partnership with General Hubbard. In 1903 the Central extended its line into the western coffee districts by completing a thirty-mile branch from Patulul to Mazatenango. By joining forces, Keith and Hubbard created a de facto railroad monopoly in 1904, eight years before Keith legally incorporated all Guatemalan railroads into the International Railways of Central America. Hubbard evidently had decided to invest in Keith's enterprise before Farquhar even signed the contract. On January 5, 1904, the American consul reported to the State Department that "it is understood that the same interests are backing this line [the Northern Railway] as control the Guatemala Central from San José and that it will be operated under the same management."[44]

Neither Keith nor Hubbard saw much sense in having two different companies manage one small transoceanic railroad. Competition surely would have ruined the Central, which was already in financial straits, but Keith also recognized that his railroad could not operate profitably if it did not acquire the coffee freight of the western highlands, which was then shipped out on the Central. Hence, the two men established a mutually beneficial partnership before construction on the Northern Railway began. A U.S. diplomat reported in 1906 that a tariff war between the Central and the Northern line was not likely because the same parties that controlled the Central had also invested in the new road.[45]

Keith entered the Guatemalan railroad business with the intention of monopolizing the railroad network. In the 1904 concession he acquired the right to purchase or consolidate with other railroad companies, a provision that Estrada Cabrera reaffirmed informally in 1907 and formally in 1908.[46] As Keith's lawyers later explained, the 1904 contract marked the beginning "of a project which Mr. Keith and Sir William Van Horne, his associate, conceived for consolidating the existing railways in Guatemala and extending them by concessions for additional lines so as to establish a continuous International Railways system from the frontier of Mexico . . . throughout Central America to the Isthmus of Panama."[47]

Naturally, the lawyers understated Keith's ambitions to take control of the region's entire transportation network, including port and shipping facilities. By 1904, Keith and UFCO had acquired three of the region's few deep-water ports: Bocas del Toro in Panama, Puerto Limón in Costa Rica, and Puerto Barrios. If Keith completed his dream of a Central America united by rail, he would place UFCO in a position to prevent rival banana planters from gaining access to the market on competitive terms.[48]

Given UFCO's competitive advantage in Central America, one would think that the world's financial institutions would have provided him with all the capital he needed to complete a small railroad in Guatemala. He found U.S. bankers strangely uninterested in his project, however, and therefore turned to German capitalists. In 1905, Farquhar, vice president of the Guatemala Railway Company, secured a $2.7 loan from the Deutsche Bank of Berlin.[49]

Construction began shortly thereafter. Keith hired engineer Virgil G. Bogue, who had served his uncle Henry Meiggs in Peru in the 1870s, to direct the construction effort. Knowing the difficulties that landslides presented to the route between El Rancho and the capital, Bogue decided to leave the Motagua River valley and push through the less dangerous Sanarate Valley. Farquhar supervised the project and brought in engineers who had worked for him in Cuba. As Silvanus Miller had done successfully in the 1890s, Farquhar subcontracted for the building of various parts of the line and employed hundreds of Indian laborers drafted into service by the government. Neither Keith nor Van Horne spent much time in Guatemala; thus, maintaining good relations with the dictator was Farquhar's most difficult and important task. Although he hired some black laborers for the construction crews, he relied heavily on the Indians conscripted by the government.[50]

An outbreak of yellow fever in the summer of 1905 nearly paralyzed the entire construction effort. The American minister reported in September 1905 that yellow fever had made "disastrous progress" in the lowlands, with residents of Zacapa and Gualán hit particularly hard. In response, the government established a strict military cordon around the area, and private citizens, including American diplomats, sent medicines and supplies to Zacapa.[51]

Although officials claimed that the quarantine worked, several months later one knowledgeable observer reported that Indians continued to die from yellow fever. Kenneth Champney, an American *finquero* in the Verapaz region, lost many of his workers to the Northern Railway. Champney left a vivid, though hardly sympathetic, explanation of how the labor drafts devastated the Indians: "When a man is taken for the railway it means with going and coming, a loss of six weeks, to begin with. But it mostly means more. It is very likely to mean six months lost: and often it means a dead Indian. You see the man comes back sick. It is next to impossible for Indians of this climate to cross the Polochic Valley without getting fever; a bad sort of fever and apt to be rapid. A week or so after a man is back we ask for him and learn that he is buried. At the best he is an invalid; no good to us and no good to his family for a long time."[52]

Indians quickly learned that they should resist conscription at all costs, and many of them emigrated to Belize to escape a death sentence on the Northern Railway. The reconcentration of laborers on the railway, coupled with Indian flight, deprived Champney of his workers since the government took workers away from his and other fincas. In May 1906, Champney complained about the loss of his Indian laborers to Keith's enterprise and asked the American minister to intercede on his behalf: "We are planting coffee; we are not building railways; we have nothing to do with the Northern Railway Company. They are a private concern, like our own, and no matter what public or private influence they may enjoy, we have no notion of doing other peoples' work gratis with the very laborers that we have lawfully paid and contracted for our own work. The United Fruit Company might as reasonably ask us to plant bananas for them."[53]

As a result of financial problems, yellow fever, and harsh working conditions, Farquhar's crews had graded only twenty-one miles of section six by February 1906.[54] Several months later former President Barillas and his ally, Salvadoran Minister of War Tomás Regalado, led rebel armies into Guatemala. To meet the challenge the government transferred some of the railroad workers to the battle front. After the United States and Mexico arranged a truce between the warring factions in July 1906, the government sent workers back to the railroad crews. But as a direct result of the war, Keith's financiers withdrew their support. The large German interests in Guatemala became involved in a serious dispute with the dictator, and the Deutsche Bank, concerned about political instability, refused to make further advances to the Guatemala Railway. Farquhar attributed the cutoff to "a quarrel of the Guatemalan Government with the large German interests."[55]

Knowing of the company's financial difficulties, Estrada Cabrera gave Keith an additional six months in which to complete the line. Keith and Van Horne, who had been preoccupied with events in Cuba and elsewhere, now had to give their undivided attention to the task of financing the Northern Railway because they would lose the 1904 concession if they did not secure alternative financing soon. Although they were both wealthy men, Van Horne had invested far more money than he had anticipated in Cuba and could ill afford a heavier expenditure on a railroad already behind schedule and short on funds. He and Keith could provide the capital from their own funds if they had assurances that the government would respect its obligations and provide the company with its complete cooperation. Hoping to receive such guarantees, Keith and Van Horne traveled to Guatemala City by steamship, railroad, and mule. They met the dictator in April 1907, and in less than two hours the men resolved ten important issues. While there is no record of the decisions reached at this fateful meeting, Keith later claimed that Estrada Cabrera promised that he would permit the consolidation of the Guatemala Railway and the Central. Moreover, he agreed that the flexible terms granted to them in the 1904 concession would apply to all of the railroads.[56]

In other words, Estrada Cabrera winked at Keith's monopolistic designs. No wonder Van Horne had such high praise for the caudillo's decisiveness: "I am particularly pleased at the fair and liberal manner in which the terms of our contract have been carried out by the Government of Guatemala. Our experience in this regard has been very much more satisfactory than with any Anglo-Saxon government with which I have had to do, and we have not been bled to the extent of one dollar by any-body connected with the administration."[57] Consequently, Van Horne, Keith, and Hubbard put up $7 million of their own cash to complete the railroad, with Keith alone contributing $6 million. To raise the money, Keith, who at one point owned about three fifths of UFCO's stock, sold all but 10 percent. To cover his share of the new outlays, Van Horne sold some of his properties in Mexico and elsewhere.[58] Although both men assumed a large personal risk, their company had already acquired lands, lines, a wharf, and rolling stock worth at least as much through the 1904 concession.

The infusion of cash put the crews back to work and restored the nation's confidence. Construction continued without interruption until its conclusion nine months later. As the workers pushed toward Guatemala City, Estrada Cabrera prepared to mark the long-awaited event with a two-week national holiday, even postponing the October opening of the national fair so that it could open simultaneously with the railroad. To dignify the contribution made by American capital to Guatemalan progress, the United States dispatched a special envoy, General George W. Davis, who witnessed Estrada Cabrera drive in the gold spike on January 19, 1908. The first train from Puerto Barrios chugged into Guatemala City shortly thereafter, and Guatemala finally had a transoceanic railroad.[59]

Notes

1. Rafael Arévalo Martínez, *¡Ecce Pericles! Historia de la tiranía de Manuel Estrada Cabrera*, 2 vols., 2d ed. (San José, Costa Rica: Editorial Universitaria Centroamericana, 1971), 1:44–46 (author's translations); Catherine Rendon claims that Estrada Cabrera went into the meeting unarmed ("Manuel Estrada Cabrera," 116–17).

2. William F. Sands, *Our Jungle Diplomacy* (Chapel Hill: University of North Carolina Press, 1944), 72, 85; "General Barillas Murdered," *New York Times*, April 8, 1907. On Estrada Cabrera's consolidation of power see Rendon, "Manuel Estrada Cabrera," 119–28.

3. "Annual Report on the Republics of Guatemala, El Salvador, Honduras, and Nicaragua for 1919," in Kenneth Bourne and D. Cameron Watt, eds. and comps., *British Documents on Foreign Affairs. Reports and Papers from the Foreign Office Confidential Print, Part II, Series D, Latin America, 1914–1939* (Bethesda, MD: University Publications of America, 1990), 246.

4. "Report of Major General George W. Davis to the Secretary of State of the United States of America," March 30, 1914, SD 814.77/45; Sands, *Jungle Diplomacy*, 90.

5. Dana G. Munro to White, December 12, 1923, SD 814.001/c11/68; Benton McMillen (American minister to Guatemala) to State, May 12, 1920, SD 814.00/477; Rendon, "Manuel Estrada Cabrera," 60.

6. McCann, *An American Company*, 45. McCann was UFCO's director of public relations from 1952 to 1974.

7. Thomas and Ebba Schoonover, "Statistics for an Understanding of Foreign Intrusions into Central America from the 1820s to 1930," *Anuario de Estudios Centroamericanos* 15:1 (1989): 98.

8. General Electric officials claimed that the money was payment for Estrada Cabrera's interest in the Empresa Eléctrica de Escuintla. A copy of the check is in Geissler to State, February 25, 1926, SD 814.6463Em7/120; the company's explanation is in Geissler to State, February 25, 1926, SD 814.6463/120.

9. Jackson, "Technological Development," 201.

10. "Railway and Steamship Enterprises in Guatemala," *Consular Reports*, vol. 57, no. 213 (June 1898): 218–19.

11. W. Godfrey Hunter (U.S. minister to Guatemala) to State, November 12, 1898, and Hunter to State, September 7, 1900, Diplomatic despatches.

12. Jackson, "Technological Development," 201; "Railways in Guatemala," *New York Times*, March 11, 1899.

13. Milton A. Kallis to Victor A. Kramer and W. Perry Epes, December 20, 1952, DOJ, File 60-166-56, 3; Hosmer, "Guatemala," *Consular Reports*, vol. 27, no. 97 (September 1888): 421; "Guatemala Has a Boom," *New York Times*, November 10, 1899.

14. Hunter to State, August 27, 1900, Diplomatic despatches.

15. Anderson, "Development of Export Transportation," 366–69; James C. McNally (consul general), "Guatemalan Northern Railway," *Consular Reports*, vol. 64, no. 242 (November 1900): 401–2; Hunter to State, September 7, 1900, Diplomatic despatches.

16. Jackson, "Technological Development," 206–7; "Guatemala Railway Contract," *Consular Reports*, vol. 65, no. 246 (March 1901): 369–70.

17. Hunter to State, December 12, 1900, Diplomatic despatches.

18. *New York Times*, December 27, 1900.

19. Bauer Paiz, *Como opera el capital yanqui*, 205–7.

20. McNally to David J. Hill (assistant secretary of state), October 30, 1901, U.S. Department of State, Despatches from U.S. Consuls in Guatemala, 1824–1906 (hereafter cited as Consular despatches).

21. [Untitled report on the construction of the Northern Railway], Archivo General de Centro América, Guatemala City, Guatemala (hereafter cited as AGCA), B129, legajo 22183, Ferrocarril del Norte [no expediente]; Jackson, "Technological Development," 208–9; Leslie Combs to State, May 15, 1903, Diplomatic

despatches; Combs to State, July 18, 1903, Diplomatic despatches; Combs to State, August 5, 1903, enclosed, Juan Barrios M. (minister of foreign relations) to Combs, August 4, 1903, Diplomatic despatches.

22. IRCA memorandum, April 1921, AGCA, B129, legajo 22190, "Ferrocarril Zacapa-Frontera" [no expediente]; "Transfer of Principal Concession," June 11, 1904, in International Railways of Central America, *International Railways of Central America, Concessions, Contracts and Decrees, 1877–1912* (Boston: Press of George H. Ellis Company, 1913), 21.

23. Davidson B. McKibbin, "Percival Farquhar: American Promoter in Latin America, 1900–1914" (Ph.D. diss., University of Chicago, 1950), 15–19, 28–29; Charles A. Gould, *The Last Titan: Percival Farquhar, American Entrepreneur in Latin America* (Stanford: Institute of Hispanic American and Luso-Brazilian Studies, Bolivar House, Stanford University, 1964), 30–31.

24. Gould, *Last Titan*, 52–53; Combs to State, January 6, 1904, Diplomatic despatches.

25. Wagner, "Actividades empresariales de los alemanes," 113–14; Rendon, "Manuel Estrada Cabrera," 65; General manager, Guatemala Central Railroad, to President Manuel Estrada Cabrera, December 31, 1903, AGCA, Personal Papers of Manuel Estrada Cabrera.

26. Gould, *Last Titan*, 52.

27. Because Estrada Cabrera handled these negotiations personally, the ministry of development did not conduct its usual thorough review of the project. If there were any documentation on the Farquhar negotiations, Estrada Cabrera most likely had the documents destroyed.

28. Bauer Paiz, *Como opera el capital yanqui*, 154–55; Ross, "Construction of the Interoceanic Railroad," 451–52.

29. Paiz, *Como opera el capital yanqui*, 115–26. For an English translation of this contract see SD 814.77/90.

30. Miguel Angel Asturias, *The Green Pope*, trans. Gregory Rabassa (New York: Delacorte Press, 1971), 134.

31. Gould, *Last Titan*, 53.

32. "Guatemala Railway Company. Railway Loan Agreement," April 1, 1905, JL 1, Box 7, Folder 51, PICO records.

33. Kemmerer and Dalgaard, "Inflation, Intrigue and Monetary Reform," 27; William Heimke to Francis B. Loomis, July 27, 1909, U.S. Department of State, Numerical File, 10859/17-19, (hereafter cited as SDNF followed by file number).

34. González Dávison, *El régimen liberal*, 35; Jones, *Guatemala*, 236–37; Rendon, "Manuel Estrada Cabrera," 83; "Guatemala Loan Projects," SD 814.51/112; David Hepburn Dinwoodie, "Dollar Diplomacy in Light of the Guatemalan Loan Project, 1909–1913," *Americas* 26:3 (1970): 240.

35. Ministro de Gobernación B. Alvarado to Ministro de Fomento, May 24, 1922, AGCA, B129, legajo 22190, "Ferrocarril Zacapa-Frontera" [no expediente]. In this letter the payoff is confirmed, but the original is not attached and no date is given for the transaction. It is possible that Keith made the payment at a later date, perhaps 1915, as a means of extricating his company from some difficulties with the government.

36. Minutes of meeting between Rafael Rodezno and Keith with the minister of development [April 1921], AGCA, B129, legajo 22189 [no expediente]; IRCA memorandum, April 1921, AGCA, B129, legajo 22190 [no expediente].

37. For a listing of Estrada Cabrera's properties in the department of Izabal see Clarence B. Hewes to State, October 9, 1923, enclosure, annexes A & B, SD 814.00C11/56; Edward Reed (vice consul), to W. S. Hemingway, April 28, 1920,

U.S. Department of State, RG 84, Consular Post Records, General Correspondence, Livingston (hereafter cited as Consular post records).

38. Leon H. Ellis (chargé d'affaires ad interim) to State, October 20, 1925, SD 814.001c11/81.

39. Anderson concurs in the importance of the 1904 railroad concession. See "Development of Export Transportation," 391.

40. Ross, "Construction of the Interoceanic Railroad," 451; Robert Lansing and Lester Woolsey (IRCA attorneys) to State, October 9 and 12, 1922, SD 814.77/ 165 and 814.77/167; United Fruit Company, minutes of directors' and stockholders' meetings, September 13, 1904, DOJ, File 60-166-56, Series 537, IRCA-60. This series contains hundreds of documents originally submitted in the case of Ripley v. IRCA, 188 N.Y.S. 2d 62. The Department of Justice subpoenaed many of the exhibits presented in this case and filed them haphazardly in series 537. Where possible, subsequent references to one of these documents will include the number assigned to it by the Department of Justice (i.e., IRCA-60).

41. "United Fruit Company and The Guatemala Railway Company, Traffic Agreement, September 15, 1904," DOJ, 60-166-56, Series 443.

42. Kallis to Kramer and Epes, December 20, 1952, DOJ, 60-166-56, 19.

43. Bradley Palmer (secretary, UFCO) to Secretary of State Philander C. Knox, October 8, 1909, SDNF, 10859/25-26.

44. Alfred A. Winslow to Loomis (assistant secretary of state), January 5, 1904, Consular despatches.

45. Philip Brown to State, February 20, 1906, Diplomatic despatches.

46. Minutes of meeting between Rodezno, Keith, and minister of development [1921], AGCA, B129, legajo 22189.

47. "The Case of the International Railways of Central America," SD 814.77/ 92, enclosure no. 1.

48. Ruddick, "A Study in Monopoly," 14.

49. Gould, *Last Titan*, 53–54; "Guatemala Railway Company, Railway Loan Agreement," and "Guatemala Railway Company to the Mercantile Trust Company," May 1, 1905, JL 1, Box 7, Folder 51, PICO records.

50. Gould, *Last Titan*, 54.

51. Brown to State, September 2, 1905, Diplomatic despatches.

52. Combs to State, May 9, 1906, Diplomatic despatches.

53. Ibid.

54. Brown to State, February 20, 1906, Diplomatic despatches.

55. Gould, *Last Titan*, 57; Walter Vaughan, *The Life and Work of Sir William Van Horne* (New York: The Century Company, 1920), 318.

56. Ross, "Construction of the Interoceanic Railroad," 66; minutes of meeting between Rodezno, Keith, and minister of development [1921], AGCA, B129, legajo 22189 [no expediente].

57.Vaughan, *Life and Work*, 319–20.

58. IRCA memorandum, April 1921, AGCA, B129, legajo 22190; "The Case of the IRCA," 814.77/92, p. 11; Ripley v. International Railways of Central America, 188 N.Y.S. 2d 62, p. 69; Vaughan, *Life and Work*, 318.

59. Ross, "Construction of the Interoceanic Railroad," 453–54.

4

Minor Keith and Caudillo Politics

Minor Keith was not just the man who built or acquired most Central American railroads and founded the world's largest banana company; he was also known as the uncrowned king of Central America, the green pope, and the Cecil Rhodes of Central America. The man who carved out empires from tropical jungles became so powerful that he is one of the most important figures in modern Central American history. Miguel Angel Asturias has captured and promoted the legendary Keith with an immortal description: "The Green Pope [Keith] lifts a finger and a ship starts or stops. He says a word and a republic is bought. He sneezes and a president, whether general or lawyer, falls. . . . He rubs his behind on a chair and a revolution breaks out."[1]

In the fifteen years that it took to build the ninety-three-mile line from Puerto Limón to San José, over five thousand men, including three of Keith's brothers, died from malaria, yellow fever, or exhaustion. Keith not only survived but also found his fortune and his calling. While the railroad was under construction he planted banana trees along the route to provide freight for the empty cars that soon would be rolling over it toward Puerto Limón. The banana business became so profitable that he expanded plantings into present-day Panama and Colombia. When Keith set his sights on Guatemala he was the multimillionaire vice president of United Fruit, with banana and railroad enclaves in Puerto Limón; Bocas del Toro, Panama; and Santa Marta.[2]

Keith was not a Wall Street tycoon who exploited the tropics from a Manhattan office. He spent most of his life in Central America where he learned to fight, swear, and drink with the ruffians employed on his railroads, some of them veterans of the William Walker filibustering expeditions. Keith earned the respect of his men by sweating it out on the front lines; he once rode out to pay his employees with nothing more than a bottle of whiskey. He convinced the men that he was good for the money he owed them, then treated them each to a shot "before he gulped an entire bottle, without once lifting it from his lips."[3]

Apocryphal or not, Keith survived his early years in the tropics because of a strong constitution (or at least an indestructible liver), good fortune, and an ambition that drove him out of poverty. Although he will always be associated with the banana business, he would have preferred to be remembered as the man who built a railroad network connecting Panama to the United States and intersecting the Central American republics. As his nephew later explained: "Keith envisaged the five republics united by steel bonds of mutual economic interests upon which might be based an eventual political consolidation, a United States of Central America, much as had been attempted three quarters of a century before."[4]

The Costa Rica Railway represented only the southern portion of a network that Keith planned to extend throughout the isthmus. In 1887 his agents lobbied the Nicaraguan government for the rights to build a line from Puerto Limón to Lake Nicaragua and negotiated with the Hondurans to complete the transoceanic railway.[5] Keith never acquired the concessions he wanted in the middle republics, but Guatemala and El Salvador sanctioned his projects in 1908, with concessions that authorized Keith to build a branch off his Guatemala Railway from Zacapa to the Salvadoran border and thence to La Union on the Gulf of Fonseca.

The same man who made the construction of the Guatemalan line possible, however, also frustrated Keith's efforts to complete his Central American railroad, for Estrada Cabrera granted concessions with more respect than that with which he observed them. While the unpredictable caudillo allowed Keith to consolidate all Guatemalan railroads into the International Railways of Central America in 1912, he prevented him from raising the money required to build the Zacapa branch. As a result, IRCA never became the Central American network that Keith intended it to be; it was founded as and remained a network of Guatemalan railroads that served the monopolistic interests of United Fruit.

The completion of the transoceanic railroad in January 1908 did not satisfy Estrada Cabrera, who was "railroad mad," according to Daniel B. Hodgsdon, manager of the Guatemala Central. Hodgsdon knew that Estrada Cabrera and Keith shared an interest in a branch from Zacapa to the Salvadoran frontier, but the similarities stopped there. Keith was a practical businessman, while Estrada Cabrera was an impractical politician. Keith and Hodgsdon recognized that the volume of banana traffic on the Guatemalan Railway was not yet sufficient to make it profitable. Although Hodgsdon felt strongly that the economic conditions of early 1908 did not warrant any further railroad construction, railroad madness prevailed.[6]

For all his business sense, Hodgsdon's political sensitivity was even better, and he predicted that a liberal railroad contract could be secured from the government. On February 19 his colleague, Fred Gooding Williamson, manager of the Guatemala Railway, signed a concession with the minister of development for the construction of a line from Zacapa to the Salvadoran frontier. In addition to specifying terms of construction, it formalized the verbal agreement already reached by Keith and Estrada Cabrera. Article 1 stipulated that the Zacapa branch and any other lines previously acquired, or that might be acquired in the future, would be considered part of the Guatemala Railway and governed by the same generous terms of the 1904 Farquhar contract.[7]

Although business conditions did not warrant additional construction, Keith and his associates in United Fruit desperately wanted this contract. In 1904, United made its first improvements in the dock at Puerto Barrios, and four years later Keith initiated a thorough renovation that included a 600-foot concrete and steel wharf capable of handling four ships simultaneously, buoys, and lights for both the harbor and wharf.[8] To Keith and his associates in United the Zacapa concession formed part of a projected rail network that would bring Guatemalan and Salvadoran commerce to its steamships anchored at Puerto Barrios. As it did elsewhere, United sought control of Guatemalan ports and railroads in order to control access to the market. Bradley Palmer, UFCO lawyer and secretary, informed the State Department that United intended to join Puerto Barrios and La Union, El Salvador, the region's only natural harbors, with a first-class transoceanic railway. Palmer inadvertently revealed the ties that subordinated Keith's Guatemala Railway to United Fruit when he wrote as general counsel of UFCO, which did not have the rights to build the line to La Union; Keith possessed those rights, but there was never any practical distinction between his railroad and UFCO.[9]

Van Horne and Hubbard, who each owned one third of the Guatemala Railways, found little room in the vast empire that Keith was creating for United. After they helped him put the finishing touches on his railroad monopoly, they sold their interests in the firm and pursued other adventures. Between 1908 and 1910, Van Horne rearranged the railroad's tenuous financing while Hubbard eliminated their Pacific coast competitors.

With the company operating in the black and scheduled to repay the Deutsche Bank $1.2 million on May 1, 1908, the Americans had no option other than to refinance their debt. Van Horne and Farquhar arranged to replace the German debt with a $1.2-million loan at 7 percent interest from Scottish financier Robert Fleming, who had recently bought control of the Cuba Railroad. Farquhar left the Guatemala project shortly thereafter and initiated his own railroad project in Brazil. The completion of the line and the financial reorganization of the company did not boost Van Horne's sagging interest in the Guatemala project, either. He admitted that the Guatemala Railway had become his bête noire and cut his ties to Keith and the railroad several years later.[10]

Hubbard's last contribution to the enterprise was the acquisition of the Occidental Railroad, the Central's main competition along the Pacific coast. Both of these railways had grown from small, noncompetitive lines serving different ports (San José and Champerico), to rivals eager to extend their lines along the coast as they bid for the traffic of the rich coffee districts. When the Central connected with the Occidental at Mazatenango in 1903, only a short distance between Ayutla on the Mexican border and Retalhuleu remained in the Guatemalan portion of the projected Pan American Railway, a grandiose scheme that would link Canada to Tierra del Fuego by rail.[11]

Although neither the Occidental nor the Central had much interest in the Pan American Railway, both of them wanted to establish a rail connection with Mexico. In 1906 the government authorized the Occidental to begin construction on an extension from Caballo Blanco (a point south of Retalhuleu) to Coatepeque, just twenty-one miles from the Mexican border. The Central claimed preferential rights of construction under its concessions, but the government decided the dispute in favor of the Occidental. The owners of the Occidental, the Aparicio family, evidently acquired the Caballo Blanco-Coatepeque concession only to prevent the Central from securing it and thereby decreasing the value of their own line, which they were eager to sell. Hodgsdon advocated the acquisition of the Occidental in 1908, but Hubbard prohibited him from pursuing it because he could not raise the money until the U.S. bond market recovered.[12]

Hodgsdon complied with those orders while he outmaneuvered Occidental in the bid for control of the Pacific railways. In May 1908 he acquired a concession to complete the extension from Coatepeque to the Mexican border. By signing this contract, Hodgsdon prevented the Occidental from extending its line to the Mexican border and decided the competition in favor of the Central. The Occidental capitulated in the spring of 1909, when Hubbard purchased a controlling interest and placed it under the jurisdiction of his Pacific Improvement Company. One year later the Central acquired the Ocós Railway, a small, inconsequential line owned by Schwartz and Company, thereby giving the Central control of the entire western railroad network.[13]

Were it not for Hubbard's association with Keith, the Central would have been in a position to divert traffic away from Puerto Barrios. Once the two sections of railroad from Caballo Blanco to the border were completed, the American consul predicted in 1908, barring tariff manipulations by the railroad, all produce from southwestern Guatemala would be shipped across the Isthmus of Tehuantepec on Pan American and Mexican railroads to Coatzacoalcos on the Gulf Coast.[14]

However, Hodgsdon and Hubbard were already considering the means by which they could capture the coffee freight and ship it out of Puerto Barrios. Hodgsdon realized that the Central would have lost business to competitive lines if the Occidental had built the connection to the Mexican border. Even before the rail connection with Mexico was completed, some *finqueros* had loaded their coffee at Champerico or Ocós, shipped it to southern Mexico, reloaded it on the Tehuantepec railroad, and delivered it to Coatzacoalcos. To prevent the further loss of coffee freight through Coatzacoalcos, Champerico, or Ocós, Hubbard acquired the Occidental, and he did so with the intention of transporting coffee on the Central and Guatemala Railway to Puerto Barrios, over three hundred miles away from its traditional Pacific ports. Hodgsdon explained that with the Occidental owned by the Central, "a volume of tonnage could be routed over it and the Guatemala Railway at fairly profitable rates, not a pound of which is it possible for us to obtain the way the road is now operated."[15]

Many observers, Keith foremost among them, were disappointed when the *finqueros* did not take advantage of the completion of the Northern Railway to ship their coffee through Puerto Barrios. Until Keith's freight rates compelled them to do otherwise, the *finqueros* of the western districts shipped their coffee through San José, Champerico, and Ocós. In April 1909 the American consul in Livingston reported that because the bulk of the coffee was still being shipped out of the Pacific ports, Keith's Guatemala Railway had become "something of a White Elephant."[16]

Until 1911 the railroad did not show the profits that Keith had anticipated. The poor and uncharacteristic performance of the company disturbed his financiers, particularly Fleming, who had extended Keith a short-term loan in 1908. To retire this debt and secure permanent financing through the sale of bonds in London, Keith would have to show a profit. While British investors may have had confidence in his ability to manage a railroad, many had doubts about the financial stability of Guatemala, which still had not repaid a British debt incurred in the 1820s. Although the debt had been rescheduled in 1895, the Guatemalans fell into default just a few years later. Palmer explained the financial predicament that Keith faced in 1909: "The interest of these bonds [1895 English bonds] has not been paid for many years, and the London bankers who are interested in the railway have stated that it will be impossible to bring out a public issue of railway bonds until the national debts have been respected and the national credit restored."[17]

The effort to place the railroad on a sound financial basis brought Keith and Palmer to Guatemala in March 1909 with a proposal to reorganize the country's finances. Although they had little interest in banking they had concluded that the success of their enterprises would not be assured without a comprehensive financial and monetary reform. They proposed to refund the external debt and modernize facilities at Puerto Barrios through the issuance of $17.5 million in 5 percent bonds, create a national bank, and stabilize the currency through a $12.5-million loan. Once the reform was implemented, Keith could proceed with his plans to build the Zacapa branch to the Salvadoran border in accordance with the 1908 concession.[18]

Keith and Palmer spent two months in Guatemala trying to convince Estrada Cabrera that he should implement a financial reform and accept their proposal. They argued that, as the owners of the Guatemala Railway, they should be given preference for making the loans, inasmuch as the government had guaranteed the company a 5 percent return on its $4.5-million investment. Since the company had lost money in its first three years, the government owed $1.25 million to Keith, who left thinking that he had convinced the dictator to work with him rather than with other groups that did not have such a large financial interest in putting Guatemalan finances on a sound basis.[19]

Shortly after Keith's departure agents of the Windsor Trust Company of New York proposed a $10- to $12-million financial reform package and requested a concession on all mining properties for which the government had not already issued titles. Acting on behalf of American mining interests that included Congressman William Sulzer of New York and former Lieutenant Governor A. E. Spriggs of Montana, the Windsor agents obtained the concession by admitting Estrada Cabrera into their syndicate. American Minister William F. Sands heard the details of this arrangement from other American citizens who feared the loss of their own mines. Sands vigorously protested what he called a "rancid transaction," but he resigned after the State Department refused to challenge a powerful congressman.[20]

In August 1909 the J. and W. Seligman banking house of New York, which had the strongest political connections within Guatemala, proposed yet another financial reform package. The Seligman representative in Guatemala was Adolfo Stahl, the head of the American syndicate, who, in collaboration with the dictator, profited from the country's deflated currency and chaotic financial conditions. Although Estrada Cabrera negotiated with the Keith and Windsor groups, he would most likely defer to Stahl on this and all other financial matters, since the caudillo favored him "without the question of a doubt," the American minister predicted.[21]

Keith and Palmer utilized their Washington connections to apply pressure on Estrada Cabrera through diplomatic channels. In the summer of 1909 they solicited the support of Sands, Secretary of State Philander C. Knox, and President William Howard Taft. At a meeting in Massachusetts, Palmer discussed Keith's plans to stabilize Guatemalan finances, and in order to secure U.S. support, he offered to seek modifications in the concessions that would give the United States the right to intervene militarily in order to keep the transoceanic line open.[22]

Although the State Department knew the full, sordid details of the financial swindles in which two of the three groups engaged, it showed no favoritism toward any of them. By early January 1910 the Windsor group had lost interest in the financial reform package; hence, the State Department encouraged the Keith and Seligman interests to pursue a financial reform package together. Keith and Palmer held a series of discussions with the Seligman group, but they could not agree on the issue of managerial control as long as Stahl represented Seligman. Keith held Stahl and his syndicate responsible for the "hopeless state of bankruptcy" and wanted him eliminated from the negotiations, or at least placed in a position from which he could no longer control the country's finances.[23]

The dictator would consider no proposal that diminished Stahl's influence or substantially reformed the financial system that benefited him and his close associates. Rather than accept a reform package financed by a reputable international banker, Estrada Cabrera preferred the system whereby he took out short-term loans that evidently profited him and the syndicate. In March 1910, Keith, exasperated by Guatemala's corruption, threatened to abandon his plans for future development, and Palmer warned the president that a disaster would occur if the government incurred a large indebtedness without making the necessary financial reforms because no further investments would be justified until the country's credit was permanently restored.[24]

Despite the threat from the country's largest investor, Estrada Cabrera accepted another loan from Stahl. In September he convened a special session of the legislature to formally reject all three financial reform packages on the grounds that they prejudiced the country's financial interests and violated its sovereignty. Sands concluded that Estrada Cabrera opposed Keith's proposals because he did not want "to give greater power and influence to Mr. Keith than he already possesses through the United Fruit Company, the railroads of Guatemala, and the steamship company on the Atlantic coast."[25]

Keith and Palmer continued to advocate a financial reform package, but they did so through British contacts. They took up the case with the Council of Foreign Bondholders in London, convinced that the settlement of the English debt was the first step toward a financial reform that would ultimately benefit their interests. Although the British minister settled the old debt by delivering an ultimatum to Estrada Cabrera in March 1913, the government did not carry out a financial reform until the mid-1920s.[26]

Keith's interest in pursuing a financial reform waned as the Guatemala Railway began to show a profit. The earnings of the railroad jumped from $464,005 in 1910 to $778,062 in 1911, partly because of an increase in banana exports from 633,291 to 1,004,569 bunches. Yet an examination of the railway's revenues reveals that it was much more than a private banana line. Bananas ranked third as a source of company revenues, behind imported commodities and other exports. The railway had become the primary carrier of Guatemalan commerce by 1911, and this, rather than the expansion of the banana industry, explains the initial success of the railroad.[27]

In view of the railroad's success, Keith requested a loan of £4.5 million, but the London bankers approved a loan of only £1 million on the condition that Keith would use it to purchase the Central Railroad, improve the wharf at Puerto Barrios, and reduce the steep grades coming out of the port area. The loan could not be used to finance the construction of the Zacapa branch to El Salvador because Keith could finance that project by collecting the $1.25 million that the government owed him. In January 1912, Palmer informed the State Department that tentative arrangements for the consolidation of the railroads had been made.[28]

On February 8, Hubbard sold Keith the Central for $2.1 million in cash and $3.5 million in bonds bearing 3.5 percent interest. Keith founded the International Railways of Central America on April 19 and transferred all the property, rights, and privileges of the Guatemala Railway to it. Palmer signed onto the deed of transfer as a witness, a formality that demonstrated that the same interlocking directorates and traffic agreements that had existed since 1904 still linked the two companies. The general manager of the Central, A. D. Shepard, certainly knew that United Fruit was behind this transaction. As he explained the deal to an associate, "The Pacific Improvement Company has sold all its interest in the Guatemalan Central Railroad Company, and other properties in Guatemala to Minor C. Keith and John H. Dunn, who, I understand are acting for the International Railways of Central America, or, in other words, the United Fruit Company."[29]

In public, IRCA and UFCO officials deliberately concealed the extent to which they collaborated in Guatemala. IRCA's lawyers, for example, argued in 1921 that the two companies were connected only by privately executed agreements that served the interests of both firms: "The United Fruit Company has never had any control over the International Railways in any manner. When the line east of Guatemala City was built, it opened lands available for banana cultivation which the United Fruit Company acquired and planted to bananas. Naturally, the United Fruit Company has shipped its agricultural products to the seaboard over this railway as there was no other outlet, but this relation has been a purely business one."[30]

To be sure, Keith personally owned a majority interest in IRCA from 1904 to 1928. The main instrument linking the two companies during these twenty-four years was the 1904 traffic agreement, a "purely business arrangement." Yet the antitrust lawyers of the Department of Justice recognized that before 1928, UFCO had effective control over IRCA through traffic agreements that guaranteed the former rates and services available to no other banana company. When the New York State Supreme Court awarded $4.5 million to a group of minority IRCA stockholders, it attached little significance to the absence of stock ownership in IRCA by UFCO because the fruit company controlled the railway by means that still allowed it to secure unfairly low freight rates for the banana traffic.[31]

Aside from the traffic agreement, interlocking directorates and some joint stockholders assured the functional unity of the two firms. Until 1928, Keith, the founder and president of IRCA as well as founder and vice president of UFCO from 1899 to 1924, was the primary link between the two companies. Preston, president of United Fruit from 1899 until his death in 1924, sat on IRCA's board of directors from 1912 to 1924 and held 7,000 shares of IRCA stock. Palmer, besides being Keith's personal friend, was a director of IRCA (1912–1924 and 1930–1946), a director and secretary of UFCO, and legal counsel to both firms.[32] With the same people managing both companies, functional distinctions between the two companies disappeared.

Financial control of IRCA, however, rested with Keith until 1928. From 1912 until 1927, Keith personally held 15/26 of IRCA stock. Fleming, the Scottish investment banker who rescued the company from financial ruin in 1908, owned 7/26. Despite denials by United the record shows that the company had, for a least a brief time, a financial interest in IRCA. In 1923, at Keith's request, UFCO purchased some IRCA stock on condition that Keith could buy these shares from it at cost plus interest. Keith exercised his option in May and, together with Fleming, bought 4,825 shares of preferred and 27,940 shares of common stock previously held by UFCO.[33]

The absence of stock ownership prior to 1928 provided UFCO with a legal basis to defend itself against antitrust lawyers and hostile Guatemalan politicians, even though the companies could not deny that their economic interests were closely related. In 1923, Victor Cutter, vice president of United Fruit, denied having much knowledge about UFCO's holdings in IRCA but admitted that his company's relations with the railroad "have always been, and still are, very friendly."[34]

The legal distinctions that Cutter, Keith, Preston, and Palmer carefully maintained did not alter the Guatemalans' perception that UFCO and IRCA operated as one company in their country. UFCO and IRCA officials acted as if they were part of the same team; whenever the Guatemalans challenged their economic interests, they spoke with one voice and often hired the same legal counsel. The first significant challenge to the railroad monopoly that Keith and his UFCO colleagues built surfaced shortly after Keith organized IRCA. The dictator who sanctioned the 1904 concession suddenly turned on Keith and prevented him from consummating the railroad network of which he dreamed.

On August 23, 1912, F. G. Williamson, general manager of IRCA, requested the Guatemalans' formal approval of the company's new name and all the properties it had acquired. What was once only the Guatemala Railway, with a line connecting Guatemala City to Puerto Barrios, was now a railroad monopoly subservient to UFCO, but the consolidation and reorganization of the railroad was clearly authorized by the 1904 concession. Williamson simply asked the government to recognize the company's new name and transfer the titles of the recently acquired properties to him.[35]

By November 6, Williamson still had not received the documentation he had solicited, and the London bankers were getting worried. Until the government recognized the rights of IRCA to do business in Guatemala, the bankers could not proceed with the registration of a bond issue because they needed the deeds and titles of all the different companies that IRCA now possessed. The processing of those documents, Williamson discovered, was now stalled by bureaucrats who grew increasingly hostile toward the company. Sensing that something had gone terribly wrong, Williamson respectfully requested the diplomatic intervention of the United States.[36]

Within the Ministry of Development, bureaucrats dared to question the wisdom of policies that allowed foreign concessionaires to monopolize the railroad network. In 1912 the ministry reviewed a railroad project submitted by Hiram Eastman, who proposed to build a line from San Felipe (a junction on the Occidental line) to Chiantla via Quezaltenango. As compensation, Eastman requested privileges that had become fairly standard articles in railroad concessions. Vicente Saenz, commissioned by the ministry to analyze the proposal, refused to yield another inch to foreign entrepreneurs and implicitly criticized the concessions that had allowed Keith to monopolize the railroad network. Saenz, arguing that all monopolies violated the constitutional article guaranteeing the freedom of industry, urged the government to reevaluate its railroad development policy. In the past, he argued, the government had not accurately predicted the consequences of liberal concessions, which he described as "the bitter fruits of absolute monopoly; the frightening increase in the internal debt; the mountains of gold; the length of the contracts; the slow and sly, but secure and effective absorption [of competitive lines], to lead us to our death. Such a skillful and appropriate economic policy!"[37] On Saenz's recommendation the Ministry of Development rejected Eastman's proposal.

Shortly thereafter the government approved another proposal on the grounds that a new line would bring some competition into the railroad business. Mrs. W. S. Timmins, representing unnamed bankers in Boston, proposed to invest $80 million in a line from Livingston across the country to Champerico, with a dubious extension to Flores in the Petén. Timmins met personally with Ministry of Development officials and evidently impressed them with the idea of incorporating the Petén into the productive life of the country. Undoubtedly, her offer to turn over to the president stocks valued at $1 million in gold also earned the support of the bureaucrats, who approved the project with the stipulation that Timmins could not sell the railroad to any other party without specific government authorization.[38]

From these two decisions one may deduce that the Guatemalans had learned at least two valuable lessons from Keith: either they should have demanded more money from him, or they should not have let him acquire all the railroads. Some bureaucrats, such as Saenz, articulated an antimonopolistic position founded on solid constitutional precepts; most of them, however, simply implemented decisions made by Estrada Cabrera, who considered himself above the law. Although Williamson and the American minister suspected that the caudillo had orchestrated the stalling tactics that frustrated IRCA, neither one knew why he was doing it.

Keith had fulfilled all but the obligation he had assumed in the Méndez-Williamson contract to complete the Zacapa branch within four years. Although Keith had commissioned the surveys for the proposed route, he failed to initiate construction by the deadline of February 1910. By that date the company had installed only a switch at the Zacapa junction in an inauguration ceremony held on Estrada Cabrera's birthday, November 21, 1908. One reason for Keith's delay, according to Williamson, was that Keith wanted to acquire all the Pacific slope lines before he began work on the Zacapa line.[39]

Estrada Cabrera's refusal to reform the country's financial system also prevented Keith from raising the capital required to build the railroad. Keith's London bankers would not loan him the money as long as the government failed to stabilize its finances and retire the $1.25-million debt, an amount sufficient to finance construction of the Zacapa branch. Even if the bankers had approved Keith's earlier request for a £4-million loan, they could not process it until the government released the titles and recognized IRCA's right to do business in Guatemala. Since the caudillo had obviously obstructed the Zacapa project, one must doubt his allegations that Keith had failed to comply with the contracts; he was exploiting an issue created by his own obstructionism.

On November 28, 1912, the American chargé d'affaires, Hugh R. Wilson, pleaded with the minister of foreign affairs to remove the obstacles thrown in the path of an American enterprise. In a decree issued two days later the government officially recognized that the newly formed International Railways of Central America had absorbed the Central Railroad and intended to build or acquire other lines.[40] The government apparently recognized Keith's railroad monopoly.

Four months later Guatemalans were publicly threatening to hang Williamson from the nearest tree. During the nine months in which he lobbied on behalf of IRCA, he had become a nuisance to bureaucrats and a target of ridicule for journalists, neither of whom expressed sentiments contrary to those of their dictator. His popularity plummeted in April 1913 after he settled a minor labor dispute by firing the workers' leaders. One newspaper labeled Williamson "the most harmful man that has landed on Central American soil" and incited the people to riot: "Guatemala is the victim and shall continue to be so, until its governments act with energy or its people rise in body to lynch their oppressors who steal their daily bread and then mock at their hunger and misery."[41]

Secretary of State William Jennings Bryan directed Wilson to express his strong concern for the security of American life and property. On April 22, Wilson met the minister of foreign affairs, who assured him six days later that the government would give its full protection to American interests. Wilson accepted the promises but left suspecting that the government remained hostile toward Williamson and IRCA because it probably instigated the attacks against the company.[42]

Indeed, for the next seven months the dictator, adopting tactics used by General Barillas in the 1880s, refused to satisfy IRCA's demands. The government denied or ignored repeated requests by IRCA officials and American diplomats to register IRCA's titles, deeds, and mortgages and to settle the $1.25-million debt. In a related issue the government stalled on United Fruit's request to register lands it had acquired between 1910 and 1912. In November, IRCA's lawyers reluctantly asked the State Department to send a special U.S. representative to Guatemala, at their expense, to demand Guatemala's compliance with its contractual obligations.[43]

On January 22, 1914, President Woodrow Wilson appointed a special agent to Guatemala, retired Major General George W. Davis, who had attended the inauguration of the Guatemala Railway six years earlier. In contrast to that festive occasion, Wilson now instructed Davis to resolve the controversies affecting the railway and other American interests. Immediately after his appointment, Davis went to New York for a meeting with Keith and UFCO's general manager. When he left for Guatemala on February 2 he was already convinced that the two companies had "reason and justice in their complaints." Keith had essentially bought diplomatic intervention on behalf of IRCA and UFCO; he could not have defended IRCA any better than Davis, who carried the weight of presidential authority with him. Since the 1904 contract gave Keith the right to purchase and consolidate with all other railroads in the country, IRCA was not only legitimate but also more efficient than smaller companies, Davis argued, because Keith had united all the lines into "one great transcontinental system" that was more economical than the four separate ones that had existed prior to the consolidation.[44]

Davis quickly learned that Estrada Cabrera was orchestrating the bureaucratic delays that had frustrated IRCA for one year. When he arrived in Guatemala in mid-February, he held only a few discussions with the minister of foreign affairs before he realized that only direct negotiations with the caudillo could resolve the dispute. It took him much longer to learn that Estrada Cabrera was a master of deception. When the two men discussed the case on March 11, Estrada Cabrera agreed to register the lands recently acquired by UFCO and promised to settle the other issues a few days after the companies complied with Guatemalan laws. The tone of the two-hour meeting was not friendly enough to disguise a hostility to the American interests that, Davis predicted, would manifest itself in further annoyances and an insistence upon the strictest observance of technicalities.[45]

Davis met with the president for the last time on March 14 and secured Estrada Cabrera's promise to record IRCA's titles as soon as the government inspector issued a favorable report on the railroad. As for the transfer of the Central Railroad to IRCA, the government would recognize it upon receipt of a document that showed exactly what properties IRCA had acquired from the Central. Although Davis received no pledge to settle the debt to IRCA, he left Guatemala on March 19 believing that his assistant, E. M. Lawton, could settle the dispute based on the caudillo's ambiguous statements.[46]

Years of experience had taught Estrada Cabrera how to frustrate foreign diplomats. On April 2 he explained to Lawton that the weighty issues involved in the case required careful study that could take up to three months. Government officials insisted that they could not register the deeds and mortgages until their engineers concluded an inspection of the line and IRCA submitted deeds of conveyance for every parcel of private land taken for the right of way. Although the government already had this evidence in the public registers, Williamson agreed to furnish all the necessary documents, a process that could take at least another three months. Estrada Cabrera assured Lawton that he had ordered his subordinates to expedite affairs by lending "more than customary aid" to the railroad.[47]

One wonders how long it would have taken if the bureaucrats had not been ordered to accelerate the paperwork, for they consumed another year processing documents that they already possessed and inspecting a railroad that had been fully operational for over five years. The government's tactics exasperated the American minister, who thought only a categorical demand by the State Department would end the dispute. "The only way you can bring anything here to a satisfactory conclusion," William Hayne Leavell argued, "is by the exercise of an infinite patience, a courtesy that will not be provoked, and by having at your disposal a not inconsiderable section of eternity."[48]

Estrada Cabrera was obviously toying with Keith and the American diplomats. He reached the height of absurdity in October 1914 when the government made its only effort to resolve any of the issues General Davis had left behind. In the 1904 contract the government had granted the railway a mile of Puerto Barrios shoreline, one hundred yards wide, but the government had not transferred the land to IRCA, ostensibly because it could not afford to buy it. In October the government offered a 100-yard strip of land from high tide out toward the open sea—a useless strip of water.[49]

Keith subsequently realized that this inane dispute required his personal attention; he suspected that it had something to do with the sharp increase in railroad freight rates and profits that followed his consolidation of the railroad network. The railroad's rate policies, governed by the 1904 concession, set maximum tariffs three to four times higher than the concession under which the Guatemala Central had operated for decades. Because the contract also guaranteed the railroad administrative autonomy—that is, freedom from government intervention—the company could manipulate the tariff structure within these high maximum rates as it saw fit. Hence, after Keith purchased the Central he established highly prejudicial freight rates to encourage shipments of coffee over the northern section of the railroad to Puerto Barrios. For the next forty years the rate structure discouraged shipments out of the Pacific ports; at times the rates for shipping coffee out of San José were three times higher than the cost of shipping it out of Puerto Barrios. As a result Pacific Mail, which had dominated Pacific shipping since the 1860s, lost business to United Fruit's steamships. Faced with diminishing profits and the intimidating prospect of competing with United Fruit, Pacific Mail withdrew from the Pacific business in 1914.[50]

Thus, Keith established himself as the arbiter of Guatemalan commerce. He, rather than the Guatemalan minister of development, implemented a rate policy that shifted Guatemala's commerce away from the southern coast and Pacific Mail to the northern coast and United Fruit. In 1906, before the completion of the Northern Railway, commercial traffic was divided between five different ports. Of the 558 ships that cleared Guatemalan ports in 1906, 162 left from San José, 143 from Puerto Barrios, 124 from Champerico, 85 from Livingston, and 44 from Ocós. By 1910, two years after the completion of the railroad, Puerto Barrios had become the country's leading port, handling 65 percent of imports and 27 percent of exports. In 1915 the figures increased to 77 percent of imports and 41 percent of exports.[51]

IRCA officials claimed that they established the new rates in order to give coffee planters the option of shipping through Puerto Barrios, thereby reducing transit time to the eastern markets of the United States and avoiding the costs of shipping through the Panama Canal. Some *finqueros* and merchants evidently did not care to have this option, as a group led by the owners of the Champerico wharf petitioned the government for equitable rates in July 1914. They complained that IRCA charged three times more to ship coffee from Retalhuleu to Champerico, less than thirty miles away, than from Retalhuleu to Puerto Barrios, a distance of four hundred miles. If the rates were equalized the *finqueros* would continue to ship through the Pacific port, as they had done before the Central acquired the Occidental Railroad.[52]

Although the Ministry of Development did not approve the new rate structure (indeed it would have liked to have rejected it in May 1914), it had no legal means of compelling IRCA to change its policies. If the former lines of the Central and the Occidental were still governed by their original concessions, the ministry could have blocked the rate increase, but since the Méndez-Williamson contract of 1908 authorized Keith to administer all railroads under the terms of the Farquhar concession, the new rate policy was as legal as it was discriminatory. Thus, in December 1914 the Ministry of Development rejected the pleas of the *finqueros* and merchants to restore equitable rates on the railroad. The ministry favored a political solution to the rate problem, meaning negotiations with Keith, but a legal remedy was not available since IRCA had violated only a provision of the 1895 railroad law that set a timetable for notifying the public of rate increases.[53] The new rate policy allowed IRCA to capture the coffee trade, and its profits, shown in Figure 1, jumped more than 50 percent between 1911 and 1912, the first year in which IRCA operated all Guatemalan railways under the new rate schedule.

The wealth generated by the railroad complicated Keith's political problems, for not only did he have to contend with bureaucrats who wanted to negotiate rates downward, but he also had to deal with an envious caudillo who could justifiably claim partial responsibility for IRCA's sudden profitability. If Keith did not settle accounts with the dictator, the bureaucrats would continue to badger the railroad and prevent Keith from consummating his dream of a Central American railroad. With special agent Davis removed from the scene, Keith had to negotiate his own problems because Minister Leavell apparently showed little inclination to intervene in Guatemala's internal affairs. Leavell's attitude suited Estrada Cabrera perfectly, for it allowed him "to keep a tight hand on the United Fruit Company and Mr. Minor Keith's other enterprises, and to remind these powerful corporations from time to time that they must cultivate his goodwill or suffer serious consequences," according to the British minister.[54]

Figure 1. International Railways of Central America Profits, 1908–1937

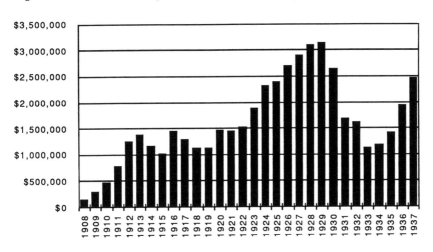

Source: Chester Lloyd Jones, *Guatemala: Past and Present* (1940, reprint, New York: Russell & Russell, 1966), 257–58.

Keith arrived in mid-February 1915 and spent nearly three months pleading for the liberation of his company from a troublesome bureaucracy. Keith voluntarily ceded the mile of shoreline that the government refused to surrender and signed a new mail contract with the government; in return, Estrada Cabrera approved a 150 percent rate increase on the Pacific section of the railroad.[55] While Keith failed to obtain assurances that the government would retire the $1.25-million debt and register the deeds, he evidently restored amicable relations with the caudillo, for there were no major disputes between them for the next five years.

Given the paucity of documentation, one can only speculate about the informal agreement that Keith concluded with Estrada Cabrera. A financial inducement could have been involved, as evidence shows that Keith gave Estrada Cabrera five hundred shares of IRCA stock at some point.[56] It is likely that Keith gave him the stock (or some other kind of payment) in order to resolve the three-year dispute over deeds and title registrations. General Davis suspected that Estrada Cabrera had been trying to extort Keith all along:

> It seems to have been the policy of the Government to embarrass the corporation by delaying action on requests for a fulfillment of contractual obligations, and by raising technical questions respecting registration of documents, the motive seemingly being to so harass, annoy and impede as to constrain the corporation to make concessions, in other words, to purchase again the property rights they have already earned legitimately and renounce just claims against the Government, abate charges or concede favors; in other words, to submit to extortion and blackmail or further jeopardize what they have.[57]

Estrada Cabrera created the controversy in order to bring Keith back to the negotiating table, where he could discreetly discuss rates and his personal interest in IRCA's profits. The three-year controversy did not originate in the antimonopolistic critiques of the Ministry of Development or the *finqueros'* requests for the restoration of equitable freight rates; for the next five years nobody dared to challenge the rate policy or the president who approved it for $50,000 worth of IRCA stock. Keith's failure to build the Zacapa branch did not ignite the controversy either. Estrada Cabrera had approved the concession in 1908 to increase trade with his neighbor, but he soon realized that the railroad would facilitate an invasion of Salvadoran troops. The fact that military forces could move in either direction evidently escaped the wily caudillo, and Keith tried to assuage his fears of a foreign invasion. In 1909, Palmer had proposed an amendment to the railroad contracts that would give the United States the right to intervene to keep the railroad open, thereby discouraging any Salvadoran military action. According to Boaz Long, who represented IRCA in the early 1920s and later served as ambassador to Guatemala, Estrada Cabrera withheld the money he owed Keith and delayed the mortgage registrations so that Keith would not be able to establish rail connection with El Salvador.[58]

The caudillo obtained what he wanted from Keith—more money and no Zacapa line—without delivering the titles, deeds, or subsidies. In the months after Keith's departure, he expected the United States to demand the immediate settlement of these issues, but the ultimatum never came. In 1919, Estrada Cabrera agreed to settle the debt with IRCA at $1.4 million, but the government never paid one penny of it. Partly because of Estrada Cabrera's obstructionism, Keith would not live long enough to complete the Zacapa branch, but he saw IRCA become a tremendous financial success. Even without rail connection to El Salvador, IRCA was worth $55 million in 1920, and its earning potential was limited only by Guatemala's capacity to produce and consume freight that IRCA cars could carry to and from Puerto Barrios.[59] It monopolized rail transport from coast to coast, controlled the company's main port, and had a close and profitable relationship with United Fruit and a powerful though unpredictable dictator. Together, they could repress any challenges to their hegemony.

Notes

1. Miguel Angel Asturias, *Strong Wind*, trans. Gregory Rabassa (New York: Delacorte Press, 1968), 112.
2. Stewart, *Keith and Costa Rica*, 11–19.
3. Wilson, *Empire in Green and Gold*, 59.
4. John Keith Hatch, *Minor C. Keith: Pioneer of the American Tropics*, (N.p), 63.
5. Henry C. Hall (minister to Guatemala) to State, March 14, 1887, Diplomatic despatches.
6. Daniel B. Hodgsdon to General Thomas H. Hubbard, February 1, 1908, JL 17, Box 14, Folder 1, PICO records.
7. IRCA, *Concessions, Contracts and Decrees, 1877–1912*, 27.
8. Anderson, "Development of Export Transportation," 382–83.
9. Bradley Palmer to Henry M. Hoyt, November 18, 1909, SD 814.77/1; Kendrick, *A Report upon International Railways*, 26–27.
10. Gould, *Last Titan*, 57–58; "Guatemala Railway Company; Loan Agreement of 1908," JL 1, Box 7, Folder 51, PICO records; Vaughan, *Life and Work*, 329.
11. Ross, "Construction of the Railroads of Central America," 327–85.
12. Adolfo Meyer (president, Occidental Railroad) to Secretaría de Fomento, March 19, 1906, and Hodgsdon to Fomento, March 25, 1906, AGCA, B129, legajo 22179, expediente 942; Hubbard to A. D. Shepard (general manager, Central Railroad), February 19, 1908, JL 17, Box 14, Folder 1, PICO records.
13. Kendrick, *A Report upon International Railways*, 24–25; Major William Heimke (minister to Guatemala) to State, May 18, 1909, SDNF, 14992/3–4. The acquisition of the Ocós followed a bitter legal contest for control of the railroad. See "Ferrocarril Central," AGCA, B129, legajo 22181.

14. William Owen (vice consul, Guatemala City) to State, July 25, 1908, SDNF, 14992/1.

15. Hodgsdon to Hubbard, January 29, 1908, JL 17, Box 14, Folder 1, PICO records.

16. Edward Reed (consul, Livingston) to F. R. Jekyll, April 9, 1909, Livingston, General Correspondence, Consular post records.

17. Palmer to State, October 8, 1909, SDNF, 10859/25–26.

18. Ibid., July 28, 1910, SDNF, 18857/10; Dinwoodie, "Dollar Diplomacy," 242; Palmer to George Wickersham (attorney general), March 23, 1909, SDNF, 18857/1; memorandum, "Guatemala Loan Projects," SD 814.51/112.

19. Heimke to Francis B. Loomis, July 27, 1909, SDNF, 10859/17–19; memorandum, Arthur Frazier (secretary of legation, San Salvador), SDNF, 10859/ 32–33.

20. Dinwoodie, "Dollar Diplomacy," 242; Sands, *Jungle Diplomacy*, 185–89.

21. Heimke to Loomis, July 27, 1909, SDNF, 10859/17–19.

22. Keith to William F. Sands, August 25, 1909; SDNF, 10859/15–16; Palmer to Sands, August 27, 1909, SDNF, 10859/17–19; Palmer to Secretary of State Philander C. Knox, October 8, 1909, SDNF, 10859/25–26.

23. Palmer to Estrada Cabrera, September 3, 1909, SDNF, 10859/15–16; Palmer to State, January 22, 1910, SDNF, 10859/54; Palmer to Knox, October 11, 1909, SDNF, 10859/27; memorandum, November 8, 1909, SDNF, 10859/34–35.

24. Palmer to State, March 7, 1910, enclosed, Palmer to Estrada Cabrera, March 7, 1910, SD 814.51/64.

25. Sands to Knox, September 29, 1910, SD 814.51/109; memorandum, "Guatemala Loan Projects," SD 814.51/112; Dinwoodie, "Dollar Diplomacy," 244.

26. Palmer to Knox, January 13, 1912, SD 814.51/153; Palmer to Knox, February 6, 1912, SD 814.51/158; Peter Calvert, "The Last Occasion on which Britain Used Coercion to Settle a Dispute with a Non-Colonial Territory in the Caribbean: Guatemala and the Powers, 1909–1913," *Inter-American Economic Affairs* 25:3 (1971): 72–73.

27. Guatemala Railway Company, *Annual Report of the Guatemala Railway Company, 1911*, 21; International Railways of Central America, *Annual Report, 1920*.

28. "The Case of the IRCA," 18–19, SD 814.77/92; Palmer to Knox, January 13, 1912, SD 814.51/153.

29. "Memorandum of Agreement," February 8, 1912, and "Guatemala Central Railroad Company to International Railways of Central America," April 24, 1912, JL 1, Box 7, Folder 51, PICO records; A. D. Shepard to R. J. Keown, Jr. (Union Oil Company), June 24, 1912, JL 17, Box 14, Folder 1, PICO records.

30. "The Case of IRCA," 8, SD 814.77/92.

31. Milton A. Kallis to Victor H. Kramer and W. Perry Epes, December 20, 1952, DOJ, File 60-166-5619; Ripley v. International Railways of Central America, 188 N.Y.S. 2d 62, 71.

32. Arthur Nicholson (secretary, United Fruit) to Jerome N. Frank (chairman, Securities and Exchange Commision), February 3, 1941, DOJ, File 60-166-56, series 537, IRCA-34; [list of UFCO and IRCA officeholders] DOJ, File 60-166-56, series 537, IRCA-173; Henry M. Keith (vice president, IRCA) to A. J. Barnaud (district manager, Bureau of Foreign & Domestic Commerce), July 12, 1923, SD 813.77/5.

33. Wheeler (ambassador to Great Britain) to State, June 28, 1923, SD 813.77/ 3; Keith to Barnaud, July 12, 1923, SD 813.77/5; Nicholson to Frank, February 3, 1941, DOJ, File 60-166-56, series 537, IRCA-34.

34. E. S. Gregg (Bureau of Foreign and Domestic Commerce) to Mr. Monroe, State Department, July 9, 1923, SD 813.77/7.

35. "Report of General Davis," March 30, 1914, enclosure no. 1, George W. Davis to Estrada Cabrera, February 28, 1914, SD 814.77/45.

36. Hugh R. Wilson (minister to Guatemala) to State, November 26, 1912, SD 814.77/31.

37. Vicente Saenz to Ministerio de Fomento, May 21, 1912, AGCA, B129, legajo 22170, expediente 1415.

38. Wilson to State, August 13, 1912, SD 814.77/29; Adolfo García Aguilar et al. to Ministerio de Fomento, September 3, 1912, AGCA, B129, legajo 22170, expediente 154.

39. Fred G. Williamson to Keith, October 14, 1908, AGCA, B129, legajo 22189, [no expediente]; Bauer Paiz, *Como opera el capital yanqui*, 149; R. S. Reynolds Hitt (minister to Guatemala) to State, January 26, 1912, SD 814.77/23.

40. Wilson to State, December 6, 1912, enclosure no. 2, Luis Toledo Herrarte (minister of foreign relations) to Wilson, December 2, 1912, SD 814.77/33.

41. Wilson to State, April 21, 1913, enclosure, *La Campaña*, April 19, 1913, SD 814.77/37; John Gray (Delaware Corporation Company) to William Jennings Bryan (secretary of state), April 18, 1913, enclosure, Williamson to Hon. Manuel Estrada Cabrera, SD 814.77/56.

42. Wilson to State, April 29, 1913, SD 814.77/39.

43. Bryan to Davis, January 28, 1914, SD 814.77/42a; Gray to Boaz Long (chief, Latin American Bureau), November 7, 1913, SD 814.77/41.

44. Bryan to Davis, January 28, 1914, SD 814.77/42a; "Report of General Davis," 3–4, SD 814.77/45.

45. "Report of General Davis," 3–4, SD 814.77/45.

46. Ibid., 11–16.

47. E. M. Lawton (consul, Tegucigalpa) to State, April 6, 1914, SD 814.77/47.

48. William Hayne Leavell (minister to Guatemala) to State, April 20, 1914, SD 814.77/49.

49. Leavell to State, October 15, 1914, SD 814.77/52.

50. "Trade Opportunities and Panama Canal," October 6, 1913, Consular post records, Guatemala City, 1913, vol. IV, 610; for a detailed analysis of IRCA's rate policies see Bauer Paiz, *Como opera el capital yanqui*, 139–49; Handy, *Gift of the Devil*, 84; Dana G. Munro, *The Five Republics of Central America* (New York: Oxford University Press, 1918), 69; Anderson, "Development of Export Transportation," 263.

51. Great Britain, Foreign Office, Board of Trade, *Guatemala: Report for the Year 1906 on the Trade and Resources of Guatemala*, 14–15; Stuart Lipton (consul general, Guatemala) to State, May 2, 1916, SD 814.51/261.

52. "The Case of IRCA," 22, SD 814.77/92; Cía. de Agencias de Champerico to Señores J. Lisser y Cía., July 22, 1914, AGCA, B129, legajo 22184, expediente 1683.

53. Untitled memorandum, Ministerio de Fomento, AGCA, B129, legajo 22181, expediente 1644; [untitled memorandum], Ministerio de Fomento, AGCA, B129, legajo 22184, expediente 1683.

54. Alban Young (British minister to Central America) to Sir Edward Grey, January 24, 1915, in Bourne and Watt, eds., *British Documents on Foreign Affairs. Latin America, 1914–1939*, 20.

55. Leavell to State, May 25, 1915, SD 814.77/53.

56. B. Alvarado (ministro de Gobernación) to Ministerio de Fomento, May 24, 1922, AGCA, B129, legajo 22190 [no expediente].

57. "Report of General Davis," 12, SD 814.77/45.

58. Palmer to Estrada Cabrera, September 3, 1909, SDNF, 10859/15–16; Robert Lansing and Lester Woolsey to State, January 6, 1923, enclosed, Long to Lansing and Woolsey, January 5, 1923, SD 814.77/211. Long claimed that he received this information directly from Estrada Cabrera and confirmed it with Adrian Recinos, a member of his cabinet.

59. Lansing and Woolsey to State, January 6, 1923, exhibit A, Long to Lansing and Woolsey, January 5, 1923, SD 814.77/211; Lansing and Woolsey to State, enclosed, "Protest Filed by International Railways of Central America with Government of Republic of Guatemala," May 21, 1921, SD 814.77/90; IRCA, *Annual Report, 1920.*

5

United Fruit, Cuyamel, and the Battle for Motagua, Part I

The pioneers of the Central American banana industry considered themselves members of an epic generation of modern conquerors who introduced capitalist civilization to backward societies by cultivating bananas, building railroads, dredging harbors, installing sanitation facilities, and combating tropical diseases. They worked in an inhospitable Caribbean environment that claimed thousands of lives, and those individuals who subdued the frontier assumed heroic proportions, at least in the works of their chroniclers. Bradley Palmer, for example, extolled Keith's contribution to Costa Rican civilization by claiming that the country's progress in the late nineteenth century was due to him alone.[1]

Victor Macomber Cutter shared the rugged characteristics of Keith and the other pioneers, but, as a second-generation Banana Man, he never had to endure the rigors that existed on the Caribbean frontier. Born near Lowell, Massachusetts, in 1881, this poor boy worked his way through a Phi Beta Kappa from Dartmouth in 1903. One year later he began his career with United as a timekeeper in Costa Rica, despite Andrew Preston's warning that life in the tropics was especially lonely and uncomfortable for a New Englander. Cutter had little difficulty adapting to and excelling in plantation agriculture, as evidenced by his quick climb up the corporate ladder. When United decided to open a new division in Guatemala, it chose Cutter as its first manager.[2]

The appointment gave Cutter the opportunity to prove that he was cast in the same heroic mold as the industry's pioneers. Keith had subdued the Costa Rican environment two decades before Cutter arrived there; he was in the process of conquering eastern Guatemala when Cutter assumed command of the banana plantations. By the time he met diplomat Hugh Wilson on the docks of Puerto Barrios in 1911, the Dartmouth graduate looked and acted the part of the successful tropical manager. Six feet tall, weighing two hundred pounds, and dressed in white, Cutter struck Wilson as a character out of an O. Henry novel, with a shyness that belied a volatile temperament and a love of adventure that his position either required or nurtured. Wilson wrote: "His handling of negroes was remarkable. He excelled in everything they admired. He could fight the wildest of them, he could outshoot them, his endurance was unlimited and his occasional flash of ferocious temper kept them cowed. Such qualities were necessary. These negroes from Jamaica were cheerful and reasonably industrious, but full of liquor they became dangerous. Cutter would face them down in their worst moments."[3]

After he had established the Guatemalan division, Cutter was transferred to Honduras where he met his nemesis, Samuel F. Zemurray. While the two men were roughly the same age, Zemurray belonged in spirit to the first generation of banana men. Like Keith, he worked his way up a corporate ladder of his own making and earned his fame and fortune without a high-school education. Born in 1877 to a poor Russian family, he emigrated to the United States in 1892 with nothing but ambition. The teenager took a job at his uncle's general store in Selma, Alabama, where he made his first venture into the banana business. He went to the docks of Mobile, bought $150 worth of "ripes" (bananas that have ripened in transit and must be sold immediately or discarded), and loaded them in a railway express car, hoping to get back to Selma before the cargo rotted. When he realized that the ripes would not make it back to Selma, Zemurray offered a free bunch of bananas to any telegraph operator who notified local grocers that he was coming through with a shipment of bananas. As the train made its way to Selma, Zemurray sold his ripes to grocers at the railway station and made it home with a $35 profit. He repeated that trip so many times over the next three years that he had saved over $100,000 by the time he was twenty-one.[4]

Zemurray gradually made his way to New Orleans, a port and a market dominated by United Fruit. Hoping to replicate his Selma success, he asked UFCO officials for a contract to sell the ripes that they were discarding on the docks. United's agents granted the contract thinking that the young man could not possibly sell the bananas before they ripened. When the Banana Man began selling the fruit in the local markets and cutting into company profits, they politely asked him to relinquish the contract. Zemurray agreed to do so on the condition that United provide him with some financial assistance.[5]

He went on to establish the Cuyamel Fruit Company, a multimillion-dollar enterprise that displayed the aggressive, innovative spirit of its founder, who acquired a reputation as one of the toughest hombres in the business. He neither respected Cutter's Ivy League credentials nor feared his employer. The banana business never rewarded passivity; the quick exhaustion of banana lands made expansion imperative. In pursuit of land and profits, Cuyamel and United came to blows in the Motagua River valley, a no-man's-land claimed by two companies as well as two countries. In 1915, when Zemurray began building a railroad from his Honduran plantations toward the river, he ignited the battle for Motagua, a banana war that lasted fourteen years and brought Honduras and Guatemala to the brink of conventional war on several occasions. While the international dispute had its origins in poorly defined colonial boundaries, competition between UFCO and Cuyamel triggered and sustained the hostilities. The offensive that Zemurray launched in 1915 struck at the heart of UFCO's Guatemalan empire; if United had not repelled Cuyamel's incursion, it would have lost the monopoly on the banana business that it had only recently established.

Before United Fruit developed its massive plantations in eastern Guatemala, there was a clear distinction between the cultivation of bananas, in which competitive practices prevailed, and marketing, a field dominated by the Oteri and Macheca steamship lines. After United acquired the lines in 1899, it showed no interest in expanding into banana cultivation in Guatemala, for it had highly productive plantations in Costa Rica, Colombia, and Jamaica. UFCO initially confined its activities to marketing bananas produced by private planters in eastern Guatemala. The first contract that it signed with the Estrada Cabrera government, in fact, contained no provision for the cultivation of bananas; it only authorized United to purchase bananas from private planters at rates supposedly regulated by the government. In October 1901, United terminated the mail contract because the government failed to pay the monthly subvention for the conveyance of its mail, but it continued to provide weekly service between Puerto Barrios, where its agents purchased fruit from independents, and New Orleans, from which United distributed Guatemalan bananas through its marketing network.[6]

After Keith acquired the rights to complete and operate the Northern Railway, however, United decided to develop its first plantations. With its control of Keith's railroad and the port, United had the power to deny independents access to the market, and it was only a matter of time before it would dominate the banana business. Moreover, UFCO began banana cultivation on terms that no private planter could match. Before it planted any trees, it secured a traffic agreement from Keith's railroad that gave it a 50 percent discount on banana shipments and the right to specify the times and places at which it would deliver its bananas to the railroad, which was obligated to give United precedence in the use of its cars and the docks at Puerto Barrios. Independents could not hope to obtain any comparable agreements from the railroad, for it also promised not to encourage any competition in the banana business.[7] In a separate transaction, Keith gave United fifty thousand acres of land valued at roughly $1 million, ostensibly to encourage it to plant bananas. Hence, a railroad, a port, and land—the three vital ingredients for a banana operation—came into United's possession free of charge.

Even with its investment secured and minimized, the banana trust developed its plantations cautiously, planting only 9,650 acres between 1906 and 1909. In 1910, when banana exports reached a record 1,225,000 bunches, United decided to use its considerable financial muscle to expand the acreage under cultivation and eliminate actual or potential competitors. Independent planters either succumbed to the lure of United's millions or recognized that competition with the giant was futile. UFCO purchased 76,000 acres from private planters between 1910 and 1913, increasing its total landholdings to 126,189 acres. Cutter, who directed this $5-million project that included a hospital, warehouses, tramways, housing, an ice factory, and commissaries, transformed eastern Guatemala into a huge plantation, with banana trees flanking both sides of the IRCA line for fifty miles through the Motagua River valley, which was, for all practical purposes, UFCO territory.[8]

Private planters remained in the area, but only the strongest planters stayed in the business, and they operated on terms set by United Fruit. Soon after establishing the plantations, Cutter doubled the prevailing wage for field workers, thereby forcing competitors to match his wage or lose their employees. The Jamaicans, most of whom were left destitute after they completed the Northern Railway, appreciated the seventy-five cents per day that Cutter offered, but the move also reduced the profits of the independent planters and forced some of them out of business. Other planters survived by accepting United Fruit's offer to purchase their bananas at set prices, but the contracts under which they operated made them subservient to UFCO. The nominally independent planters often found their fruit rejected by United's agents on the docks because the bananas were allegedly below standard.[9]

United's dominance extended even to the the area around Lake Izabal, where planters had been able to avoid direct confrontation with United by shipping their fruit down the Rio Dulce to Livingston, a small port that United did not control. Some European steamships occasionally called at Livingston to load coffee coming out of the Verapaz region, but they had little interest in competing with United in the banana trade. Without their own shipping facilities, these planters also had to accept contracts with United. In 1913 the U.S. consul in Livingston reported that UFCO monopolized the fruit produced by the independent farmers. Over the next few years, as United's plantations in the Motagua River valley came into full production, exports from Livingston dropped and the private planters were virtually eliminated.[10]

Hence, within a period of seven years, UFCO developed a monopoly on the cultivation and marketing of bananas in eastern Guatemala. None of the private planters offered much resistance to it, for there was little hope of competing with a firm that controlled the railroad, port, and ships that linked the plantations to the external market. The Banana Man, however, had his own railroad and port in Honduras; his access to the U.S. market was limited but not blocked by United Fruit. Moreover, he had a personal score to settle with Victor Cutter and United Fruit, a company with which he had collaborated between 1905 and 1913.

During this time, Zemurray managed one of only three nominally independent companies that United Fruit allowed to remain in the banana business. Immediately after its creation, United Fruit pursued a policy of stifling or eliminating competition by collaborating with or acquiring rival firms. By 1906 it had purchased fifteen of the eighteen firms engaged in importing bananas. With the three remaining firms, United reduced competition by buying a majority interest and not assuming management. United purchased a 60 percent interest in the Hubbard-Zemurray Steamship Company, a 51 percent share of the Atlantic Fruit Company, and a 50 percent interest in the Vaccaro Brothers Company. In each case, United left managerial responsibilities in the hands of the company's founders, Zemurray, Joseph DiGiorgio, and Joseph Vaccaro, respectively. By taking a controlling share of the capital and leaving management in the hands of others, Preston hoped to broaden his sources of supply without violating antitrust legislation.[11]

The arrangements also benefited Zemurray, DiGiorgio, and Vaccaro, each of whom expanded their operations and established reasonably profitable enterprises within an industry dominated by one firm. The Hubbard-Zemurray Company grew from a minor shipping company marketing Honduran bananas through United's Gulf coast distribution network, into a major banana farmer. In 1910, Zemurray acquired his first lands by purchasing the properties of William F. Streich of Philadelphia, who possessed a 1902 concession from the Honduran government for the cultivation of 12,235 acres on each side of the Cuyamel River.[12] Behind Zemurray came revolution and United Fruit.

United had been unusually unsuccessful in convincing Miguel Dávila, president of Honduras, to authorize a concession that would give it control of a transoceanic line, a port, and the banana lands around the line, an arrangement similar to that which had allowed it to eliminate independent planters in eastern Guatemala. Beginning in 1908, UFCO's agents lobbied for the rights to complete and operate the National Railroad, connecting Puerto Cortés to the Gulf of Fonseca. Since the 1850s the Hondurans had tried a number of different means to complete the railroad, but by 1910 only forty miles of track had been laid from Puerto Cortés. United's proposal encountered serious opposition from private farmers and nationalistic Hondurans who realized that if United gained control of the railroad, it would be in a position to dictate freight prices and thereby eliminate the planters who had dominated the northern coast since the late nineteenth century.[13]

When Dávila approved a financial reorganization package recommended to him by Secretary of State Philander C. Knox, Zemurray and United Fruit recognized that they would never obtain the liberal concessions they sought.

The Knox plan called for an overhaul of the country's finances and a thorough reform of the customs houses under the supervision of an official appointed by the American president. As the package would be underwritten by a loan from the Morgan banks, Zemurray saw that the government would not likely approve the typical banana concession that included long-term tax exemptions for the construction of docks, railroads, tramways, and telegraph facilities.[14]

While the plan would have stabilized Honduran finances, Zemurray viewed it as a threat to his private interests. He explained: "I was doing a small business buying fruit from independent planters, but I wanted to expand. I wanted to build railroads and raise my own fruit. The duty on railroad equipment was prohibitive—a cent a pound—and so I had to have concessions that would enable me to import that stuff duty free. If the banks were running Honduras and collecting their loans from customs duties, how far would I have gotten when I asked for a concession?"[15]

Sometime in the fall of 1910, Zemurray lobbied in the State Department against the loan package. Zemurray later claimed that Wilbur Carr, director of the consular service, had assured him and his associate Dr. Virgil C. Reynolds, a former vice consul in La Ceiba, that the United States would not interfere with a revolutionary movement led by Manuel Bonilla, the former president of Honduras who was then plotting Dávila's overthrow with Zemurray's financial support. Carr denied ever meeting with Zemurray or making such a statement, although he acknowledged having had a general discussion about Honduran politics with Dr. Reynolds.[16]

If Zemurray thought that the State Department would look favorably on another Central American revolution, he was mistaken. One purpose of stabilizing the Honduran financial system was to promote political stability, a difficult goal given the ready supply of arms, ammunition, mercenaries, and disgruntled but ambitious former presidents. In defiance of American foreign policy, Zemurray forged a personal friendship and political alliance with Bonilla, who had taken refuge in the French Quarter of New Orleans following an ill-fated invasion in July 1910. Borrowing money from Zemurray, Bonilla bought a yacht called the *Hornet*, rerigged it for military operations, loaded it with arms, and recruited a small army commanded by General Lee Christmas and Colonel Guy "Machine Gun" Maloney. On January 10, 1911, Christmas and Maloney invaded Honduras and joined the Bonilla forces, which had already taken Trujillo; Maloney took La Ceiba with only six men, and Tegucigalpa fell without a fight.[17] Bonilla became president, and Knox's financial reorganization plan was dead.

Although the U.S. government never took legal action against Zemurray or United Fruit, the evidence implicates both companies in a conspiracy to break U.S. neutrality laws and overthrow the Honduran government. Both companies had the motivation to depose the Dávila government, and Zemurray admitted his involvement in the Bonilla revolution. Indeed, he protested the seizure of the *Hornet* by the U.S. Navy, claiming that the State Department had promised that it would not interfere with Bonilla's revolution. Independent planters in Honduras charged that UFCO and Zemurray financed and supported the Bonilla revolution in order "to secure concessions of valuable unimproved fruit lands, the Inter Oceanic Railroad, . . . and the right to finance the Republic, thus enabling them to acquire complete control of the banana business of the country, as they have done in other of the Central American Republics." Estrada Cabrera believed that UFCO had an understanding with Bonilla and pointed out that it was in a position to furnish money, war materiel, and men from its Guatemalan division. The U.S. consul at Livingston confirmed that IRCA delivered a shipment of small arms to the Bonilla forces at Puerto Barrios and that 125 to 150 men recruited from the plantations joined the rebels. While UFCO denied any involvement, one must remember that it held a 60 percent interest in Zemurray's firm. Knox viewed the evidence strong enough to warrant a thorough investigation of the entire affair.[18]

In any case, the Bonilla revolution did not produce all the benefits that Zemurray and United had anticipated from a change in government. In fact, it produced some hostilities in the U.S. government, and Andrew Preston had no desire to give the Department of Justice any more reason to investigate allegations of its criminal behavior. Hence, United sold its interest in Hubbard-Zemurray, Atlantic, and Vaccaros by September 1911, but it maintained a close working relationship with Zemurray for two years thereafter, primarily because he was so close to the Bonilla government that he could obtain practically anything he asked for, according to his own financial agent.[19]

Zemurray asked for many things, for himself and for his friends, all of whom shared an interest in carving out distinct enclaves in northern Honduras. In August 1911, Bonilla appointed him the fiscal agent of Honduras with the authority to negotiate a $500,000 loan that would defray all the expenses of the recent revolution, including the loan he had made to Bonilla. On March 4, 1912, he received the rights to select an additional 24,700 acres in the vaguely defined region between the Cuyamel River and the Guatemalan frontier. Several months later, Hubbard and Zemurray reorganized all these properties as the Cuyamel Fruit Company of New Orleans, a $5-million enterprise in which Zemurray held a majority interest. Zemurray secured another concession that authorized the development of banana plantations in the vicinity of Tela, but he transferred this to the Tela Railroad Company, a UFCO subsidiary. Zemurray knew how to return a favor. Through another subsidiary, the Trujillo Railroad Company, UFCO began the development of lands around Trujillo. With the Vaccaro Brothers (later the Standard Fruit Company) operating in the region around La Ceiba, the northern coast of Honduras had been carved into four distinct banana zones by three U.S. companies.[20]

Ironically, the man who had led the conquest of the banana lands found himself in the weakest position. United Fruit's prosperous plantations in the Motagua River valley bordered Zemurray's lands to the north and west; to his east, Zemurray faced the Vaccaros and UFCO. He eventually would have to fight one of these companies for more land, since hurricanes, diseases, and soil exhaustion kept the average commercial productivity of a plantation down to ten years.[21] While Zemurray could probably win a fight with the Vaccaros, he was most likely to engage United Fruit, for his concession gave him the right to lands between the Cuyamel River and the Guatemalan border. Unfortunately, nobody knew where that border actually was.

Since 1847, Guatemala and Honduras had been trying to establish a definite boundary between their countries based on the territorial divisions established by the Royal Ordinance of Intendentes in 1786. Because subsequent boundary commissions could not ascertain the extent of each intendency, a diplomatic dispute simmered from independence until 1895, when the two countries created a commission to analyze the colonial documents and recommend a definitive boundary line. The commissioners could not get very far with their work because the Guatemalan authorities would not permit the Honduran engineers to survey what they considered Guatemalan territory. As far as they were concerned, Guatemalan territory may have included lands adjacent to Tegucigalpa; some Hondurans claimed lands on the shores of Lake Izabal.[22] A bilateral settlement of the boundary dispute seemed unlikely in 1914.

Nevertheless, the border conflict would have remained within the diplomatic arena indefinitely were it not for the bitter rivalries that erupted soon after the American companies had established their spheres of influence. Although the disputed territory extended 125 miles from the junction of the borders of Honduras, El Salvador, and Guatemala to the Gulf of Honduras, and one hundred miles between the boundary of British Honduras and the Ulua River, the battlefront in the banana war was limited to the right bank of the Motagua River, an area to which both Cuyamel and United claimed concessionary rights (see Map 3). As they were collaborating for their mutual benefit between 1905 and 1913, the two companies informally acknowledged the disputed territory as a neutral zone.[23]

The tenuous peace began to unravel in early 1913 when Keith's agent, René Keilhauer, submitted a proposal to the president of Honduras that provided for the settlement of the country's foreign debt, the imposition of a one-cent tax on banana exports, the transfer of the wharf at Puerto Cortés and the National Railroad, the rights to extend the line to the Gulf of Fonseca, and a grant of 370,650 acres. Other than an annual rent payment of $50,000, Keilhauer's plan offered little material incentive to the Hondurans, who only recently had taken possession of the National Railroad and would

Map 3. Battle for Motagua

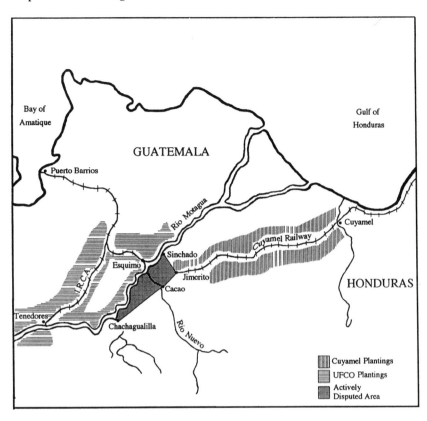

not likely part with a forty-mile line to which Honduran nationalists attached great symbolic importance. Keilhauer informed the American minister that he could overcome these political difficulties "by the judicious distribution of a considerable sum of money."[24]

If Bonilla approved the project, Keith and his UFCO associates would have an iron grip on the nation's infrastructure. Keith had already acquired the rights to build a railroad from Trujillo to Tegucigalpa and to complete the Pan American railroad across southern Honduras. As the concessions included large grants of land, the use of national resources lying in and contiguous to the zone of the railroad, exemptions from port duties, and exclusive rights to build and maintain wharves at Puerto Cortés and the Bay of Fonseca, Keith was bidding for nothing less than control of the best railroads and ports in the country. To gain control of the national railroad, he also requested authorization to establish a bank of emission with the exclusive privilege of banking all government funds. In the opinion of the U.S. minister to Honduras, the concession Keith sought "constitutes an outright gift of the country to the United Fruit Company."[25]

In fact, the concession may have cost Keilhauer more than United had anticipated, for it upset the balance of power, alienating its competitors and some Honduran politicians. The consul at Puerto Cortés warned his superiors that approval of the plan to settle the debt and cede the National Railroad to Keith would incite violent attacks against American property and people, for the people of his district were already hostile toward United Fruit. But Keilhauer applied discreet pressure at the center of power in Tegucigalpa, where he worked on Dr. A. A. Ramirez Fontecha, the Spanish consul whom Bonilla entrusted with the delicate negotiations involving multimillion-dollar concessions. Rumors circulated that Fontecha had extracted a high price from Keilhauer, but he was apparently worth it, for Bonilla evidently supported Keith's project.[26]

United's bid for total control destroyed what remained of the working alliance between it, Cuyamel, and the Atlantic Fruit Company, among which there existed a rough productive parity in the Puerto Cortés district. If Keith gained control of Puerto Cortés and the National Railroad, however, Cuyamel and Atlantic would either have to accept rates and schedules set by United Fruit or export their fruit by another means. Recognizing their precarious situation, Atlantic Fruit officials made preparations to abandon the district entirely.[27]

Zemurray, on the other hand, was in the process of developing thirty-seven hundred acres along the Cuyamel River, the heart of his company's enterprise. Since the concessions under which he operated allowed him to build railroads, tramways, and wharves in and around Omoa, Zemurray was not totally dependent upon the National Railroad for the transportation of his bananas to market, but until he completed the railroad to Omoa and built adequate port facilities there, he exported his fruit through Puerto Cortés. UFCO's acquisition of the concession, therefore, would alter the balance of power in the banana districts and represent a decisive political defeat; Zemurray evidently had lost some influence over the Bonilla government, for the president was ready to approve Keith's project before he died in March. Were it not for Bonilla's death, Keith probably would have obtained the contract he wanted, but without the strongman in office, Keilhauer could not overcome the legislators' grave reservations about the concession; the assembly adjourned in April without taking any action.[28]

Bonilla's death did not diminish Keith's interest in Honduran railroads; it only compelled him to change his political strategy. He solicited the support of the State Department and resubmitted his proposal in early 1914, claiming that he was in a position to negotiate on behalf of the British bondholders, who were willing to accept any debt settlement that he arranged. Zemurray could not accept UFCO control of Puerto Cortés, for he needed an outlet for the fruit produced on his Cuyamel plantations. Consequently, Zemurray entered the political fray in early 1914, when he submitted his own proposal for the construction and operation of the National Railroad. The split between former private collaborators had now become publicly hostile, Keilhauer and Keith reportedly "hot after Zemurray at every turn."[29]

From Zemurray's perspective, the hostilities were justified in the name of self-defense, for his fruit would rot on the trees in northwestern Honduras if he did not block United Fruit's concessions. While he pressed in the political arena to have either UFCO's concession rejected or his own approved, Zemurray invoked his existing concessionary rights and initiated construction of a railroad from Omoa along the coast toward his plantations. The move precipitated a bitter conflict with the Morse Timber Company of Louisiana, which also claimed the right to build in that area, and United Fruit, which wanted to prevent Zemurray from obtaining an outlet for his bananas. Morse took Zemurray to court and, for the most part, won recognition of its rights, but Zemurray's lawyers tied the case up in the appeals process while the government allowed Cuyamel to lay several miles of track and erect a wharf at Omoa. Rumors circulated that UFCO had assisted Morse in this conflict, but the only substantial evidence came from Zemurray, who alleged that United Fruit had used its connections in the banking industry to force the early payment of one of his loans. With the survival of his company at stake, in the spring of 1914 he secured relief from an unidentified European financier.[30]

The Banana Man was displaying the characteristics that made him a legend in the business, dodging bullets by relying on his own resourcefulness and political charm. He could not match the dollars that UFCO's agents could toss around, which may explain why he lost influence over Bonilla, but his decisive and bold personality, not to mention his money, appealed to many Hondurans, including Bonilla's successor, Francisco Bertrand. Despite UFCO's incessant lobbying, he refused to surrender the National Railroad or block the construction of the Cuyamel Railroad, either of which would have denied Zemurray an outlet to the Caribbean. A grateful Zemurray told Bertrand three years later: "Once more I repeat to you, that you can always count on me as a sincere friend, for I shall never forget the good treatment I received from you and your government that spring of 1914 when I was really in serious difficulties."[31]

For the remainder of his administration, Bertrand dealt with an increasingly powerful United Fruit that was determined to block Zemurray's expansion. In January 1915, Keith was still lobbying for the rights to the National Railroad, and the American minister worried that UFCO was plotting a change in government to achieve its objectives. The competition between Cuyamel and United intensified thereafter, partly because the conflict had already generated serious personal animosities that compounded the corporate rivalries. Joseph Montgomery, Zemurray's trusted lieutenant, attributed part of the dispute to a personal rivalry that had developed almost as soon as Zemurray met Victor Cutter. Shortly after Preston reassigned Cutter to the new Honduran divisions in 1914, Zemurray quickly showed up the man who had developed a reputation as a hot-tempered fighter and a skilled administrator. According to Montgomery, Cutter was "asleep at the switch" when Zemurray secured two contracts for banana lands that UFCO should have obtained. The two men were personal enemies for the next twenty years.[32]

Zemurray could not long remain within the narrow confines that United had been trying to impose upon him because disease and soil exhaustion would eventually take his lands out of production. United would have liked to keep Cuyamel's plantations limited to the region between its Tela and Bananera divisions, an area that Zemurray may have been able to accept if UFCO and Guatemala had recognized the Motagua as the boundary. Zemurray had a Honduran concession that authorized cultivation and railroad construction between the Cuyamel River and the Guatemalan border. Since Estrada Cabrera also claimed the rights to authorize plantings and construction in the area, Zemurray recognized that he would have to placate or at least neutralize the caudillo before he moved into the region.

Beginning in 1913 either Zemurray or his agents solicited permission from Guatemala to plant in the disputed area and construct thirty-three miles of railway. As such a concession would not contradict what Honduras had already sanctioned, Zemurray reasoned, it should not provoke an international controversy. To his great disappointment, the caudillo refused to meet him, despite numerous trips to La Palma, the dictator's private residence. He dealt only with Luis Ferro, the president's "special agent," who was evidently instructed to stall Zemurray. On a spring day in 1915,

Zemurray was waiting to see the dictator at La Palma when the chief of staff told him that because of other pressing obligations, the president could not receive him. The Banana Man calmed his fury and left a message for the dictator: "Inform the president that the concession that was being requested of him, one with ample benefits for Guatemala, I will obtain from another party, and I will be remembered."[33] He left for Honduras the next day.

Zemurray realized that he did not need Guatemala's approval, for he had a Honduran concession that allowed him to push his railroad all the way to the Guatemalan border. In the summer of 1915 he initiated construction on an extension of the Cuyamel Railroad from its termination at Jimerito to Sinchado, a village just three miles shy of the Motagua. Guatemalan authorities notified the company that it would have to terminate construction because it had no authorization to build on Guatemalan territory. Arguing that it was working on Honduran territory under a valid concession from that government, Cuyamel ignored the warnings, despite reports that one thousand troops were mobilizing on the other side of the river. Cuyamel appealed to the Honduran government for protection, but Bertrand told his friend that his troops would not defend Cuyamel in disputed territory. In the early fall, General Luis Monzón, commander of Livingston, stopped work on the line and urged Cuyamel to apply for the appropriate authorization from Guatemala City.[34]

Since Zemurray had recently been denied the concession he sought, he received the invitation cautiously, but Cuyamel recognized that it might be easier and cheaper to bribe its way out of the controversy rather than fight the combined power of Estrada Cabrera and United Fruit. Keith had recently resolved his differences with the caudillo through some illicit arrangements, and he had undoubtedly earned the goodwill of the chief executive. For a small fee, Zemurray could get his piece of the action, but Estrada Cabrera could not offer a significant land or railroad concession, for Keith and United would not voluntarily yield their monopoly on the banana business of the Motagua River valley. On October 28, Guatemala authorized Cuyamel to build only one mile of railroad, but it did not approve the cultivation of bananas in the disputed area.[35]

For the next eighteen months, Zemurray suspended work on the railroad extension to the Motagua while he modernized and expanded his plantation network in or near the disputed territory. He spent $500,000 clearing lands, draining swamps, building roads, and installing irrigation systems. According to Zemurray, when the investment had reached "formidable proportions" and therefore could not be abandoned, emissaries from Estrada Cabrera appeared on the scene and attempted to collect property taxes from the company, claiming that it operated on Guatemalan territory. Zemurray recognized this for what it was—extortion—and refused on the grounds that he was cultivating Honduran land under legitimate titles. The Guatemalans persisted, however, convincing Zemurray that he could liberate himself from their "petty annoyances" by offering a financial gratification in Guatemala City. Zemurray dispatched a representative to Guatemala with instructions to purchase a pledge of noninterference from the president, believing that it was the most convenient way out of the conflict. To his surprise, the representative found that the dictator asked only that Cuyamel acknowledge Guatemalan jurisdiction over the disputed territory and offered any terms and privileges that Zemurray would care to specify in a concession.[36]

While he wanted to placate the Guatemalan government, Zemurray rejected the offer because he did not want to offend Bertrand, who had already promised to protect Cuyamel's right to cultivate in the area. His plantings had reached the Cuyamelito River at a point called Colón, about six miles south of the Motagua and nineteen from the sea; Honduras did not consider this part of the actively disputed territory and until 1917, Guatemala apparently concurred, for it had not protested the plantings. There was, however, a powerful force working behind the scenes, for United Fruit claimed that it had legitimate titles to the lands along the Cuyamelito River. The caudillo was apparently willing to sacrifice United or play it off Cuyamel, but when Zemurray refused to play that game, he decided to work on United's behalf.[37]

On February 11, 1917, General Monzón ordered Cuyamel to vacate Guatemalan territory if it failed to present the legal titles that authorized its work. Cuyamel refused to comply with the order, claiming that the boundary convention of 1914 permitted cultivation in the disputed territory. The Guatemalan commander at Sinchado moved into the area, ordered Cuyamel to withdraw, and arrested several Honduran citizens. President Bertrand informed Washington that he was prepared to defend his country's sovereignty with military force. From Puerto Cortés, the Honduran military dispatched a hastily recruited and poorly trained force of five to seven hundred men, expecting to engage Guatemalan troops on the border.[38]

Only sixty of these Honduran troops actually reached Cuyamel's property, and they were quickly withdrawn at the request of the American minister, John W. Ewing, who believed that United had instigated the Guatemalan intervention in order to weaken Cuyamel. Ewing suggested that Cuyamel's productive plantations aroused the jealousy of "a powerful competing interest [UFCO] whose methods are not always most scrupulous." Neither Honduras nor Guatemala was prepared to fight a banana war, however, and each requested U.S. mediation; by February 28 the danger of a military clash had been averted.[39]

Although the armies backed off and the two countries eventually agreed to suspend activity in the disputed area under a status quo agreement, competition between Cuyamel and United still threatened to bring the two countries into armed conflict. In addition to the conflict over lands near the

Motagua, the companies were still lobbying the Honduran government for a concession on the National Railroad. By March, Zemurray had reportedly gained the upper hand in this political struggle by gaining the support of San Pedro Sula planters and the president, but Bertrand did not force the issue because UFCO allies in the legislature remained strong. Fearing that the intercorporate struggles would trigger another military confrontation, the State Department supported the diplomatic efforts to which Guatemala and Honduras recommitted their countries in September. On November 12 the U.S. government offered its services as mediator and invited both countries to send representatives to Washington for negotiations.[40]

Before negotiations began, Estrada Cabrera wanted to establish a secure presence on the right bank of the Motagua and check the advance of Cuyamel. The government colonized six families near the Sinchado garrison in March, hoping that a civilian presence would solidify the military claim that it already had established. Although the Hondurans protested the move as a violation of the status quo, they were committed to a peaceful resolution of the dispute through the decisive intervention of the United States. In the absence of such decisiveness, Guatemala intervened militarily in late December, ostensibly to prevent further construction on an extension of the Cuyamel Railroad. One hundred Guatemalan troops occupied the newly opened road from Jimerito to Rio Nuevo and prevented any further construction; another force moved near Omoa, deep into territory always recognized as Honduran. In January 1918, Guatemalan troop strength in the disputed territory was increased to four hundred, all of them encamped near the Rio Nuevo bridge. Guatemalans had never intervened in the disputed area with such military force, but the Hondurans entrusted the defense of their sovereignty to the United States. By these actions, the caudillo made it clear that he intended to incorporate the south bank of the Motagua River and expel Cuyamel.[41]

With the two countries closer to war than they had ever been, Secretary of State Robert Lansing compelled both governments to withdraw their forces while the United States attempted to mediate a negotiated solution to the crisis. On January 9 the Honduran foreign minister proposed a withdrawal of Honduran forces south and east of the Merendon mountains and the relocation of Guatemalan troops north and west of the Motagua River. While Guatemala immediately accepted the idea of a neutral zone, Estrada Cabrera insisted on the suspension of Cuyamel's development work prior to any withdrawal. Lansing demanded that the two countries disassociate the question of Cuyamel's concessionary rights from the boundary dispute, believing that it could be resolved after a permanent boundary had been fixed. Estrada Cabrera, concerned that Cuyamel's activities would establish a Honduran claim to the area south of the Motagua, refused to withdraw his troops until Cuyamel terminated its plantings and railroad construction. The caudillo relented on this issue only after Lansing had informed him that the United States would not tolerate Guatemalan interference with the production of a food item that was essential to the war effort.[42]

On January 29, Lansing formally invited both countries to send representatives to a boundary conference in Washington. The Hondurans accepted and withdrew their forces by February 12; the Guatemalans agreed to send a negotiator to Washington but kept their troops in place, despite Lansing's repeated requests for their withdrawal. In September he ordered Cuyamel to terminate its development work and dispatched some troops to enforce his decree.[43]

Meanwhile, special representatives of Guatemala and Honduras debated the boundary question in Washington with the friendly mediation of Boaz Long. The conference lasted two years, and its most significant contribution to the resolution of the dispute was a survey of the disputed area that clarified the issues involved and the amount of territory actually disputed. In 1919 a team of American specialists conducted a topographical and economic survey of the region. Their studies revealed that economic interests fueled the conflict; there were 178 square miles tied up by overlapping land grants and another forty-six miles of railroad right-of-way that were actively contested.[44]

Diplomats could not resolve hostilities generated by international businessmen. Given the intensity of the competition between the two fruit companies, only direct negotiations between the firms could reduce tensions in the area. The neutral zone created in early 1918 helped to reduce the possibility of an accidental outbreak of war, but it did not eliminate the fundamental causes of the conflict. The two companies secretly arranged a truce without the knowledge or participation of Guatemala, Honduras, or the United States. The two companies established the groundwork for a truce on January 8, 1918, when United Fruit's executive committee authorized an advance of $765,000 to the International Railways of Central America for the purchase of seventeen thousand shares of Cuyamel stock. Although Zemurray retained majority ownership, the investment lessened tension between the two companies and brought the first phase of the battle for Motagua to a temporary end. Eventually, Zemurray suspended work on his railroad and plantations in the area; he even refused to purchase bananas from independent farmers.[45] Since the status quo agreement worked out with American mediation would have allowed Cuyamel to continue work in the area, Zemurray's refusal to press his claims to the banana lands must have been covered by a private agreement he made with United Fruit. In any case, both companies respected the neutral zone for six years.

Zemurray always recognized the conflict over the Motagua River valley as a war between two rival companies. Without their interest in the lands, the dispute between Honduras and Guatemala would have remained within the diplomatic arena. To solve it, Zemurray once suggested that he and Keith use their influence over the Honduran and Guatemalan governments to establish a permanent boundary, for he suspected that Estrada Cabrera would never negotiate in good faith as long as he suspected that he could exploit the issue for his own benefit. While nothing came of this effort, Zemurray met Bradley Palmer in Washington sometime in the fall of 1919, hoping to engage in frank discussions with one of the few men in United Fruit whom he respected. Zemurray, a man of action who liked straight-talkers, evidently made it clear that the resolution of the dispute required United's acceptance of Cuyamel's presence in the disputed territory; Palmer was prepared to acknowledge Zemurray's right to do business in the area, but the deal was never consummated.[46]

This was a banana war, triggered by rival companies and fought by egocentric businessmen and the caudillos who exploited the issue for their personal benefit. In February 1919, while Guatemalan negotiators demanded recognition of the Merendon mountain range as the border, Estrada Cabrera sent Ferro back into the field to offer, according to Zemurray, "almost anything he [Zemurray] wanted in the way of concessions" if he could convince the Honduran representative in Washington, Policarpo Bonilla, to accept the Motagua River as the boundary. The incredulous Zemurray secured Bonilla's assent, but Ferro never delivered the written proposal that he had requested.[47] Neither Cuyamel nor Honduras ever came closer to incorporating banana lands on the right bank of the Motagua.

Notes

1. Bradley Palmer to Philander C. Knox, April 13, 1909, SDNF 18857/2–3.
2. Wilson, *Empire in Green and Gold*, 206–9.
3. Hugh Wilson, *The Education of a Diplomat* (London: Longmans, Green and Company, 1938), 36–37.
4. Pringle, "A Jonah Who Swallowed the Whale," *American Magazine* 116 (September 1933): 114; Kobler, "Sam the Banana Man," 87.
5. Kepner and Soothill, *Banana Empire*, 100–101; Wilson, *Empire in Green and Gold*, 200.
6. Jones, *Guatemala*, 213; Bauer Paiz, *Como opera el capital yanqui*, 205–6; Alfred A. Winslow (consul general), "Banana Industry of Guatemala," August 31, 1903, *Consular Reports*, vol. 73, no. 279 (December 1903).
7. "United Fruit Company and The Guatemala Railway Company, Traffic Agreement, September 15, 1904," DOJ, 60-166-56, Series 443.
8. United Fruit Company, *Eleventh Annual Report*, 1910, exhibit B; Frederick Upham Adams, *Conquest of the Tropics: The Story of the Creative Enterprises Conducted by the United Fruit Company* (Garden City, NY: Doubleday, Page & Company, 1914), 197–98; George A. Bucklin, Jr. (consul general), "Annual Report on Commerce and Industry, 1912," Consular post records, Guatemala City, 1913,

vol. 4, 610; Victor Cutter to R. S. Reynolds Hitt, February 22, 1913, U.S. Department of State, RG 84, Diplomatic Post Records, Guatemala City (hereafter cited as Diplomatic post records), 1913, vol. 5, 852.

9. Cutter to William Owen, (vice consul), October 4, 1913, Consular post records, Guatemala City, 1913, pt. 5, 861.1; Edward Reed (consular agent, Livingston) to William P. Kent (consul general, Guatemala), October 8, 1908, Consular post records, Livingston, Official Correspondence; Kepner and Soothill, *Banana Empire*, 256–60.

10. Reed, "Report. Trade and Investment," March 15, 1913, Consular post records, Guatemala City, 1913, vol. 4, 610; Reed, "Trade Report," May 31, 1919, Consular post records, Livingston, 1919, pt. 2, 600; Arthur C. Frost (consul general), "Annual Report on Commerce and Industries of the Republic of Guatemala for 1920," October 4, 1921, Consular post records, Guatemala City, 1921, pt. 4, 600; Nancie L. Solien González, *Black Carib Household Structure: A Study of Migration and Modernization* (Seattle: University of Washington Press, 1969), 33–38.

11. Milton A. Kallis to Victor H. Kramer and W. Perry Epes, December 20, 1952, DOJ, File 60-166-56, 4, 7; Wilson, *Empire in Green and Gold*, 200–201; House, Committee on the Merchant Marine and Fisheries, *Proceedings of the Committee on the Merchant Marine and Fisheries in the Investigation of Shipping Combinations under House Resolution 587*, 62d. Cong., 2d sess., 1913, 783–99; Thomas L. Karnes, *Tropical Enterprise: The Standard Fruit and Steamship Company in Latin America* (Baton Rouge: Louisiana State University Press, 1978), 18.

12. Kepner and Soothill, *Banana Empire*, 101; John W. Ewing (minister to Honduras) to State, April 20, 1914, SD 815.77/219.

13. C. Andrews et al. to State, January 30, 1911, SD 815.00/1127; E. Dox et al. to Knox, February 18, 1911, SD 815.00/1145.

14. Dana G. Munro, *Intervention and Dollar Diplomacy in the Caribbean, 1900–1921* (Princeton: Princeton University Press, 1964), 225–27; Kepner and Soothill, *Banana Empire*, 106.

15. "United Fruit," *Fortune* 7:3 (March 1933): 31.

16. Claude Dawson (consul, Puerto Cortés) to State, February 20, 1911, SD 815.00/1153; memorandum by Wilbur Carr, March 1, 1911. In the oft-quoted *Fortune* article, Zemurray also claimed that Knox called him in for a discussion of the loan project, but there is no record of any meeting between Knox and Zemurray in the State Department files.

17. The most authoritative account of this episode is Munro, *Intervention and Dollar Diplomacy*, 217–31; for a more entertaining, though less informative, account see Hermann Bacher Deutsch, *The Incredible Yanqui: The Career of Lee Christmas* (New York: Longmans, Green and Company, 1931).

18. Dawson to State, February 20, 1911, SD 815.00/1153; Andrews to State, January 30, 1911, SD 815.00/1127; Hitt to State, January 21, 1911, SD 815.00/1049; Reed to George A. Bucklin, Jr. (consul general, Guatemala City) January 20, 1911, and Reed to commanding officer, USS *Tacoma*, January 29, 1911, Consular post records, Livingston, Official Correspondence; Knox to attorney general, February 6, 1911, SD 814.00/1049.

19. Kallis to Kramer and Epes, December 20, 1952, DOJ, File 60-166-56, 7; Charles D. White (minister to Honduras) to State, October 12, 1911, SD 815.77/67 1/2.

20. J. Butler Wright to State, August 30, 1911, SD 815.51/301; Ewing to State, April 20, 1914, SD 815.77/219; Kepner and Soothill, *Banana Empire*, 111–12;

Walter LaFeber, *Inevitable Revolutions: The United States in Central America* (New York: W. W. Norton, 1983), 43.

21. Kepner and Soothill, *Banana Empire*, 32.

22. Gordon Ireland, *Boundaries, Possessions, and Conflicts in Central and North America and the Caribbean*, 2d ed. (New York: Octagon Books, 1971), 86–89.

23. David Hepburn Dinwoodie, "Expedient Diplomacy: The United States and Guatemala, 1898–1920" (Ph.D. diss., University of Colorado, Boulder, 1966), 128; Ray Fox (consul, Puerto Cortés) to State, March 6, 1928, SD 714.1515/589.

24. White to State, January 14, 1913, SD 815.77/164.

25. Ibid., March 5, 1913, SD 815.77/169.

26. David J. D. Myers (consul, Puerto Cortés) to State, February 19, 1913, SD 815.77/166; White to State, March 5, 1913, SD 815.77/169.

27. Myers to White, March 5, 1913, enclosure no. 4, Reed to Myers, February 27, 1913, SD 815.77/171.

28. Myers to State, February 15, 1914, SD 815.77/209; White to State, April 17, 1913, SD 815.77/173.

29. Myers to State, February 15, 1914, SD 815.77/209.

30. Ewing to State, September 23, 1914, SD 815.77/236; Ewing to State, April 20, 1914, SD 815.77/219; Lewis Sanders (Morse Timber Company) to William Jennings Bryan, December 11, 1914, SD 815.77/247; John A. Gamon (consul, Puerto Cortés) to State, August 27, 1915, SD 815.77/255.

31. Zemurray to R. F. Broussard (senator, Louisiana) June 15, 1917, enclosed letter of Zemurray to Francisco Bertrand, May 9, 1917, SD 714.1515/58.

32. Ewing to State, January 15, 1915, SD 815.77/251; Wilson, *Empire in Green and Gold*, 207; "Ill Feeling between the United Fruit Company and the Cuyamel Fruit Company in Honduras," April 8, 1929, SD 815.6156.

33. Carlos Salazar, *Memoria de los servicios prestados a la nacion, 1908–1944*, 2d. ed. (Guatemala: Grupo Literario Editorial, 1987), 197–98; Kepner and Soothill, *Banana Empire*, 118.

34. Gamon to State, August 27, 1915, SD 815.77/255; Fox to State, March 6, 1928, SD 714.1515/589.

35. Ewing to State, June 11, 1917, SD 714.1515/22; Gamon to State, August 27, 1915, SD 815.77/255; Ewing to State, March 7, 1917, SD 714.1515/19.

36. Zemurray told his story to the minister to Honduras. See Ewing to State, February 29, 1917, SD 714.1515/13; and ibid., February 15, 1917, SD 714.1515/12.

37. Ibid., February 15, 1917, SD 714.1515/12; ibid., March 5, 1917, SD 714.1515/14.

38. Ibid., March 7, 1917, enclosure no. 1, General Monzón, Jefe Político y Comandante de Armas, Livingston, to Greeley, February 11, 1917, and no. 4, Greeley to Comandante Local y Juez Municipal, El Cinchado, February 13, 1917, SD 714.1515/19; Alberto Membreño (Honduran minister) to State, February 19, 1917, Department of State. *Papers Relating to the Foreign Relations of the United States*, 1917 (hereafter cited as *FRUS*, followed by year), 761–62; Walter F. Boyle, (consul, Puerto Cortés) to State, February 26, 1917, SD 714.1515/16.

39. William Hayne Leavell to State, March 8, 1917, SD 714.1515/17; Ewing to State, February 20, 1917, SD 714.1515/13; Joaquin Méndez (Guatemalan minister) to State, February 21, 1917, *FRUS, 1917*, 763; Membreño to State, February 19, 1917, *FRUS, 1917*, 761–62; Ewing to State, February 28, 1917, *FRUS, 1917*, 763–64.

40. Ewing to State, March 15, 1917, SD 815.77/262; Ireland, *Boundaries*, 89.

41. Ewing to State, January 8, 1918, *FRUS, 1919* 1:85–86; Boyle to State, January 4, 1918, SD 714.1515/62; Lansing to Walter Clarence Thurston (chargé d'affaires, Guatemala), January 9, 1917, SD 714.1515/57.

42. Ewing to State, January 8, 1918, *FRUS, 1919* 1:85–86; Lansing to Ewing, January 9, 1918, *FRUS, 1919* 1:86–87; Lansing to Thurston, January 29, 1918, *FRUS, 1919* 1:94.

43. Thurston to State, February 2, 1918, *FRUS, 1919* 1:95; Curtis to State, February 14, 1918, *FRUS, 1919* 1:97; Leavell to State, February 20, 1918, *FRUS, 1919* 1:97–98; Zemurray to Stabler, February 26, 1918, SD 714.1515/92; State to Thurston, February 5, 1919, *FRUS, 1919* 1:100.

44. The minutes of these meetings and the documentation presented can be found on microfilm. See SD 714.1515/520, reels 18–23. For a summary of the economic survey see Ashmead (executive of the Guatemala-Honduras Economic Survey) to Boaz Long, September 5, 1919, *FRUS, 1919* 1:107–13.

45. Kallis to Kramer and Epes, December 20, 1952, DOJ, File 60-166-56, 8; George P. Share (vice consul, Puerto Cortés) to State, September 7, 1923, SD 714.1515/394.

46. Zemurray to Stabler, February 26, 1918, SD 714.1515/92; Dinwoodie, "Expedient Diplomacy," 143.

47. John R. Bradley to State, March 8, 1920, SD 714.1515/160; Thurston to State, March 15, 1919, SD 714.1515/164; Long to Johnson, October 1, 1919, SD 714.1515/209.

6

The Democratic Interlude

In the last years of his regime, Estrada Cabrera became increasingly isolated from and intimidated by his own people. Suffering from diabetes and often drinking heavily, he refused to venture more than a few miles outside of the capital, and he rarely received visitors. His power rested on a group of loyal generals that contained three future presidents—Lázaro Chacón, José María Orellana, and Jorge Ubico—and on the widespread perception that the United States supported him. As he became more brutal and apparently incompetent, the State Department looked more favorably upon a peaceful transfer of power to another strongman, but to the end it opposed the violent overthrow of the dictator.[1]

The Unionist party, a political coalition founded in December 1919 to promote Central America's reunification, actually advocated the immediate termination of the twenty-two-year-old tyranny, by armed rebellion if necessary. Led by Conservatives tied to the landed oligarchy (Manuel Cobos Batres, Emilio Escamilla, Pedro Aguirre, and José Azmitia), the Unionists also attracted support among the urban proletariat, artisans, students, and industrialists.[2] In January and February 1920 at least three opposition newspapers blasted the decrepit regime in increasingly strident tones, but none threatened the aged caudillo more defiantly than *El Obrero Libre*. On March 21, Silverio Ortiz, president of the Liga Obrera, warned Estrada Cabrera that he represented sixty thousand laborers who would no longer tolerate his repression: "We do not want blood to spill. . . . We have to arrange things peacefully. Understand it well, we are strong enough so that we could . . . destroy the tyranny. But no. We are all Guatemalans and harmony must prevail. A civil war would end Guatemala. The hour for you and for the people has sounded. There is no other option: the people will triumph."[3]

Indeed, the broadly based popular movement would have overthrown the Liberal regime were it not for the obstinacy of the American government. On April 5 the Americans vaguely threatened intervention when Benton McMillin, the minister to Guatemala, warned that the United States would oppose a revolutionary change in government. Believing that the

Americans had closed one of their options, the Unionists then allied with dissident Liberals in the legislature led by Adrian Vidaurre. The two parties worked out a compromise whereby they would appoint Carlos Herrera, a Liberal and a wealthy landowner known more for his managerial skills than his commitment to liberalism, the provisional president of a bipartisan government. With four seats in the new cabinet reserved for Liberals, the agreement appropriated the idealistic and reformist impulses that originally characterized the Unionist movement. To Ortiz and the workers, it represented the first betrayal of the Unionist cause.[4]

Hence, the Unionist rebellion against Estrada Cabrera succeeded only in removing a dictator; it did not overturn forty-nine years of Liberal rule. A legislature dominated by Liberals declared the old caudillo insane and appointed Herrera provisional president on April 8. Although workers and students defeated the remnants of the dictator's army in the week thereafter, they were denied total victory by the Unionist leadership. No reprisals were taken against those who had collaborated with the regime, and the diplomatic corps escorted Estrada Cabrera to the safety of the military academy, his prison for the next few years.[5]

Nevertheless, the political-military campaign against the dictator opened a crack in the Liberal order that was not sealed until General Ubico reimposed a stern Liberal dictatorship in 1931. Herrera began the 1920s promising to restore constitutional democracy and to respect basic political rights. Despite the authoritarian tendencies displayed by him and his two successors, political parties still published their programs in a free press; worker organizations fought for the right to organize, strike, and bargain collectively; the legislature occasionally defied presidential authority; and, for the first time since 1904, Guatemalans openly attacked United Fruit's monopoly.[6]

Through these ten years of relative political liberty, a democratic interlude between two dictatorships, United retained its monopoly, but democracy did not serve it as well as dictatorship had. Given the opportunity to criticize American enterprise, Guatemalans obstructed UFCO's efforts to obtain the liberal concessions it sought. United lobbied successfully for the lease of lands in the Motagua River valley, but popular opposition forced Keith to accept substantial modifications in the Zacapa concession and prevented him from gaining control of the central bank. In 1921, when Herrera annulled one of IRCA's concessions, and again in 1923, when the workers of Puerto Barrios struck for better working conditions, the democratic challenge reached crisis proportions. Fortunately for United Fruit, it still had enough corrupt and authoritarian friends in the executive branch and the military to contain the reformist and nationalistic movements of the 1920s.

Popular hostility toward United Fruit surfaced only after the Unionists defeated Estrada Cabrera. In the Unionist platform and the political manifestos of the era, there are few if any references to foreign monopoly, for the opposition targeted its immediate enemy, the dictatorship. With the dictator removed, the people expressed their many grievances against the railroad, fruit, and electric companies, but Herrera initially promised to respect and promote American investment. The State Department delayed recognition of the new government until it confirmed the political orientation of the new regime; some diplomats feared the influence of pro-German officials within the Herrera government, primarily Emilio Escamilla, the minister of war. On June 24, 1920, the same day on which he received U.S. diplomatic recognition, Herrera agreed to repay a $1.4-million debt to IRCA over the next three years. In September his brother reaffirmed the government's commitment to respect the rights and properties of the railroad and the electric company, which had been acquired by the Electric Bond and Share Company of New York (EBASCO).[7]

Herrera's policy toward American enterprise reflected the ambiguities of an oligarchy dependent upon foreign capital. As a prosperous sugar planter, he appreciated the material improvements that American investment brought to Guatemala, but he opposed the monopolistic practices that obstructed the country's economic development. The oligarchy, whether Liberal or Conservative, had a vested interest in liberating its commerce from the monopoly on rail and port facilities held by UFCO and IRCA. To the extent that the Herrera government challenged American enterprises, it was rooted in the antimonopolistic traditions established by Barrios, Barillas, and Reyna Barrios in the late nineteenth century.

The democratic opening of 1920 gave Herrera and the oligarchies the opportunity to renegotiate the terms under which American firms operated. In the fall of 1920 merchants and *finqueros* petitioned the Ministry of Development for relief from IRCA's tariff structure, which discriminated against all Pacific-borne commerce. Freight rates between Retalhuleu and San José were now 100 percent higher than the rates between Retalhuleu and Puerto Barrios. Since ocean freight rates from San José via the canal to New York were the same as from Puerto Barrios to New York, the tariffs were the only reason why Guatemalan coffee should not flow out of its natural Pacific outlets. IRCA had established the rates in order to channel freight through Puerto Barrios, arguing that it could not afford to send empty boxcars to that port, which handled most of the country's imports. The railroad's circuitous logic was exposed by Herbert S. Gould, the American chargé d'affaires, who pointed out that most of the country's imports would enter via the Pacific ports if IRCA had not established the discriminatory tariffs. After a decade of conflict between the railroad and the western *finqueros*, Gould reported that the Pacific ports would be ruined if IRCA's rates remained in effect.[8]

Under pressure from the planters, in December 1920 the government authorized the construction of highways parallel to the IRCA lines and cancelled a regulation that prohibited anything but a railway car from delivering freight at the wharves. Given the government's lack of capital, these were halfhearted challenges to IRCA's monopoly, but if the *finqueros* could transport their coffee to San José or Champerico by mule or oxcart, they could load their coffee on the Pacific Mail Steamship lines, now owned by W. R. Grace, and IRCA and UFCO would lose freight. If and when IRCA completed the Zacapa branch, Pacific Mail, which had dominated Pacific coast shipping for nearly fifty years, would also lose the freight of Salvadoran *finqueros*, for their coffee could be rerouted toward Puerto Barrios just as easily as Guatemalan coffee had been several years earlier. To recover its freight and prevent any further losses, Pacific Mail rallied opposition to IRCA by working through Ernest Forbes, a lobbyist who was not averse to playing hardball with corrupt politicians or rivals.[9]

Forbes discovered that the Ministry of Development was already preparing a strong legal case against IRCA and the monopoly it had constructed under the 1908 Méndez-Williamson contract. It solicited opinions from respectable lawyers of diverse political affiliations in an effort to assess the legality of the concession and IRCA's compliance with it. On the surface it appeared that Keith had failed to meet his contractual obligations, since he had not built the Zacapa branch line within the specified time period. He could claim, with considerable justification, that the line had not been built because the government had not paid its debt to the railroad or delivered the deeds and titles it required. Soon after Herrera agreed to retire the debt, Keith initiated preliminary work; by the end of 1920, IRCA had graded the Salvadoran portion of the line, but it had only established camps and assembled supplies in Guatemala.[10]

The government's hostility toward the company, however, was based on a thorough review of IRCA's concession and the railroad's impact on Guatemalan commerce. On December 29, 1920, Marcial Prem, a Liberal, submitted the first and most devastating critique of the company, the 1908 contract, and the dictator who had authorized it. Article 1 of the contract, Prem explained, extended the provisions of the 1904 Farquhar contract to all the lines that Keith acquired. Without this clause, IRCA would have had to operate its railroad under many different concessions, none of them as long or as liberal as the Farquhar concession. This article, Prem concluded, was extremely damaging to the national interest, for it essentially ceded Guatemalan railroads to a foreign company in perpetuity. In previous concessions, the government would assume ownership of the railroad when the contract expired, but in the 1904 concession, the government reserved the right to purchase the railroad after ninety-nine years. Since the company would take full and perpetual ownership if the country did not buy it, Prem interpreted Article 1 as the equivalent of a gratuitous cession of all Guatemalan railroads forever. He therefore urged the government to nullify the 1908 concession because the railroad had failed to build the Zacapa branch within the specified four-year time period. Prem recognized the importance of rail connection to El Salvador, but he recommended that the government negotiate a contract that did not allow a foreign company to monopolize transportation facilities and operate in defiance of Guatemalan laws.[11]

Over the next two months, reviews from a number of sources fortified Prem's conclusions. Marcial García Salas, a Unionist with close ties to Herrera, took exception to the provisions by which the government guaranteed a 5 percent profit to the enterprise, exempted bananas from all taxes for thirty-five years, conceded valuable lands to a company, and allowed it administrative autonomy. The contract had so seriously compromised the nation's interest and sovereignty that García Salas wondered how any patriotic Guatemalan could have approved such a harmful concession.[12]

After these reviews within the Ministry of Development, the Council of State, a presidential advisory body, commissioned its own studies and on March 30, 1921, recommended the annulment of the contract.[13] Additional support came from the country's most powerful lobby, the Asociación General de Agricultores. In April the *finqueros* exhorted the government to annul the Zacapa concession and revise the 1904 Farquhar contract: "As the International Railways works in complete accord with the Fruit Company, they try, in order to advance their interests, to send all of our imports and exports through Puerto Barrios. This effort, while it may be advantageous to the two enterprises, has truly prejudicial and harmful effects upon Guatemala, and we are obligated to save the country from this disaster that would cause us incalculable damage."[14]

Opposed by wealthy and politically influential landowners, some of whom had an interest in shipping their coffee on the Grace lines, Keith recognized the brewing controversy as the most serious threat to his enterprise since its inception. If the government cancelled the 1908 concession, he could not anticipate the new laws or regulations that would govern his railroad. The government could impose new taxes, collect old ones, or establish a commission to regulate rates and services. In any event, annulment of the contract would force Keith to renegotiate the terms under which it operated, and Herrera preferred an amicable settlement over confrontation. Keith discussed the case with Felix Castellanos, minister of development, but he refused to compromise because he felt that IRCA had fulfilled all of its contractual obligations. If the government had paid its annual subsidy and processed the titles and deeds that his company had demanded from Estrada Cabrera several years earlier, the line to El Salvador would have been completed already, Keith argued.[15]

Keith's defensible position had little impact on the Herrera government because other, less honorable motives, influenced it. There were, to be sure, sincerely nationalistic reformers who wanted to reduce IRCA's power, but others in the administration saw an opportunity to exploit the rivalry between UFCO and W. R. Grace for personal gain. Grace's agent in

Guatemala, Ernest Forbes, spent the first half of 1921 in Guatemala promoting Grace's commercial interests by encouraging Guatemalans to cancel IRCA's concessions; he later boasted that he had secured the cancellation of the 1908 concession with bribes totaling $50,000. García Salas, one of the Unionist lawyers who had recommended annulment, claimed that Herrera and his advisers threatened to cancel the concession only to "shake out of the interests involved all the cash that could be obtained."[16]

When the government gave Keith the opportunity to match Forbes, however, he would not submit to extortion. According to Keith's lawyers, Herrera had no choice but to carry out his threats after Keith refused to "grease palms." While one would expect Keith to make such an allegation, statements by Forbes and García Salas indicate that some illicit motivations influenced Herrera, who annulled the 1908 Mendez-Williamson contract on May 13, 1921.[17]

While Herrera's act struck at the legal foundation of IRCA's monopoly, it was only a modest effort to modify the terms that governed the railroad's operations. Herrera did not nationalize IRCA or deny its right to do business in the country; in subsequent negotiations with the company, the Guatemalans expressed a willingness to revise the 1904 and 1908 concessions. Although American diplomats protested Herrera's unilateral action, they also recognized the necessity of amending IRCA's contracts. Gould argued: "I am convinced that the railway situation in this country would never be tolerated by a body such as our Interstate Commerce Commission or any of the state railway commissions. And I am further convinced of the sad fact that the one reason which prevents the government from taking steps to better the situation is the fear of the influence of the United Fruit Company in Washington."[18]

Indeed, United wielded extraordinary influence over the State Department through Lansing and Woolsey, the law firm of former Secretary of State Robert Lansing, with whom Keith had tangled just a few years earlier when Keith supported the Tinoco government of Costa Rica despite Lansing's opposition to his unconstitutional regime. As an ally, Lansing gave Keith access to and a degree of control over the information that flowed into and the policies that emerged from the State Department. On the day that Herrera annulled the concession, Lansing and Woolsey requested diplomatic assistance, and without waiting for any additional information, from either its own representatives or the Guatemalan government, the State Department promptly ordered the American minister to make the strongest possible protests to the government.[19]

In his own protest of May 21, Keith charged that the annulment was illegal and vowed to hold the government responsible for all pecuniary damages it caused. At the same time, he adopted a conciliatory tone when he privately suggested ways that he and Herrera could resolve what could become an international dispute. Keith understood that the Guatemalans objected primarily to Article 1 of the 1908 contract, by which IRCA received the right to operate all railroads under the Farquhar contract. Although Keith vowed never to renounce that right and preferred to have the concession reinstated, he urged Herrera to consider purchasing the old track known as the Central Railroad (San José to Guatemala City and subsidiary lines). If the government did not accept the terms he offered, Keith advised Herrera to consider nationalizing the entire line by purchasing it outright from him.[20]

As he did not believe that Herrera would take any action unless the United States pressured him to do so, Keith lobbied for diplomatic assistance through Lansing and Woolsey. Throughout the crisis the prestigious firm virtually dictated American policy; it even drafted instructions to the American minister and then asked the State Department to forward the message at the company's expense. In late October one bureaucrat objected to the impropriety of private attorneys suggesting how the State Department should or should not reply to communications from foreign governments because that was a decision made solely by the secretary of state.[21]

Nevertheless, the State Department practically adopted the IRCA case, despite appeals from another American company, W. R. Grace, which lobbied the State Department through the San Francisco Chamber of Commerce. In August the chamber asked the department not to support IRCA's efforts to have the concession reinstated because it was not appropriate for it to support a company that monopolized trade. If IRCA completed the Zacapa line and applied its discriminatory rates to Salvadoran commerce, the chamber predicted that United Fruit, which controlled the railroad, would impose a virtual embargo on all freight movement by way of San Francisco. Coffee previously exported to San Francisco would be diverted to the eastern United States, while California flour and lumber exports to Central America consequently would decline. The State Department rejected the plea because the Guatemalan government had annulled legitimate rights without just cause.[22]

With American diplomats supporting his position, Keith had little reason to soften his original demand for the full and immediate reinstatement of the concession. Herrera, on the other hand, never intended to alienate the American government and had to deal with pro-American factions within his own coalition government. Hence, he adopted a conciliatory position after he issued the decree, and in October he accepted IRCA's proposal to negotiate with the semiofficial mediation of the American minister.[23]

Before the negotiations began, the nationalistic coalition that had brought Herrera into power disintegrated, as Liberals and Conservatives renewed their traditional conflicts over a range of issues, including the IRCA controversy. Herrera's hostility to American enterprise left him vulnerable to attacks from those who did not want to antagonize the U.S. government (primarily Liberals) or United Fruit. A clear sign of Herrera's weakness came at the end of the summer, when he capitulated to the Liberal demands for the removal of the minister of war, Escamilla, who had offended Generals Orellana and Ubico by attempting to reduce the size and influence of the army. On November 11, with rumors of an impending coup paralyzing the government, Keith withdrew his previous offers to sell all or part of the railroad to the government.[24] There was no reason for Keith to compromise when the Liberals were about to reverse the moderately reformist tendencies of the Herrera government.

The long-anticipated reactionary coup began at midnight, December 6, and ended five hours later with Herrera's resignation. Support within the army was so complete that not even Herrera's personal guard resisted. A provisional junta composed of Generals Orellana, José María Lima, and Miguel Larrave rescinded the Unionist constitution, reconvened Estrada Cabrera's legislature, and invalidated all legislative acts passed since April 1920. The coup was clearly a victory for the old Liberal guard that had been loyal to Estrada Cabrera. Orellana was a personal favorite and protégé of Estrada Cabrera, and he quickly emerged as the most powerful junta member. He reinstated former administrators of the Estrada Cabrera regime, including Generals Chacón and Ubico, the latter becoming the minister of war.[25] Orellana, Chacón, and Ubico dominated Guatemalan politics for the next twenty-three years.

While some Guatemalans have argued that Washington ordered the removal of Herrera in order to protect the American monopolies, there is no evidence that UFCO, IRCA, EBASCO, or the State Department instigated the coup.[26] Keith certainly had the means and the motive to support a rebellion, but without evidence to the contrary, it is doubtful that Orellana worked on his behalf, since he refused to reinstate the original concession. American diplomats, moreover, were initially dismayed by the coup and withheld diplomatic recognition for several months. The American minister considered the coup a tragic setback for democracy: "I regard the whole transaction as very unfortunate for Guatemala. The people had a freedom of press and citizenship greater than they have had under any President for generations. So far as I can judge the masses of the people were content with this situation. There was complaint, it is true, against President Herrera for not being firm enough, and this was not without justification as recent events demonstrate."[27]

Although it is unlikely that American interests initiated the coup, the United States assisted Orellana's efforts to consolidate power. The summer before Herrera's removal, the Unionists had drafted a constitution for a reunited isthmus that established a provisional federal council with the authority to suppress rebellion in any of the member states. In December the council discussed the possibility of restoring Herrera's democratic government. The United States, concerned about Mexican influence over the projected union, warned the other Central American states not to intervene in Guatemala's internal affairs.[28]

Hence, Orellana knew that the United States, while it did not immediately recognize his government, opposed any move to restore Herrera and the Unionists to power. In the two months after the coup, Orellana persecuted the workers' movement, arrested one half of the Unionist leadership, expelled the archbishop, and suppressed peasant rebellions, yet American criticisms of his unconstitutional origins and repressive practices vanished. On February 1, 1922, Undersecretary of State Sumner Welles informed the Guatemalan foreign minister that the United States would recognize the Orellana government provided that it was confirmed in a popular election and agreed to settle the disputes with IRCA and the electric company to American satisfaction.[29]

With the military controlling the electoral machinery and silencing the opposition, Orellana's confirmation in elections held on February 22 was a foregone conclusion. In the days before the elections, the military crushed rebellions in at least twelve communities, including the Conservative stronghold of Antigua, but the electoral process still eliminated one of the obstacles to American recognition. Although Orellana failed to make specific pledges on the IRCA settlement, the State Department recognized his government on April 17, after he agreed to submit a new electric company contract to the legislature, initiate negotiations with IRCA based on the cancellation of the Herrera decree, and protect and promote American investments.[30]

Even with the military solidly behind him, Orellana could not completely reverse the democratic gains that had been made in the previous two years. The press, legislature, and workers' movements continued to criticize the Yankee monopolies, and Orellana, who evidently held a measure of respect for an independent legislature and a free press, attempted to placate the nationalistic opposition by co-opting it. In March he angered the State Department and IRCA by appointing a committee that included Prem and Castellanos, both of whom had supported the cancellation of the Zacapa concession a year earlier, to review the Zacapa dispute. Orellana could not back down from the confrontation with the American monopolies without weakening his political position at home because opposition to IRCA, UFCO, and EBASCO was becoming a defining characteristic of Guatemalan nationalism.[31]

Orellana's commitment to American enterprise, however, exceeded his commitment to the nationalistic opponents of the Yankee firms. In May he asked the legislature to reinstate the original Zacapa concession, and an enraged mob of workers and Conservatives forced the representatives to table the bill. Evidently, the government's repression had not silenced the democratic challenge. If he were to follow the model of his mentor, Estrada Cabrera, Orellana would subordinate or disband the legislature and rule by decree. However, neither the Conservative opposition nor the Liberal party, in which an ideological division was developing between traditionalists and progressives, would tolerate a return to the dictatorial practices of the past. Since Liberals and Conservatives had recommended the annulment of IRCA's Zacapa concession, Orellana was compelled to continue negotiations with IRCA and its supporters in the State Department. Boaz Long, a former State Department official, represented IRCA in negotiations held in the spring of 1922, but the parties deadlocked over its demand for compensation for losses it suffered as the result of Herrera's unilateral abrogation of a valid concession.[32]

In a vain effort to soften State Department support for IRCA, Orellana appointed Prem as his special emissary to Washington in the summer of 1922. The selection of Prem definitely appealed to the railroad's harshest critics, for he had established the case against IRCA in December 1920, but his harsh criticisms of Keith won him little sympathy. For weeks, Prem lobbied the State Department, providing it with information about the railroad's monopolistic practices that the American government had either ignored or dismissed. In the interest of promoting better relations between the two countries, Prem asked the department to analyze Guatemala's position carefully:

> The fact is that the business done in Guatemala has not always been based on good morals and honesty. It is very natural and just that he who intends to do business should think of obtaining a profit proportionate to the capital invested and the risk to be run. This is honorable, decorous, and worthy; but if, in order to secure exaggerated and hoggish concessions which will cause the ruination of the poor country with which they are contracted, appeal is made to bribery, we can not help indignantly and sternly rejecting this corrupt and shameful mode of procedure as being contrary to the development of the good relations and confidence which must prevail between friendly countries which desire to increase their business.[33]

Keith's lawyers indignantly protested the defamation of Keith's character, denying that he or any other company official had ever resorted to bribery or other outrageous acts in the conduct of business. However, they charged that the Guatemalans had not always played fairly either, particularly during the dictatorship, when Estrada Cabrera attempted to extort money from the firm. The lawyers dismissed Prem's allegations as those of a "cranky child" and impugned his motives by alleging that he was on the payroll of the Pacific Mail Steamship Company, which opposed the construction of the Zacapa branch for its own commercial interests.[34]

The diversionary tactic worked well for IRCA, since the State Department never investigated allegations of Keith's improprieties. If it had, Prem could have divulged embarrassing details about his relations with Estrada

Cabrera, for the Unionists had uncovered incriminating documents when they sacked La Palma in April 1920. Prem rested his case on the injustice of Keith's 1904 railroad concession. He argued that "there was not a thing that Mr. Keith could think of asking of the Guatemalan government that was not granted him with the greatest of willingness. The list of concessions and privileges which were granted to him is endless and almost frightful. We ask that this contract be read attentively, for it is the best defense of Guatemala."[35]

To the State Department, allegations of Keith's corrupt practices and the unjust terms of his concessions were irrelevant. The diplomats sustained Keith's demand for the reinstatement of the concession with equitable compensation for losses IRCA had suffered, which Keith estimated at $3 million. Popular opposition to the railroad, however, prevented the legislators from accepting an indemnity payment to the railroad. Hence, in the fall of 1922 negotiators contemplated alternative solutions to a political impasse caused by a strong legislative opposition that demanded substantial revisions to the contract. The new American minister, Arthur Geissler, and IRCA's negotiator, Bayard Pruyn, reconsidered the nationalization option that Keith had first suggested to Herrera in May 1921. Geissler and Pruyn recommended that the government purchase the entire line through a bond issue of $20 to $30 million, estimating that the government could repay the loan within a few years.[36]

Neither Keith nor the State Department considered nationalization a viable solution to the dispute. While Keith had once suggested such an option, he believed that he could maintain his highly profitable railroad and secure an adequate concession from the Orellana regime. Pruyn and Geissler, however, thought that Keith would have to compromise, if only because Guatemalans could not pay any indemnity unless they tapped a new source of income. Since Keith rejected a Guatemalan proposal to impose a transit tax on the railroad, in late September Geissler and Pruyn recommended that IRCA and the government share the profits derived from the Zacapa railroad. If Keith accepted a profit-sharing clause and an indemnity of $1.25 million, the case would be closed. The proposal infuriated Keith, who quickly rejected it and recalled Pruyn to New York for consultation.[37]

Evidently, Pruyn convinced Keith that political conditions in Guatemala, namely the emergence of a nationalistic movement opposed to foreign monopolies, compelled him to adopt a more conciliatory position. When Pruyn resumed negotiations on January 23, 1923, he discovered that the contract had become a divisive issue within the executive branch and the Liberal party, pitting Minister of Foreign Relations Adrian Recinos against Minister of War Ubico, who was reportedly preparing a military coup. With Orellana playing the politically uncomfortable role of a president subservient to a foreign monopoly, the stevedores of Puerto Barrios went on strike on

February 3, their demands including the termination of the foreign monopolies that strangled the country's commerce. The strike exacerbated tensions in the government and attracted widespread support behind a nationalistic banner. On February 18, Pruyn advised Keith to settle the contract on the terms that Orellana offered because the collapse of the Liberal party, and perhaps the government, was imminent.[38]

A revolt at the garrison of Palencia on March 2 shook the Orellana regime and served notice that the rumors of a military coup had some foundation in Guatemala City.[39] Recognizing that Orellana could not offer any more without suffering serious political consequences, IRCA signed a new contract with the government on March 9. Keith reversed his earlier positions and accepted a $1.25-million indemnity payment and two unprecedented provisions: an equal distribution of the profits derived from the Zacapa branch, and the government's right to inspect IRCA's account books.[40]

The contract still did not satisfy the political opposition. In the following week, rumors of a coup swirled around Prem, the long-time IRCA critic who had become a nationalistic symbol. Prem's contention that Orellana's foreign policies impaired Guatemala's sovereignty and independence struck a responsive chord among the Puerto Barrios strikers, Conservatives, and dissident elements within the Liberal party. On the advice of the American minister, Orellana silenced Prem and his supporters by reinforcing the capital's garrisons, and the rebellion that was supposed to begin on March 14 or 15 never materialized. The crisis within the executive branch ended a week later with Orellana's dismissal of the entire cabinet and the appointment of ministers that he controlled more effectively.[41]

While Orellana had asserted his authority over the cabinet, he lacked control of the legislature, where considerable opposition to his policies remained. At least a part of that opposition was fueled or funded by W. R. Grace, which lobbied against the contract through Dr. Forbes, who had purchased a few votes in favor of annulment just two years earlier. If the government approved the new contract, Grace's subsidiary, Pacific Mail, would lose freight to IRCA and UFCO, since the companies would reroute Salvadoran coffee out of Puerto Barrios on the Caribbean side. Despite the State Department's opposition to any interference by Grace, Geissler received information from high government officials that the steamship interests had "expended large sums of money" to defeat the new contract. Geissler had no firm evidence of bribery, but he knew that "such evidence is seldom obtainable in cases of that character."[42]

Partly as a result of Forbes's lobbying, the renegotiated contract encountered stiff legislative opposition. When the assembly considered the new contract in April 1923, a crowd of one thousand cheered on the legislators who opposed the contract. After a week of raucous debates, the legislature returned the contract to the executive branch for revisions.

Critics of the contract pointed out that it contained a $1.475-million indemnity to IRCA without any compromise on the issue of the railroad's high and discriminatory tariffs, one of the main complaints of the *finqueros*. Keith, who wanted to raise rates, saw little advantage in fighting over this issue because the government's ability to regulate tariffs was "only apparent, not real." He agreed to resolve the rate issue at a conference to be convened within three months. By a vote of 38 to 18, the legislators passed the contract on May 21, 1923, with a list of interpretations that clarified some details of the contract, including the standardization of rates on the Pacific lines.[43]

In retrospect, the compromises Guatemala extracted from Keith were relatively insignificant, but it was a small victory for a young democratic process. It showed that the legislature and popular opinion could influence contract negotiations, which had always been the exclusive domain of an authoritarian executive. The process demonstrated the value of democracy, for Keith could not obtain the liberal concessions to which he had grown accustomed during the Estrada Cabrera dictatorship. Given the popular opposition to the railroad, and that an American minister and an IRCA negotiator advocated nationalization, Orellana could have demanded tougher terms, but he was beholden to United Fruit.

The government never brought Keith to the negotiating table to discuss tariff revisions, yet Orellana obediently accepted his responsibility to pay IRCA's $1.475-million indemnity and retire its outstanding debts. In the summer of 1923, Pruyn convinced Orellana to pay the railroad's total claims of $2.5 million through the issuance of bonds. The following March the legislature authorized Orellana to negotiate a loan, and the government received its first offer from the Anglo-London-Paris National Bank of San Francisco, a front for Schwartz and Company, part of the corrupt American syndicate that dominated Guatemalan finances during the Estrada Cabrera dictatorship. In an effort to recover its losses, Schwartz offered a loan and a financial reform package that did not include any provisions for paying off IRCA. When it appeared that the government was going to accept a loan from the San Francisco bank, Keith, who had competed with Schwartz and Company two decades earlier, stepped forward with a financial reform package of his own.[44]

Keith recognized that he had acquired such a bad reputation that Guatemalans would reject any proposal that bore his name or that of United Fruit. To disguise his interest in Guatemalan finances, Keith secretly commissioned Dr. Edward Kemmerer, the "money doctor," who served as a financial adviser to a number of Latin American republics during his illustrious career. Having worked on a financial reform project for Guatemala in 1919, Kemmerer knew the country and its economic problems well. In 1924 he accepted a commission from Pruyn to develop a plan to place Guatemala on the gold standard, establish a central bank, and retire the government's debts by floating an $8-million loan. On June 5, 1924, Kemmerer met with Keith and his assistant Henry Price in New York to discuss details of the project. He left for Guatemala three weeks later on a United Fruit ship, but only Orellana knew that Kemmerer represented Keith.[45]

Although Kemmerer was warmly received by the government, officials procrastinated and delayed action on his proposals. Financial reform was a top priority of the government, but it was not eager to rush into any contract offered by foreign investors. Kemmerer suspected that the hidden interests of some officials made financial reform a matter of sophisticated intrigue. The financial stabilization package he had developed, aside from affecting the powerful Schwartz interests, provided for the appointment of a customs agent, and that meant an end to graft income for some individuals. Because corruption permeated all levels of the bureaucracy, Kemmerer doubted whether any reform could pass solely on its merits. He left Guatemala on September 13, having accomplished nothing more significant than suggesting the *quetzal* as the name of the country's currency.[46]

While Kemmerer explained Guatemala's procrastination as a result of corruption, there were other, more serious factors at work. To his credit, Orellana was determined to carry out a comprehensive reform without another foreign loan. In 1923 he had initiated a financial reform program based partly on the plan Kemmerer had submitted in 1919. Orellana raised the tax on coffee by fifty cents to fund the creation of the Caja Reguladora, an institution that would become the sole bank of issue when it accumulated gold reserves of $2.8 million. With the economy prosperous and coffee prices high, government revenues increased and Orellana implemented his own financial reform. On November 26, 1924, the government issued a new currency (the quetzal) and placed it on par with the U.S. dollar. Existing banks lost their right to issue notes, and the government finalized plans to establish the country's first true central bank.[47]

Consummation of the deal depended on the continued boom in the coffee market and Orellana's ability to resist Keith's tempting offers. Keith had been prepared all along to underwrite the entire financial reform, and in January 1925, he returned to make one last, discreet effort to obtain control of Guatemalan banks and recover a debt that was incurred nearly two decades earlier. While he claimed that his only interest in banking was to collect his company's debts, stabilize the currency, and promote the country's development, the plan he promoted would have given him control of the central bank and the customhouses,[48] in addition to the railroads and ports he already controlled. Orellana recognized the political and economic consequences of Keith's ambitions and refused to yield. They had a friendly meeting in late January and discussed a number of topics, including a new railroad into the Petén and the possibility of Keith's financing the government's admirable reforms. Orellana thanked him for the kind offer, then reaffirmed his commitment to reorganize the financial system without any foreign assistance.[49]

Unlike in 1904, when Keith had negotiated with a government struggling with an economic depression, Orellana negotiated from a position of strength, for he could afford to resist Keith's efforts to gain control of the central bank. In March 1925, Keith dropped his efforts to finance the reform package and concentrated on gaining control of the central bank by other means. He developed a plan to purchase a controlling interest in the new bank with Schlubach, Sapper and Company of Germany, Speyer and Company of New York, and local Guatemalan investors. Keith knew that the government would eventually offer some shares to the general public, and he was willing to associate with any responsible investor to obtain control. When Orellana finally announced the creation of the central bank in June 1926, Guatemalan investors subscribed for one half of the shares, and he prohibited any group from owning more than 25 percent of the stock. Orellana had prevented Keith from securing nearly absolute control of Guatemala's economic infrastructure.[50]

It was another small victory for democracy. If Orellana had not tolerated a relatively free press and legislative branch, he would not have been restrained by popular hostility to Keith and the railroad. Democracy and economic prosperity adversely affected United Fruit's political relations with the host government; it always obtained more generous concessions from the dictator of an impoverished or economically stagnant country. One can only wonder how much further the Guatemalans would have challenged United if their authoritarian presidents had been even more nationalistic and less corrupt.

General Lázaro Chacón assumed the presidency after Orellana's death in September 1926, and quickly earned a reputation as the country's most venal president. Representatives of American companies claimed that they had never seen anything like the corruption of the Chacón administration, neither in scope nor in the amounts of money demanded by high officials. Chacón's finance minister, Felipe Solares, confirmed that the annual budget included a line for $100,000 in "extraordinary expenses" for the president, a substantial sum to be sure, but only a fraction of the amount he could make through extortion. In almost every government contract, Solares admitted that the contractors paid "commissions" to the appropriate officials. Chacón's successor, General Ubico, charged him with stealing over $20 million, an allegation that Solares could deny only by saying that it represented the accumulated malfeasance of several administrations.[51]

Chacón received some of that amount by extorting IRCA, which had been unable to collect the $2.5 million the government had agreed to pay it in 1923. To collect this debt, IRCA commissioned the services of a special agent, Colonel Fred W. Wilson, who came to Guatemala in 1921 as a collector of debts for Amsinck and Company of New York, a firm associated with the Schwartz group. The British consul described Wilson as a "generally unpopular" fellow who was "justifiably distrusted in government circles." Even Charles Myers, who became vice president and manager of IRCA in 1928, described Wilson as "a first class shyster and a crook."[52]

Soon after Chacón became president, he told Solares to settle the debt with IRCA, but he also let it be known that he expected compensation for his services. Wilson informed Chacón's agent that he wanted Chacón's demand for a kickback put in writing because he would have to convince the IRCA management that the payment was required. To Myers's disappointment, IRCA accepted the extortionate demand and paid Chacón an undisclosed amount before he settled the $2.5-million debt on May 31, 1927. Geissler was annoyed that a case in which the State Department had taken a direct interest was settled by the payment of bribe money.[53]

The termination of a fifteen-year controversy allowed IRCA to proceed with the construction of the Zacapa branch to El Salvador. The question of financing construction costs set in motion the events leading to the transfer of managerial control of the railroad from Keith to United Fruit. In the spring of 1927, Prentice Gray, manager of the J. Henry Schroder Banking Corporation, visited Guatemala to gather information he needed to evaluate IRCA's request for a $7-million loan. While Gray had few doubts about the company's financial strength, he wondered how well the firm would do once Keith, who was nearly eighty years old, passed away or retired. In either event, Gray shared United Fruit's interest in keeping managerial control in friendly hands.[54]

The State Department also took note of the line of succession, because it feared British or German acquisition of the company. Schroder was technically an American company, but in most quarters it was considered a British firm, and it was closely tied to Schlubach, Thiemer and Company of Hamburg. The American consul, Philip Holland, warned the State Department that IRCA could come under British or German control. If this occurred, he argued, it would be a "great loss of the prestige, commerce, and influence of the United States. The commerce of all Central America is interwoven and to a large extent dependent upon and can be controlled by the International Railways of Central America."[55]

United Fruit had no interest in seeing the railroad come under the control of persons who did not continue the preferential treatment that IRCA gave it through a series of traffic agreements. A railroad subservient to it had been a deadly tool in UFCO's competition against independent planters on the Caribbean coast, and it would be just as effective against the independent planters who were then developing banana plantations on the Pacific coast. In the competition with these planters, United Fruit wanted to maintain control of rail and port facilities in the area, for it could then deny independent planters access to markets on competitive terms. As Bradley

Palmer explained to Schroder, United wanted to maintain control of the railroad: "We want protection for [the] future and believe you can assist in affording this at the same time accomplishing for yourselves two great advantages, namely wider market and greater value for your present investment." Palmer pledged to promote Schroder's economic interests by undertaking a program of expanding the banana business in Central America, particularly in Guatemala.[56]

Thus, Palmer, Keith, and Schroder worked out a voting trust agreement that satisfied the needs and interests of all parties. The agreement disguised the amount of control that UFCO actually exercised but assured it completely effectual direction. Keith sold his two hundred thousand shares to a trust organized by and on behalf of United Fruit and Schroder. United purchased only seventy-one thousand shares (17.8 percent), but it exercised command by arrangement with Schroder and Robert Fleming, Keith's associate since 1908. As part of the deal, Keith gave Palmer the resignations of four IRCA directors after he received payment for his shares. He remained president of the board until his death in 1929, but managerial control resided with officers appointed by United Fruit and Schroder.[57]

By this trust agreement, United retained control of IRCA without revealing that it managed the railroad. By doing it through third parties, United hoped to silence rumors that it was acquiring control of the railroad. "United Fruit" does not even appear in the trust agreement; the name of Old Colony Trust Company was used in its place. However, UFCO had a private agreement with Old Colony in which the latter agreed that it would only make appointments at the direction of United Fruit, without naming or advertising the name of the company for which it operated.[58]

Schroder would have preferred to publicize United Fruit's acquisition of a large block of IRCA stock because the news would have strengthened investor confidence in the stock that it planned to market in London. He asked for UFCO's permission to issue a news release that said only that United Fruit had bought a substantial although not controlling interest in the common stock of a railway whose net earnings had increased over 150 percent since 1920. Victor Cutter, who became president of United Fruit in 1924, denied the request because he thought that it would be better for IRCA to stand on its own record rather than to depend on UFCO. He also believed that "it would be advantageous for all companies operating in Latin America to avoid any appearance of merging into or with other businesses."[59]

Privately, IRCA and UFCO officials conceded that United Fruit had assumed the management of the company. Keith resigned the presidency and Henry Price, who had once coveted the position for himself, was retained on a temporary basis to assure an orderly transition. Fred Lavis became the new president of IRCA, and with United's approval he appointed a new administrative team. For example, in November 1928, Lavis asked George P. Chittenden, vice president of United Fruit, if he should retain the services of Colonel Wilson, the "shyster" who had arranged the debt settlement in May 1927. In December 1928 he informed Chittenden that he had accepted the resignations of Pruyn and Edward Hyde from the board of directors and was waiting for Palmer to make the other two appointments.[60] IRCA was not and would never become a UFCO subsidiary, but United indirectly managed the railroad.

The consequence of all these deliberate deceptions was simply that United Fruit retained its domination of IRCA after Keith retired. For twenty-five years, Keith had been the personal link between two companies, with traffic agreements and joint directorships supplementing the control that Keith personally assured. The voting trust replaced Keith and prevented the railroad from falling into hostile hands. Lavis assured the State Department that neither British nor German investors had acquired IRCA, for the fruit company and its bankers retained effective control of the railroad. The main change in IRCA's structure was that control of its stock was no longer mainly in American hands. Fleming and Schroder would, because of the stock they controlled, influence the company's policies.[61]

Nevertheless, UFCO still carried the most weight with the company's management. Even Palmer, who was anxious to preserve the illusion that IRCA and UFCO were independent entities, informed Secretary of State Frank B. Kellogg that United had acquired a substantial interest in IRCA and owned the Costa Rican railway system. Palmer disclosed this information because he wanted Kellogg to approve UFCO's plan to complete the Zacapa branch to El Salvador. Palmer, who had been with Keith since the earliest days and assumed responsibility for completing the project on behalf of his personal friend, advised Kellogg of United Fruit's intention to bridge the remaining gaps in the Central American railroad network. Before it proceeded, however, Palmer wanted to know the views of the State Department, particularly with respect to its plans to build across Nicaragua, which was then embroiled in a civil war.[62]

As long as IRCA remained in American hands, the State Department had no objection to establishing rail connection between El Salvador and Guatemala. With all obstacles to construction removed, IRCA secured two loans totaling $11 million and began work. IRCA inaugurated service between Zacapa and San Salvador in December 1929, but Keith died six months before IRCA completed the line that had vexed him for twenty years. The man who did the most "to steer the destinies of the Caribbean countries," if we accept the hyperbole of one obituary, failed to fulfill his dream of uniting Central America by steel rails.[63]

While Guatemalan dictators and democrats had conditioned the development of United Fruit, American diplomats and capitalists had deluded themselves into thinking that they shaped Guatemala's destiny. The country's

most brutal dictator sanctioned the concession that allowed Keith to monopolize railways, and the limited democratic opening of the 1920s blocked
his efforts to extend his influence to Guatemalan financing. Without timely
assistance from Guatemala's corrupt and authoritarian rulers, Keith and
United would have found it much more difficult to extract liberal concessions from the government, eliminate competitors, and suppress challenges
to its authority. Because some politicians placed a higher priority on personal aggrandizement than the country's long-term economic development,
United maintained its power and prerogatives throughout the democratic
interlude. A few sincere nationalists, Marcial Prem and Marcial García
Salas among them, questioned the company's contribution to Guatemalan
development, but the ruling elite never took the democratic challenge
beyond the political and diplomatic arena. In early 1923, United's workers
moved the struggle to the hot and humid front lines at Puerto Barrios.

Notes

1. González Dávison, *El régimen liberal*, 44; R. S. Reynolds Hitt to Wilson
(assistant secretary of state), April 4, 1911, SD 814.001/3; Stabler to Robert
Lansing, August 6, 1919, SD 814.509; George W. Baker, Jr., "The Woodrow
Wilson Administration and Guatemalan Relations," *The Historian* 27:2 (February
1965): 164; Wade Kit, "The Fall of Guatemalan Dictator, Manuel Estrada Cabrera:
U.S. Pressure or National Opposition," *Canadian Journal of Latin American and
Caribbean Studies* 15:29 (1990): 115–18.
2. On the history of the Unionist movement see Arévalo Martínez, *¡Ecce
Pericles!*, vol. 2; Rafael Montúfar, *Caída de una tiranía* (Guatemala: Sánchez y de
Guise, 1923); Carlos Figueroa Ibarra, "Contendio de clase y participación obrera en
el movimiento antidictatorial de 1920," *Política y Sociedad* 4 (July–December
1977): 20–25; idem, "La insurrección armada de 1920 en Guatemala," ibid. 8
(July–December 1979): 91–92.
3. Cited in Arévalo Martínez, *¡Ecce Pericles!* 2:188 (author's translations).
4. Benton McMillin to State, April 6, 1920, SD 814.00/381; Arévalo Martínez,
¡Ecce Pericles! 2:210–18, 380.
5. McMillin to State, April 30, 1920, SD 814.00/471; William Krehm, *Democracies and Tyrannies of the Caribbean* (Westport, CT: Lawrence Hill & Company,
1984), 31–32.
6. Gleijeses, *Shattered Hope*, 10; Ralph Lee Woodward, Jr., *Central America:
A Nation Divided*, 2d. ed. (New York: Oxford University Press, 1985), 209;
Joseph A. Pitti, "Jorge Ubico and Guatemalan Politics in the 1920s" (Ph.D. diss.,
University of New Mexico, 1975); Hector Perez-Brignoli, *A Brief History of
Central America*, trans. Ricardo B. Sawrey A. and Susana Stettri de Sawrey
(Berkeley: University of California Press, 1989), 108.
7. Arévalo Martínez, *¡Ecce Pericles!* 2:83–236; González Dávison, *El régimen
liberal*, 40–44; McMillin to State, May 12, 1920, SD 814.00/477; Colby to President Wilson, June 12, 1920, SD 814.00/485a; Colby to American legation, Guatemala, June 21, 1920, SD 814.00/487a; Baker, "Wilson Administration," 167;

memorandum, Dr. Rowe, July 8, 1920, SD 814.00/493; McMillen to State, September 22, 1920, SD 814.00/510.

8. Herbert S. Gould (chargé d'affaires ad interim) to State, November 22, 1920, SD 814.00/513; Gould to State, December 28, 1920, SD 814.00/517.

9. Dr. Ernest Forbes to Wilbur Carr (assistant secretary of state), December 22, 1920, SD 814.00/523; Lawrence Clayton, *Grace: W. R. Grace & Co.: The Formative Years, 1850–1930* (Ottawa, IL: Jameson Books, 1985), 269–70; Arthur Geissler to State, April 9, 1923, SD 814.77/214; Dana G. Munro to Francis White, April 11, 1923, SD 814.77/215; for an example of Forbes's character and the tactics he used to frustrate the former German owners of the electric company see Forbes to Carr, December 22, 1920, SD 814.00/523.

10. "Protest Filed by IRCA," May 21, 1921, SD 814.77/90; Lester Woolsey to State, June 10, 1921, SD 814.77/60; IRCA, *Annual Report, 1920*; Lansing and Woolsey to State, August 23, 1921, enclosure no. 4, Keith to Ministerio de Fomento, April 22, 1921, 814.77/78.

11. Francisco Sánchez Latour to William Phillips (undersecretary of state), July 11, 1922, enclosure, *Documentos relativos al contrato del ferrocarril Zacapa a la frontera de El Salvador*, document no. 4, memorandum of Dr. Marcial Prem to Señor Ministro de Fomento, December 29, 1920, SD 814.77/141.

12. Sánchez Latour to Phillips, *Documentos relativos al contrato*, document no. 6, Marcial García Salas to Ministro de Fomento, January 15, 1921, SD 814.77/141.

13. Ibid., document no. 7, Lic. Don Rafael Ponciano and Elfego J. Palanco to Consejo de Estado, February 9, 1921; document no. 8, Lic. Salvador Falla, José Ernesto Zelaya, J. de D. Castillo, and Jorge Morales U. to Consejo de Estado, March 30, 1921.

14. Asociación General de Agricultores to Ministerio de Fomento, April 1921, AGCA, B129, legajo 22190 [no expediente], (author's translations).

15. Sánchez Latour to Phillips, *Documentos relativos al contrato*, document no. 57, Keith to Ministro de Fomento, April 22, 1921, SD 814.77/141.

16. Forbes to Carr, December 22, 1920, SD 814.00/523; Geissler to State, April 7, 1923, enclosure 1, W. E. Mullins to John B. Pruyn, February 23, 1923, SD 814.77/220; Phillips to Geissler, January 16, 1923, SD 814.77/180b; Lansing and Woolsey to State, January 6, 1923, enclosed, Boaz Long to Lansing and Woolsey, January 5, 1923, SD 814.77/211.

17. Lansing and Woolsey to State, January 6, 1923, enclosed, Long to Lansing and Woolsey, January 5, 1923, SD 814.77/211; Sánchez Latour to Phillips, *Documentos relativos al contrato*, document no. 13, SD 814.77/141.

18. McMillin to State, June 23, 1921, enclosed, minister of foreign relations [Felix Castellanos] to McMillin, June 15, 1921, SD 814.77/74; Gould to State, December 28, 1920, SD 814.00/517.

19. LaFeber, *Inevitable Revolutions*, 56–58; Woolsey to State, May 13, 1921, SD 814.77/63; McMillin to State, May 17, 1921, SD 814.00/542.

20. "Protest Filed by IRCA," May 21, 1921, SD 814.77/90; Sánchez Latour to Phillips, *Documentos relativos al contrato*, document no. 96, General Manager (IRCA) to Ministro de Fomento, November 11, 1921, enclosure, Keith to President Herrera, May 21, 1921, SD 814.77/141.

21. Woolsey to State, June 10, 1921, SD 814.77/69; Henry P. Fletcher to Lansing and Woolsey, October 28, 1921, SD 814.77/86.

22. Alvey Adee (second assistant secretary) to Lewis Haas (San Francisco Chamber of Commerce), November 2, 1921, and D. Grady to Haas, August 4, 1921, SD 814.77/80.

23. Lansing to Fletcher (undersecretary of state), October 4, 1921, SD 814.77/ 88; Julio Bianchi (Guatemalan ambassador to the United States) to Charles Evans Hughes (secretary of state), October 8, 1921, SD 814.77/85.

24. McMillin to State, July 13, 1921, SD 814.00/551; Pitti, "Ubico and Guatemalan Politics," 29–32; Sánchez Latour to Phillips, *Documentos relativos al contrato,* document no. 96, General Manager (IRCA) to Ministro de Fomento, November 11, 1921, SD 814.77/141.

25. McMillin to State, December 7, 1921, SD 814.00/587; Rendon, "Manuel Estrada Cabrera, 324–26; Kenneth Grieb, *Guatemalan Caudillo: The Regime of Jorge Ubico, Guatemala, 1931–1944* (Athens: Ohio University Press, 1979), 6–7.

26. Manuel Galich, *Guatemala* (Havana: Casa de las Américas, 1968), 31; Bauer Paiz, *Como opera el capital yanqui,* 150.

27. McMillin to State, December 7, 1921, SD 814.00/587.

28. Pitti, "Ubico and Guatemalan Politics," 64–65; Dana G. Munro, *The United States and the Caribbean Republics, 1921–1933* (Princeton: Princeton University Press, 1974), 119–21; Thomas Karnes, *The Failure of Union: Central America, 1824–1975* (Tempe: Arizona State University, Center for Latin American Studies, 1976), 219–20.

29. Pitti, "Ubico and Guatemalan Politics," 76–83; González Dávison, *El régimen liberal,* 47; Sumner Welles to undersecretary [Fletcher], February 1, 1922, SD 814.00/675. The dispute with EBASCO centered on the company's efforts to obtain a fifty-year concession for the operation of the electric company.

30. Pitti, "Ubico and Guatemalan Politics," 82–83; Fletcher to Charles B. Curtis, (chargé d'affaires ad interim), February 16, 1922, SD 814.77/94; Sánchez Latour to Welles, March 9, 1922, SD 814.6463Em7/57; Richard Southgate to State, April 17, 1922, SD 814.00/682; Munro to White, September 6, 1922, SD 814.77/ 209.

31. Long (special IRCA representative) to Munro, March 31, 1922, SD 814.77/ 161; Southgate to State, April 28, 1922, SD 814.77/110. One study of Guatemalan nationalism disputes the existence of a coherent nationalism prior to 1900, but there is no adequate study of the development of nationalism in the twentieth century. See Steven Paul Palmer, "A Liberal Discipline: Inventing Nations in Guatemala and Costa Rica, 1870–1900" (Ph.D. diss., Columbia University, 1990). Bauer Paiz, *Como opera el capital yanqui,* reflects the nationalist sentiments that fueled policy toward American enterprises during the Guatemalan Revolution.

32. Pitti, "Ubico and Guatemalan Politics," 83; Welles to Lansing and Woolsey, February 15, 1922, SD 814.77/94; Long to Fletcher (acting secretary of state), March 6, 1922, SD 814.77/99; Southgate (chargé d'affaires ad interim) to State, March 7, 1922, SD 814.77/96; Southgate to State, April 6, 1922, SD 814.77/104; Southgate to State, April 12, 1922, SD 814.77/107; Southgate to State, May 5, 1922, SD 814.77/113.

33. Sánchez Latour to Phillips, enclosure, memorandum no. 1, Marcial Prem, "Sobre el Ferrocarril de Zacapa a la frontera de El Salvador," July 11, 1922, SD 814.77/141.

34. Lansing and Woolsey to State, October 12, 1922, SD 814.77/167.

35. Sánchez Latour to Phillips, memorandum no. 1, Prem, "Sobre el Ferrocarril," July 11, 1922, SD 814.77/141.

36. Southgate to State, May 5, 1922, SD 814.77/113; State to American legation, September 11, 1922, SD 814.77/143.

37. State to American legation, September 11, 1922, SD 814.77/143; Geissler to State, October 12, 1922, SD 814.77/159.

38. Bayard Pruyn to Keith, February 18, 1923, SD 814.77/191.

39. "Una nueva revuelta en Palencia," *Diario Nuevo*, March 5, 1923.

40. Keith to State, January 4, 1923, SD 814.77/176; Geissler to State, March 8, 1923, SD 814.77/202.

41. Geissler to State, February 20, 1923, SD 814.00/727; Geissler to State, March 16, 1923, SD 814.00/729; "El Señor Presidente de la República nombra su nuevo gabinete," *Diario de Centro América*, March 21, 1923.

42. Geissler to State, April 7, 1923, SD 814.77/220; Munro to White, April 11, 1923, SD 814.77/215; Geissler to State, April 27, 1923, SD 814.77/227.

43. Geissler to State, April 27, 1923, SD 814.77/226; Munro to White, May 11, 1923, SD 814.77/240; Hughes to American legation, May 13, 1923, SD 814.77/229; Geissler to State, May 22, 1923, SD 814.77/243.

44. Kemmerer and Dalgaard, "Inflation, Intrigue," 28–29.

45. Paul W. Drake, *The Money Doctor in the Andes: The Kemmerer Missions, 1923–1933* (Durham: Duke University Press, 1989); Kemmerer and Dalgaard, "Inflation, Intrigue," 30–32.

46. Kemmerer and Dalgaard, "Inflation, Intrigue," 32–33; Lansing and Woolsey to State, January 2, 1925, SD 814.51/481.

47. Pitti, "Ubico and Guatemalan Politics," 127–50. For a more detailed examination from an economist's perspective see John P. Young, *Central American Currency and Finance* (Princeton: Princeton University Press, 1925).

48. Geissler to State, January 22, 1925, enclosure no. 1, memorandum of conversation between Keith and Ellis (secretary of legation), SD 814.51/494.

49. Geissler to State, January 8, 1925, SD 814.51/485; Geissler to State, January 20, 1925, SD 814.51/486.

50. Ellis to State, March 12, 1925, SD 814.51/503; Geissler to State, December 4, 1926, Consular post records, Guatemala City, 1926, vol. 4, 851.6; Pitti, "Ubico and Guatemalan Politics," 150.

51. Pitti, "Ubico and Guatemalan Politics," 358–59; Geissler to State, January 31, 1929, SD 814.1561/14; Hawks to State, September 14, 1927, SD 814.154/39; Pitti, "Ubico and Guatemalan Politics," 360.

52. A. Clark Kerr, memorandum, January 26, 1927, in Bourne and Watt, eds., *British Documents on Foreign Affairs, Latin America, 1914–1939*, 314–15; Geissler to State, December 27, 1929, enclosure no. 1, SD 814.51/647.

53. Geissler to State, December 27, 1929, enclosure 1, memorandum by Geissler, December 11, 1929, SD 814.51/647; Pitti, "Ubico and Guatemalan Politics," 359.

54. Philip Holland (consul general) to State, April 6, 1927, SD 813.77/20.

55. Ibid.

56. Bradley Palmer to London, June 14, 1928, DOJ, File 60-166-56, Series 537, IRCA-63 [or PX 3682].

57. "International Railways of Central America, Voting Trust Agreement," August 1, 1928, DOJ, File 60-166-56, Series 537, IRCA-191 [PX 3499]; Arthur E. Nicholson (secretary, United Fruit) to Jerome Frank (chairman, Securities and Exchange Commission) February 3, 1941, DOJ, File 60-166-56, Series 537, IRCA-34.

58. Palmer to Prentice Gray (J. Henry Schroder Banking Corporation), July 7, 1928, DOJ, File 60-166-56, Series 537, IRCA-65.

59. Schroder to Palmer, September 14, 1928, and Victor Cutter to George S. Beal (vice president, Schroder), September 18, 1928, DOJ, File 60-166-56, Series 537, IRCA-67.

60. Fred Lavis to George P. Chittenden, November 24, 1928, DOJ, File 60-166-56, Series 537, IRCA-70; Lavis to Chittenden, December 7, 1928, DOJ, File 60-166-56, Series 537, IRCA-71.

61. Munro to White, June 5, 1929, SD 814.77/25.

62. Palmer to Francis B. Kellogg, August 8, 1928, SD 814.77/24.

63. "Empire Builder," *The Nation*, July 3, 1929, 5; Geissler to State, December 11, 1929, SD 813.77/29.

7

The Puerto Barrios Strike

In 1914 there could not have been much to do on a Saturday night in Quirigua, a small United Fruit Company town in Guatemala, famous for its modern hospital and its location near the ruins of a pre-Columbian civilization. If you were not a sick worker or a curious archaeologist, you were likely to pass the time rolling dice and gambling, which is what a few Jamaican men and ladinos (Guatemalans of mixed blood) did on May 9. One of the Jamaican gamblers, a Mr. Esson, relieved the Guatemalans of their money, either "by his good play or loaded dice." On his way home that evening, Esson was murdered.[1]

Esson's compatriots had good reason to believe that the losing party of ladinos killed their friend. The following morning a party of at least twelve Jamaican men, armed with machetes and a few revolvers, set out to avenge Esson's murder, for few people—white, ladino, or black—relied on the court system for justice. The Jamaicans allegedly killed two ladinos. To prevent an endless cycle of reprisals, United Fruit officials requested military intervention from Adolfo Quevedo, the military commander of the department of Izabal. Believing that an army of sixty Jamaicans was about to kill all native Guatemalans, Quevedo called in reinforcements from other garrisons and dispatched his troops to the Quirigua plantations.[2]

At 4:30 A.M. on May 12 the commander divided his forces into three squadrons and attacked the Jamaicans' living quarters, firing on anyone in sight. A few returned the fire, but most ran for their lives. When the shooting stopped, two Jamaicans lay dead, another two wounded, and the soldiers had captured several others. According to Victor Cutter, the young manager of United's new division, the attack was a premeditated massacre: "In the opinion of every one who saw the occurrences, the entering of the farms with armed soldiers without warning and without any definite plan as to capture of criminals, with indiscriminate shooting which followed, amounted to cold-blooded murder of several Jamaican negroes."[3]

Racially motivated violence had accompanied the development of railroads and the banana industry in the department of Izabal since the 1880s. Economic growth required and attracted large numbers of Jamaicans, black

Americans, ladinos, and smaller numbers of Italians, Indians, and white Americans, each with his own language, culture, and racial prejudices. United Fruit cleared the natural jungle and created a social jungle with a broad diversity of racial and ethnic groups intertwined in a capitalist enclave containing the seeds of class and anti-imperialist struggle.[4] United Fruit exploited the cultural diversity of its laborers to maintain discipline and repress wages, but it could not long contain the growth of a labor movement. While black workers saw their friends beaten and even lynched by both whites and ladinos, they shared with their Guatemalan colleagues an interest in organizing and acting collectively for mutual benefit. Jamaicans and ladinos served white managers of a multinational corporation; they worked long hours for low wages in an unhealthy climate; they both complained about poor medical care and housing. However, in the most significant strike against United Fruit prior to the 1944 revolution, ethnic rivalries impaired the struggle for social and economic justice.

On February 3, 1923, two hundred stevedores at Puerto Barrios refused to load a banana boat because they wanted higher wages, better medical service, and an end to the company's alleged preference for hiring black laborers. Thousands of workers from the plantations, hospitals, and electrical plants walked out in support of the dockworkers, and they added another demand—an end to United Fruit's monopolization of the port, railroad, and banana business. The company's race-based hiring practices disappeared from the workers' agenda, as labor leaders began to transform a spontaneous strike led by and for ladinos into a working-class challenge to American imperialism.

Although the strike of the Puerto Barrios stevedores formed part of the democratic challenge of the 1920s, the workers armed themselves with an anti-imperialist ideology and organized militancy that disturbed UFCO's white managers, the Liberal establishment, and the Conservative opposition. If United recognized the right of its workers to organize, strike, and bargain collectively, then other workers would make similar demands and management would lose its ability to dictate the terms and conditions of employment. Since Orellana also opposed an autonomous labor movement, the defense of United's interests became synonymous with the defense of his regime. For a moment it appeared that the Conservatives would forge an alliance with the workers, but the Puerto Barrios strikers challenged the structures of imperialism, and few oligarchs were prepared to launch that struggle.

The origins and conduct of this significant strike are found in and shaped by a forty-year quest for liberty and justice among the black and ladino workers who built United Fruit's Caribbean enclave. Everyone came with the hope of making a better life, but only a few of them, primarily the white men who directed the plantation regimen, actually realized their dreams. The system that crushed the aspirations of immigrant laborers also created the conditions in which a politically active rural proletariat organized to challenge United Fruit. The sporadic violence, protests, and strikes that attended the establishment of United's enclave demonstrate that the strikers of 1923 built their movement on a long tradition of resistance to exploitation.

Most of the stevedores and plantation workers were as new to the area as the white management, for Spaniards, Creoles, ladinos, and Indians preferred the more salubrious climate of the western highlands. Previous efforts to colonize the region, most notably the ambitious projects of Mariano Gálvez in the 1830s, failed to attract sufficient people or capital. Hence, the department of Izabal was relatively underpopulated and undeveloped when construction on the Northern Railway began, compelling the first construction companies to recruit their workers from New Orleans. After that initial effort ended in disaster, railroad contractors enlisted most of their workers from Belize and Jamaica, as the government could not assure an adequate supply of Indian workers through the *mandamiento* (forced labor drafts).[5]

After observing the performance of at least ten different nationalities on his Costa Rican enterprises, Keith concluded that Jamaicans, besides being accustomed to the work and acclimated to the region, accepted the plantation regime with little protest. He recruited so extensively among the Jamaicans that they outnumbered all other ethnic groups twelve to one.[6] In the late nineteenth century, many other entrepreneurs hired Jamaicans for work on railroads, plantations, and especially the Panama Canal. The increased demand for labor, combined with the depressed economies of Jamaica and the southern United States, precipitated a massive migration of black laborers, some as permanent settlers and others as seasonal workers. The formation of a black culture along Guatemala's Caribbean coast forms part of a larger sociohistorical phenomenon, a second stage in the African diaspora, involving Jamaicans and black Americans and spanning the entire Caribbean region.[7]

If the North American businessmen expected docility from their workers, they were mistaken, for the Jamaican workers came from a culture with an established tradition of organized resistance. In Costa Rica they carved out their own means of resistance through small, private landholdings and the earliest labor organizations along Central America's Caribbean coast. Between 1903 and 1905 a series of unsuccessful strikes temporarily rocked the wharf and railroad yards of the banana district, and in 1910 the workers formed their first union. Claiming a membership of several thousand, they walked off the job for several months and prevented the company from hiring scabs to replace them. Although the union was disbanded in 1913, the laborers and political observers learned the value of organizing.[8]

Since the Guatemalan division developed twenty years after the Costa Rican plantations, labor organizations naturally developed later. However, the Guatemalan workers resisted abusive labor practices of American railroad contractors in the 1890s, and flight, violence, and spontaneous work stoppages were common forms of protest. One early source of friction emanated from the contractors' failure to comply with the terms of the agreements they used to recruit workers abroad. Many who came to work on the Northern Railway in the 1890s signed contracts in which the employer consented to cover the cost of passage to Guatemala in return for a worker's promise to pay off this debt before he received any wages. Canadian engineer William T. Penney, who supervised some of the work on the line in the 1890s, admitted that the men who boarded the steamships for Guatemala were lost as soon as they embarked, for the company rarely fulfilled its contractual obligations. Penney saw many workers try to escape the wage slavery in which they found themselves, but, since few could evade the authorities or survive the swamps for long, most of them returned to camp where they occasionally suffered humiliating whippings.[9]

In the early days of the Caribbean enclave, whites also disciplined black workers through terror. On April 29, 1896, a black American named Harper was arrested after he allegedly shot and killed a white supervisor of the Northern Railway. Early the next morning a mob of about two hundred white Americans forcibly removed Harper from his prison cell and hanged him. The whites responsible for the lynching were never brought to justice, partly because the American minister, who believed that the victim was guilty, issued no protest. From this and other incidents, Guatemalan officials drew only the conclusion that they should fight crime in the area by reducing the number of blacks, who were responsible for the scandalous crimes committed on a daily basis.[10]

Since the victims of whippings and lynchings had little or no recourse to legal or diplomatic channels, the workers recognized that they had to defend themselves. In September 1898, with the government several months behind in meeting its payroll obligations on the Northern Railway, the workers terminated construction on the entire line by laying down their tools and refusing to continue until they were paid. Estrada Cabrera resolved the strike by paying them the wages they were due, but he suspended the project and dismissed the workers. Racial tensions subsequently increased and, as a result of real or alleged conflicts with the authorities, Guatemalan police imprisoned many of the stranded black workers. The Americans appealed for but did not receive adequate assistance from their consular representative at Livingston, for he complained that defending and protecting these blacks was "the most irksome part" of his duties. American diplomats grudgingly offered protection to black Americans only to discourage Guatemalans from thinking that they could also mistreat white Americans.[11]

The resumption of construction on the Northern Railway in 1901 provided a temporary solution to the region's unemployment problem. Although the government supplied the contractors with hundreds of Indian laborers, disease and overwork compelled many of them to avoid the labor drafts by emigrating to British Honduras, which was described as "a hive of Indians" in 1906. Jamaicans, however, preferred work on the railroad to labor on the Panama Canal because mortality rates there in the 1880s were so high that the governor of Jamaica placed near-prohibitive restrictions on emigration to Panama. To maintain a labor supply for its Central American plantations, United Fruit lobbied the governor of Jamaica to reject President Theodore Roosevelt's request to lift the restrictions.[12]

After the completion of the Northern Railway, some of these former railroad workers took jobs on United's new plantations, but the company continued to recruit in Jamaica and Belize. Unlike the Guatemalan *finqueros*, United assumed the primary responsibility for finding, controlling, and disciplining its labor force; it did not want the host state to interfere with its labor practices. Local authorities often collaborated with the American owners, but the enclave nurtured its own means of administering justice and regulating labor relations, living conditions, health care, and social life. In March 1906, for example, a black man named John Williams allegedly shot and killed a white man during a barroom brawl. Guatemalan police apprehended Williams several days later and placed him on a train to Zacapa, where the Guatemalan courts would try him. As the train was en route, a mob of white men bribed the prisoner's guards, removed Williams from the train, and murdered him. The American minister, Leslie Combs, did not protest this case to the Guatemalan authorities because he, like the lynchers, believed that Williams deserved the punishment.[13]

Several days later twelve of Williams's compatriots requested diplomatic assistance from Combs. While they did not dispute the charge that Williams had killed the man, they passionately defended every person's right to a fair trial. If no action were taken against the responsible parties, the men feared a repetition of the lynching: "In such case if the white man be allowed to (by bribing the Government with a few dollars) do as they please, then we poor colored men will become as targets for not only them, but the natives as well too, so we beg you to please take some steps towards this, so that in the future we may have liberty and justice."[14] Combs ignored the petition.

In United Fruit's enclave, the white men could do almost anything they pleased because the state had virtually abdicated its sovereignty over the region. United Fruit ran the docks, set train schedules, owned most of the land, employed more people than any firm in the country, stocked the commissaries with essential supplies, provided medical service, and even maintained its own private police force. Local police and judicial authorities had little choice but to collaborate with this powerful enterprise because it drove the region's economy. Unable to appeal to American diplomats and abused or ignored by Guatemalan officials, black workers lived and worked in an enclave managed by a private foreign enterprise as a company fiefdom, in which corporate interests and customs governed the lives of all employees. Only the steel rails of IRCA tied the Bananera division to the rest of Guatemala; the laws of American capitalism governed the culturally diverse population of eastern Guatemala.

Even before United Fruit developed its plantation system, the Caribbean coast displayed racial, linguistic, cultural, and economic traits distinct from the rest of the country.[15] United accentuated the distinctive characteristics of the region, for it brought in English-speaking, predominantly Protestant, West Indian laborers to develop a productive enterprise tied directly to the international capitalist system. Moreover, the concessions that governed IRCA and UFCO gave custom the force of law, as the contracts granted them administrative autonomy over their enterprises. While this provision was subject to interpretation, in practice United insisted that, among other things, it had the exclusive right to regulate and discipline its labor force.

Hence, labor patterns and laws that prevailed in the western highlands did not generally apply to United's plantations. In the highlands, Indian labor coerced by the *mandamiento* or debt servitude provided the work force on the coffee plantations, and government officials intervened where necessary to provide the *finqueros* with a sufficient supply of labor. In the event of a dispute, the Indian workers and their Guatemalan employers could appeal to the government, which had an adequate military presence to assure order in the rural areas.[16] On the Caribbean coast, United recruited and disciplined its own laborers, and, while a degree of debt servitude may have been imposed on some workers through the commissary system, United hired its laborers on a daily wage or contract system; it did not enlist or control its work force through the *mandamiento*, debt peonage, or vagrancy laws. Labor disputes rarely went beyond the enclave, as the government had little interest in protecting black workers, and United only appealed to the national government when it could not repress the conflict on its own.

Despite the claims of United and its apologists that the wages and conditions of employment on its enterprises were much better than those offered on any other farm, the West Indian laborers did not compare their status to that of the Guatemalan Indians in the highlands. They analyzed their conditions from within the context of the enclave, a perspective that highlighted the contradictions between a white managerial class and a black working class. A white minority in Puerto Barrios and company headquarters at Bananera governed the enclave. Of the forty-three hundred people employed by United in 1914, only three hundred were white, and they filled all the managerial positions.[17]

The white managers lived in comfortable houses equipped with running water, electricity, and whatever modern conveniences they could acquire; the black employees lived in bunkhouses or huts that were set apart from the whites' living quarters. Blacks could look at but not enter the front yard of any white residence; they were expected to yield the right-of-way and remove their hats when talking to white people. Even access to the hospital was determined by race. Although black workers had 2 percent of their pay deducted to cover hospital charges at Quirigua, they had no provisions for sick leave written into their contracts. When a white person fell ill, he would be sent to the hospital immediately and receive full pay for all the time spent under a doctor's care. A person of color, however, may not have been so quickly dismissed from his plantation chores to receive medical treatment, because workers engaged on a contract or day-labor basis were not entitled to full-time hospital treatment.[18]

All labor conflicts therefore contained elements of racial and class antagonisms. In December 1909, for example, a group of Jamaicans looted two commissaries at the Dartmouth and Cayuga farms. UFCO operated about twelve stores on its farms, and workers complained about the prices it charged for food and merchandise, for, if they did not buy their necessities in the commissary, they would usually have to do without them. When an angry force of six hundred Jamaicans threatened to continue the assault on company property, United Fruit requested military intervention, but the local commander refused to arrest the rioters because he feared that he might spark even greater violence. The authorities allowed whites and ladinos the revenge they exacted in early January, when a group of four ladinos lynched William Wright, a Jamaican supposedly involved in the recent disturbances. Guatemalan authorities arrested one ladino on suspicion of murder but released him several days later. United Fruit then hired him as a farm superintendent.[19]

Native Guatemalans only sought jobs with United Fruit after West Indian laborers had already performed the most difficult tasks of the banana industry, clearing jungle and planting bananas. The unhealthy climate and the lack of economic opportunities had kept most ladinos away. Hence, once United had organized the plantation system, built the hospital, and installed sanitation facilities, Guatemalans found the jobs attractive. In 1914, with a small number of ladinos working at Puerto Barrios and the banana plantations, the Guatemalan government attempted to influence United's hiring practices by imposing a cash deposit of fifty dollars on each immigrant laborer.[20]

Nevertheless, the government lacked the willingness and ability to regulate effectively United's labor practices. Under the Liberal regimes, work was not so much a right as it was an obligation, as labor legislation provided coercive means to guarantee coffee planters a steady supply of labor. A law of 1894 theoretically abolished forced labor under the *mandamiento*, but Estrada Cabrera's government still drafted thousands for work on coffee estates and public-works projects. Existing legislation, in any case, was designed to regulate relations between *patrón* and Indian workers on the coffee fincas; there were no laws or regulations applicable to the free-labor system that prevailed on the banana plantations.[21] Some of the legislation could have been applied to United's enterprises, but the government preferred to let UFCO manage its own affairs.

The government had an interest in preventing the development of workers' organizations on any of the company's enterprises, particularly in the city, where the development of a railroad union could have inspired other laborers to form their own organizations. The absence of legislation establishing a workers' right to organize, strike, and bargain collectively, combined with the paternalistic attitude of the government, obstructed the formation of autonomous labor groups. During the Estrada Cabrera regime the government permitted a number of mutual-aid societies (each one had to appoint him the honorary vice president), but the dictator viewed labor organizations as subversive and prohibited workers from establishing truly independent unions with the right to strike.[22]

Thus, United Fruit's management determined wages and working conditions, and workers had few means to influence what the company offered. Given that work on most of the firm's divisions was sporadic and often irregular, it preferred to pay its workers on a contract, task, or hourly basis, thereby avoiding the necessity of maintaining a large labor force on the payroll around the clock. Management assigned employees a certain task and paid the workers when they completed their chores; the length of time required to complete the assignment did not affect their pay. In 1914 fieldhands working under contract could earn $1 to $1.25 per day for clearing land and tending and cutting fruit. The task or contract system, according to company officials and their apologists, worked better than a wage system because the Jamaicans and Indians, who were otherwise inclined to idleness and irresponsibility, would not perform their duties if left alone among the vast banana plantations.[23]

Laborers lived and worked at the mercy of management, working only when needed and at the pace set by their employers. Workers had to be prepared to hit the fields at a moment's notice because the harvest depended entirely on the arrival and departure times of the steamships. After the district supervisor received a definite schedule, he ordered the farm managers to deliver a certain quantity of stems at a specified time to the loading station. The farm manager then ordered three-man cutting gangs out into the fields at 5:30 A.M., and they would not return until they had cut all the fruit requested by the district supervisor. On the railroad yards and the docks, management set working hours according to the arrival and departure times of ships and trains. Stevedores had to wait until the sirens called them to work, at any time of day or night. When the alarm sounded the workers had to rush to the docks because management handed out jobs on a first-come, first-serve basis. If they were lucky enough to secure one of the jobs, they were one of the few UFCO employees to receive wages, which in 1914 amounted to 12.5 cents per hour for a ten-hour day.[24]

United Fruit once attempted to convert the stevedores to a contract system, but the workers, despite the near certainty of government intervention, struck in defense of the wage system. On January 14, 1914, United Fruit instituted a contract system whereby the workers would receive twenty cents for each one hundred stems carried from the railroad cars to the conveyor belts that lifted the bananas on board. At the end of the day the laborers expressed widespread dissatisfaction with the new system. One man carried 656 stems and thereby earned $1.31, but, since several others carried no more than 200 stems, the contract system reduced their daily wages.[25]

In response to the workers' complaints, United offered thirty cents per 100 stems. UFCO's manager, G. M. Shaw, believed that any good man could carry 700 stems in a ten-hour day. Knowing that their most productive worker loaded only 656 stems, the workers rejected Shaw's offer and went on strike. According to Joaquin Hecht (a consular official and later a United Fruit employee), the striking stevedores—and those who supported them—threatened the entire white community: "If the strikers would have had the intention of killing off every white man and destroy the property of foreign companies, they could have done so with impunity, as the authorities would not have turned a hand. In all probability the authorities would have taken to the woods." Since the local commander was overwhelmed by the workers' show of force, Shaw appealed personally to Estrada Cabrera, but the astute caudillo recognized the danger of a more violent confrontation and asked United to return to the wage system in return for his pledge to expel the strike leaders.[26]

This incident demonstrated the value of united, militant action. When they acted in sufficient numbers, the workers could drive a wedge between United and the government. The organization of the plantation system into fincas of one thousand acres, however, minimized contact between the workers of the various units, for workers from different farms met only when they obtained their weekly supplies.[27] Contact between the port and railroad workers was even less frequent because the workers were separated by a considerable distance, and, as more ladinos acquired jobs at Puerto Barrios, cultural differences between the stevedores and the plantation workers also retarded the development of a labor movement.

The most effective deterrent to collective action and organization, however, was the constant threat of military intervention, either by the Guatemalan military or the American marines. Management relied in the first instance on the local police and military, but, as the 1914 strike demonstrated, it could not rely on government intervention. Hence, when railroad and plantation workers threatened a general strike in late 1918, the State Department instructed the legation to contact an American warship off the Pacific coast in the event that the Guatemalans could not control the situation.[28]

Without the threat of military reprisals, workers could extract meaning-ful compromises from management. During the Unionist rebellion of April 1920, for example, railroad workers and stevedores in Puerto Barrios went on strike, and the company had no choice but to accept the workers' demands for an increase in their wages from $1.50 to $3.00 per day because the fighting in the capital precluded military intervention by either Guate-malan or American forces.[29] Following Estrada Cabrera's resignation the workers who had fought the tyranny demanded political compensation for their contribution to the restoration of democratic rule. Bakers, carpenters, railroad workers, and other urban laborers founded unions, mutual-aid societies, and the country's first Communist party to promote and defend their interests. The railroad workers became one of the most active and militant of all the new worker organizations, a tradition maintained in the October revolution of 1944. In May 1920 they went on strike, demanding higher pay and official recognition of their newly formed union, the Union Ferrocarrilera, as the legal representative of all railroad employees.[30]

Herrera suppressed the strike with the support and encouragement of the managers, one of his first betrayals of his allies in the Liga Obrera. Defining the railroad as a public service enterprise vital to the public welfare, he decreed that the state had a responsibility to repress all strikes that threatened the national interest. The government thereby established a legal foundation for preventing railroad and dock workers from organizing and striking, as the state assumed the responsibility for keeping the railroads and ports in operation.[31]

Nevertheless, the railroad workers, led by those in Escuintla, continued to press for legal recognition of their union and higher wages. IRCA dismissed some of the men who joined the union, although the company claimed that it had dismissed the workers solely as a cost-saving measure. In truth, IRCA refused to employ any union member because it had adopted a strict policy of dealing directly and individually with each worker; it would not recognize the rights of its employees to organize and bargain collectively.[32] United Fruit and IRCA held firmly to this policy for the re-mainder of the Liberal period, and the government usually supported them.

In October 1920 representatives of the Liga Obrera met with Herrera to present their case for the workers' right to organize and strike, but the president refused to support any additional social reforms. The following year the government decreed that any public demonstrations that did not have the advance approval of the government would be illegal and that its organizers would be held responsible for the public disorders that ensued. After the government slowed the process of legalizing mutual-aid societies, syndicates, and unions, a group of radicals formed the Union Obrera Socialista, a precursor to the Communist party.[33]

Herrera's successor, General Orellana, persecuted the young labor movement throughout his five-year tenure, recognizing the potential political impact of a new alliance between the organized and increasingly militant workers and the Conservatives. His minister of war, Jorge Ubico, cracked down on working-class leaders following the coup of December 1921 and again after an aborted military coup in August 1922.[34] The government's repression did not silence the new labor organizations, but it compelled many of them to adopt a conciliatory attitude toward government. Of the different confederations and parties that vied for the allegiance of the working classes, the Federación Obrera de Guatemala, an organization committed to working within the system and subsidized by the government, claimed the most membership. In any case, the working-class organizations in Guatemala City, composed of and representing artisans and radical intellectuals and having neither the manpower nor the resources to do much more than propagandize, made hardly any inroads into the vast United Fruit work force.

The strike of the Puerto Barrios stevedores, therefore, began independently of and adopted objectives and tactics different from those advocated by the Guatemala City organizations. Most of those groups, including the Communist party, fought for limited objectives within the established legal and political systems; none of them used the strike as an effective weapon in its negotiations with management and the government. By terminating all work on the only pier at Puerto Barrios, the stevedores caused immediate damage to United Fruit's export business and threatened to paralyze Guatemalan commerce, because 79 percent of the country's imports and 71 percent of its exports passed over that wharf.[35] Thus, when the stevedores refused to load a cargo of thirty-six thousand banana stems, they threw down the gauntlet before United and General Orellana.

The strike began without any previous notice on the morning of February 3, 1923, when the stevedores refused to carry bananas from the railroad cars to the conveyor belts. Management immediately tried to break the strike by bringing in other workers to load the fruit, but the strikers physically interfered with the scabs and brought all loading to a complete stop.[36] United then recruited about three hundred blacks from the banana farms, but about two hundred strikers prevented all but a few of them from getting out to the wharf, and some of the farm workers evidently refused to break the strike. For forty-eight hours the scene at the pier was tense and occasionally violent, but the local authorities rejected United Fruit's demands to clear the docks of all strikers. On February 5, United sent off a ship with only six thousand stems, leaving about thirty thousand stems rotting in seventy railroad cars. That same day, Orellana sent military reinforcements to Puerto Barrios.[37]

Ladinos evidently led the strike, for their initial demands included an end to United's alleged preference for hiring Jamaicans. The racial issue won the workers some supporters in Guatemala City, but it gave management a weapon to use against the workers. By recruiting black farm workers to break the strike, management attempted to exploit the racial divisions among the laborers, but this tactic, even if it had worked in other labor disputes, offended nationalistic sentiment. While few contemporary commentators accepted the right of labor to organize and strike, they could all rally behind the patriotic workers who challenged the anti-Guatemalan labor policies of a foreign company. An editorial in *El Excelsior* denounced the company's labor policies and urged the government to defend Guatemalan workers, whose labor was generally superior to that of black immigrants.[38]

Consequently, it was in the interest of both management and labor to downplay the significance of racist labor practices and demands. After the ship left, the labor leaders went into the countryside to convince all UFCO employees to join the strike, knowing that their success depended on their ability to prevent United from recruiting more scabs. Assuming that three fourths of United Fruit's five thousand workers were black, the strikers would have difficulty gaining support if they continued to demand an end to United's alleged preference for hiring Jamaicans.[39] The leaders therefore de-emphasized the racial factors and concentrated on the material issues that had prompted the strike. On February 6 the strikers sent their first petition to General Orellana, and it included no reference to the company's discriminatory hiring practices. The stevedores demanded an increase in their pay from one-half cent per bunch to one cent per bunch of bananas loaded on the ships, with double time for overtime and vacation days. In addition, they demanded better and more efficient medical attention, issues that would incite enthusiasm among all United Fruit employees. The workers complained that poor workers often died before being admitted to the hospital because they had to fill out so many forms prior to receiving medical attention.[40]

In their petition of February 6 the workers also appealed to the political and economic interests of the entire nation. Although they may have acted spontaneously in response to their immediate material concerns, the workers viewed their strike as a patriotic and historic effort to recover a measure of the rights and powers that Estrada Cabrera had abdicated to UFCO and IRCA through several concessions that allowed the companies to monopolize railroads, shipping, and the banana business. The workers argued that the concessions violated the constitutions of both countries because they allowed United to restrict the liberty of commerce guaranteed by the laws of the United States and Guatemala. Puerto Barrios, the workers argued, should be owned and operated by the state, not by a private foreign company. If the government did not discriminate against the commerce of any nation, trade and productivity would expand substantially.[41]

The strikers sent a similar memorandum to U.S. Minister Arthur Geissler and requested his help in their struggle against United's monopoly. The paper, signed by Genaro Ochoa and Julio Molina, made it clear that the workers welcomed American investment as long as the companies complied with Guatemalan laws and promoted economic growth. They even asked Geissler to invite other shipping companies to call at Guatemalan ports, promising to load their ships before any UFCO steamer. The workers opposed the unconstitutional behavior of UFCO and IRCA, two companies linked by a common interest in stifling Guatemalan commerce. The time had come, Ochoa and Molina argued, to terminate a pernicious monopoly that annihilated Guatemalan liberties, crushed commerce, and obstructed the country's progress and economic welfare.[42]

Ochoa and Molina helped to transform a spontaneous work stoppage into a nationalist crusade against United Fruit, the symbol of economic imperialism throughout Latin America. The conversion was partly the result of an enlightened leadership that emerged after the strike began. UFCO and the government believed that either foreign agitators or persons not employed by the company were responsible for the strike. Jorge Fergusson, who was not employed by United Fruit, admitted that he had drafted the workers' petitions, but he denied that he or any other outsiders had instigated the strike. United Fruit's monopolization of commerce and its abusive labor policies, he explained, were sufficient motivation for the Guatemalan workers.[43]

Around issues like these the stevedores could attract broad support outside of the Puerto Barrios region. Media backing for the strikers had been lukewarm as long as the strike was viewed solely as a labor-management conflict. Editors sympathized with the poor pay and working conditions, but they usually denied the right of the workers to organize and prevent other people from working. Since the workers also represented the legitimate grievances of a poor, developing country against a rich and powerful foreign corporation, the editor of *El Excelsior* urged Guatemalans to consider the case more seriously because it was a patriotic issue that affected the interests of the entire country.[44]

Nevertheless, racial animosities weakened the workers' cause. Hundreds of workers from the Quirigua hospital, electrical plant, and United Fruit plantations joined the strikers between February 5 and 10; by then between eight hundred and two thousand strikers had stopped the movement of all freight at the port. While R. K. Thomas claimed that these workers had virtual control of United's property, the position of the strikers was still precarious, for it was reported on February 10 that two thousand Belizeans and Jamaicans were prepared to replace the ladino workers on the docks. Moreover, because of strong government pressure to keep the railroad in operation, the strike had failed to enlist the support of railroad workers across the country.[45]

Nevertheless, the Orellana regime and United Fruit viewed the strike as a serious threat to their political and economic interests. A successful strike against the country's largest employer, particularly one with a powerful political lobby in Guatemala City and Washington, could inspire workers throughout the country. Although the local authorities had initially refused to intervene, Orellana sympathized with and protected the interests of capital, not those of a labor force that included several thousand black immigrants. A few days after the strike he replaced the governor with General Enrique Arís, a man with a reputation for brutality and connections with American corporate interests. In 1907 he was removed from his post as governor of the department of Izabal for pistol-whipping three black Americans who had committed no offense. The Guatemalan courts did not punish the general because he was a favorite of Estrada Cabrera and American corporations. Workers denounced General Arís as a tyrant and terrorist who served United Fruit, pointing out that Arís was quartered in the fruit company's hotel, where United attended to his every need.[46]

Thus, General Orellana presented two faces to the workers. On the one hand, the deployment of additional troops under the command of General Arís demonstrated his intention to restore order. On the other hand, he invited the strike leaders to the capital for direct and personal discussions. On the evening of February 14, a delegation of workers led by Ochoa and Miguel Bardales met with Orellana. After expressing his desire to protect the interests of the workers and listening to their complaints about the abusive behavior of General Arís, Orellana convinced them to accept a proposal for a government-sponsored mediation effort.[47]

The plan called for the appointment of a six-member commission composed of three representatives from the striking workers and three appointed by United. Orellana dispatched an official mediator to Puerto Barrios with a provisional proposal that called for a guarantee that United Fruit would not dismiss any of the strikers, the appointment of a Guatemalan at the Quirigua hospital, the improvement of sanitary conditions, a detailed study of UFCO wage scales, and a promise that Guatemalans would have an option on all the jobs then held by blacks, provided that they were qualified for the position. Upon the approval of the proposal, the workers would return to the docks with the understanding that they could resume the strike on March 15 if the conditions of the agreement had not been implemented.[48]

On February 17, Ochoa and the other negotiators presented the plan to the workers. Although it did not include a guaranteed pay increase, the strikers were inclined to accept the proposal and give the government a chance to work on their behalf. However, some of them had already been told by United Fruit that their services were no longer needed because soldiers were doing the work of the stevedores. Once these soldiers were removed from the docks, the workers agreed to return to their jobs. They were beginning to act like a union, and on February 18 they formed the first Sindicato de Bananeros and appointed an executive council of ten persons that included Ochoa and Molina. The stevedores went back to work on February 19, and the plantation workers followed suit the next day.[49]

Three weeks of fruitless negotiations followed. The stevedores continued to press for a 100 percent wage increase, but they dropped their insistence that the company cease preferential hiring of black laborers, and this may have attracted more workers to the movement. On March 3, Thomas informed Geissler that the stevedores and plantation workers would strike again on March 15, with a force of perhaps five thousand men, the total of all the company workers, black and ladino. Even when threatened with a complete shutdown of the entire division, United Fruit refused to negotiate. From the beginning to the end of the conflict, United claimed that it could replace its entire work force if the strikers did not accept the terms of employment that it offered.[50]

United had little use for workers or political leaders who challenged the company's labor policies. Thomas dismissed most of the worker's demands as Communist propaganda, and he even described the pro-labor sympathies of Minister of Development Rafael Ponciano as Bolshevik when Ponciano's only crime had been to urge Thomas to make wage concessions to the laborers. Thomas held firm to the policy that United maintained until the revolution of 1944: "The Company has contracted with each one of the laborers individually and not as members of a labor organization. The Company does not recognize for carrying on its work, the personnel of such organizations as those have for their principal object, in the case under review, the prevalence of force over right. The Company will continue treating with the laborers individually who accept the usual terms fixed by it in regard to employment."[51]

On March 3 government officials informed Geissler that they could not prevent another strike if the company did not adopt a more conciliatory attitude. General Orellana urged United Fruit to negotiate in good faith because the workers' positions merited serious consideration. If the company did not negotiate, Orellana feared a general walkout, possibly extending into Honduras, and, in that event, he would have to intervene militarily. On March 10, Geissler characterized the president as "oppressed by the thought that many poor fellows may have to die."[52]

While Orellana may have preferred a negotiated settlement, he was prepared to use force because he related the Puerto Barrios strike to the general political and military opposition he confronted closer to home. Rumors circulated that the workers were prepared to join a military rebellion led by Marcial Prem, whose nationalistic credentials were strengthened by his representation of Guatemala at the conference of Central American states convened by the United States in December 1922. Prem voted for the general treaty of peace and amity that the conferees drafted, but he cast a separate, negative vote on a treaty establishing a commission of inquiry that would investigate international conflicts. Prem viewed the inclusion of the United States on this panel as a humiliating form of intervention because the Americans were not signatories to the general peace treaty. For this minor act of defiance, Prem became, like the Puerto Barrios workers, a symbol of Guatemalan resistance to U.S. imperialism.[53]

Prem's vote focused attention on Orellana's pro-American positions. Orellana had requested an American military adviser and U.S. arbitration of the Guatemala-Honduras boundary dispute, and he had approved concessions to IRCA and the Empresa Eléctrica. Critics charged that he had impaired the sovereignty of Guatemala. By mid-March, criticisms had blossomed into rumors of a military coup instigated by influential politicians in the lawyers' association. It was widely rumored and reported in the press that the lawyers would raise the banner of armed revolt at a meeting scheduled for the night of March 14, when Prem would be the featured speaker. Orellana received reports that the Puerto Barrios workers would strike on that day or the day after, and then rebels would attempt a coup in Guatemala City. In anticipation of the coup, Orellana brought in five hundred additional soldiers to the capital and transferred eight hundred to Puerto Barrios.[54]

The coup in the capital never materialized, largely because of the intervention of the United States. On March 13, Geissler met with Orellana and his secretary of foreign affairs and helped them prepare a counterstrategy. Geissler advised Orellana to expose the fallacy of Prem's supposedly nationalistic positions and publicize his knowledge of the lawyers' intentions to launch a coup after their meeting. That night, *El Excelsior* published an article that followed the minister's suggestions. It also announced the arrival of the USS *Tacoma* at Puerto Barrios on March 14. At Orellana's request, Geissler had invited the commander of the *Tacoma* to make a "routine visit" to the capital.[55]

With their plans exposed, Prem and the lawyers canceled the meeting scheduled for March 14. What little tolerance Generals Orellana and Arís had for the workers was now exhausted. Even though United Fruit had not engaged in meaningful negotiations, on March 14 the government ordered the expulsion óf twenty foreign citizens who had allegedly incited the disorder in Puerto Barrios. Early the next morning the *Tacoma* anchored in Puerto Barrios, and the captain and forty-five men boarded the train to pay their respects to General Orellana in Guatemala City. The show of force evidently worked, as the day passed without a strike and the labor leaders were sent without incident to Bluefields, Nicaragua.[56]

The arrest and expulsion of the strike leaders may have sparked a violent confrontation. According to Mario López Larrave, troops under the command of General Arís killed several workers, wounded many others, imprisoned twenty-two leaders, and expelled the rest of them from the country, but there is no evidence to substantiate this report. If there was any

violence, it did not affect the operations of Puerto Barrios. The port operated normally several days before and after the March 15 deadline; two
ships anchored at and three ships departed from the port on March 16, one of
them carrying a load of seven thousand bunches of bananas. On March 23
the Ministry of War transferred General Arís to another post. His mission
had been completed.[57]

While the details of the repression have not been established, it is
nevertheless clear that the military intervention of the Guatemalan government and a show of force by the U.S. Navy resolved the conflict. Guatemalan soldiers had acted as scabs in the early days of the strike, and on the day
before the strike was scheduled to resume, eight hundred reinforcements
arrived. The army expelled the strike leaders, and United Fruit resumed
business as usual. It was neither the first nor the last time that the government dispatched troops to restore order, but military intervention on this
scale had not been seen before.[58]

For the next twenty-one years, United's workers did not dare to con-
front the military power of the state. The government restricted the right of
workers to strike under all circumstances, but prohibited strikes in all public
services. Since United Fruit and IRCA carried the mail, operated the tele-
graphs, and ran the railroads, the government would not tolerate any more
strikes against the company. The conclusion reached by Piero Gleijeses is
inescapable. Dictatorship served UFCO well in Guatemala, and the intervention of 1923 was one of the government's most significant contributions
to the company. From then until 1944, the company faced no more labor
agitation. It was "an aloof feudal lord entrenched in its outlying domains
and respected by the weak sovereign of the land."[59]

The anti-imperialist, antimonopolist, and democratic sentiments that
fueled the 1923 strike, however, were not snuffed out by the military
intervention. In the revolution of 1944 the railroad and plantation workers
resumed the offensive that had been repulsed on the docks of Puerto
Barrios. Within one week of Ubico's resignation, IRCA workers formed the
Sindicato de Acción y Mejoramiento Ferrocarrilero, which became the most
influential union in the country. Alarik A. Bennet, a Jamaican, led the farm
workers of Izabal in the Sindicato de Empresa de Trabajadores de la United
Fruit Company. Juan Domingo Segura, a Zambo of predominantly African
ancestry, led the stevedores of Puerto Barrios.[60] The military intervention
had taught the workers to fear the power of the state, but perhaps it also had
demonstrated the value and necessity of organizing in defense of their
common interests.

Notes

1. Roger P. Ames (consular agent) to William Owen (vice consul), May 17, 1914, Diplomatic post records, 1914, vol. 2.

2. Minister of foreign relations to William Hayne Leavell, May 15, 1914, enclosure, "Asunto de Quirigua," by Adolfo J. Quevedo, Diplomatic post records, 1914, vol. 2, 350/10.

3. Victor Cutter to Leavell, May 13, 1914, Diplomatic post records, 1914, vol. 2, 350/1.

4. Charles David Kepner, *Social Aspects of the Banana Industry* (1936, reprint, New York: AMC Press, 1967), 157.

5. William J. Griffith, *Empires in the Wilderness: Foreign Colonization and Development in Guatemala, 1834–1844* (Chapel Hill: University of North Carolina Press, 1965); H. Remsen Whitehouse to State, March 25, 1885, enclosure, protest of Con Hickey, December 24, 1884, Diplomatic despatches; Macgrane Coxe (minister to Guatemala) to State, June 1, 1897, Diplomatic despatches.

6. Bourgois, *Ethnicity at Work*, 47–48; Stewart, *Keith and Costa Rica*, 67; Wilson, *Empire in Green and Gold*, 51–52.

7. Roy Simon Bryce-Laporte with Trevor Purcell, "A Lesser-known Chapter of the African Diaspora: West Indians in Costa Rica, Central America," in *Global Dimensions of the African Diaspora*, ed. Joseph Harris (Washington, DC: Howard University Press, 1982), 221–23; Schoonover, *United States in Central America*, 111; Bourgois, *Ethnicity at Work*, 46–51.

8. Chomsky, "Plantation Society," 202–34.

9. Coxe to State, June 1, 1897, Diplomatic despatches; William T. Penney, "Notas y comentarios sobre acontecimientos y experiencias vividos durante mis viajes por México y Centroamérica," *Mesoamérica* 16 (1988): 375.

10. Penney, "Notas y comentarios," 377–78; Pierce M. B. Young (minister to Guatemala) to State, May 22, 1896, Diplomatic despatches; Coxe to State, June 1, 1897, Diplomatic despatches; Coxe to Olney, November 11, 1896, enclosed, Muñoz (minister of foreign relations) to Coxe, October 31, 1896, Diplomatic despatches.

11. W. Godfrey Hunter (minister to Guatemala) to State, November 12, 1898, Diplomatic despatches; James C. McNally (consul general) to David J. Hill (assistant secretary of state), June 15, 1901, enclosed, Edward Reed (vice consul, Livingston) to W. G. Hunter, Jr. (vice and deputy consul general), June 1, 1901, Consular despatches; Schoonover, *United States in Central America*, 128.

12. Leslie Combs to Elihu Root, May 9, 1906, Diplomatic despatches; Michael Conniff, *Black Labor on a White Canal: Panama, 1904–1981* (Pittsburgh: University of Pittsburgh Press, 1985), 25.

13. Schoonover, *United States in Central America*, 119; Combs to State, April 3, 1906, Diplomatic despatches.

14. Combs to State, April 3, 1906, enclosed, Robert Bostic et al. to Combs, March 25, 1906, Diplomatic despatches.

15. On the unique cultural history of Izabal see González, *Black Carib Household Structure*; Azzo Ghidinelli, "Aspectos Económicos de la Cultura de los Caribes Negros del Municipio de Livingston," *Guatemala Indígena* 7:4 (1972): 71–152; Alfonso Arrivillaga and Alfredo Gómez, "Antecedentes históricos, movilizaciones sociales y reivindicaciones étnicas en la Costa Atlántica de Guatemala," *Estudios Sociales Centroamericanos* 48 (1988): 35–47; and Patrick Warner, "Garifuna Genesis: The Sad Story of a Displaced People," *African Commentary* 2:3 (March 1990): 26–28.

16. For more on the labor history of the coffee plantations see Julio Castellano Cambranes, *Coffee and Peasants in Guatemala: The Origins of the Modern Plantation Economy in Guatemala, 1853–1897* (Stockholm: Institute for Latin American Studies, 1985); David McCreery, "Debt Servitude in Rural Guatemala, 1876–1936," *Hispanic American Historical Review* 63:4 (1983); and idem, "An Odious Feudalism," ibid., 99–117. Comparisons between the two systems are difficult because more research is required on the labor history of the banana plantations, but an important contribution is Kepner, *Social Aspects of the Banana Industry*.

17. Gerald Harris (commerical agent), "Business of Eastern Guatemala," Consular post records, Guatemala City, 1914, pt. 3, 610.

18. John L. Williams, "The Rise of the Banana Industry and Its Influence on Caribbean Coutntries" (M.A. thesis, Clark University, 1925), 35, 119; George Bennett (manager, UFCO) to Robert Janz (vice consul), January 23, 1931, Consular post records, Guatemala City, 1931; pt. 8, 850.4.

19. Kepner and Soothill, *Banana Empire*, 319–22; Reed to Jefe Político, December 23, 1909, Consular post records, Livingston, Official Correspondence; Reed to Owen, February 16, 1910, Consular post records, Livingston, Official Correspondence.

20. Harris, "The Business of Eastern Guatemala," Consular post records, Guatemala City, 1914, pt. 3, 610; in Costa Rica a similar transition from Jamaican to mestizo labor took place. See Bryce-Laporte, "A Lesser-known Chapter," 227–28.

21. McCreery, "Odious Feudalism," 105–8; Frank Griffith Dawson, "Labor Legislation and Social Integration in Guatemala: 1871–1944," *American Journal of Comparative Law* 14 (1965–66): 129–35; Jones, *Guatemala*, 166–67.

22. Arturo Taracena Arriola, "La Confederación Obrera de Centro América (COCA): 1921–1928," *Anuario de Estudios Centroamericanos* 10 (1984): 81–83; Archer Bush, *Organized Labor in Guatemala, 1944–1949: A Case Study of an Adolescent Labor Movement in an Underdeveloped Country* (Hamilton, NY: Colgate University, 1950), pt. 3:1; Woodward, *Central America*, 208.

23. Adams, *Conquest of the Tropics*, 202.

24. Williams, "Rise of the Banana Industry," 27–29; Bush, *Organized Labor*, pt. 2:30–31; G. M. Shaw (general manager, UFCO) to Leavell, January 20, 1915, Diplomatic post records, 1915, vol. 5, 850.4/2.

25. Shaw to Leavell, January 20, 1915, Diplomatic post records.

26. Joaquin Hecht (acting consular agent) to Stuart Lupton (consul general), January 29, 1915, Diplomatic post records, Guatemalan legation, 1914, vol. 4.

27. Bush, *Organized Labor*, pt. 2, 11.

28. Walter Clarence Thurston to State, December 7, 1918, SD 814.00/289; Thurston to State, December 10, 1918, SD 814.00/290; Thurston to State, December 12, 1918, SD 814.00/291; Thurston to State, February 19, 1919, SD 814.5045/2.

29. Reed to Harry Johnson, April 25, 1920; Reed to Mrs. Henri Jekyll, April 21, 1920; Reed to Mrs. Payne, April 26, 1920, Consular post records, Livingston, General Correspondence; Mario López Larrave, *Breve historia del movimiento sindical guatemalteco* (Guatemala: Editorial Universitaria, 1976), 18.

30. Antonio Obando Sánchez, *Memorias: la historia del movimiento obrero* (Guatemala: Editorial Universitaria, 1978), 25–35; Arturo Taracena Arriola, "El primer Partido Comunista de Guatemala (1922–1932); diez años de una historia olvidada," *Anuario de Estudios Centroamericanos* 15:1 (1989): 49; idem, "Presencia anarquista en Guatemala entre 1920 y 1932," *Mesoamérica* 15 (1988): 1–23; idem, "Confederación Obrera," ibid. 15 (1988): 81–93.

31. Taracena, "El primer Partido Comunista," 49.

32. [Untitled memorandum], AGCA, B129, legajo 22191, expediente 2912; general manager (IRCA) to Ministerio de Fomento, April 26, 1921, AGCA, B129, legajo 22190, [no expediente].

33. Taracena, "El primer Partido Comunista," 50–52.

34. Pitti, "Ubico and Guatemalan Politics," 76–84.

35. Philip Holland (consul general), "Annual Report on Commerce and Industries of the Republic of Guatemala for 1923," June 6, 1924, Consular post records, Guatemala City, 1924, pt. 4.

36. Arthur Geissler to State, March 10, 1923, enclosed, R. K. Thomas (manager, United Fruit) to Geissler, March 7, 1923, SD 814.504/9; Geissler to State, February 10, 1923, RG 84, Diplomatic post records, Guatemala legation, 1923, vol. 3, 850.4UFCO; "Como fue la huelga en Puerto Barrios," *El Diario Nuevo*, [Guatemala] February 4, 1923.

37. Geissler to State, March 10, 1923, enclosed, Thomas to Geissler, March 7, 1923, SD 814.504/9; "Sigue desenvolviendose la huelga de Puerto Barrios," *El Imparcial*, February 6, 1923; "El paro en Puerto Barrios," ibid., February 8, 1923.

38. "Doscientos cargadores del muelle de Puerto Barrios se han declarado en huelga," *El Excelsior*, February 5, 1923; Bourgois argues that UFCO exploited racial animosities throughout the Caribbean in order to control the workers. See *Ethnicity at Work*, 58.

39. Figures on the racial composition and distribution of the workforce are speculative. In 1918 the U.S. consul estimated that three fourths of United Fruit's employees were Jamaican blacks. See William Thomas Lee (American consul) to State, April 15, 1918, Consular post records, 1918, pt. 2, 600.

40. "Protesta de los huelguistas de Puerto Barrios," *El Imparcial*, February 9, 1923.

41. Ibid.; Genaro Ochoa et al. to Geissler, February 13, 1923, Diplomatic post records, Guatemala legation, 1923, vol. 3; Ochoa et al. to Presidente Orellana, AGCA, B129, legajo 22091, expediente 3361.

42. Ochoa to Geissler, February 13, 1923, Diplomatic post records, Guatemala legation, 1923, vol. 3.

43. "¿Lideres extraños al obrerismo agitaron a los huelguistas," *El Imparcial*, February 20, 1923.

44. "La huelga en la costa norte," *El Diario Nuevo*, February 7, 1923; "El cariz que presenta la huelga en la actualidad," *El Excelsior*, February 17, 1923; "Otro aspecto de la huelga," ibid., February 19, 1923.

45. Geissler to State, March 10, 1923, SD 814.504/9; "La huelga de trabajadores en Puerto Barrios," *El Imparcial*, February 5, 1923; Taracena, "El primer Partido Comunista," 50; Geissler to State, February 10, 1923, Diplomatic post records, 1923, vol. 3, 850.4UFCO; Geissler to State, February 15, 1923, Diplomatic post records, 1923, vol. 3, 850.4/UFCO.

46. Schoonover, *United States in Central America*, 121–23; "Protestan contra el General Arís los trabajadores del norte," *El Imparcial*, February 19, 1923 (quoting from a letter from the workers to Orellana, February 14, 1923).

47. "Hoy volverán al trabajo los huelguistas del norte," *El Imparcial*, February 15, 1923.

48. "Teoricamente, concluyó la huelga," ibid., February 16, 1923.

49. "Actividades del obrerismo capitalino para solucionar la huelga del norte," ibid., February 21, 1923; "Vuelven al trabajo en Puerto Barrios," ibid., February 19, 1923; "Esta mañana volvieron a sus puestos los huelgistas de Quirigua y Playitas," *El Excelsior*, February 20, 1923.

50. Geissler to State, March 3, 1923, Diplomatic post records, 1923, vol. 3, 850.4UFCO.

51. Geissler to State, March 10, 1923, enclosed, Thomas to Geissler, March 7, 1923, SD 814.504/9.

52. Geissler to State, March 3, 1923, Diplomatic post records, Guatemala legation, 1923, 850.4UFCO; Geissler to State, March 10, 1923, Diplomatic post records, 1923, 850.4UFCO.

53. Geissler to State, February 20, 1923, SD 814.00/727; for Prem's criticisms of the treaty see *El Diario Nuevo*, February 19, 1923.

54. Geissler to State, March 16, 1923, SD 814.00/729; "Temores de que estalle una revuelta en la ciudad," *El Imparcial*, March 14, 1923.

55. Geissler to State, March 16, 1923, SD 814.00/729; "Los trabajadores de Puerto Barrios preparan una nueva huelga," *El Excelsior*, March 13, 1923.

56. "Se suspende la sesión de esta noche en la Asociación de Abogados," *Diario de Centro América*, March 14, 1923; *El Guatemalteco*, March 27, 1923; Geissler to State, March 16, 1923, SD 814.00/729; "Llegará hoy a esta capital la oficialidad del Tacoma," *El Excelsior*, March 15, 1923.

57. López Larrave, *Breve historia*, 18–19. No account of any confrontation in March 1923 could be found in the newspapers, U.S. consular reports from Puerto Barrios, or the despatches from the Jefe Político of the department of Izabal. See *El Diario Nuevo*, March 17, 1923; and Guatemala, *Memoria de la Secretaría de Guerra, Año 1924*, 23, 49.

58. Taracena Arriola, "El primer Partido Comunista," 50. Taracena argues that it was the first military intervention, but a number of military confrontations occurred before this, the most notable one the attacks on the Jamaican workers in 1914.

59. López Larrave, *Breve historia*, 22–23; Gleijeses, *Shattered Hope*, 92.

60. Bush, *Organized Labor*, pt. 2:22 and pt. 3:2.

8

The Battle for Motagua, Part II

In late May 1929, Sam Zemurray went to Boston to negotiate a truce with his longtime rival, Victor Cutter. For the previous fifteen years the two men had been locked in personal and corporate combat, and now they were attempting to resolve hostilities that had benefited neither. It could not have been easy for Zemurray to make the trip, for he was not a man inclined to accept anything less than total victory. He was an innovative, flamboyant, hard-hitting businessman with a foul mouth and a hot temper who never shied away from confrontation. His flashy style had earned him the respect of many Hondurans, with whom he had spent most of his life. Cutter had lived eleven years in Central America and professed a love for the Caribbean, but his reserved mannerisms and conservative managerial style identified him as a New Englander. As a division manager he had demonstrated his courage and fighting skills, but he was much more comfortable managing United's vast empire from his office in Boston. He often referred to Zemurray as "that little fellow" from Honduras, though Zemurray probably stood as tall as Cutter. On several occasions, that little big man had taken on and defeated Cutter, affirming his reputation as the Banana Man. Cutter never understood nor appreciated the temperamental Zemurray, and the Banana Man despised him.[1]

Zemurray relished the rivalry with Cutter and United Fruit. When the two companies were competing for business worth millions of dollars, he said that he enjoyed "poking the giant's knees with his little shovel."[2] But the competition between the two firms reached crisis proportions after the truce between the two companies collapsed in 1924. As the two fruit companies drove Guatemala and Honduras to the brink of war, the State Department intervened to bring the battle for Motagua to a peaceful end. Knowing that Cutter and Zemurray could terminate the hostilities as easily as they had begun them, American diplomats encouraged Zemurray to negotiate his differences with Cutter. The origins, conduct, and conclusion of this banana war revealed the nature of politics and the structure of power in the banana lands of Central America. Decisions made in corporate boardrooms in New Orleans and Boston caused armies of poor young soldiers to defend the illusory sovereignty of both Guatemala and Honduras. The battle for Motagua was not much of a war, but it was the best battle two corporate rivals could arrange.

Despite the failure of diplomatic efforts to resolve the territorial conflict, Guatemala, Honduras, United, and Cuyamel respected the neutral zone from its creation in 1918 to late 1924. Guatemala and Honduras withdrew from the boundary conference in early 1921, but they still expressed a willingness to negotiate their differences while they respected the status quo. Zemurray deliberately avoided provocative actions in the neutral zone for five years, even to the extent of refusing to purchase bananas raised by squatters in the disputed territory. In the meantime he strengthened his company's position in Honduras by leasing the National Railroad under the controversial terms of the Antichresis contract of 1920. Six years earlier, Zemurray and Keith had competed for the rights to extend the line across Honduras, but because United and Cuyamel were observing a truce, the lease evidently did not trigger a resumption of hostilities.[3]

With the line under his control, Zemurray obtained a monopoly on the fruit cultivated by independent planters along the railroad and on the lands bordering the Ulua and Chamelecon rivers. He improved Puerto Cortés and made it Cuyamel's principal port; the company planted two thousand acres in sugarcane and applied the latest management techniques and technology to the entire enterprise. In 1924, Zemurray inaugurated the finest irrigation system in the tropics, despite the critics who said it could not be done. When he harvested five million bunches of the largest bananas ever seen, few people doubted that Zemurray was the most aggressive and innovative man in the banana business.[4]

Cuyamel was still only as large and productive as United Fruit's Tela division, but within its sphere of influence, it was impregnable. Irving B. Joselow, a Lithuanian American, learned of Zemurray's power when he tried to break into his territory in early 1922. Joselow arrived in Honduras with the objective of making arrangements for the purchase of bananas from independent planters along the National Railroad. He intended to ship these bananas to New York and market them through some dissatisfied United Fruit distributors. It was a plausible plan, with the exception that Zemurray had no reason to allow Joselow access to the railroad and port that he controlled.[5]

If Zemurray had allowed Joselow to export bananas to New York, he would have broken an informal agreement whereby the two companies eliminated competition in the American market. United and Cuyamel had an understanding that Cuyamel could operate in the Puerto Cortés district free of UFCO interference, provided that Cuyamel only shipped its fruit to

New Orleans and stayed out of United's Atlantic coast markets. To maintain their marketing agreement, officers of both companies informed the American consul that they had made arrangements so that Joselow would not get a single bunch of bananas out of the country. Against this combination, Joselow did not have a chance.[6]

Given the nature of the banana business, it was only a matter of time before the two companies came into conflict over banana lands in the Motagua River valley. With his plantations falling to disease, Zemurray would have to expand his plantings, and the only ways to go were north and westward toward the Guatemalan border and into United Fruit territory. In early 1923, Cuyamel began planting bananas on some lands in the neutral zone, invoking its rights under the 1912 Honduran concession that gave Zemurray the right to exploit lands between the Cuyamel River and the Guatemalan border. To the State Department, Cuyamel's activities were permitted under the terms of the status quo, but the Guatemalans never withdrew their demand that Cuyamel suspend all its work until the establishment of a permanent boundary. In April, Guatemalan authorities stopped Cuyamel because Zemurray did not have authorization from their government to plant. Through the American minister to Guatemala, Orellana expressed his inclination to approve Zemurray's request for a concession to cultivate bananas in the disputed territory, provided that Cuyamel pay an export tax.[7]

The battle for Motagua was never just about historical territorial claims; it was about control of the banana business. United Fruit, as the dominant force in the entire industry, determined the amount of competition it would tolerate. The unwritten golden rule of United's policy in Guatemala stated that it would never accept competition within Guatemalan territory, and United's demarcation of the nation included lands on the south or right bank of the Motagua River. By 1922 independent planters in that area had developed a productive capacity of about two hundred thousand stems per year, and all of this fruit was shipped out of the country by IRCA and UFCO. Abraham Curry, an independent who operated three motor launches and twelve barges on the Motagua, welcomed Zemurray into the region, for he wanted to ship his fruit out of the mouth of the Motagua River, thereby avoiding United's high transport costs through Puerto Barrios. Curry believed that Zemurray could obtain Guatemalan authorization to extend his business into the area by making the appropriate payments to the local authorities.[8]

Having been led to similar beliefs by Estrada Cabrera's agents, Zemurray received Guatemala's approaches with the appropriate skepticism, recognizing that the new president may have issued a sincere though indirect invitation for Cuyamel to invest in the country. In the three years since the removal of the dictator, Guatemalans had expressed substantial dissatisfaction with UFCO and IRCA, and nationalistic opposition compelled General

Orellana to maintain a discreet distance from the foreign monopolies. Hence, Zemurray may have sensed an opportunity to break the alliance between United and the Liberal establishment. In late 1923 he arranged a temporary deal whereby Cuyamel could operate in the disputed territory provided that it recognized and paid an export tax levied by the Guatemalan government on bananas shipped out of the area.[9]

There was evidently no firm alliance between Orellana and United Fruit. Each pursued its own interests and either one would have sacrificed the other for a higher goal, because neither ideology, nor nationalism, nor loyalty fueled the conflict as much as banana money. The country that received the disputed territory in any arbitral award would claim the rights to either tax or extort from the American banana companies. The U.S. minister to Honduras, Franklin E. Morales, recognized the conflict as a struggle over money: "The greater part of the boundary question appears to be, not the value of the land or the desire of either government to benefit its nationals by its final acquisition and development, but merely its control in case an American corporation should start operations and thus afford a source of easy money. It is a well-known and generally-admitted fact that native politicians would much rather make one dollar by graft than ten honestly with the same expenditure of time and effort."[10]

Zemurray knew that his company would save money if it paid taxes to one government instead of two. In January 1924, Zemurray approached the Guatemalan government through Joselow, who had joined him after he failed to break into Zemurray's sphere of influence in and around Puerto Cortés. Joselow agreed to lobby the Guatemalan government on behalf of Cuyamel on the condition that he and Zemurray would jointly operate whatever concession he acquired. He solicited the government's approval for Cuyamel's lease of a strip of land, one hundred meters wide, along both banks of the Motagua River, from the El Rico bridge to the Caribbean, sixty miles away. The proposal also included authorization to build a railroad linking the Cuyamel Railroad to the IRCA line in Guatemala. Joselow hoped that the proposal would not revive the border dispute since Zemurray would have two concessions for the same land.[11]

Not to be outdone, UFCO and IRCA sought Guatemala's approval to move into the same area, under virtually identical terms. Joaquin Hecht, a former superintendent of Puerto Barrios who allegedly earned a small fortune through smuggling, lobbied on behalf of United Fruit. Although he was not considered very scrupulous in his dealings, his method of operation was appropriate for the task at hand. Hecht asked for the lease of a strip of land one hundred meters wide along the lower Motagua River and for permission to construct a twelve-mile railroad branch from the Huron plantation to the Chachagualilla River in the neutral zone. At about the same time, IRCA requested—ostensibly to acquire more freight for its lines—

authorization for a thirty-five-mile branch from Morales, across the river to a point on the Rio Nuevo, where it would connect with the Cuyamel line.[12]

With each company seeking Guatemalan approval for its encroachment upon the territory of its rival, the corporate truce was evidently unravelling, but if Guatemala took sides in the competition, it would give a distinct advantage to one company and thereby increase the likelihood of a military confrontation between Guatemala and Honduras. To prevent a resumption of hostilities, Secretary of State Charles Evans Hughes ordered Geissler to express American hopes that neither Guatemala nor Honduras would grant a concession in the neutral zone. In late June, Geissler received Orellana's assurances that he would not approve either concession before a boundary settlement.[13]

Nevertheless, United's determination to incorporate the coveted banana lands into its domain and check, once and for all, Cuyamel's advance into the area, overrode any concerns about official American foreign policy. Hecht withdrew the company's request for rights to build a railroad into the territory, although he insisted that the territory was not a part of the neutral zone. Zemurray, while he needed the new lands as much as United, opposed a resumption of the corporate warfare. He asked the American minister in Tegucigalpa to go to Boston and negotiate an end to the rivalry between the two companies, but the State Department rejected the idea.[14]

United Fruit evidently had more influence over General Orellana than did the secretary of state. On November 7, Orellana approved a concession that gave UFCO the right to cultivate to a depth of one hundred meters both banks of the Motagua River from the Caribbean to the El Rico bridge. Before this contract, UFCO cultivated bananas along the north or left bank of the upper Motagua from Tenedores inland toward Los Amates (see Map 3). By the terms of the new lease, the independent planters who cultivated both banks of the lower Motagua, from Tenedores toward the sea, and others who cultivated lands in the upper Motagua, would lose title to their lands. These farmers, some of whom had been in business for forty-five years, protested the 1924 concession as an unconstitutional usurpation of their lands by the government. The government acted under the authority of an agrarian law that reserved the banks of all navigable rivers for the state, but the farmers claimed that the Motagua was not navigable.[15]

Their protests were in vain. For only $6,000 per year, UFCO acquired the right to cultivate thirty square kilometers of excellent banana land in the department of Izabal and the neutral zone. It accepted the first tax on banana exports, a paltry one cent per bunch, but Orellana exempted the company from all other state and municipal taxes. The contract authorized UFCO to develop and extend its plantations throughout the zone and build or acquire all phone, telegraph, and rail lines required for the operation of these plantations, with the understanding that any materials imported for these projects would be tax-exempt as well. The government gave United the right to build a port at any location on the Gulf of Amatique and allowed the company to engage in any activities designed to improve coastal shipping facilities. Finally, the concession gave UFCO the exclusive right to organize and administer its affairs. Through this contract, according to Alfonso Bauer Paiz, United Fruit "obtained the dominion of the Atlantic coast."[16]

By approving the contract, Orellana implicitly rejected the option of restoring competitive practices to the banana business. Cuyamel wanted to move into the area to cultivate its own bananas, build a railroad extension to the Motagua, and purchase bananas grown by independents along the river. If Orellana had wanted to stimulate agricultural production in the area, benefit Guatemalan planters, placate the United States, and avoid a resumption of hostilities with Honduras, he would have conceded the lease to Cuyamel. By giving the lease to United, which already controlled rail and transport facilities, he gave UFCO carte blanche to repulse the competitive threat coming from the neutral zone.

Cuyamel evidently lacked the political influence that United Fruit brought to bear on the negotiations with the Guatemalan government. Despite the popular animosity toward United Fruit that had caused political problems for Orellana on more than one occasion, the general rebuffed Cuyamel. One must suspect that a degree of graft was involved in the negotiations. Bauer Paiz, who served as minister of economy in the 1940s, suspected that United acquired the contract through some unscrupulous and deceptive lobbying. To Joselow, Zemurray's negotiator, Orellana's approval of United's proposal suggested that "the powers that be finally succumbed to the lure of the filthy lucor [*sic*] and betrayed their country."[17]

In any case, by approving United's proposal, Orellana effectively declared war on Cuyamel and Honduras, for the lease of disputed territory could only be received as a deliberate provocation. The secretary of state had asked Orellana not to approve either concession because to do so would carry an explicit claim to Guatemalan sovereignty on the right bank of the Motagua, the most hotly contested area in the disputed territory. Orellana evidently wanted to establish a Guatemalan presence in the territory and preempt the arbitral proceedings to which his government had committed at the Washington Conference of 1923; he wanted to strengthen his claim on the disputed territory before an arbitrator decided the issue for him.[18]

Even though the lease was not ratified until 1927, it sparked another round of war between Cuyamel, United, and the governments that supported them, for United Fruit quickly moved into the disputed territory as if it were fully authorized to do so. While Zemurray broke the spirit of the truce by planting in the neutral zone, he wanted to avoid another outbreak of hostilities with United. By acquiring the Motagua lease contract, United Fruit started the second battle for Motagua. The American consul at Puerto Cortés argued that "it is doubtful if the act of the United Fruit Company to petition, and of the Guatemalan Government to grant, this concession could stand without severe censure."[19]

The battle for Motagua resumed shortly after Orellana approved the concession. In early 1925, Zemurray began cultivating lands in the neutral zone through nominally independent planters and claimed his right to do so under a Honduran concession that antedated United's Guatemalan concession by twelve years. Twelve Cuyamel affiliates, whose plantations around Omoa and Cuyamel had been lost to disease, planted the right side of the Cuyamel Railroad between Jimerito and Cacao and were clearing lands toward Sinchado. Zemurray assisted the squatters with loans aggregating $4,500. While Cuyamel had an established policy of loaning money to independent planters, the company had never assisted planters in disputed territory.[20]

Although company officials never admitted it, United Fruit provided financial assistance to its own independents in the neutral zone. Between January and September of 1925, planters loyal to United planted a thirty-mile stretch of land along the right bank of the Motagua and also cleared land around Sinchado to block Cuyamel from gaining access to the river. United denied providing any assistance to these planters, but their sudden movement into the heart of the disputed territory suggests that United financed and organized them. The American consul, Ray Fox, concluded that "no such influx of planters into this particular area within so identical a period of time would have been accomplished voluntarily."[21]

Hence, the need for new banana lands brought both companies into the neutral zone, and another round of military confrontations ensued. Competition went beyond standard business practices when United brought in military forces that Cuyamel could not match. In October 1925, 120 Guatemalan soldiers crossed the Motagua in United Fruit launches and established a base camp at Sinchado. From that point the troops could defend both Guatemala's claim to the disputed territory and United's assumed right to cultivate there. The troops intimidated Cuyamel's planters, prohibited them from clearing any new lands without their promise to sell their fruit to UFCO, and arrested some of the squatters who resisted.[22]

The main objective in this banana war was not the lands on the right bank but the river itself. United Fruit wanted to cultivate in the neutral zone and maintain its monopoly on the fruit grown by independents along the Motagua River. To do that it was imperative to prevent Cuyamel from establishing a railhead on the Motagua River. If the Cuyamel Railroad were extended to the river, it would be able to divert banana traffic away from Puerto Barrios and ship the fruit out over the Cuyamel line to Puerto Cortés in Honduras. Both United and the Guatemalan government, which had recently imposed a one-cent tax on banana exports, wanted to prevent Cuyamel from diverting any share of its commerce to a Honduran port. Guatemalan troops prevented Cuyamel from extending the railroad to the

river in 1917, and the defense of the river remained the main priority of
United and Guatemala. If Zemurray resumed work on the line, UFCO
would defend its domain with all the resources at its command, but Cuyamel
did not renew work on the railroad in 1925, despite United's claims that it
had. Zemurray confined his activity in the neutral zone to financing independent planters.[23]

Unlike United, Orellana was willing to consider an extension of the
Cuyamel Railroad to the Motagua. In late October his foreign minister,
Roberto Lowenthal, encouraged Zemurray to reapply for a concession
because Orellana was prepared to award Cuyamel a contract to extend the
line to the river.[24] Having been deceived by the Guatemalans before, Zemurray
suspected a trap and did not pursue contract negotiations. Recognizing that
the most convenient way to settle the controversy, or at least contain the
conflict, was through a secret agreement with United, Zemurray negotiated
terms of a truce with his adversary sometime after Guatemalan soldiers had
begun harassing his planters in the neutral zone. While the terms of this
secret agreement have not been divulged, they probably included a promise
by Zemurray not to extend the Cuyamel Railroad, and they reduced tensions
between the two companies in late 1925.[25]

The hot-tempered Zemurray could not long sustain a truce with a
company managed by a man he distrusted. The truce unraveled in 1926
when he asked the Honduran government for authorization to build a bridge
across the Tela Railroad into UFCO territory. United Fruit officials publicly
denounced the proposed concession as a violation of their concessionary
rights while they privately assured Zemurray that they would not actually
lobby against the concession in order to maintain the truce.[26]

When the Honduran legislature rejected the contract in April 1926, an
infuriated Zemurray attributed his defeat to United Fruit's political manipulations. If UFCO had contributed to the rejection of the concession, it would
have been a betrayal of the corporate truce and a deliberate breach of faith,
but the Hondurans rejected it because of Zemurray's numerous violations
and abuses of his concessionary rights. He had come under heavy criticism
for the so-called clandestine railroad branches, small feeder lines that the
company had built without previous government authorization. To settle the
controversy over these lines, Zemurray included provisions in his contract
for the cancellation of the government's $1.5-million debt to the National
Railway, but a majority of congressmen viewed the concession as an insult
to national honor, and they repudiated it.[27]

Zemurray, personally offended by Victor Cutter and United Fruit,
subsequently resumed the offensive against UFCO in the neutral zone and
throughout Central America. He would no longer be content with the
acquisition of lands in the disputed territory or the extension of his railroad
into UFCO territory. Zemurray now aimed at a greater share of the banana
business, and, to this end, he forged alliances with other companies that

could wage war on several fronts simultaneously. In April 1926 he and the Vaccaro Brothers created the Banana Distributing Company of Delaware to improve their marketing system in the United States. He also tried to extend his plantings and contracts with independent operators throughout the banana-producing regions. In Colombia, Costa Rica, and Jamaica, Cuyamel collaborated with the Atlantic Fruit and Sugar Company; in Mexico, it worked with the Standard Fruit and Steamship Company (formerly the Vaccaro Brothers); in Guatemala and Honduras, it engaged UFCO's formidable armies by itself. Through these alliances, Zemurray hoped to divert some of United's independent banana business into Cuyamel's marketing network and increase his share of the American market [28]

As the banana companies instigated heated political debates throughout the region, they nearly dragged Hondurans and Guatemalans into a war for their rights to exploit the Motagua River valley. Company lobbyists, politicians, and reporters portrayed the border conflict as a matter of national honor, with Cuyamel urging Honduras to defend its sovereignty by force of arms if necessary, and United rallying Guatemalan nationalists, despite its official protestations of neutrality.[29] Since Zemurray's claim to the neutral zone rested on a Honduran concession, the only means by which United could defend its claim to the area was through a Guatemalan concession, and it was the lease of the Motagua riverbanks from Guatemala that triggered another military confrontation in 1927. Notwithstanding appeals from the United States and Honduras, United Fruit refused to relinquish its rights under the 1924 concession because a renunciation of the contract might be construed as a departure from its policy of strict neutrality in the border dispute.[30]

For all practical purposes, United Fruit allied with the generals who governed Guatemala, knowing that it would need military assistance to repulse a move by Cuyamel into the area. A concession carried only a claim to lands; it would take an army to enforce that claim to disputed territory. Without a Guatemalan army behind it, United would have to engage Cuyamel solely in the economic and political arenas. On these levels, Zemurray could compete admirably, but since he could not count on Honduran military support, the balance of power favored United Fruit. In September 1926, just months after the truce between Cuyamel and United Fruit had broken down, Guatemalan troops took virtual control of the neutral zone, arrested some Cuyamel affiliates, and allegedly warned all planters that fruit grown in the area had to be exported through Puerto Barrios because they were operating on Guatemalan soil.[31]

By the mid-1920s, United had built a network of political alliances strong enough to bring military forces to its defense in the neutral zone. Many Guatemalans shared United's interest in incorporating the disputed territory, but few of them recognized the private interests that influenced their government's policy toward the border conflict and the banana rivalry that triggered it. In 1927, Chacón demanded and received a substantial kickback for agreeing to retire IRCA's $2.5-million debt.[32] United Fruit preferred more discreet and less expensive means of buying political influence, such as placing prominent politicians and government officials on the company payroll as lawyers, including Dr. José Matos and Carlos Salazar, both of whom served as United Fruit attorneys and later occupied the post of minister of foreign relations. United retained Matos's legal services in 1924, and Chacón appointed him minister of foreign relations in November 1926. Matos continued to receive his $200-per-month UFCO salary for several months after his appointment and relinquished it only after Arthur Geissler raised the question of ethics with George Bennett, United's manager. While Bennett agreed that the relationship compromised Matos and removed him from the payroll, he maintained the company's contacts by hiring the foreign minister's brother as his replacement.[33]

Without influential friends in high places, United could not have overcome the political opposition to its activities that occasionally surfaced in the legislature. Before May 2, 1927, the date on which the Guatemalan legislature approved an amended version of the 1924 contract, none of United Fruit's activities in the neutral zone was sanctioned by Guatemalan law. Hence, Orellana had no constitutional authority to dispatch troops into the area to enforce United's titles. If he had requested legislative approval for the contract, the representatives may have rejected it, for they were showing a surprising amount of resistance to presidential authority and foreign capital. In the spring of 1927 a coalition of Recinistas (supporters of Adrian Recinos) and Ubiquistas (supporters of Jorge Ubico) in the legislature rejected several foreign contracts that Chacón favored.[34]

Yet when the Motagua concession came up for debate, United already had de facto possession of both banks of the river. The legislators could either legalize an existing reality or offend nationalistic sentiments by rejecting the contract and thereby weakening Guatemalan claims to the disputed territory. With the Guatemalans eager to strengthen their territorial claims, the legislators approved another liberal concession to United Fruit. The legislators exacted some minor amendments to the original proposal, the most significant one an increase in the annual rental fee from $6,000 per year to $14,000, but popular interest in incorporating the new lands superseded the representatives' concerns about contract terms, and they approved the concession on May 2.[35]

By acquiring the concession, United Fruit gained a distinct advantage over Cuyamel on the battlefield, for having endorsed United's move into the disputed territory, the legislature could be expected to support any military measures required to defend Guatemalan sovereignty. Zemurray recognized that the action of the Guatemalan legislature required a bold and risky counterattack. Just a few weeks after the contract's ratification, he resumed work on the railroad extension that had been suspended for thirteen years in the interests of maintaining peace in the border zone. Construction crews now aimed at completing a tramline from the Quimistan plantation to a point near the confluence of the Motagua and the Chachagualilla rivers. If Cuyamel established a railhead there, it would compete directly with United Fruit's railhead at Esquimo, on the opposite bank of the river, from which United loaded its bananas on IRCA cars for shipment out of Puerto Barrios.[36]

Zemurray's drive toward the river brought the battle for Motagua to a climax, for United's high command could not accept a competitive railhead on the river. Despite periodic disturbances, the rival banana powers had recognized an uneasy truce in which their plantations could coexist in the disputed territory, as long as Cuyamel stayed off of the river. Zemurray's projected tramline upset the status quo because it would allow him to divert tens of thousands of bananas away from United. Independents had moved onto the right bank with the assistance of United Fruit, but if Zemurray's tramline reached the river, he might lure them away from United because Cuyamel always paid fifty cents per stem from independent planters while United paid only thirty-five cents. Once Cuyamel had established a railhead on the Motagua, United would either have to raise its price fifteen cents or lose the business of the independent planters.[37]

In defense of their respective banana companies, Guatemalan and Honduran forces mobilized. In late May the Hondurans established or reinforced a garrison at Chachagualilla, a move that the Guatemalans protested as a violation of the neutral zone. The Hondurans argued that Guatemala had violated the status quo first when it ratified the UFCO contract; hence, they prepared to defend their claims to the disputed territory. To prevent hostilities and to stall a Honduran plan to submit the conflict to American arbitration, Chacón dispatched Virgilio Rodríguez Beteta as a minister plenipotentiary to Honduras with instructions to negotiate an immediate Honduran withdrawal from the Chachagualilla garrison.[38]

While diplomats talked, the banana men fought for position in the border zone and ultimately decided the fate of the disputed territory. Through nominally independent planters, United Fruit gained control of the entire right bank of the Motagua. Honduran officials investigated the region in August and discovered at least thirteen plantations in full production on the right bank, all of them Guatemalan. Having witnessed bananas being loaded on launches all along the river for shipment to Puerto Barrios, where the planters paid their export taxes, the inspectors concluded that "under present conditions the river is considered as Guatemalan and all the laborers who live on the fincas have Guatemalan employers and are under the Guatemalan authorities."[39] Subsequent investigations by the American consul at Puerto Cortés validated the Honduran survey of the disputed area. While it was true that the only direct UFCO planting was at the La Tienda farm near Esquimo on the left bank, independent planters tied financially to it cultivated the whole right bank. Cuyamel established its own plantation at Chachagualilla and financed independent farmers as well, but the planters tied to it cultivated the lands around Jimerito and Cacao, while UFCO or planters affiliated with it controlled both riverbanks.[40]

Hence, United had effective possession of the right bank when Zemurray attempted to break through the lines and establish a railhead on the Motagua. On February 10, 1928, after Zemurray's railroad crews had laid about three hundred yards of track toward the Motagua River, the Guatemalans protested the action as a violation of the status quo agreements and warned that they were prepared to use whatever means were necessary to defend their national interests. On February 13, fifty Guatemalan soldiers invaded Chachagualilla, captured the Honduran commander of its garrison, and prohibited further work on the line. Instead of protesting the attack on a Honduran outpost, President Miguel Paz Barahona called in a senior official of Cuyamel and ordered him to suspend work on the railroad because the company lacked authorization to build any lines in the region.[41] At that moment, the Banana Man lost the battle for Motagua.

Nevertheless, Guatemala and Honduras were on the brink of a potentially disastrous banana war that the United States hoped to prevent. American diplomatic pressure compelled both countries to accept bilateral negotiations mediated by the U.S. minister to Costa Rica, Roy T. Davis. Delegations from both countries met at Cuyamel, Honduras, from April 14 to April 23, hoping to fix a provisional boundary, but the conference yielded only a call to submit the border dispute to binding arbitration. Carlos Salazar, the head of the Guatemalan delegation to the Cuyamel conference, viewed this outcome as a success for his country because he felt that a settlement at that time would have given the right bank of the Motagua (and the UFCO plantations within it) to Honduras.[42]

Although the Cuyamel conference failed to establish a permanent boundary, it at least restored a temporary truce, for Honduran and Guatemalan troops were withdrawn from the area. Since President Paz was not willing to provide Cuyamel with military support, Zemurray's last hope of winning the battle against United was to install a president willing to fight his battles. With elections scheduled for 1928, Zemurray recognized an opportunity to return power to the Liberal party, which traditionally exchanged political favors for Cuyamel's financial support. United promoted its interests through the National party led by the charismatic caudillo Tiburcio Carías Andino. In the presidential elections of 1923, Carías had received a plurality of votes, but after the Liberal congress denied him the election, he launched an armed rebellion. Through the intervention and mediation of the United States, Carías laid down his arms and accepted Paz as a compromise candidate.[43]

During the Paz administration, Zemurray's substantial efforts to buy influence in the legislative and executive branches failed. United and Cuyamel installed expensive lobbies in Tegucigalpa to promote their interests by providing expensive entertainment and sordid services to influential politicians and, according to the American minister to Honduras, George Thomas Summerlin, they accepted bribery as a necessary corollary to the banana business.[44] Notwithstanding the temptations of the banana lobbyists, Cuyamel scored few points with the government. In October 1927 the legislature, in which supporters of UFCO and Carías had gained considerable influence, rejected a railroad concession that Cuyamel had been seeking for several years. Many of them were still upset about the so-called clandestine branches that Cuyamel had built without government authorization. Zemurray consequently withdrew his expensive lobby because it had cost him a tremendous amount of money yet produced little value in return.[45]

Zemurray subsequently turned to a strategy that had served him much better earlier in his career: revolution. In the 1928 elections, the Liberals nominated Vicente Mejía Colindres to contest General Carías, and whatever the outcome, both parties would have to be prepared for the normal postelection military confrontation. Realizing that a Carías victory would seal his fate in the Motagua region, Zemurray began smuggling in arms for his supporters in the Liberal party. Compelling evidence of arms shipments through Puerto Cortés led the State Department to institute a rigid surveillance of all Cuyamel ships leaving New York or New Orleans. As a result, New Orleans port authorities confiscated a $50,000 shipment of rifles, automatic shotguns, tear gas, and ammunition destined for Honduras in early May 1928. Although the subsequent prosecution did not establish Cuyamel's complicity in the operation, the smuggler was defended in court by Joseph Montgomery, a former New Orleans district attorney and Zemurray's right-hand man.[46]

Even without the weapons, the Liberal candidate won the presidency, and United Fruit's general respected the outcome, despite pleas from his supporters to launch another rebellion. Nevertheless, it was not a total victory for Cuyamel because Carías remained the president of a congress dominated by the National party.[47] With the government divided between the two parties, Zemurray would not be able to enlist Honduran support in his efforts to reverse the gains already made by United Fruit in the disputed area.

Zemurray had no choice but to sue for peace. For several months after the election, Cuyamel lobbyists and its allies continued to fight United in the newspapers and banana fields throughout Central America. The fray became particularly vicious in Costa Rica, where Cuyamel's anti-United Fruit propaganda fanned enough anti-American sentiments that the State Department felt compelled to terminate the banana war between the two American companies. Believing that the competition between United and Cuyamel had impaired American interests, Assistant Secretary of State Francis White brought the two parties to the negotiating table in April 1929.

American diplomatic and consular officials had believed for some time that a resolution of the differences between the two companies would facilitate a boundary settlement, or at least reduce the likelihood of war. In 1928, Ray Fox, the consul at Puerto Cortés, argued that the dispute could be settled "somewhere between New Orleans [headquarters of Cuyamel] and Boston." White agreed that direct negotiations between Cuyamel and United Fruit offered the most prudent means of settling the boundary dispute and other regional problems.[48]

In White's meetings with representatives of both companies he discovered a willingness to make peace. While each still blamed the other for instigating the conflict, both recognized that the rivalry had gone beyond acceptable boundaries and that neither party would benefit by the continuance of hostilities. To resolve the conflict, Montgomery suggested that he and a United Fruit representative negotiate the terms of a truce that would then be ratified by Zemurray and Bradley Palmer, who was United Fruit's chairman of the board. Although Victor Cutter was president of United Fruit, Montgomery wanted any arrangement approved personally by Palmer, the real power in Boston and a man whom Zemurray respected and trusted.[49]

The State Department urged the rivals to take advantage of the friendly relations that existed between Zemurray and Palmer to bring about a quick settlement of a conflict that benefited neither public nor private U.S. interests.[50] The State Department's mediation ultimately produced much more than the diplomats originally expected. To negotiate a cease-fire to the banana war, Zemurray traveled to Boston in May 1929. Given Zemurray's deep bitterness toward Cutter, it could not have been easy for him to acknowledge, in surprising detail, some of the wrongs committed by him or in his name, and offer his hand in peace. Cutter apparently did not offer a reciprocal confession. Instead, he asked Zemurray why he had not come to United Fruit before he launched the war. If he had just spoken with him, he would have been assured that United had not lobbied against the railroad concession Zemurray had solicited from the Honduran government in 1926. Zemurray admitted that he "saw red" after the Hondurans rejected the contract and that he then took the offensive against United Fruit.[51]

Cutter agreed that it was time to make peace, and the two men reached a preliminary truce wherein they agreed to an immediate cessation of hostilities and promised not to resume hostilities without a face-to-face meeting at which they would try to resolve the situation amicably. According to United Fruit Vice President George P. Chittenden, the two men also concluded a marketing agreement that would encourage Zemurray to "play the game" with UFCO. Since for some time Cuyamel's productive capacity had exceeded that of its marketing network, the company was dumping off lower-priced bananas just to break even, and as a result it had destabilized the banana market. In an effort to restore order to the market, Zemurray and Cutter arranged a deal whereby United would market some of Cuyamel's bananas. Chittenden confidentially admitted to Assistant Secretary White that a merger of the companies would be the most effective means of establishing a permanent peace between the two rivals. White explained: "He [Chittenden] said that of course, speaking frankly, a merger between the two Companies would be the ideal thing but that might run afoul of the Sherman Act and hence they had made a marketing arrangement within the terms of that law which would be beneficial to both." Chittenden still worried that Zemurray would respect the peace only as long as it was profitable for him to do so.[52]

On November 15, 1929, United Fruit and Cuyamel arranged the merger that Chittenden once viewed as a probable violation of federal antitrust laws. United purchased the goodwill, lands, assets, and properties of Cuyamel and its subsidiary, the Cortés Development Company, for three hundred thousand shares of United Fruit stock.[53] At the time, Cuyamel operated thirteen steamships, managed the most productive banana plantations in Central America, and accounted for 12.7 percent of the U.S. market, a distant second to United's 52.6 percent. With Cuyamel's assets added to its own, United Fruit's share of the banana market rose to 60 percent in 1930 and remained between 60 and 70 percent for the next twenty years. Since the agreement had as its primary purpose the cessation of competition between the two companies, UFCO solicited the legal opinions of three law firms. One of them concluded that it was a close call as to whether the agreement violated the Sherman Act because at the time of the consolidation, the two firms accounted for 65 percent of banana sales. Knowing this, United's board of directors still authorized the incorporation of Cuyamel's assets on December 20, 1929.[54]

Legend has it that Bradley Palmer talked Zemurray into accepting this deal over twelve bottles of ale in a British pub. It could not have been too difficult to convince an inebriated Zemurray to accept three hundred thousand shares of United Fruit stock valued at $32 million, but he also had to promise that he would never again compete with United Fruit. As the largest individual stockholder in United Fruit, the Banana Man would not likely cut his own throat by renewing the war at some later date. Zemurray lost the battle, won the peace, and retired to his estate near New Orleans, hoping to spend some time with his family.[55]

The defeat of Cuyamel in the battle for Motagua confirmed the hegemony of United Fruit on Guatemala's Caribbean coast. Zemurray's bid to develop plantations and build railroads in the area once offered some hope that competitive conditions would be restored to the banana business, but the Guatemalan government evidently preferred monopoly over free trade. In the absence of Cuyamel, independent Guatemalan planters were forced to accept whatever contract terms United offered. According to these planters, United always reserved the exclusive right to rescind its contracts when it was necessary and convenient to the company. In the summer of 1929, with

Cuyamel in full retreat, the planters pressed their cases in court, alleging that the unilateral character of the contracts violated Guatemalan law.[56]

Even these planters knew that it would take more than a court decision to reduce the power that United had obtained in the coastal districts. Besides controlling the port and railroad facilities on which the banana business depended, UFCO exercised administrative autonomy in all of its enterprises, and many of the government officials were actually subordinate to it, not the government in Guatemala City. When the planters appealed to the local authorities for assistance for the Liga de Defensa de Pequeños Agricultores, an organization formed to fight the arbitrary practices of UFCO, they found no support. The planters charged that in the department of Izabal, United was the government and the local authorities were only lambs that served it.[57]

The conditions of the banana planters in particular, and the state of the economy in general, could have been improved considerably had the government granted the lease of the Motagua riverbanks to Cuyamel instead of to United Fruit. There were obviously alternatives to the monopoly that UFCO had acquired, but two Guatemalan caudillos opted to reinforce rather than weaken it. As for the border dispute, it simmered for several years longer, tightly capped by diplomatic activity in Washington. The Guatemalans and Hondurans eventually settled the boundary dispute by submitting it to the arbitration of a tribunal chaired by Charles Evans Hughes, chief justice of the United States. A quick look at a map of present-day Guatemala shows that Guatemala received the area between the right bank of the Motagua River and the Merendon range in what was once part of Honduras. The acquisition of this territory is due, in no small part, to United Fruit's triumph over Sam Zemurray in the battle for Motagua.[58]

Notes

1. Pringle, "A Jonah Who Swallowed the Whale," 114; Wilson, *Empire in Green and Gold*, 206–11, 220–25, 260–65; McCann, *An American Company*, 20–24. Although Wilson downplays the hostilities between the two men, Joseph W. Montgomery, Zemurray's legal representative, confirmed the personal hostilities to the State Department. See memorandum of conversation, Francis White (assistant secretary) and Montgomery, April 8, 1929, SD 815.6156/34 1/2.

2. Pringle, "A Jonah Who Swallowed the Whale," 91.

3. Ireland, *Boundaries*, 90; George P. Share (vice consul, Puerto Cortés) to State, September 7, 1923, SD 714.1515/394; John Brady (consul, Puerto Cortes) to State, February 21, 1919, SD 815.602C99; Kepner and Soothill, *Banana Empire*, 123.

4. Albert H. Gerberich (vice consul, Puerto Cortés) to State, February 3, 1922, SD 815.6156J77/2; Wilson, *Empire in Green and Gold*, 222–25.

5. Gerberich to State, February 3, 1922, SD 815.6156J77/2.

6. Gerberich to State, March 4, 1922, SD 815.6156/16.

7. Arthur Geissler (American minister) to State, April 23, 1923, SD 714.1515/380.

8. Share to State, September 7, 1923, SD 714.1515/394.

9. Franklin E. Morales to State, December 11, 1923, SD 714.1515/397.

10. Ibid.

11. Gerberich to State, February 3, 1922, SD 815.6156J77/2; Geissler to State, February 6, 1924, SD 714.1515/400; Geissler to State, January 29, 1924, SD 714.1515/399; Geissler to State, May 15, 1924, SD 714.1515/404; Irving B. Joselow to Geissler, April 25, 1924, Diplomatic post records, Guatemala City, 1924, vol. 5, 860/C&UFC.

12. A. Clark Kerr, memorandum, January 26, 1927, in Bourne and Watt, eds., *British Documents on Foreign Affairs, Latin America, 1914–1939*, 314; Geissler to State, June 2, 1924, SD 814.602/Un3; Aylward to Ministro de Fomento, July 31, 1924, AGCA, B129, legajo 22192, expediente 3667.

13. Charles Evans Hughes to American legation, June 26, 1924, SD 814.602Un3/1; Geissler to State, June 27, 1924, Diplomatic post records, 1924, vol. 5, 860/C&UFCo.

14. Geissler to State, July 15, 1924, Diplomatic post records, 1924, vol. 5, 860/C&UFCo; "Activities of Cuyamel," November 22, 1928, SD 815.6156/26.

15. Oscar De León Aragón, *Los contratos de la United Fruit Company y las compañías muelleras en Guatemala* (Guatemala: Ministerio de Educación Pública, 1950), 45, 74.

16. Bauer Paiz, *Como opera el capital yanqui*, 213.

17. Ibid; Joselow to Geissler, December 1, 1924, Diplomatic post records, 1924, vol. 2, 715.

18. McFadden to White, October 23, 1925, 714.1515/475.

19. Ray Fox to State, March 6, 1928, SD 714.1515/589.

20. Ibid., October 26, 1925, SD 714.1515/444.

21. Ibid.

22. Leon H. Ellis (chargé d'affaires ad interim, Guatemala) to State, October 8, 1925, SD 714.1515/424; Fox to State, October 21, 1925, SD 714.1515/428.

23. Lawrence Dennis (chargé d'affaires ad interim, Honduras) to State, October 24, 1925, enclosure 2, Pemberton (Cuyamel officer) to Ministerio de Relaciones Exteriores (Honduras), October 19, 1925, SD 714.1515/445; Fox to State, October 21, 1925, SD 714.1515/428.

24. Ellis to State, October 31, 1925, SD 714.1515/448.

25. Memorandum of conversation, White and Joseph Montgomery, April 8, 1929, SD 815.6156/34 1/2; memorandum of conversation, White and George P. Chittenden (vice president, UFCO), June 4, 1929, SD 815.6156/36 1/2.

26. Memorandum of conversation, White and Chittenden, June 4, 1929, SD 815.6156/36 1/2.

27. George T. Summerlin (minister to Honduras) to State, April 14, 1926, SD 815.77/329.

28. Karnes, *Tropical Enterprise*, 177; Geissler to State, February 22, 1928, SD 714.1515/568.

29. Kepner and Soothill, *Banana Empire*, 117–121; Krehm, *Democracies and Tyrannies*, 83–84; Virgilio Rodríguez Beteta, *No es guerra de hermanos sino de bananos; como evite la guerra en Centroamérica en 1928* (Guatemala: Universidad de San Carlos de Guatemala, 1969), 31.

30. Lansing and Woolsey to State, October 5, 1927, SD 714.1515/536; Rodríguez Beteta, *No es guerra de hermanos*, 115–21, 141–48.

31. Montgomery (Cuyamel) to State, September 22, 1926, SD 714.1515/468; Ellis to State, October 20, 1925, SD 714.1515/474.

32. Geissler to State, December 27, 1929, SD 814.51/647; Pitti, "Ubico and Guatemalan Politics," 359; Henry B. Price (vice president, IRCA) to State, November 7, 1927, SD 814.51/606.

33. Memorandum by Geissler, January 11, 1927, Diplomatic post records, 1927, vol. 8, 861.5United Fruit Company; González Dávison, *El régimen liberal*, 53. On Salazar's ties to United see Fay Allen Des Portes, memorandum of telephone conversation, February 4, 1938, SD 814.773/34.

34. Pitti, "Ubico and Guatemalan Politics," 268.

35. De León Aragón, *Los contratos de la United Fruit Company*, 79.

36. Geissler to State, May 20, 1927, SD 714.1515/506; Fox to State, October 26, 1925, SD 714.1515/444.

37. Fox to State, March 6, 1928, SD 714.1515/589; Geissler to State, May 20, 1927, enclosure no. 3, memorandum submitted by George S. Bennett (manager, UFCO), May 19, 1927, SD 714.1515/506.

38. Rodríguez Beteta, *No es guerra de hermanos*, 11, 115–21, 141–48; Summerlin to State, August 7, 1927, SD 714.1515/522.

39. Summerlin to State, September 7, 1927, enclosure, copy and translation of report from Indalecio Ferrera and Samuel García to Señor Comandante de Armas, Puerto Cortés, August 25, 1927, SD 714.1515/534.

40. Fox to State, March 6, 1928, SD 714.1515/589.

41. Summerlin to State, February 13, 1928, *FRUS, 1928* 1:712–13.

42. Ireland, *Boundaries, Possessions, and Conflicts*, 90; Salazar, *Memoria de los servicios prestados*, 92.

43. James Dunkerley, *Power in the Isthmus: A Political History of Modern Central America* (London: Verso, 1988), 67–68; James A. Morris, *Honduras: Caudillo Politics and Military Rulers* (Boulder: Westview Press, 1984), 9.

44. Summerlin to State, October 4, 1927, SD 815.615/7; "Activities of Cuyamel," November 22, 1928, SD 815.6156/26.

45. "Activities of Cuyamel," November 22, 1928, SD 815.6156/26.

46. "Central American Cache Found in House Downtown," *New Orleans Times Picayune*, May 4, 1928; Summerlin to State, May 21, 1928, SD 815.113/293.

47. Mario Posas and Rafael del Cid, *La construcción del sector público y del estado nacional de Honduras, 1876–1979* (San José: Editorial Universitaria Centroamericana, 1981), 63; Morris, *Honduras*, 8.

48. Memorandum of conversation, White and Montgomery, April 8, 1929, SD 815.6156/34 1/2; Fox to State, SD 714.1515/589.

49. Memorandum of conversation, White and Montgomery, April 8, 1929, SD 815.6156/34 1/2.

50. Memorandum of conversation, Judge William K. Jackson (UFCO), Lester H. Woolsey, and Dana G. Munro, April 16, 1929, SD 815.6156/33 1/2.

51. Memorandum of conversation, White and Chittenden, June 4, 1929, SD 815.6156/36 1/2.

52. Ibid.

53. "Memorandum of Agreement between Cuyamel Fruit Company and United Fruit Company," DOJ, File 60-166-56, Series 347.

54. Milton A. Kallis to Victor H. Kramer and W. Perry Epes, December 20, 1952, DOJ, File 60-166-6.

55. "United Fruit," *Fortune*, 26–28; Kepner and Soothill, *Banana Empire*, 133.

56. "Nuevos y terribles aspectos que encierran los contratos de la empresa frutera en el norte de la República natal," *Renovación Obrera* [Guatemala City], June 30, 1929.

57. "Los efectivos resultados de nuestra campaña en favor de los pequeños agricultores de la zona norte de Guatemala contra la acción explotadora de la United Fruit Co.," ibid., August 7, 1922; "La frutera suborna a los moradores de una población, en su bien," ibid., August 27, 1929.

58. Ireland, *Boundaries, Possessions, and Conflicts*, 92–93.

9

Expansion to the Pacific

In April 1927, Victor Cutter tried to explain to the scholars at the American Academy of Political and Social Science in Philadelphia that the era in which U.S. capitalists had exploited the tropics had been replaced by an epoch of general industrial and commercial development. As he spoke, United Fruit's exploitation of a legitimate border dispute had Guatemala and Honduras on the brink of war, but he attempted to put the best possible face on the company's operations. He boldly asserted that "all past troubles involving diplomacy have been caused by small, irresponsible companies and individuals, and by unjust concessions, sometimes improperly obtained; or by entrance of foreigners into countries where governments were unstable and revolutions frequent. Fortunately, these conditions do not exist today."[1]

The speech may have played well in the scholarly halls of Philadelphia, but the banana republics remained the same volatile places where entrepreneurs, such as Keith and Zemurray, managed private fiefdoms and paid few, if any, taxes to the host government. Presidents still demanded cuts of the banana business, laborers struck for higher wages, and occasionally Boston overlooked some of the seamier sides of the business, as it did when General Lázaro Chacón demanded a kickback from IRCA in 1927. United Fruit's triumph over Cuyamel in the battle for Motagua showed how little the company actually played by the rules and how far removed Cutter was from the reality of the tropics.[2] The banana business was still a dirty game that often rewarded foul players with large profits.

United Fruit did not create the rules of the game, but it played by them for forty-five years. While it acquired and defended its concessions by collaborating with corrupt and authoritarian governments, by the late 1920s it had already established the means by which it could eliminate competition without resorting to some of the ignoble tactics characteristic of its early days in Guatemala. United's control of the infrastructure made it a political and economic force that neither the government nor local businesses could ignore. United enjoyed the support of key political figures, managed its enterprises without government interference, controlled rates and services on the country's railroads and ports, and had virtually unlimited financial backing from Boston and political support in Washington. As Zemurray discovered, there was little room for competition within Guatemala.

United was powerful enough to fight a two-front war simultaneously, for while it engaged Zemurray on the Caribbean it also confronted European competitors on the Pacific. In the early 1920s, European capitalists purchased over four hundred thousand acres, acquired a concession to build rail and port facilities in the area, and made plans to market their fruit in California. In 1928, to eliminate this threat, United formed a wholly owned subsidiary, the Compañía Agrícola de Guatemala (CAG), and negotiated with the government for the rights to develop its own plantation network on the Pacific coast. Corporate objectives conflicted with the interests of nationalistic Guatemalans who wanted to break United's monopoly, by either supporting United's European competition or developing their own plantations on the Pacific coast. Despite its formidable power, UFCO still required the assistance of another general on a white horse, Jorge Ubico, because only a dictator could reverse the democratic gains of the 1920s and repress opposition to or competition with United Fruit's empire.

Although the fertile plains between the Pacific coast and the mountains can sustain a wide variety of crops, a series of problems impaired the development of large-scale export agriculture. To compensate for sporadic but occasionally heavy rainfall, farms required expensive irrigation and drainage facilities. As the region was underpopulated, companies would have to attract a work force, and by the 1920s, Jamaican labor was no longer available in sufficient numbers because the government opposed black immigration. Infrastructure was inadequate or poorly maintained. Planters faced either a long haul overland to Puerto Barrios for marketing in the traditional Atlantic and Gulf Coast ports or a precarious journey over one of the piers jutting out into the Pacific Ocean to a California market that was not then as attractive as it is now. The development of plantations along Guatemala's Pacific coast, requiring heavy investment in infrastructural development, was not a high priority for the conservative Victor Cutter.[3]

For nearly ten years he even tolerated the presence of two strong competitors on the Pacific coast. In 1918 the Klein-Simpson Fruit Company, a wholesale fruit distributor from Los Angeles, purchased 5,500 acres near port San José and planted 2,000 acres in bananas. On October 14, 1921, Klein-Simpson reorganized as the California-Guatemala Fruit Corporation, although its first banana shipments to California could have commenced a year earlier. In the spring of 1922 heavy rains wiped out nearly one half of the banana crop, but the company persisted under United's watchful eyes. In March 1923 the company successfully marketed a load of bananas in

California, proving that the fruit would not ripen before it completed the nine-day journey.[4]

Sometime that year the Mexican-American Fruit and Steamship Corporation, a joint venture of Atlantic Fruit and the Vaccaro Brothers, acquired the California-Guatemala Fruit Corporation as part of its effort to secure new sources of supply and expand its share of the American market. United had no interest in letting two of its three main rivals succeed in either endeavor, for it lacked both Pacific coast plantations and a distribution network in California. Until 1927, when it opened a division headquarters in San Francisco, UFCO supplied the California market with Caribbean bananas shipped by rail from Galveston and New Orleans. United still had powerful weapons in its business arsenal. With the initial costs of production on the Pacific side exceeding those of the Caribbean plantations by three times, the California-Guatemala could not engage in a price war with United. To prevent its rivals from gaining a competitive edge in the California market, United glutted the market, lowered banana prices, and forced the firm to suspend operations in August 1925, after it had spent nearly $2 million.[5]

The California-Guatemala firm resumed exports sometime thereafter, but it never expanded its plantings beyond two thousand acres. A more credible challenge to United Fruit surfaced in 1923, when Arthur Wallenberg of Sweden purchased four hundred thousand acres on the Pacific coast. He had convenient access to all the capital he might need through his uncle Knut Wallenberg, who owned one half of Hambros Bank of London. The Wallenbergs united with a group of European capitalists to develop a modern, diversified enterprise, complete with ancillary railroads and ports, on the southern coast.[6]

The success of the enterprise depended upon Wallenberg's ability to secure and maintain government support. If he did not build his own railroads and port, he would have to depend upon the goodwill of IRCA and UFCO, and only the most naive competitor would expect IRCA to offer reasonable rates and reliable services for the 321-mile trek to Puerto Barrios. Bananas not grown under UFCO contract would likely rot in IRCA boxcars or on the wharves before the stevedores loaded them onto any UFCO steamer. Given that IRCA controlled the piers at San José and Champerico, neither of which could handle a large volume of banana traffic anyway, the Wallenbergs requested authorization to build their own port at Concepción del Mar, a point between the aforementioned ports. In October 1923, Orellana authorized Wallenberg's request but unlike the concessions that defined the operations of Puerto Barrios, the government would supervise the new port and keep it open to all carriers on equal terms. The concession did not include tax exemptions, land grants, or the administrative autonomy that UFCO enjoyed. According to American diplomats, Wallenberg obtained this relatively modest contract by distributing approximately $50,000 in bribes to government officials.[7]

For his first venture into Guatemalan politics, Wallenberg certainly displayed no aversion to the seamy tactics that Keith had employed years before him, but he lacked the skills required of a serious UFCO competitor. An investigation into his European background revealed that he was considered the black sheep of an otherwise excellent and successful family. Knut Wallenberg, however, formerly the Swedish minister of foreign affairs and a director of Sweden's leading bank, financed the project along with Axel de Bildt, the manager of a large European shipping concern. In mid-1924, Arthur Wallenberg transferred his land and concession to a stock company formed by a group of millionaires who were prepared to invest their money in banana plantations, a port, and a railroad spur to the main IRCA line.[8]

While this European venture has been interpreted as a significant and promising challenge to United's monopoly, Wallenberg and de Bildt never wanted to compete directly with UFCO.[9] In June 1924, Thomas Fitzhugh Lee, an American investment banker who had unsuccessfully promoted oil exploration in Guatemala earlier that year, invited the Europeans to join a financial syndicate being organized by Minor Keith, for whom Lee worked confidentially on the loan and financial reorganization package he pursued with the Orellana administration. De Bildt recognized the value of such a combination and agreed to meet Lee and his associates in New York in November. Keith accepted the inclusion of the Europeans in the loan and banking project, but he considered that venture separate from the rail and banana business the Europeans were developing.[10]

Geopolitical factors drove the Europeans to seek an alliance with Keith. United Fruit dominated Guatemala's infrastructure and the State Department conditioned its domestic policies. According to Lee, de Bildt explained to him that the Europeans "felt their operations in Guatemala might be more safely conducted as a minority interest with a strong American group, since Central America was undoubtedly regarded as within the sphere of influence of Washington." To secure Keith's collaboration, neutralize United Fruit, and placate the State Department, de Bildt proposed to take whatever share of the loan and bank that Keith organized.[11]

Lee then arranged a meeting between Arthur Wallenberg and Keith in January 1925, when Keith was scheduled to present his financial package to Orellana. Keith delayed his departure from New Orleans in order to discuss the banking project with Arthur Wallenberg, but there was no compelling reason for him to collaborate with him in any other endeavor. Wallenberg offered Keith a position on his board of directors in exchange for a seat on IRCA's board. Given that Wallenberg's company had not yet constructed a mile of railroad or exported one banana stem, Keith saw nothing to gain and rejected the proposal, although he agreed to inspect Wallenberg's properties while he was in Guatemala. According to Lee, Keith also promised to withhold his financial reform package while the Europeans presented their own plan to Orellana.[12]

On March 1, just two weeks after Wallenberg imported the first material for the construction of a nine-mile railroad from the coast to some point along the IRCA line, Keith inspected the project to fix the point at which he would allow a connection with his railroad. He also heard Wallenberg's desperate plea to bring him and United Fruit into his scheme to build a port at Concepción del Mar and plant fifty thousand acres of bananas. Keith concluded that Wallenberg had no definite plans for developing either the port or the banana plantations. Keith's lawyer, Henry Price, was convinced that Wallenberg was just putting on an elaborate scheme to convince either Keith or United Fruit to buy all his properties.[13]

Neither Keith nor Cutter took the unattractive bait offered by Wallenberg or Lee, who left Keith on unfriendly terms in February. If the Europeans developed their banana plantations, UFCO and IRCA still had effective tools with which to stifle or eliminate the competition. Arthur Wallenberg left Guatemala in August for personal reasons, but his departure actually strengthened the project's credibility. Wallenberg's properties and port contract came under the competent management of Guatemala Plantations Limited, in which Knut Wallenberg owned 75 percent and Sir A. Mitchelson of London controlled the remaining 25 percent.[14]

Even with skilled administrators and adequate capital, the Europeans faced the formidable obstacles of recruiting and training a labor force, installing irrigation systems, and building the necessary infrastructure. If Guatemala Plantations solved these problems, it still had to ship its fruit out of Guatemala, a difficult proposition given United's control of rail and shipping. Unless the Europeans neutralized United, Cutter would run them out of business, just as he had done to the California-Guatemala Fruit Corporation several years earlier. The American consul predicted that the Europeans could develop their plantations only if they came to terms with UFCO, a powerhouse that could "render profitable banana cultivation impossible."[15]

Thus, even after Guatemala Plantations attracted skilled management and adequate financing, the Europeans still wanted to cooperate with United Fruit. In the fall of 1925, John Hambly, general manager of the firm, and Dr. Albert Hahl, the former governor of the German colony of New Guinea, visited Boston with the intention of selling a portion of the company to United. Although Cutter decided not to invest in the new firm, he agreed, according to the Europeans, to purchase fruit from the new company.[16]

With this tenuous understanding, the Europeans laid the foundations for the modern banana business in the department of Escuintla. By 1928 the village of Tiquisate was a small company town with a hospital, a theater, and comfortable living quarters for management and three hundred

Guatemalan workers. The diversity of the enterprise impressed Guatemalan and American observers. Although it concentrated on eight hundred acres planted in bananas, it also planted one hundred acres of Cuban tobacco, three hundred acres of cacao, and fifty-five acres of Hawaiian pineapple. [17]

Although the Europeans cultivated less acreage than the California-Guatemala Fruit Corporation, they presented a greater obstacle to United because they owned more land, and as Panama disease ravaged the Caribbean plantations, United's demand for disease-free land on the Pacific coast grew. In May 1923 the government attempted to confine this root fungus to the Caribbean coast by prohibiting the transportation of banana plants, parcels of soil, or banana leaves from the northern to the southern coast. By 1925 the spread of the disease, coupled with soil exhaustion, compelled both Cuyamel and United to search for lands on the Pacific coast of Central America. [18]

The conservatism that Cutter displayed in his competition with Cuyamel served the company much better in its drive toward the Pacific than it did in the battle for Motagua. Cutter could not abandon the Caribbean plantations and initiate new ones on the other coast; he would have to assure a smooth transition that would maintain United's dominant position in the banana business. He therefore initiated a deliberate strategy patterned after the history of United's development of its Bananera division, where Keith gained control of rail and transportation facilities before Cutter moved in to develop the banana plantations. In 1926, IRCA purchased the old pier at San José for $230,000, giving UFCO the option of shipping bananas out of either Puerto Barrios or San José on terms that it virtually dictated. An experimental shipment of bananas two years earlier had already demonstrated that bananas grown on the Pacific coast could be shipped across the country in twenty-six hours, loaded on a refrigerated ship in Puerto Barrios, and marketed safely in New York. [19]

With its control of the railroad and ports, United could market its fruit in the Pacific, Gulf, or Atlantic ports on its own terms, while one of its rivals, the California-Guatemala Fruit Corporation, utilized a pier owned by IRCA. Through the voting trust agreements of 1928, United received solid assurances that the railroad would remain in friendly hands after Keith's death or retirement. Because UFCO could extract favorable rates and services from IRCA, it decided to make Guatemala the focus of a general expansion program that Cutter initiated in the late 1920s. According to Bradley Palmer, conditions in Guatemala favored rapid development, but the company would not have approved the expansion to the Pacific if UFCO or its friends did not have voting control in IRCA. [20]

Guatemala Plantations and the California-Guatemala Fruit Corporation remained in business only as long as United tolerated their competition. IRCA transported the bananas of the California-Guatemala Fruit Corporation at three cents per thousand pounds for each mile of the two-mile trek between its Los Angeles farm and the wharf at San José. By early 1928 the California-Guatemala firm had developed an annual export capacity of 433,308 stems, but competition with United was futile, given the latter's control of the railroad and port. United purchased 3,495 of the company's 3,500 shares in June 1928 and dissolved it two years later. At the same time Joaquin Hecht, now acting as United's general agent, reported that with President Chacón's assistance the company had already secured options in the name of a third party on 675,000 acres, and he was negotiating with Guatemala Plantations for the purchase of up to one million acres. The CAG was prepared to invest a total of $25,075,000 in a Pacific port, railroads, and plantations.[21]

The Europeans, who had always been eager to accept United's investment in their project, offered little resistance to the company's expansion to the Pacific. Between March 1928 and February 1929, Guatemala Plantations sold about 220,000 acres and its port concession to the CAG for $2 million. United acquired all of its Pacific coast land through private purchases; the first concession covering its southern coast operations was authorized in 1931, and it did not include a land grant. As these private land acquisitions did not require legislative approval, UFCO had a free hand to deal with landowners who refused to sell on the terms it offered. According to Charles Kepner, the company normally dealt with intransigent landowners by buying the plots and water rights surrounding their plots and forcing them to dispose of their property.[22]

By 1929, UFCO owned several hundred thousand acres but it did not cultivate any bananas. Of the 566,838 banana stems exported from the southern coast in 1929, independent planters produced 82.5 percent of them, but they sold their entire harvest to United Fruit.[23] To assure that no competitive enterprise would ever again threaten to build rail and port facilities, the CAG began lobbying for the rights to build a modern port on the Pacific. Even though United already owned the pier at San José and the 1923 Wallenberg concession, which gave it the right to build a port at Concepción del Mar, it wanted a broader concession that would establish its hegemony in the Pacific region for the next fifty years.

While Chacón approved the company's efforts to build a new port and eliminate its competitors on the Pacific coast, legislators, journalists, students, and workers sharpened their nationalistic attacks on United Fruit and prepared for another confrontation in the assembly. In March 1928, Hecht characterized Chacón as friendly to the proposed concession and the company, but the president had not won the support of his Council of State.[24] On April 18 the council approved the idea of building a modern port on the Pacific coast, but the councilors criticized the tax exemptions, water rights, and terms of operation as either too broad or vague. In particular, the councilors disliked the clause that fixed the tax on banana exports at one cent per bunch for the next fifty years and urged the government to increase the tax to two cents.[25]

Notwithstanding the councilors' objections, on April 30, Chacón's minister of development signed a port contract that addressed few of the criticisms raised by the Council of State. One clause provided for the CAG to pay, voluntarily, an additional one-half-cent export tax, but the other provisions remained virtually identical. The contract would have given the CAG the exclusive rights to build a port at a point somewhere along the Pacific coast, at its own cost, within five years. When completed, United would manage it as a private enterprise, not a national port; United Fruit ships would receive preferential treatment at the port. The government exempted the company from the payment of import taxes on all the materials required for the construction of the port, feeder lines, schools, hospitals, and all other buildings connected with its projected Tiquisate enterprises. With absolute control of the rail and port facilities that served the banana farms and the right to administer its affairs free of government interference, the concession basically authorized the establishment of another United Fruit enclave on the country's Pacific coast. Chacón and the American minister naively expected the assembly to pass the concession within a month.[26]

When the concession came before the assembly on May 2, it encountered such bitter opposition that the American minister attributed it to plotting of Cuyamel Fruit, which was then fighting United at every opportunity throughout Central America. Yet the opposition originated with Guatemalan *finqueros* who had long been dissatisfied with United's poor and expensive service on the country's only railroad. On May 16 the Confederación de las Asociaciones Agrícolas (Confederation of Agricultural Associations) submitted a detailed critique of the proposed contract. The planters worried that the concession would allow the CAG to monopolize the port and stifle or eliminate competition from independent operators, the producers who still dominated cultivation in the area. Although they did not specifically recommend the rejection of the contract, they left no doubt that they expected the legislators to demand substantial modification before they endorsed it. In late May, Hecht decided to withdraw it rather than let the political opposition fuel nationalist sentiment to its advantage.[27]

The debates surrounding the proposed concession recalled the development project of José María Reyna Barrios in the 1890s, when the landed oligarchy wanted to own and operate the Northern Railway, Puerto Barrios, and a Pacific coast port. The *finqueros* of the 1920s viewed their opposition to United Fruit's proposed contract as an effort to resurrect a patriotic and progressive program that Reyna Barrios had failed to realize. Although they recognized the construction of a modern port as a matter of "transcendental" value, they felt compelled to prevent United from expanding its control over their economic infrastructure. The planters advocated the construction of a national port accessible to the public on equal terms, hoping that the resulting competition between the fruit companies would benefit the entire country.[28]

Faced with strong opposition from influential circles, UFCO would either have to revise its proposal or intensify its political lobbying, applying all the pressure it could bring to bear on the legislature. In May, George Bennett, manager of the Bananera division, returned to Boston accompanied by José Mariano Trabanino, the first vice president of the legislature and former legal adviser to United Fruit. Trabanino belonged to the progressive wing of the Liberal party led by Ubico and criticized the foreign contracts that Chacón favored. United co-opted the young maverick by putting him on the company payroll as a legal adviser, a position he resigned after he entered the assembly, and he maintained close ties to the company. With Trabanino's advice, UFCO redrafted the concession, and Bennett returned to Guatemala in the fall convinced that he could obtain legislative approval.[29]

A military rebellion on January 17, 1929, interrupted the political process and demonstrated the danger of identifying too closely with the fruit company. Dissident colonels led approximately three thousand troops against Chacón's corrupt government and vowed to liberate the country "from that insatiable octopus, [that] great plague of barterers lacking in dignity, in talent and in patriotism, whose efforts are applied only to contriving Machiavellian plans of ruin and stagnation." Chacón's loyalists responded swiftly and brutally. Aerial assaults on Mazatenango and Quezaltenango killed two hundred and wounded another eight hundred men, women, and children. The army accepted the surrender of these cities on January 22, but the loyal generals summarily executed their rebellious comrades.[30]

In the repression that followed the aborted coup, Chacón attacked all his political opponents, including the increasingly powerful Ubiquistas within his own party. Although he failed to consolidate the dictatorial regime that some of his supporters favored, Chacón asserted greater control over the legislature, as some of its members, most notably Trabanino, were implicated in the military conspiracy. Hecht had enough influence with Chacón to protect Trabanino, but the president charged eight representatives with sedition and declared their seats vacant. Knowing that the ousted legislators opposed United's proposed port contract and that Chacón intended to rig the election of their replacements, Hecht looked forward to the installation of a new legislature filled with more men who would obey Chacón's orders.[31]

Even after a slate of Chaconistas assumed the leadership of the assembly in March, United could not obtain legislative approval of its contract. A number of deputies pounced on the contract when it was reconsidered in April, arguing that the state, not a private foreign enterprise, should build and manage a new port open to all companies on equal terms. To Hecht's dismay, the assembly created a committee to study proposals for the construction of a government port, and four of its five members had announced their support of the administration. Chacón obviously could not control his own party. If the legislators rejected the port contract, United threatened to build its own port at Concepción del Mar under the terms of the 1923 concession that it had acquired from Wallenberg. Unwilling to compromise any further, Hecht had the contract withdrawn in June.[32]

As it had done throughout the 1920s, United engaged its democratic opposition in the legislative branch by cultivating close ties with the executive. It could purchase influence through its private land acquisitions, as many government officials owned land in the Pacific coast region. Hecht paid Gustavo Herrera $120,000 for a 2,200-acre cattle ranch that his wife had inherited from her father, former President Orellana. The Herrera family represented the upper echelon of the Guatemalan oligarchy, and one of them, Manuel Maria Herrera, pushed United's port project from his post as minister of agriculture.[33]

Indirect and discreet favors allowed United to lobby government officials without raising its profile or embarrassing politicians by exposing their close ties to an unpopular foreign firm. In April 1929, Hecht and René Keilhauer, representing IRCA, paid a friendly visit to Manuel Herrera to discuss matters of general interest to the country and the companies they represented. Herrera spoke of the government's interest in extending Seventh Avenue to La Aurora, a distance of only four kilometers but still too long for a government short of funds. Hecht offered to import, at United Fruit's expense, all the materials and machinery required to build an asphalt road, and Keilhauer promised to bring one of his engineers from El Salvador to direct the construction effort.[34] Although there was no quid pro quo in this transaction, the goodwill gesture cemented ties between United and the executive branch.

United's expansion to the Pacific was not possible without an authoritarian president capable of repressing dissent, for Guatemalans could have chosen one of several viable alternatives to the UFCO port project. In 1925 and 1926 the government entertained proposals backed by the German electric company to build a Pacific port at either Ocós or Iztapa, which would have provided stiff competition for IRCA. In 1929 a California-based company expressed an interest in floating a loan to finance the construction of a government-owned port.[35] Despite the exaggerated claims of United Fruit, it was not the only company interested in developing the region's infrastructure. At least three American firms bid for the rights to build a first-class highway from San José to Guatemala City. As the projected road paralleled the IRCA line, it would have provided a competitive means of transporting bananas to San José, and for that reason, Cutter expressed disapproval for any road-building program that did not feed into the main IRCA line. In August 1929 the government approved a contract with the Warren Brothers of Boston, but it only authorized construction of twelve kilometers extending southward from Guatemala City. [36]

There had been substantial legislative support for an extensive road-building program, but Chacón defended United Fruit's interests. The legislature reflected public animosity toward UFCO, IRCA, and the government that served them. Students satirized and criticized Chacón's corrupt practices in the annual March demonstrations (*huelga de dolores*), and a political broadside circulated the following month charged UFCO and IRCA with the attempted bribery of high government officials. Legislative opposition to Chacón's foreign concessions served the public's interest in obtaining an honest review of the government's development policies. In an apparent admission of some past indiscretions, Minister Geissler advised UFCO and all other foreign companies to clean up their act. [37]

In the summer of 1929 popular discontent over the deteriorating economy was evident in the press, the annual May Day celebrations, another strike of the stevedores of Puerto Barrios, and demands for a special legislative session to draft a reform package that included amendments to the electoral process. On September 12, Chacón responded to the political challenge by suspending the constitutional guarantees of free speech, assembly, and the press on the grounds that demands for a special legislative session promoted sedition. As the suspension would last through the elections of December 1929, when one half of the legislators would stand for reelection, it was likely that United would obtain that friendly legislature that Hecht had been anticipating since the colonel's revolt eleven months earlier. [38]

The assembly that convened in March 1930 contained thirty-nine new deputies, thirty-three of them nominally Chacón supporters. The legislators elected a slate of leaders proposed by Chacón and indicated a willingness to support the government's policies, as long as they benefited the entire country and did not line the pockets of government officials. Yet the president showed no appreciation for the depth and seriousness of the criticisms leveled against him and United Fruit, for he approved a new port contract on May 23 that did not address concerns of his own ministers of agriculture and development, who had recommended the inclusion of clauses obligating the company to construct a road to the new port and a canal parallel to the coast. The government extracted some minor compromises from the CAG, one of which transferred the port to the government at the expiration of the fifty-year concession, and another that imposed a voluntary banana export tax of one cent beyond the mandatory one-cent tax imposed in the earlier contract versions. [39]

Despite all the focus on the port, United never really wanted or needed to build a modern harbor on the Pacific coast. An experimental shipment in 1924 had already proven that bananas harvested on the southern coast could be delivered quickly to Puerto Barrios for marketing in the traditional Gulf and Atlantic coast ports. If for some reason United wanted to ship out of the

Pacific, it could either build a port at Concepción del Mar under the 1923 Wallenberg concession or improve the wharf at San José, a notoriously inadequate pier that had nevertheless served independent planters for years. In 1929, UFCO and IRCA opted for the latter course of action, authorizing a $575,600 investment to improve the pier and facilities at San José.[40]

Hence, United sought the concession primarily to prevent either a competitor or the government from building a rival port. The concession also included valuable rights and privileges governing the development of the banana plantations in Tiquisate, but United could have developed the plantations without a government concession, just as the Europeans had done before it, because it already possessed the land, railroad, and port required for the expansion to the Pacific. Yet United wanted to acquire the means to stifle or eliminate competition before it initiated work in the new Tiquisate division. If United controlled all existing or potential outlets, no competitor could market its fruit profitably, for IRCA dictated rates and determined service on the railroad and the ports, and United dictated the rates IRCA charged for hauling bananas. For example, on June 30, 1930, Cutter notified IRCA that he had reduced the price for hauling bananas from the 15.33 cents per stem established by mutual agreement in 1920 to the 11.5 cents per stem rate that had been fixed in the 1913 traffic agreement.[41]

There was much more at stake than the monopolization of the banana business. Some Guatemalans recognized an opportunity to break United's control of the transportation network and for that reason promoted the construction of a government port. United opposed an open port because it would have lost a good share of the commercial traffic, primarily coffee, that IRCA transported over its lines to UFCO ships at Puerto Barrios. Hence, the heated debates about the port contract represented another chance to rid the country of United's commercial monopoly, and the legislature tabled the bill on May 31. Chacón, on the other hand, was prepared to capitulate to United, no matter what the consequences. If United built a Pacific port, the American minister predicted that it would become the country's main harbor, and with United controlling the railroad connecting it with the main IRCA line, the company "would have other commerce by the throat."[42]

The Chacón regime knew the full implications of an unamended port contract it resubmitted to a special legislative session on July 3. The minister of agriculture admonished the representatives to pass the concession quickly, for if they truly wanted to stimulate the banana industry, there were no realistic alternatives to United Fruit's proposal. The minister asked the legislators to recognize the painful reality that nobody could compete with UFCO, least of all a government that lacked the financial resources to construct and manage its own port. To increase banana production, build a new port, develop uncultivated lands, and increase government revenues, the government had to negotiate with United.[43]

Many legislators still wanted to pursue alternative development projects. Few people doubted the value of a modern port on the southern coast, but many raised legitimate questions about the legality and practicality of the proposed concession. Julio Samayoa, a member of the Council of State, questioned the authority of the government to concede coastal lands to foreigners and set the banana export tax for fifty years. Congressman Vitalino Martínez remained convinced that the government could construct its own port with a $5-million loan and retire the debt from the port revenues it collected over the first few years. Seven hundred members of the same Liberal party that Chacón nominally led pronounced against the contract before the legislature reconsidered it, arguing that it required substantial amendments to correct some of its unconstitutional provisions that only served a foreign company that took advantage of the country.[44]

As he had done for the past three years, Chacón completely misread the political situation. After four days of acrimonious debate fueled by a raucous gallery, the legislators sent the contract back to the Council of State for further study and amendment. Chacón's failure to obtain legislative approval of the foreign contracts he favored convinced the American minister that Chacón's intelligence was "so limited that he is unable to understand anything of the problems of Government."[45] Chacón just was not made of dictatorial timber.

As the country slipped into political and economic chaos, the *finqueros* began to demand an authoritarian leader who could repress the social unrest that reached disturbing levels in the summer of 1930.The most serious of these uprisings occurred at Totonicapan in July, when two thousand Indians attacked the local garrison to protest an increase in the land tax. With land values and personal income declining, *finqueros* demanded a firm response to the social and economic crisis. They advocated an economic recovery program designed to expand agricultural credit, promote infrastructural investments, maintain a cheap supply of labor, and terminate government corruption. Chacón offered a few palliatives, including a loan from the Swedish Match Company, but he obtained insufficient financing for the public works project and the agricultural development bank that the planters advocated.[46]

By November 1930, Chacón faced an increasingly vocal political opposition centered on General Jorge Ubico, a man with a reputation for brutal yet honest efficiency. The son of Liberal politician and wealthy coffee planter Arturo Ubico, godson of famed revolutionary Justo Rufino Barrios, he personally linked the landholding aristocracy to the military. In the military academy he displayed little academic aptitude, but his influential father pushed the young boy up the military and political ladder during the Estrada Cabrera dictatorship. As jefe político of Alta Verapaz (1907–1909) and Retalhuleu (1911–1919), he displayed the organizational skills and obsession with law and order that won him the praise of American diplomats and the Liberal establishment. As he was intimately connected to the dictatorship, he fled to the United States following the Unionist victory in April 1920, only to return to help General Orellana organize the coup that unseated one of Guatemala's most democratic administrations. As Orellana's minister of war (1921–1923), he persecuted Conservatives, Communists, and workers, and the president promoted him to the highest rank in the army, general of division, before Ubico retired to manage his family's fincas.[47]

In 1926 he campaigned against Chacón as the candidate of the Liberal Progressive party, an organization he founded to promote his own political career and capture the reformist sentiments of dissident Liberals and "the generation of 1920," an amorphous group of students and intellectuals whose disillusionment with the defunct ideologies of the Liberal and the Conservative parties led them to contemplate radical solutions to the country's problems. In 1926, Ubico was the preferred candidate of such distinguished reformists as Miguel Angel Asturias, Jorge García Granados, and future President Juan José Arévalo. Although Ubico lost a rigged election, he returned to private life confident that his countrymen would remember him as an incorruptible reformer and efficient administrator.[48]

As Chacón's political standing plummeted, Ubico's political star rose, for the public viewed the president's obsequious behavior toward United Fruit as sure evidence of his dishonesty. In his defense, Chacón argued that the collapse of the coffee market compelled him to support a project that would reduce the country's dependency on coffee exports by promoting banana exports and increasing government revenues. As planters pointed out, however, the country would realize even greater benefits if Guatemalans controlled the banana industry. On the pages of *Nuestro Diario*, prominent agriculturalists advocated the development of the banana industry under free-market conditions, not a monopoly dominated by United Fruit. As Guatemala's respected economist Carlos Zachrisson pointed out, the concession that Chacón favored guaranteed United Fruit a monopoly on the port and the Pacific coast banana industry.[49]

The concession would not generate much new revenue either. The government had imposed the first tax on banana exports in 1924, and even then it was only one cent per stem. In 1928 the export tax netted $60,856, or 1.97 percent of the total value of banana exports ($3,096,334); coffee exports, in contrast, paid a tax of $2,016,332, or 8.7 percent of the total value ($23,062,533). Even if the company paid the voluntary one-cent tax, government revenues would not exceed $100,000 in a good year.[50] This was hardly a significant contribution to the government's declining revenue base.

Furthermore, the construction of a modern port on the Pacific coast was not a prerequisite for the development of the banana industry in the area. In August 1930, UFCO and IRCA concluded an informal, three-year traffic agreement that established the rates and services governing the delivery of bananas to the IRCA lines for shipment at either San José or Puerto Barrios. The agreement obligated the fruit company to use its best efforts to obtain a minimum loading of three hundred stems per month.[51] Since UFCO had already made arrangements for shipping bananas through ports other than the one that it ostensibly wanted to build, the new port was essentially irrelevant to the company's plans to develop the banana business on the Pacific side. The setting of the banana export tax, the tax exemptions, and the administrative autonomy for which the concession provided, however, established the ideal conditions for the development of a new enclave on Guatemala's southern coast.

United's agents and its supporters in the executive branch framed the political debate in terms of the port, and this was ultimately to United Fruit's advantage. In September the Council of State issued another review of the concession that contained some minor amendments, but it accepted Chacón's argument that, given the government's desperate fiscal crisis, it could not negotiate a better deal with any other company. Even some independent banana planters from the southern coast opposed the various proposals to have the government finance and operate the new port because the government lacked the resources to do it. United officials often argued that they were the only company with the money and experience needed to build and manage the port, and if they were not given adequate terms, they would abandon the country and invest in countries that welcomed their investments.[52]

It was neither the first nor the last time that United threatened disinvestment in order to wring compromises from the government, and it was always an empty warning. Disease and soil exhaustion forced United to transfer some of its Caribbean productive capacity to the Pacific coast of Central and South America, and no country offered better conditions than Guatemala for the rapid development of new plantations. United had already purchased lands on the Pacific coast of Costa Rica, but political conditions were generally not as favorable as those in Guatemala. In 1930, Costa Rica approved a concession authorizing the development of a new United division on the western coast, but legislators imposed a two-cent banana export tax on the company and struggled for several years to prevent United from extending its monopoly on banana marketing to the Pacific coast. Moreover, Costa Rica's relatively open democratic system allowed for more active labor organization and radical politics than in Guatemala, as evident in the Communist party's leadership of a banana strike in 1934.[53]

United could meet its short-term needs by increasing production on some of its Caribbean plantations along the Jamaican, Colombian, and Honduran coasts, but the company's long-term development required the acquisition of new properties on the Pacific coast. As Bradley Palmer explained to his British associates, political conditions in Guatemala favored the development of United's first Pacific division in Guatemala.[54] The government either did not know or did not care to exploit its advantageous position in its negotiations with United, which was never the only company interested in Pacific coast development. In 1928, W. R. Grace initiated a modernization program designed to enlarge the footage of its Champerico pier and equip it to handle three to four ships at one time, twice the capacity it then possessed.[55] With German and American firms submitting bids for port, road, and railroad development, and Guatemalan planters dominating banana production on the southern coast, there were obviously alternatives to the project UFCO proposed, but Chacón could not see them because he was blinded by his personal commitment to the fruit company.

On December 9, Chacón approved a new contract with United, and one week later a military coup led by General Manuel Orellana unseated him. There is no evidence that United instigated or supported the coup, but Chacón's removal initiated a political change that resulted in the installation of a dictator amenable to United Fruit and acceptable to the State Department. One month earlier, UFCO had essentially recognized that Chacón's incompetency prevented it from obtaining the contract's approval when it asked the State Department to use its influence to get the Guatemalans to ratify the contract, but the State Department had refused. A stroke incapacitated Chacón just two days after he approved the contract and opened the door to Jorge Ubico, who had moved his Liberal Progressive party back to the center in an effort to regain the support of the traditional Liberal establishment. Stripped of the reformist principles associated with his 1926 presidential candidacy, Ubico became the darling of the Liberal oligarchy and American diplomats, who considered him the only man capable of resolving the crisis and restoring order.[56]

Chacón's stroke presented Ubico with a political opportunity he could not miss. As civil and military leaders debated the question of a constitutional successor to their debilitated president, Orellana took command on December 16, and Ubico sought refuge in the American legation. For over ten years American diplomats had admired Ubico and considered him excellent presidential timber, and now, with Ubico waiting in the wings, the Americans had the opportunity to install their favorite candidate. Secretary of State Henry Stimson publicly denounced Orellana as an unconstitutional leader and demanded his removal. Realizing that the Americans would not recognize his government, Orellana resigned on December 29, paving the way for Ubico to assume the presidency.[57]

The entire affair may have been orchestrated by the Ubiquistas and the United Fruit Company, with American diplomats as unwitting accomplices. William Krehm offers no evidence to substantiate his charge that Minister Sheldon Whitehouse negotiated the deal whereby Orellana agreed to step aside in exchange for $40,000 cash, a consular post for his son, an iron bridge for his farm, and the rights to raid the national lottery treasury.

Nevertheless, Joseph A. Pitti found the charges credible and has suggested that Orellana may have acted on behalf of Ubico from the start.[58]

As for United Fruit, there is good reason to believe that the company welcomed Ubico's assumption of power, knowing that he was a competent, pro-American leader, but there is no evidence that it lobbied on his behalf. One Guatemalan author claims that Ubico promised UFCO the contracts it wanted if the company helped him secure U.S. diplomatic recognition of his presidency. There is no evidence to substantiate any pre-election agreement between United and Ubico or United and the State Department. To promote its own interests in restoring political and economic stability to Guatemala, the United States considered the honest, competent Ubico the only viable replacement for the venal, incompetent Chacón. By refusing to recognize Orellana or anybody associated with the military coup, Whitehouse essentially wielded veto power over the selection of the next president.[59]

Through the mediation of Whitehouse, Orellana resigned, José María Reina Andrade became provisional president on December 31, and the United States recognized the government a week later. Reina Andrade scheduled elections for February 6 to 8, granting Ubico and his well-organized political machine a substantial advantage over his opponents, and set the new president's inauguration for February 14, a month ahead of standard procedure. For arranging such a rapid transfer of power and stepping down, Reina Andrade reportedly received a large financial reward. With money being distributed among his peers, Chacón miraculously recovered from his stroke just in time to steal $200,000 and retire to New Orleans.[60]

Ubico won the February elections by a margin of 305,841 votes to 0. While it may be true, as Kenneth Grieb maintains, that Ubico's popularity was undeniable, he did not build his administration on democratic foundations. Like his dictatorial colleagues in the neighboring countries, Ubico emerged from and responded to a severe political and economic crisis by applying authoritarian tactics to a politically, ideologically, and financially bankrupt government. With the acquiescence of the planter class, the military, the political establishment, and the State Department, he reimposed a political order that saved the oligarchies and foreign companies from the popular democratic forces that had stymied traditional Liberal politics during the 1920s.[61]

While the Chacón administration can hardly be held up as an honest and democratic model, the legislative branch had provided a forum for a vigorous political debate and analysis. In General Ubico's Guatemala, as in Napoleon's France, the general was the state. Ubico's profile, in fact, resembled the great French revolutionary, and he cultivated the similarities by placing at least seven busts and eight paintings of Napoleon in his homes.[62] Although Ubico never basked in the glory that comes with battlefield heroics, he applied military discipline to the government, imposing himself at the head of a streamlined hierarchy in which power and policy flowed from him. To Ubico the separation of powers, because it permitted and indeed encouraged criticism of the chief executive, bred inefficiency; in the new order, the legislature would pass the laws and foreign contracts that its superior officer ordered it to approve.

Within a few months of his election, Ubico swept the bureaucracy clean of corrupt and inefficient employees, forced the supreme court to resign en masse, and imposed his slate of presidential designates on the legislature; Reina Andrade, the man who had arranged the transition from Orellana to Ubico, became president of the legislature and appointed Ubiquistas to key positions.[63] Ubico wiped the political slate clean and installed an efficient but authoritarian government. Nobody could have been more thankful than United Fruit.

Unfettered by a political opposition, Ubico rammed United Fruit's contract through the legislature in May 1931. He claimed that the contract he submitted contained substantial improvements over the previous drafts, since his efficient government had extracted the maximum concessions from the CAG and had offered the minimum privileges in return. In fact, the basic provisions of the contract remained: a fifty-year contract, a one-cent export tax with another one-cent voluntary tax, tax exemptions on all materials required to build the port, and preferential treatment for UFCO ships that called at the port. Alfonso Bauer Paiz characterized the concession as one of the most harmful ever imposed upon Guatemala.[64]

General Ubico terminated three years of political debate and delivered the Pacific coast to United Fruit, reaffirming the value of authoritarian rule to the company. José María Reina Andrade had once spoken persuasively against the contract, but in 1931, as president of the assembly, he supervised its ratification. He and many others fell silent, not because Ubico improved the terms of the contract but because they had already abdicated their rights as independent legislators. Manuel Galich has argued that the legislators' submission to Ubico involved some of the most cowardly and sordid interests in the country's history. While the American commercial attaché admitted that high government officials had received payoffs for the ratification of previous contracts, he proudly reported that "no financial considerations were involved and it was merely the fact that the President felt that the contract would be a good thing for Guatemala that obtained its passage."[65] Even without recourse to allegations of bribery, one can conclude that United obtained from a dictatorial regime what it could not secure from an independent legislature.

The Ubico regime repressed the nationalistic and democratic forces that had resisted United's efforts to grab Guatemalan commerce, particularly the banana business of the southern coast, "by the throat." UFCO controlled the nation's infrastructure from Puerto Barrios on the Caribbean to San José on the Pacific, with a subservient railroad linking its five hundred thousand acres to each coast. With a friendly dictator in command, it was firmly entrenched in the country's political and economic system; United Fruit was now the "octopus," whose tentacles reached into every corner of the country and squeezed independent banana planters out of business.

Notes

1. Victor M. Cutter, *Trade Relations with Latin America* (Boston: United Fruit Company, 1929), 21.

2. Wilson, *Empire in Green and Gold*, 264.

3. Arthur Geissler to State, April 15, 1926, Diplomatic post records, 1926, vol. 7, 860.2; Philip Holland (consul general), to American legation, November 4, 1925, Consular post records, Guatemala City, 1925, vol. 5, 860.2.

4. "California-Guatemala Fruit Corporation," DOJ, File 60-166-56, Series 330; Arthur C. Frost, "Banana Raising on the Pacific coast of Guatemala," December 30, 1921, Consular post records, Guatemala City, 1921, pt. 5, 861.5; Frost, "Data on Banana Culture in Guatemala," September 6, 1922, Consular post records, Guatemala City, 1922, pt. 6, 861.5; "Ensayo de exportación de banano de la Costa Sur," *El Excelsior*, March 15, 1923; "El primer embarque de banano por la Costa Sur dio buen resultado," *El Imparcial*, April 10, 1923.

5. Karnes, *Tropical Enterprise*, 146–49; "California-Guatemala Fruit Corporation," DOJ, File 60-166-56, Series 330; Holland to American legation, November 4, 1925, Consular post records, Guatemala City, 1925, vol. 5, 860.2.

6. Frost to State, May 5, 1923, Consular post records, Guatemala City, 1923, vol. 3.

7. E. M. Lawton to State, June 8, 1920, SD 814.1561; Frost to State, September 25, 1922, SD 814.1561/1; Frost to State, December 21, 1922, SD 814.1561/2; Clarence B. Hewes to State, October 17, 1923, SD 814.56/0.

8. Holland to State, March 4, 1925, Consular post records, Guatemala City, 1925, vol. 5, 860.2; Robert Woods Bliss to State, February 10, 1926, Consular post records, 1926, vol. 7, 860.2; Geissler to State, June 25, 1924, Consular post records, Guatemala City, 1924, vol. 5, 860Lee.

9. Bauer Paiz, *Como opera el capital yanqui*, 224–25.

10. Kemmerer and Dalgaard, "Inflation, Intrigue," 29; State to Geissler, January 19, 1924, and Geissler to State, February 27, 1924, Consular post records, Guatemala City, 1924, vol. 5, 860.Lee; Geissler to State, January 22, 1925, enclosure no. 1, memorandum of conversation, Minor C. Keith and Leon H. Ellis, January 19, 1925, SD 814.51/494.

11. Thomas F. Lee to Dr. Arthur N. Young (economic adviser, State Department), January 28, 1925, SD 814.51/496.

12. Geissler to State, January 22, 1925, enclosures no. 3–7, Consular post records, Guatemala City, 1925, vol. 4, 851.6; Geissler to State, January 22, 1925, enclosure no. 1, memorandum of conversation, Keith and Ellis, SD 814.51/494.

13. Holland to State, March 4, 1925, Consular post records, Guatemala City, 1925, vol. 5, 860.2.

14. Lee to Geissler, February 23, 1925, Consular post records, Guatemala City, 1925, vol. 4, 851.6; Holland to Geissler, August 12, 1925, Consular post

records, Guatemala City, 1925, vol. 5, 860.2; Holland to American legation, November 4, 1925, Consular post records, 1925, vol. 5, 860.2; Bliss to State, February 10, 1926, Consular post records, 1926, vol. 7, 860.2.

15. Holland to American legation, November 4, 1925, Consular post records, 1925, vol. 5, 860.2.

16. Bliss to State, February 10, 1926, Consular post records, Guatemala City, 1926, vol. 7, 860.2; Holland to legation, November 4, 1925, Consular post records, Guatemala City, 1925, vol. 5, 860.2.

17. Report of H. Eric Trammell (vice consul), enclosed, Inspector of Agriculture of Retalhuleu to the Director General of Agriculture, January 25, 1928, Consular post records, Guatemala City, 1928, vol. 11, 861.

18. Augustus Ostertag (vice consul), "Panama Disease on North Coast Banana Plantations, Guatemala," November 14, 1923, Consular post records, Guatemala City, 1923, pt. 18, 816.2; Fox to State, October 26, 1925, SD 714.1515/444.

19. AGCA, B129, legajo 22198, expediente 5125; Holland to State, March 14, 1924, Consular post records, 1924, vol. 5, 861.5.

20. Bradley Palmer to London, June 14, 1928, DOJ, File 60-166-56, Series 537, IRCA-63 [PX 3682].

21. "California-Guatemala Fruit Corporation," DOJ, File 60-166-56, Series 330; H. T. Heyl (manager, Guatemala division) to George P. Chittenden (vice president, United), May 21, 1932, DOJ, File 60-166-56, Series 537, IRCA-91 [PX 5163]; Geissler to State, March 17, 1928, SD 814.52Cía Agrícola de Guatemala/1.

22. Geissler to State, February 14, 1929, SD 814.1561/15; Kepner, *Social Aspects*, 85.

23. J. H. Wilson (manager, UFCO) to G. K. Donald (consul general), March 21, 1930. Consular post records, Guatemala City, 1930, pt. 6, 600 Bananas.

24. Geissler to State, March 17, 1928, SD 814.52Cía. Agrícola de Guatemala/1.

25. Guatemala, Secretaría de Agricultura, *Apertura de un Puerto Moderno en el Pacífico, Memorandum del Señor Ministro de Agricultura al Señor Presidente de la Comisión Extraordinaria de Fomento de la Asamblea Nacional Legislativa, 1930,* annex no. 3, "Dictamen del Consejo de Estado," April 18, 1928, SD 814.1561/31, Sheldon Whitehouse (minister to Guatemala) to State, July 28, 1930.

26. De León Aragón, *Los contratos de la United Fruit Company,* 86; Geissler to State, May 4, 1928, SD 814.52CAG/2.

27. Geissler to State, May 4, 1928, SD 814.52CAG/2; Geissler to State, May 31, 1928, SD 814.52CAG/5; "Exposición de los agricultores ante la asamblea legislativa," *El Imparcial,* May 24, 1928.

28. *Diario de Guatemala,* June 20, 1928.

29. Pitti, "Ubico and Guatemalan Politics," 317; Geissler to State, July 24, 1928, enclosed memorandum by Stanley Hawks (secretary of legation), July 23, 1928, SD 814.52CAG/7; Hawks to State, November 12, 1928, SD 814.52/CAG/8.

30. Geissler to State, January 29, 1929, enclosure, "Revolutionary Proclamation: Justice, Progress, Honesty and Liberty to the People of Guatemala," SD 814.00 Revolution/31; Pitti, "Ubico and Guatemalan Politics," 309–29.

31. Geissler to State, January 30, 1929, SD 814.00Revolution/29; Hawks to State, March 8, 1929, SD 814.1561/17; De León Aragón, *Los contratos de la United Fruit,* 86.

32. Geissler to State, May 2, 1929, SD 814.1561/21; Pitti, "Ubico and Guatemalan Politics," 360–61.

33. Geissler to State, February 14, 1929, SD 814.1561/15; further research is required on United's land acquisitions to determine the extent to which the purchases influenced government officials. On the Herrera family and Guatemala's leading families see Susanne Jonas and David Tobis, eds., *Guatemala* (Berkeley: North American Congress on Latin America, 1974), 210–51.

34. Geissler to State, April 20, 1929, SD 814.154/77.

35. Holland to State, June 19, 1925, SD 814.156/1; Geissler to State, April 2, 1926, SD 814.156/2; Geissler to State, May 7, 1929, SD 814.1561/22.

36. Geissler to State, September 24, 1928, SD 814.154/67; Geissler to State, August 31, 1929, SD 814.154/82; Geissler to State, February 19, 1929, SD 814.154/ 74; Geissler to State, August 31, 1929, SD 814.154/82.

37. Geissler to State, June 30, 1929, SD 814.154/80; Pitti, "Ubico and Guatemalan Politics," 358–62.

38. Taracena, "El primer Partido Comunista," 59; Geissler to State, December 6 and 14, 1929, SD 814.52CAG/10 and 11; Pitti, "Ubico and Guatemalan Politics," 370–72, 386.

39. Pitti, "Ubico and Guatemalan Politics," 386; Sheldon Whitehouse to State, April 30, 1930, SD 814.1561/25.

40. Robert Janz (vice consul), "Annual Review of Commerce and Industries for the Year 1930," January 28, 1931, Consular post records, Guatemala City, 1931, pt. 5, 600; "El embarque de banano en San José," *El Excelsior*, May 29, 1930; AGCA, B129, legajo 22198, expediente 5125; memorandum to Palmer and Cutter, May 29, 1930, DOJ, File 60-166-56, Series 537, IRCA-76.

41. Cutter to IRCA, June 30, 1930, DOJ, File 60-166-56, Series 443.

42. Whitehouse to State, April 30, 1930, SD 814.1561/25.

43. Whitehouse to State, May 5, 1930, SD 814.1561/27; Guatemala, *Apertura de un Puerto Moderno en el Pacífico*, 4.

44. *Diario de las Sesiones de la Asamblea Legislativa de la República de Guatemala*, vol. 8 (1930): 819, 828; De León Aragón, *Los contratos de la United Fruit Company*, 13.

45. Whitehouse to State, July 15, 1930, SD 814.1561/30; Hawks to State, March 21, 1930, SD 814.00/1010; Whitehouse to State, July 9, 1930, SD 814.00/ 1013.

46. Whitehouse to State, July 31, 1930, SD 814.00/1015; Whitehouse to State, August 7, 1930, SD 814.00/1016; Pitti, "Ubico and Guatemalan Politics," 398–99.

47. Grieb, *Guatemalan Caudillo*, 5–7; Krehm, *Democracies and Tyrannies*, 34–35; Handy, *Gift of the Devil*, 89–92.

48. Pitti, "Ubico and Guatemalan Politics," 198–241; Handy, *Gift of the Devil*, 90–92.

49. Kepner and Soothill, *Banana Empire*, 159; De León Aragón, *Los contratos de la United Fruit Company*, 12–13.

50. Kepner and Soothill, *Banana Empire*, 213; De León Aragón, *Los contratos de la United Fruit Company*, 92–93.

51. Informal agreement of August 7, 1930, DOJ, File 60-166-56, Series 443, [PX 9].

52. Guatemala, *Diario de las sesiones*, vol. 8 (1930): 832; Kepner and Soothill, *Banana Empire*, 222.

53. Kepner and Soothill, *Banana Empire*, 77–82; Chomsky, "Plantation Society," 313–22.

54. Palmer to London, June 14, 1928, DOJ, File 60-166-56, Series 537, IRCA-63 [PX 3682].

55. Trammell, "Report on the Facilities and Regulations of the Port of Champerico," September 21, 1928, SD 814.1561/9.

56. Thurston (division of Latin American affairs), memorandum, November 13, 1930, SD 814.1561/36; W. J. McCafferty (chargé d'affaires ad interim) to State, November 13, 1930, SD 814.00/1020; Grieb, *Guatemalan Caudillo*, 6–11.

57. Grieb, *Guatemalan Caudillo*, 3–10; Pitti, "Ubico and Guatemalan Politics," 431–36; Handy, *Gift of the Devil*, 92–93; Rafael Arévalo Martínez, *Ubico* (Guatemala: Tipografía Nacional, 1984), 23–29.

58. Krehm, *Democracies and Tyrannies*, 33; Pitti, "Ubico and Guatemalan Politics," 449, 458.

59. J. Humberto Aguilar Peralta, *Vida y muerte de una dictadura: el drama político de Guatemala* (México: Linotipográfica Nieto's, 1944), 20; Grieb, *Guatemalan Caudillo*, 5.

60. Grieb, *Guatemalan Caudillo*, 5; Pitti, "Ubico and Guatemalan Politics," 467; Fay Allen Des Portes (minister to Guatemala) to State, January 9, 1937, SD 814.00/1291; Report of Lt. Col. Fred T. Cruse (military attaché), January 21, 1931, SD 814.00/1056.

61. Grieb, *Guatemalan Caudillo*, 11; Woodward, *Central America*, 215.

62. Krehm, *Democracies and Tyrannies*, 38.

63. Grieb, *Guatemalan Caudillo*, 12–13.

64. Whitehouse to State, June 1, 1931, SD 814.1561/37; for a full critique of the concession see Bauer Paiz, *Como opera el capital yanqui*, 224–75.

65. De León Aragón, *Los contratos de la United Fruit Company*, 15; Merwin L. Bohan (commercial attaché) to Bureau of Foreign and Domestic Commerce, June 9, 1931, Diplomatic post records, 1931, 861United Fruit.

10

The Octopus

The stock market crash of October 1929 ended three years of growth in which United averaged a spectacular 10 percent annual rate of return on its investment. The acquisition of Cuyamel the next month seemed to give it the ability to withstand the economic crisis into which the world plunged, for it absorbed its chief rival and increased its share of the American market to 60 percent, leaving the Standard Fruit and Steamship Company a distant second in the business with only 15 percent of the market. With nearly two million acres in nine different countries and a fleet of one hundred vessels, United entered the depression in a position to determine not only its own future but that of the entire industry as well.[1]

A sharp fall in the demand for bananas reduced U.S. imports from 65,134,000 bunches in 1929 to 39,613,000 bunches in 1933, when prices averaged 85.7 percent of their 1926 level. Under Victor Cutter's conservative regime, United reduced costs and streamlined its operations, but, as if the market sensed a mismatch between Cutter and the demands of the economic crisis, the value of United Fruit's stock dropped from 158 per share in January 1929 to 10 1/4 in June 1932.[2]

The precipitous decline alarmed all stockholders, but it infuriated the largest shareholder, the irascible Samuel Zemurray. From his comfortable Louisiana estate, Zemurray watched the value of his UFCO assets fall from $20 million in January 1930 to only $2 million in June 1932. Instinctively, he blamed his misfortunes on Cutter's incompetence, but his dislike of Boston and the other directors kept him away from the boardroom for two years, even though the amount of shares he controlled gave him a dominant voice on the board of directors. Unable to tolerate the ruin of his reputation and wealth by a bunch of New Englanders who knew little about tropical business, Zemurray set out for Boston to put the company's affairs in order. He found the directors debating a request from a division manager to spend $10,000 on an irrigation ditch. Zemurray could not understand the directors' preoccupation with what he considered a trivial issue. The Banana Man suggested that if they could not trust a manager's good sense to authorize an expenditure of only $10,000, they should hire another manager.[3]

At the board meeting of July 13, 1932, Zemurray announced that he wanted to be appointed managing director in charge of operations. The silence he received from the other directors reflected hostility from the old clique that surrounded Cutter, Daniel Gould Wing, chairman of the First National Bank of Boston, and former Massachusetts governor Channing H. Cox. It was a dramatic and ironic moment in the history of the banana business, with Zemurray challenging his old adversary from within the same dark-paneled boardroom where Cutter once plotted the war against him. While Zemurray owned only one tenth of the total UFCO shares, he had sufficient support among the other shareholders to make opposition to his demands futile. In one fanciful account, Zemurray flung a handful of proxies down on the table before he shouted at the other directors: "You gentlemen have been fucking up this business long enough. I'm going to straighten it out."[4] Apocryphal or not, the account captures the character of the decisive man who took command of United Fruit in 1932.

Zemurray's temper flared up only when someone such as Wing or Cutter deliberately provoked it; otherwise, he was a calm, handsomely dressed gentleman who enjoyed the arts and hunting almost as much as he delighted in managing all aspects of the banana business. Zemurray quickly reorganized his management team without recriminations, although Wing, Cox, and Cutter vacated their positions in order to make room for some of Zemurray's old Cuyamel lieutenants, such as Hillyer V. Rolston and Joseph Montgomery. Then he returned enthusiastically to the tropics to impose his managerial style and strategies on UFCO's moribund empire, which was still worth nearly $200 million. Within two weeks of Zemurray's corporate coup d'état, the value of United Fruit stock had doubled.[5]

Under Zemurray's management, UFCO acquired an aggressive character that reflected the innovative personality of its managing director. His reforms stabilized the company, but it took many years for UFCO to return to the high profit levels of the 1920s. As shown in Figures 2 and 3, the net worth of United Fruit and its annual profits did not reach predepression levels until 1945. When the depression passed, United had successfully reallocated a portion of its productive capacity to the Pacific coast of Guatemala and Costa Rica. United developed its new Guatemalan division first because its control of IRCA and close connections to the Ubico dictatorship allowed it to dictate when and how it expanded, despite its recently acquired obligation to construct a Pacific port by 1936. The onset of the depression compelled United to postpone its plans to develop the Tiquisate division and build the port. Guatemalan banana production had fallen from a high of 6.1 million stems in 1927 to 5.2 million in 1932.

The depression hurt IRCA much more than UFCO because the former derived a major portion of its net revenues on the long-haul business it received from transporting coffee from the Pacific side to Puerto Barrios.

Figure 2. Net Worth of United Fruit, 1926–1951

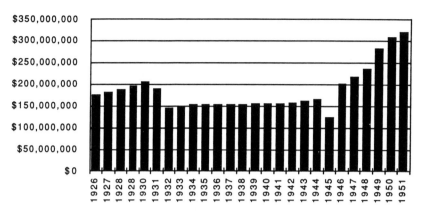

Source: U.S. Department of Justice, Anti-Trust Division, *United States v. United Fruit Co.*, Civil No. 4560, File 60-166-56, memorandum, Milton A. Kallis to Victor H. Kramer and W. Perry Epes, "Banana Investigation," December 20, 1952, 43.

Figure 3. United Fruit's Annual Profits, 1926–1951

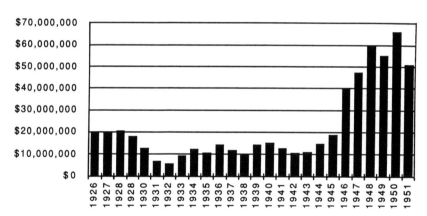

Source: U.S. Department of Justice, Anti-Trust Division, *United States v. United Fruit Co.*, Civil No. 4560, File 60-166-56, memorandum, Milton A. Kallis to Victor H. Kramer and W. Perry Epes, "Banana Investigation," December 20, 1952, 43.

The price of coffee fell to one third of the peak level achieved in the 1920s and stayed there throughout the decade. As a result, the volume and value of coffee shipped in IRCA cars brought down the railway's revenues and forced it to cut costs by eliminating some jobs and rejecting government requests for it to accept a small tax. The sharp decline in the coffee traffic allegedly brought IRCA to the verge of bankruptcy by 1933. Profits declined from $3.1 million in 1929 to a low of $1.1 million in 1933 (see Figure 1), a rate of return sufficient to allow the company to pay some dividends to its preferred stockholders.[6]

United Fruit determined the solution to IRCA's financial problems because it controlled the railroad and required its services for Bananera and the Tiquisate division it still planned to develop. Under the terms of the 1928 voting trust agreement, UFCO exercised managerial control through the appointment of directors to the IRCA board. Until 1930, United supervised IRCA's operations through its own officers, George P. Chittenden and John L. Simpson, who attended IRCA board meetings on a regular basis. From 1930 to 1934, Bradley Palmer, chairman of United Fruit's executive committee and a large shareholder, also sat on IRCA's board. In 1935, IRCA appointed Arthur A. Pollan, the general manager of United Fruit's tropical divisions, a special adviser to the company and retained his services with a fee. Through Pollan, United Fruit exercised practical control over IRCA. According to the New York Supreme Court: "No matter of importance to UFCO was ever resolved contrary to Pollan's advice."[7]

Informal contacts between the two companies were as important as the interlocking directorates. In 1930, Fred Lavis, then president of IRCA, held weekly conversations with UFCO personnel in New York and discussed all aspects of the railroad's business, particularly the urgent dilemma of establishing a rate for coffee high enough to assure adequate revenues yet low enough to maintain enough freight. United's traffic department assumed virtual control over the coffee rate, and other officials advised IRCA on personnel matters, taxes, pensions, customshouse arrangements in El Salvador, the Pacific Railway of Nicaragua, and the company's annual reports. The only difference between the advice that United gave to Lavis and that which it gave to one of its own division managers was that UFCO counseled the president of IRCA, but it ordered its managers.[8]

Through IRCA, United imposed high transportation costs on its competitors, thereby denying them access to the market on the same low terms it enjoyed. Independent planters thrived on the Pacific coast even after United acquired Guatemala Plantations and the California-Guatemala Fruit Corporation. United kept the Los Angeles plantation of the California-Guatemala firm under cultivation until 1932, when flooding convinced UFCO to abandon the farm. It eventually developed its own productive fields on the lands acquired from Guatemala Plantations, but until 1936, independents produced most of the region's banana exports and marketed them under contract with United.[9]

To those planters who attempted to break out of UFCO's monopoly, IRCA applied crippling rates. In 1932 the Berger Brothers, who cultivated a small plantation near San José, devised plans to ship independently to California after their contract with United expired, expecting IRCA to charge them the same three-cent rate it charged UFCO for shipping its bananas from the Los Angeles farm to San José. Although H. T. Heyl, United's general manager, doubted that the Bergers could succeed, given that they would not likely receive any encouragement from the government, he did not want to allow shoestring competition from any quarter, for he suspected that a successful independent venture might strengthen the Bergers's bargaining position in future contract negotiations with United. Heyl and George P. Chittenden, United's vice president, therefore established a rate of fifteen cents per stem for all independent shipments, hoping to discourage any such ventures in the future.[10]

A new traffic agreement of February 3, 1933, continued the special rates and services that United enjoyed on the Caribbean coast and extended them to the Pacific. The contract established a rate of twenty cents per United Fruit banana stem and fifty cents per all other stems shipped from the southern coast to Puerto Barrios, obligated IRCA to ship Pacific coast bananas to Puerto Barrios within twenty-four hours, guaranteed UFCO preferential service on the railroad, prohibited IRCA from encouraging competition by independent planters, and reserved these special privileges to United alone.[11]

While the president of IRCA, Charles Myers, did not even know that the railroad's concessions permitted special traffic agreements with UFCO, Zemurray understood how to exploit his control over IRCA to the limit. Myers thought that the company had only the right to fix tariffs without consulting the government, provided that the rates did not exceed the maximums stipulated in its contracts. Zemurray bet Myers a hat that IRCA's concessions allowed it to grant United Fruit or any other private shipper a discounted tariff for the movement of freight. After consulting with IRCA's lawyer, Carlos Salazar (who also happened to be an influential politician, diplomat, and later the minister of foreign relations), Myers conceded the bet.[12]

The conclusion of the 1933 traffic agreement diminished the importance of the proposed Pacific port because UFCO and IRCA established the conditions under which bananas could be shipped out of Puerto Barrios, San José, or the new port. If UFCO elected to build the port and railway lines connecting to it, article ten stipulated that IRCA would deliver all of United's bananas to the destination determined by the fruit company—either the existing ports or the junction of United's lines connecting its

Tiquisate plantations to the new port. If UFCO built its own railway line connecting the new port to the main IRCA line, it would charge IRCA rates similar to those that IRCA accorded to UFCO at ports it operated.[13] It apparently did not matter to either company if or where United built another port.

Hence, on August 15, 1933, Heyl proposed a modification of the 1931 contract that would extend the deadline for completing the port from five to twenty-five years. Heyl claimed that in the midst of a global economic crisis, United could no longer export bananas on a large scale to the west coast of the United States as the company had originally planned. Yet Heyl must have recognized a growing market for bananas somewhere, for he offered to sign more contracts with independent growers on the Pacific that would raise UFCO purchases from 1.6 million bunches to 3.2 million.[14] In essence, United asked the government to suspend its obligation to build a new port and maintain all the other provisions governing the development of its new division.

Several months later United Fruit sweetened the proposal with a $1-million low-interest loan. Although government revenues and expenditures had declined along with Guatemalan exports, the minister of finance did not jump at United Fruit's offer. He concluded that "this is a magnificent deal for the company, which undoubtedly has money deposited in banks that do not deduct interest payments from it. The government of Guatemala, with such a small loan, can not do anything worth doing, and in exchange, it will have to make monthly payments of 4,000 quetzales in principal and 3,300 quetzales in interest for the next twenty years."[15]

At this point there was still a slight chance that opponents of the proposed modifications could have extracted significant concessions from United. The American minister, Matthew E. Hanna, reported in May 1934 that treasury officials adamantly held out for a loan of at least $2 million, but United would not consider any increase. To handle the delicate negotiations with the Ubico regime, Boston dispatched Thomas Bradshaw, who informed the government that United still planned to invest millions of dollars to develop new, tax-paying plantations at Tiquisate. Despite the prospect of increased revenues, some government officials apparently suggested that the government reduce its commitment to maintain the two-cent banana export tax from fifty to twenty years. Bradshaw secured an audience with Ubico, but the general did not want to discuss the topic.[16]

Ubico was more concerned with eliminating the remnants of the political opposition to his authoritarian rule. In September 1934 the police uncovered a small cache of arms and bombs allegedly intended for use in a conspiracy to assassinate Ubico, the chief of police, and the minister of war. The security forces rounded up the suspected plotters, tortured them, and extracted the confessions that Ubico demanded. The general sent sixteen plotters before the firing squad, military courts condemned others to lengthy prison terms, guards shot prisoners allegedly attempting to escape, and sadists tortured some prisoners to death. The victims implicated prominent politicians, high-ranking military officers, and some members of Ubico's own party in the plot. Ubico forced sixty of these alleged conspirators to watch the executions in order to remind them of the fate that they could have suffered.[17]

The suppression of the September 1934 plot served as a convenient pretext for Ubico to militarize his administration even further. Post office employees, schoolchildren, and the symphony orchestra worked, played, and performed at the direction of the general. One American journalist described Guatemala as "a vast game of tin soldiers at which the Great Man amused himself."[18] Ubico eliminated or exiled his opponents, reorganized his military command, and appointed loyal generals as governors of the country's twenty-two departments. By rewarding his officers with government posts, Ubico imposed a strict military discipline throughout the country and kept the army loyal to him. The military presence in the government was so pervasive that the American military attaché wondered "Are generals in Guatemala politicians, or are politicians generals?"[19]

Following the aborted conspiracy, Ubico carefully orchestrated his reelection. Since the constitution barred a president from succeeding himself, Ubico had the constitution amended, ostensibly because the people demanded his services for another six years. When Ubico put the question to the voters in a yes-no format in mid-June 1935, only 1,227 brave souls voted not to amend the constitution to permit Ubico's reelection to a term ending in 1943. In this manner, Ubico gave his dictatorship the appearance of constitutionality, but in practice, the legislature never again dared to challenge Ubico's policies. The regular legislative sessions lasted only two months per year, and even then, the representatives held irregular meetings that lasted an average of thirty minutes each, during which time no substantial debate occurred.[20]

Had Ubico tolerated any degree of opposition in the legislature, some Guatemalans undoubtedly would have demanded the nullification of the Pacific port contract on the grounds that United had failed to fulfill its obligations. The absence of a domestic political opposition facilitated the company's expansion by strengthening its bargaining position, precisely at a time when sigatoka disease allowed Guatemala to be more demanding in the contract renegotiations. Sigatoka is a leaf fungus that deprives the banana plant of essential nutrients, resulting in premature ripening of bananas. The disease had devastated plantations in tropical Pacific islands earlier in the century and was then carried by air currents to the Caribbean. It appeared first on United's Honduran plantations and spread quickly into Guatemala and Costa Rica. As there were no known means to combat the fungus, Zemurray confronted a disease that threatened the existence of the entire banana industry.[21]

Zemurray responded to the short- and long-term implications of the crisis simultaneously. He increased funding for research on a chemical compound designed to check the spread of the disease on the existing plantations, thereby allowing the old Caribbean divisions to remain in production. Dr. Vining Dunlop, UFCO's head agronomist, experimented with something called the bordeaux mixture and produced some promising results. When he tried to explain how the chemical process arrested the airborne spore, the Banana Man interrupted him: "Please, sport, don't confuse me. You put the medicine on the leaves and that cures the disease." Although Dunlop cautioned him that the compound was still in its experimental phase, Zemurray ordered the immediate spraying of five thousand acres at a cost of $500,000.[22]

At the same time Zemurray realized that the company had to develop new sources of supply, for all plantations eventually succumbed to soil exhaustion. By 1935 he decided that the spread of sigatoka and the impending exhaustion of banana lands on the Caribbean side of Central and South America compelled United to develop plantations on the Pacific coast of Central and South America. The company did not plan an immediate relocation of its plantations from one coast to another (although it abandoned some of its Caribbean plantations), but rather a gradual move to specially selected areas. Since the main market for bananas, whether harvested along the Caribbean or the Pacific, remained on the north Atlantic seaboard, United would still have to transport the fruit of its projected divisions across Central America or through the canal.[23]

With vast tracts of uncultivated banana lands in the Pacific coast regions of Guatemala, Costa Rica, Panama, and Ecuador, United had several options available, but it selected Guatemala because of distinct advantages it had over the other sites. United's influence over IRCA's rate policy allowed it to arrange for inexpensive overland transportation to the Caribbean for marketing in the traditional Atlantic coast ports. According to John L. Simpson, a director of both IRCA and UFCO, Guatemala offered a number of special inducements for the development of a new Pacific division, "including those of water supply, political conditions and transportation."[24]

The traffic agreement of 1933 provided temporarily satisfactory arrangements for the shipment of bananas from the southern coast to Puerto Barrios. If, however, Guatemalans learned of the discounted rates UFCO enjoyed on its banana shipments across the country, a political opposition that Ubico could not repress or control could resurface, and some of the independent planters could develop into competitive enterprises. When Zemurray visited Guatemala in early 1934, he recognized a real danger in that "agitators" could capitalize on the issue of preferential rates to cause serious problems for the company.[25]

Some of these agitators came from either respected families or within the government. In April 1935 a Guatemalan named Federico Aquino, who claimed to be prepared to move 25,000 stems of bananas each week, requested information on the railroad's rates from various points on the Pacific coast to Puerto Barrios. IRCA investigators discovered that Aquino was actually a front for the *jefe político* of Puerto Barrios, who cultivated some bananas in the vicinity of that town under contract with United. As IRCA had no established rates for firms other than UFCO, Aquino was quoted the maximum rates established in the railway's concessions. This presented a politically delicate situation, for if Ubico knew of or encouraged this competition, it would not be easy to suppress. Charles Myers, evidently confident that his firm enjoyed Ubico's full support, decided that if IRCA were forced to quote rates, it would give the maximums and "face the music." The matter was brought to the attention of Arthur Pollan, United's special adviser to IRCA, and from this dispute emerged a policy to which UFCO and IRCA held for the next few years: it would always quote the maximum freight rates to any independent planters.[26]

Before United initiated the development of Tiquisate, Zemurray wanted firm assurances that he could prevent IRCA from applying the same tariffs to United's competitors and preclude any detrimental actions by an unfriendly IRCA president or board of directors. Zemurray was evidently uneasy about the potential opposition in Guatemala and from the non-United Fruit stockholders in IRCA, who might object to the low rates applied to United's freight. He believed that United could only obtain absolute control over IRCA's tariff policy by acquiring enough stock to give it a majority vote, but he recognized the political and economic value of maintaining a fine legal distinction between the two firms. Palmer argued that United could secure its interests by increasing its stock ownership in IRCA from 71,000 shares to 256,000, giving it 42 percent of the company.[27]

To arrange the protective assurances Zemurray demanded, the company solicited the opinion of John Foster Dulles, the managing senior partner of the prestigious Wall Street law firm of Sullivan and Cromwell, which provided legal counsel to UFCO, IRCA, and its banker, J. Henry Schroder. Dulles had gained his first Guatemalan experience making the legal arrangements for the acquisition of Guatemala City's electric company by the Electric Bond and Share Company of New York. In the mid-1920s, IRCA became one of Dulles's clients, and United Fruit retained the services of his younger brother and junior partner Allen, who earned UFCO's gratitude by adeptly handling its complicated lease contracts and purchasing a large block of United's shares. John Foster Dulles helped to draft the port contract of 1930 and the 1936 concession that superseded it.[28] Knowing the interlocking legal affairs of all three companies, the Dulles brothers and Sullivan and Cromwell were in a position to provide valuable counsel on an amicable transaction preapproved by all parties. Charles Myers, IRCA's president, agreed to do everything within reason to meet United's legitimate requirements because its banana traffic was of "paramount importance" to IRCA.[29]

While Dulles analyzed the means by which United could obtain control of IRCA without formally acquiring it, the company's lobbyists negotiated United's escape from an unwanted obligation to build a Pacific coast port. Five years after the contract's approval, United had not even begun construction of the port, railroad spur, hospital, or radio and telegraph station as required by the 1930 contract. The government could extend the deadline for another two years, but it also had the right to annul it and negotiate with other interested parties. Nobody honestly expected Ubico to adopt such a radical course of action, since his dictatorial regime had presented UFCO with those special political inducements that had attracted United to Guatemala's Pacific coast in the first place. He had always been friendly to United Fruit, and he looked favorably on the company's plans to expand production, since his financially strapped government would receive additional tax revenue from banana exports.[30]

Ubico gave the company what it wanted and much more in two separate agreements of March 3, 1936. He renewed the Pacific port contract with minor modifications that changed United Fruit's obligation to build a port to a nonexclusive right to build a port until 1981. To keep all the other provisions of the 1930 contract intact, United forfeited the $50,000 performance bond it had deposited with the government. It was a small price to pay for a contract that fixed a two-cent maximum export tax (with one half of that voluntary) until 1981, exempted the company from import taxes on construction materials, reaffirmed United's administrative autonomy, and gave it the right to develop all the facilities required for the banana plantations. In exchange, United Fruit loaned the government $1 million at 4 percent interest for six years, the same loan that Ubico's minister of finance had considered ridiculous two years earlier, and gave the government thirty-five thousand acres of diseased and exhausted land from its Atlantic coast properties.[31]

To those who once wanted to construct a public port, this concession insulted the national honor. Although the government claimed to have extracted meaningful concessions from the company, United did not promise to do anything that it had not yet already planned. It pledged to develop the plantations within two years, a timetable that coincided nicely with Zemurray's plans to escape the spread of sigatoka. The government took pride in the fact that United promised to build no less than twenty miles of railroad to connect the new banana plantations with IRCA, but this plan had been in the works since 1933.[32]

At least Ubico and his apologists could point out that the government received a badly needed loan. True enough, the government needed capital and United Fruit offered a short-term, low-interest loan, but United approved the loan with the understanding that the government would divert part of it to retire a $2-million debt to IRCA. The railroad's financial condition was as bad as the government's, and United needed both institutions stabilized before it developed the Tiquisate division. Hence, United loaned the government $1 million, IRCA canceled over $1.6 million in claims against the government, and Ubico promised to pay $400,000 to IRCA. The remaining $600,000 could be used to finance the construction of the caudillo's ostentatious national palace.[33]

United Fruit freed itself from the obligation to build a port, maintained the rights and privileges it wanted to develop the Tiquisate plantations, provided financial relief to IRCA, and soothed the caudillo with a $1-million loan. The second accord of March 3 extended the company's lease of the Motagua riverbanks until 1981 and increased the rental fee from $14,000 to $34,000 annually. It set the tax on banana exports at one and one-half cents per bunch until 1949, when it would be raised and held at two cents per bunch until 1981. While some apologists contended that the export tax contributed desperately needed revenue to the government, United obtained a long-term fixed tax at rates below those of coffee and bananas exported from the southern coast. Moreover, the Costa Rican government had established a two-cent export tax in 1930 and had guaranteed that rate for only twenty years.[34] Given the importance that United attached to the development of Pacific coast properties, Ubico could have demanded a higher tax and a shorter term, but in the absence of truly democratic institutions, nobody could even encourage him to demand greater compromises from the government.

In this case, there is no evidence of any bribes, extortionate demands, or U.S. diplomatic pressure during the negotiations. According to general manager Heyl, the negotiations were conducted amicably and without the exertion of any pressure from either party.[35] Perhaps no inducements were involved in the 1936 negotiations. Even if both parties conducted honest negotiations, the contract was not approved by an independent legislature representing the interests of the people, and partly for that reason, the contracts served a foreign banana company, not the independent Guatemalan planters who operated on the southern coast.

Company officials and their apologists have offered various explanations for the 1936 accords. According to Kenneth Grieb, Ubico recognized that United Fruit could not afford to undertake the construction of the port, and he still obtained badly needed financial relief for his government without discouraging United's investment.[36] If United could not afford to construct a new harbor, how could it loan the government money? How could it afford to acquire a controlling stock interest in IRCA just six months after Ubico approved the contract? In September, United purchased 185,000 issues of IRCA's common stock for $1,750,000, giving UFCO

42.6 percent of the company, an amount sufficient to constitute a majority of votes at all subsequent IRCA meetings and prevent IRCA from changing its directors or policies without United's approval. At the same time, UFCO paid IRCA $2,165,000 and agreed to invest $5 million for ten new locomotives and three hundred banana cars that IRCA would put at the service of the CAG. United also agreed not to build a port on the Pacific coast so as to ensure the movement of bananas from the new divisions over IRCA's lines to Puerto Barrios.[37]

The most sophisticated apologists, Stacy May and Galo Plaza, argue that IRCA initiated the transaction in order to save itself from certain ruin. IRCA had been losing money since the depression reduced the substantial revenues it derived from the long-haul traffic of coffee from the western highlands to Puerto Barrios. If United Fruit built a new port on the Pacific, the coffee freight would flow out of the new port and IRCA would go bankrupt.[38]

In fact, IRCA's profits started an upward swing in 1934, and IRCA still could have diverted the coffee traffic to Puerto Barrios after UFCO constructed a new port, for the company maintained its right to establish discriminatory or special tariffs within the maximum rates set by its contracts. The New York Supreme Court concluded that United's promise not to build a new port offered no practical value to IRCA. United Fruit rejected the idea of building a port because it was economically unattractive given the satisfactory rates and services already provided to it on IRCA's existing facilities. References to the port's importance to IRCA are conspicuously absent from all the extensive documentary evidence of the period leading to the 1936 contracts. The court concluded that all United's talk about the proposed port "was a mere sham to give some validity to the low rates being exacted from the IRCA."[39]

A new traffic agreement of September 1936 consummated United's elaborate sham. Like earlier traffic agreements, it guaranteed United preferential rates and services that the railroad denied to other firms. For the delivery of bananas from Tiquisate to Puerto Barrios, IRCA agreed to charge United $60 per boxcar and its competitors $130 per car. By mutual agreement in 1948 and 1952, UFCO accepted increases in its rates to $75 and $90, but independents still paid $130 for their shipments. While United argued that these rates were just compensation for the money it invested in IRCA, the special arrangements aroused hostility among independent planters in Guatemala and IRCA's minority stockholders. In 1949 minority stockholders of IRCA filed suit against United Fruit, claiming that it underpaid IRCA for shipping bananas. Ten years later, a New York judge awarded the IRCA plaintiffs $4.5 million in damages, calling the IRCA rates "unfair and unconscionable."[40]

Under Guatemalan law, however, United Fruit could rearrange its corporate structure and charge whatever rates it determined. UFCO officials admitted that the purchase of IRCA stock was done with the full knowledge and approval of the Guatemalan government. Ubico would not present any obstacles to the development of United Fruit's new division; indeed, he was quite proud of the way his government facilitated the company's growth. In the 1936 accords, Ubico reaffirmed the company's sole and exclusive right to organize, regulate, and administer all of its properties. With that reaffirmation, Zemurray could develop the Tiquisate plantations as he saw fit, and he decided to make the new division the first completely mechanized banana farm in Central America.[41]

The Tiquisate division began planting in December 1936, several months after UFCO had obtained adequate assurances that it would control IRCA's rate policies. United's control of the port and railroad reduced the risks normally associated with the first few years of a banana plantation, when competition, storms, politics, or disease often obstruct a company's development. One of the factors that inspired the move to the Pacific—sigatoka disease—followed United to the other coast. Minister Fay Allen Des Portes reported in November 1937 that with sigatoka ravaging the new plantations, United Fruit was on the verge of abandoning all operations in both Guatemala and Honduras.[42]

Zemurray gambled and won again. United spent $14 million installing an impressive overhead sprinkler system through which it sprayed bordeau mixture over the plants once every two weeks, hoping that this experimental mixture would stop the spread of sigatoka. To their surprise, Dr. Dunlop's mixture did more than just stop the disease. It also acted as a tonic and increased the weight of the fruit. The larger bananas sold at a higher price and compensated the company for the 100 percent increase in the cost of production.[43]

Tiquisate became a valuable gem in United's vast Caribbean empire. Following an inspection of the new division in April 1940, Des Portes described it as "an outstanding example of efficiency."[44] Six thousand people, most of them Indians from the highlands, found employment on one of Tiquisate's seventeen farms. Like Bananera on the Caribbean side, Tiquisate became a company town, complete with clubs, recreation facilities, stores, and schoolhouses, with one third of the population employed by the CAG. Unlike Bananera, Tiquisate was modern, efficient, and mechanized, the symbol of a new era in the banana industry, when airplane dusting, chemical agents, and irrigation systems replaced some of the labor-intensive work of underpaid field hands.[45]

As shown in Figure 4, Guatemalan banana exports (virtually all of them shipped out of the country by United Fruit) reached all time highs when the Tiquisate plantations came into full production and peaked at 10.6 million stems in 1939. The increase placed Guatemala just behind Honduras in total exports and among the top five sources of supply for the bananas consumed in the United States.[46]

Figure 4. Guatemalan Banana Exports, 1908–1944 (in Stems)

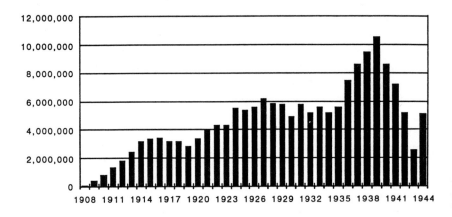

Sources: Guatemala, Secretaría de Agricultura, *Apertura de un Puerto Moderno en el Pacífico: Memorandum del Señor Ministro de Agricultura al Señor Presidente de la Comisión Extraordinaria de Fomento de la Asamblea Nacional Legislativa* (Guatemala, 1930); Bulmer-Thomas, *Political Economy of Central America*, 51; International Bank for Reconstruction and Development (World Bank), *The Economic Development of Guatemala*, 49.

Thus, in the late 1930s, United Fruit operated two huge divisions in Guatemala and had the capacity to produce much more than the ten million stems exported in 1939. The CAG owned about 320,000 acres but only cultivated 18,000. Company officials claimed that they needed a large reserve of land in case floods, blowdowns, or diseases destroyed their plantations. While the amount of land needed to provide sufficient security is debatable, the devastation wrought by natural disasters is not. In the summer of 1940 a violent storm destroyed an enormous section of banana trees at Tiquisate.[47]

United's vast reserves of land and capital enabled it to withstand natural disasters and at the same time keep land away from potential competitors. In some cases UFCO's sheer size made it impossible for planters to compete, and United did not have to resort to drastic measures to eliminate them. Once the CAG's multimillion-dollar investment was in full production, private farmers who could not afford to produce a fruit of equal quality had to abandon their plantations. By 1940 the independent planters of the region, who once dominated production, had been relegated to a position of secondary importance.[48]

Yet United was anything but a passive giant that crushed its small competitors simply by rolling over and suffocating them. Under Zemurray it was an aggressive bully, highly intolerant of any competition and relentlessly hostile to any rival, no matter what its size or potential. United Fruit deliberately stifled and eliminated competition along the Pacific coast, and it did so with the tacit approval or at least ignorance of Ubico, who protected foreign capitalists much more than his own entrepreneurial class.

Despite United's elaborate schemes to obtain control of the entire infrastructure of the Pacific coast, the pier at Champerico remained under the control of W. R. Grace. Since IRCA owned the railroad connecting it to the banana plantations that Guatemalans had built in the vicinity of Retalhuleu in the mid-1930s, it was not until the development of highways and trucking that private planters had their first opportunity to export bananas independently of both IRCA and UFCO. In their endeavors these private farmers enjoyed lukewarm support from the government, which was interested in highway development only to the extent that it did not alienate its benefactors in United Fruit. As a result, United was compelled to apply those drastic tactics that Sam Zemurray had anticipated when he obtained absolute control over IRCA and its tariff policies.

In June 1936 two Guatemalan entrepreneurs, José Gallardo and Eduardo Paiz, approached IRCA with plans to deliver six railway cars of bananas every twenty-four days at Champerico. The men cultivated bananas on a small plantation near Retalhuleu and arranged with other local farmers to export their fruit to San Francisco, where they were allegedly offered ten times what United Fruit paid them for bananas. Their chances of making a profit on the shipment were considerably diminished when IRCA quoted them a price of $102 per car for shipment to Champerico.[49] United would have paid a third of that to ship its bananas across the country and out of Puerto Barrios.

United used IRCA to restrain competition within the banana business, and Ubico was a willing and knowledgeable accomplice. The concessions he authorized gave United competitive advantages over all other real or potential competitors. Not everybody who entered the banana business had such broad tax exemptions and water rights, nor did they have the preferential rates and services that were afforded United Fruit. The legislators who resisted the port contract in the late 1920s could have promoted competition within the banana business, but Ubico terminated their efforts and tolerated the CAG's dominance of the Pacific coast banana business.

In late 1938, United finally faced serious competition from private Guatemalan planters who operated in the area around Retalhuleu and planned to ship bananas out of Champerico. In late December, Alfonso de la Cerda and Alfonso Alejos solicited information about the rates IRCA charged for transporting bananas from Retalhuleu to Champerico. The men claimed to be acting on behalf of independent banana growers who were prepared to begin exporting about three thousand stems per week to California. Alejos had heard that the railway charged UFCO only twenty cents for delivery to Puerto Barrios, and he obviously hoped that he would be offered a similar rate, because truckers were willing to cover the distance for only ten cents per stem.[50]

The railroad, advised by UFCO officials, maintained the policy established several years earlier and quoted the men the maximum tariff of twenty-eight cents per stem. At that rate, Alejos and de la Cerda would ship their produce on trucks, which was fine with the banana trust. Jack P. Armstrong of IRCA and Heyl of UFCO agreed to let the two men try to make the shipment because they doubted that it could be done profitably. On February 19, 1939, Alejos and de la Cerda delivered several truckloads of bananas in good condition to the Champerico pier, where a former UFCO employee supervised the selection and loading of the fruit in crates on a Dutch ship bound for California. Despite working with inexperienced dock workers, they loaded 1,427 stems and sent the ship off the next morning.[51]

This shipment proved that Guatemalans could grow their own bananas, deliver them at a port, and ship them out of the country without using facilities of either IRCA or UFCO. It also demonstrated the value of government support for infrastructural development, for the shipment would have been impossible without the construction of an automobile road from Retalhuleu to Champerico. Ubico, an avid motorcyclist fond of high-speed tours around the country, had launched a road-building project using forced Indian labor; by 1937 it was possible to reach virtually every part of the country by car. A salutary consequence of the public works program was that it gave exporters an alternative to shipping their products to port by rail. Guatemalan planters encouraged the construction of short roads to the port in order to break away from United Fruit's monopoly.[52]

Other Guatemalans also desired a share of the banana business that UFCO had dominated for nearly forty years. Carlos Dorion, assistant manager of the electric company and a member of an influential family, discussed the possibilities of exporting bananas out of Puerto Barrios over the IRCA line in January 1939. He claimed that a Baltimore fruit firm was willing to send ships to Puerto Barrios to take delivery of the bananas he harvested on the Pacific side. Dorion received no encouragement from IRCA. L. F. Whitbeck, IRCA's general manager, informed him that he would apply the maximum rates to the shipment and explained the difficulties that an independent firm would face when it attempted to load bananas at the Puerto Barrios pier, where United Fruit controlled all the facilities. Dorion intimated that his Baltimore purchasers were prepared to invest in its own conveyor belts if the volume of banana business justified the expense, but Whitbeck claimed that there was no room for any extra conveyors on the pier. He urged Dorion to make arrangements with United Fruit for the delivery of his bananas, a worthless recommendation given that Dorion was already under contract with UFCO. The railroad would not make it possible for him to ship on an independent basis.[53]

Although Dorion failed in his effort to crack United's monopoly, the Alejos and de la Cerda group made several shipments over the next few months. By late April they were shipping an average of twenty-five hundred stems per week. One wonders why United Fruit was even concerned about such a small operation. At the time, UFCO was exporting over two hundred thousand stems per week.[54]

People within IRCA were also questioning the railroad's refusal to bid for the freight that it was losing to truckers. Banana shipments out of Champerico continued well into 1940, and they involved a substantial loss of revenue. The trucks that delivered the bananas to the pier at Champerico picked up imported freight, particularly salt, for their return trip. Porter King, an IRCA official who analyzed this movement carefully, wondered why the railroad deliberately lost business: "As long as we decline to handle the bananas we are in reality promoting trucking competition to and from the port and losing revenue that we might otherwise receive. We have not retarded the banana movement, but by not handling it we have allowed a situation to come into being that is now being reflected in loss of revenues on local freight and import freight as well."[55]

Such a situation would not have developed if IRCA were truly an independent firm unconnected to a larger conspiracy designed to eliminate United Fruit's competitors. The conspiracy involved government officials at the highest levels. In March 1939, for example, Ricardo Dávila Ruiz informed IRCA officials that he was prepared to ship one million stems of bananas to a concern that he refused to identify. Through Carlos Salazar, the minister of foreign relations, IRCA learned that Dávila was a front for the Standard Fruit and Steamship Company of Mexico. It was a small favor from Salazar, a former IRCA attorney.[56]

Guatemalan entrepreneurs therefore found little government support for their competition with United Fruit. In fact, the government was partly responsible for authorizing the monopoly power that the fruit company now deployed against the citizens the government was supposed to protect. The concessions governing the railroad's operations only set high maximum rates. In response to the numerous inquiries about the company's rates, which Arthur Pollan of UFCO viewed as a political ploy to discredit IRCA and UFCO, the railroad officials quoted the maximums, which were an extraordinarily prohibitive $630 per car from Retalhuleu to Puerto Barrios. Obviously, the company could not defend such a rate when UFCO was assessed only $60 per car from the Pacific coast. To prevent public embarrassment, UFCO and IRCA revised the policy so that they would cite $130 as the standard rate per car from Retalhuleu to Puerto Barrios.[57]

At these rates, independents could not ship their fruit out of Puerto Barrios profitably, if at all. The ports at San José and Champerico were available to private planters only because a highway gave them the opportunity to escape the exorbitant rates of IRCA. When the roads deteriorated, the independents would have no option but to ship their fruit over IRCA's lines, as Alejos was compelled to do in September 1939.[58]

Later that year, Encarnación Abularach tried to make arrangements for a large shipment through San José. Knowing of IRCA's high rates, Abularach did not even ask for a quote; he planned to ship the bananas to port on trucks he either owned or rented. The Independent Fruit Distributor of Los Angeles had assured him of a market in California of twenty thousand stems per month. Since there had not been any banana shipments out of San José for some time, the new traffic disturbed at least one official, who recognized that shipments through that port via trucks was even more feasible than through Champerico. King respectfully requested Armstrong to establish a rate that would deprive the truckers of freight that IRCA could handle. Instead of a competitive rate, the government intervened with a prohibition on trucking between Guatemala City and San José. The prohibition effectively denied private planters access to the market on competitive terms and reinforced the hard-line position that IRCA had maintained for years. Armstrong insisted, "We shall maintain our tariff rates absolutely."[59]

Thus, as the world moved toward the war that would thoroughly disrupt the banana trade, United Fruit's position in that business was completely secure. A few independents stayed in business despite the best efforts of United Fruit to exclude them from the market, but their production was relatively insignificant. Many aspiring planters realized that collaboration with United Fruit was much easier than competition. In 1942 independent farmers cultivated 4,695 acres near Tiquisate under exclusive contracts with United Fruit that obligated them to sell to UFCO at reduced rates in return for some assistance in developing the plantations and combating disease. In the department of Izabal, independents cultivated 3,165 acres and United kept 15,000 acres of its own under cultivation through the liberal use of chemical fertilizer. While Tiquisate remained a source of pride and inspiration to company officials, Bananera could still match Tiquisate's annual production under normal circumstances.[60]

With banana enclaves on both coasts, United Fruit was the all-powerful octopus that its critics said it was. The practices of the company on the Pacific coast showed to several Guatemalan entrepreneurs just how difficult it would be for any competitor to get a share of the banana business as long as IRCA served UFCO. While Guatemalan law allowed IRCA to establish discriminatory rates and prohibited the government from interfering in the internal affairs of UFCO, American laws and foreign policy either proscribed or contravened United's commercial practices. Ironically, the most serious attack ever launched against United began not on the banana plantations of Central America but in the halls of the State Department, where diplomats questioned the value of United's contribution to Guatemala's economic development and America's foreign policy objectives.

Notes

1. Milton A. Kallis to Victor H. Kramer and W. Perry Epes, December 20, 1952, 43, DOJ, File 60-166-6; Bulmer-Thomas, *Political Economy*, 49–50; Karnes, *Tropical Enterprise*, 178.
2. Kepner, *Social Aspects*, 69; Bulmer-Thomas, *Political Economy*, 50; Kepner and Soothill, *Banana Empire*, 264–65; "United Fruit," *Fortune*, 28–29.
3. Pringle, "A Jonah Who Swallowed the Whale," 116.
4. Accounts of this important episode vary in some crucial details, including its date and whether Zemurray assumed control through the accumulation of proxies. McCann affirms the proxy story and Zemurray's foul language in *An American Company*, 21–22; and Wilson's earlier version disputes the story of the proxies. See *Empire in Green and Gold*, 257; other details are provided in Pringle, "A Jonah Who Swallowed the Whale," 116; and "United Fruit," *Fortune*, 26.
5. Pringle, "A Jonah Who Swallowed the Whale," 114; "United Fruit," *Fortune*, 26; Wilson, *Empire in Green and Gold*, 264–66.
6. Bulmer-Thomas, *Political Economy*, 49–51; Charles Myers (president, IRCA) to Ministro de Fomento, March 24, 1931, AGCA, B129, legajo 22190 [no expediente]; Myers to Fomento, June 10, 1930, AGCA, B129, legajo 22193 [no expediente]; May and Plaza, *United Fruit Company*, 165; Jones, *Guatemala*, 258.
7. Ripley v. International Railways of Central America, 188 N.Y.S. 2d 62, p. 71; [untitled, list of UFCO and IRCA officers], DOJ, File 60-166-56, Series 537, IRCA-173 [PX 3995]; "International Railways of Central America, Minutes of Meeting of Board of Directors," May 9, 1935, DOJ, File 60-166-56, Series 537, IRCA-201 [PX 679A]; "Attendance at IRCA Board Meetings," DOJ, File 60-166-56, Series 537, IRCA-184.
8. Memorandum to Bradley Palmer and Victor Cutter, May 29, 1930, DOJ, File 60-166-56, Series 537, IRCA-76.
9. J. H. Wilson (UFCO) to G. K. Donald (consul general), March 21, 1930, Consular post records, Guatemala City, 1930, pt. 6, 600 Bananas; H. T. Heyl to George P. Chittenden, May 21, 1932, DOJ, File 60-166-56, Series 537, IRCA-91 [PX 5163].
10. Heyl to Chittenden, May 21, 1932, DOJ, File 60-166-56, Series 537, IRCA-91 [PX 5163].
11. Kallis to Kramer and Epes, December 20, 1952, 20, DOJ, File 60-166-56; "Contract between International Railways of Central America and United Fruit Company, Amplifying and Extending Previous Agreements," February 3, 1933, DOJ, File 60-166-56, Series 443.
12. Charles Myers to chairman of board of directors, IRCA, February 24, 1934, DOJ, File 60-166-56, Series 537, IRCA-94.
13. "Contract between IRCA and UFCO," February 3, 1933, DOJ, File 60-166-56, Series 443.
14. Heyl to Ministerio de Fomento, August 15, 1933, AGCA, B129, legajo 22091 [no expediente].
15. Memorandum from Ministerio de Hacienda [March 1934], AGCA, B129, legajo 22091 [no expediente].
16. Matthew E. Hanna (minister to Guatemala) to State, May 15, 1934, SD 814.1561/40; Hanna to State, June 5, 1934, SD 814.1561/41.
17. Hanna to State, September 22, 1934, SD 814.00/1156; Grieb, *Guatemalan Caudillo*, 116–17.

18. Krehm, *Democracies and Tyrannies*, 38.

19. Grieb, *Guatemalan Caudillo*, 118; Gleijeses, *Shattered Hope*, 14–15; Major A. R. Harris (military attaché), G-2 report, April 5, 1933, SD 814.00/1112.

20. Grieb, *Guatemalan Caudillo*, 118–21; Susan Ann Berger, "State and Agrarian Development: Guatemala (1931–1978)" (Ph.D. diss., Columbia University, 1986), 64–65.

21. Wilson, *Empire in Green and Gold*, 272.

22. Kobler, "Sam the Banana Man," 94.

23. John L. Simpson (vice president, J. Henry Schroder Banking Corporation [and UFCO director]) to Messrs. J. Henry Schroder & Company, May 31, 1935, DOJ, File 60-166-56, Series 537, UF-5.

24. Ibid.

25. Whitney H. Shepardson to Prentice Gray, April 11, 1934, DOJ, File 60-166-56, Series 537, IRCA-95 [PX 162].

26. Myers to chairman of board of directors, IRCA, April 11, 1935, DOJ, File 60-166-56, Series 537, IRCA-100 [PX 150]; Myers to L. F. Whitbeck (general manager, IRCA), May 3, 1935, DOJ, Series 537, IRCA-101 [PX 152].

27. Myers to chairman of the board of directors, IRCA, February 24, 1934, DOJ, File 60-166-56, Series 537, IRCA-94; Simpson to Schroder & Company, May 31, 1935, DOJ, File 60-166-56, Series 537, UF-5; memorandum, Boston conversations, May 23, 1935, DOJ, File 60-166-56, Series 537, IRCA-32.

28. Ronald W. Pruessen, *John Foster Dulles: The Road to Power* (New York: Free Press, 1982), 63–64; Leonard Mosley, *Dulles: A Biography of Eleanor, Allen, and John Foster Dulles and Their Family Network* (New York: Dial Press, 1978), 77; Jonas and Tobis, *Guatemala*, 165.

29. Simpson to Schroder & Company, May 31, 1935, DOJ, File 60-166-56, Series 537.

30. Bauer Paiz, *Como opera el capital yanqui*, 234–35; Grieb, *Guatemalan Caudillo*, 186.

31. For more extensive analysis of the contract see Bauer Paiz, *Como opera el capital yanqui*, 234–75; and De León Aragón, *Los contratos de la United Fruit*, 95–105.

32. Sidney E. O'Donoghue (chargé d'affaires ad interim) to State, March 30, 1936, SD 814.51/799.

33. O'Donoghue to State, April 29, 1936, SD 814.51/802; Jones, *Guatemala*, 228; Hanna to State, May 15, 1934, SD 814.1561/40.

34. Grieb, *Guatemalan Caudillo*, 186–87; Kepner and Soothill, *Banana Empire*, 77–80; for a copy of the contract and extensive commentary see De León Aragón, *Los contratos de la United Fruit*, 188–90, 258–60.

35. O'Donoghue to State, April 8, 1936, SD 814.6156/15; Hanna to State, May 15, 1934, SD 814.1561/40.

36. Grieb, *Guatemalan Caudillo*, 187.

37. Ripley v. International Railways of Central America, 188 N.Y.S. 2d 62, p. 70; memorandum, Boston conversations, May 23, 1935, DOJ, File 60-166-56, Series 537, IRCA-32; May and Plaza, *United Fruit Company*, 166.

38. May and Plaza, *United Fruit Company*, 166.

39. Ripley v. International Railways of Central America, 188 N.Y.S. 2d 62, p. 74.

40. May and Plaza, *United Fruit Company*, 166; Ripley v. International Railways of Central America, 188 N.Y.S. 2d 62, p. 70; "Memorandum Regarding Freight Arrangements," DOJ, File 60-166-56, Series 537, IRCA-147 [PX 244]; "UFCO Loses $4,500,000 Rail Suit," *New York Times*, June 24, 1959.

41. Arthur Nicholson to Purcell (chairman, Securities and Exchange Commission), January 23, 1943, DOJ, File 60-166-56, Series 537, IRCA-142; Wilson, *Empire in Green and Gold*, 279.

42. Fay Allen Des Portes to State, November 4, 1937, SD 814.00/1314.

43. Des Portes to State, April 26, 1940, SD 814.6156/20; Wilson, *Empire in Green and Gold*, 275.

44. Des Portes to State, April 26, 1940, SD 814.6156/20.

45. Harold L. Williamson (consul general), "The United Fruit Company Plantations at Tiquisate, Guatemala," April 1, 1941, SD 814.6156/22.

46. Kallis to Kramer and Epes, December 20, 1952, DOJ, File 60-166-56.

47. Williamson, "Notes on an Official Motor Trip," July 11, 1940, SD 814.00/1336.

48. W. E. Dunn (commercial attaché), "The Situation of the Banana Industry in Guatemala," May 4, 1942, SD 814.6156/24; Williamson, "Plantations at Tiquisate," April 1, 1941, SD 814.6156/22.

49. Whitbeck to Myers, June 16, 1936, DOJ, File 60-166-56, Series 537, IRCA-108 [PX 214].

50. Porter King to Whitbeck, December 27, 1938, DOJ, File 60-166-56, Series 537, IRCA-113.

51. Jack P. Armstrong (assistant to president, IRCA) to Shepardson (vice president, IRCA), December 28, 1938, DOJ, File 60-166-56, Series 537, IRCA-41 [PX 853]; H. W. Haase to Powers, February 20, 1939, DOJ, File 60-166-56, Series 537, IRCA-123.

52. Handy, *Gift of the Devil*, 94; Des Portes to State, February 25, 1939, SD 814.6156/17.

53. Armstrong (president, IRCA) to Shepardson, January 18, 1939, DOJ, File 60-166-56, Series 537, IRCA 119 [PX 859a].

54. Ibid., April 26, 1939, DOJ, File 60-166-56, Series 537, IRCA-43; Des Portes to State, October 25, 1939, SD 814.6156/19.

55. King, memorandum, March 15, 1940, DOJ, File 60-166-56, Series 537, IRCA-140.

56. Armstrong to Shepardson, March 4, 1939, DOJ, File 60-166-56, Series 537, IRCA-36 [PX 217]; Whitbeck to Heyl, March 14, 1939, DOJ, File 60-166-56, Series 537, IRCA-35 [PX 121]; Des Portes, memorandum of telephone conversation, February 4, 1938, SD 814.773/34.

57. Armstrong, memorandum of telephone conversation with Arthur Pollan (executive vice president, UFCO), March 20, 1939, DOJ, File 60-166-56, Series 537, IRCA-128 [PX 218]; Armstrong to Pollan, March 20, 1938, DOJ, File 60-166-56, Series 537, IRCA-13.

58. J. H. Wilson to Armstrong, September 22, 1939, DOJ, File 60-166-56, Series 537, IRCA-45.

59. King to Armstrong, November 8, 1939, DOJ, File 60-166-56, Series 537, IRCA 135 [PX 222]; Armstrong to Shepardson, December 7, 1939, DOJ, File 60-166-56, Series 537, IRCA-137.

60. Dunn, "Situation of the Banana Industry," May 4, 1942, SD 814.6156/24.

11

The United States versus United Fruit

The U.S. government has justified its support for American investment in Latin America on the grounds that it served common economic interests. In response to the critics' charges that foreign investors exploited developing countries for their own private interests, American diplomats and businessmen cited the valuable capital, technology, and expertise that investors brought into the region. Secretary of State Elihu Root explained the theory behind America's foreign economic policy in 1906: "We wish to increase our prosperity, to expand our trade, to grow in wealth, in wisdom, and in spirit, but our conception of the true way to accomplish this is not to pull down others and profit by their ruin, but to help all friends to a common prosperity and a common growth, that we may all become greater and stronger together."[1]

Preston, Keith, Cutter, and Zemurray adopted this rationale to defend their own business practices. They envisioned themselves as part of a larger American enterprise, supported by their government and welcomed by the Central American republics, designed to promote the economic development and political stability of the area. American diplomats urged the Guatemalan government to establish policies attractive to and supportive of U.S. investment, believing that development served the political, economic, and strategic interests of both countries. From Manuel Estrada Cabrera through Jorge Ubico, Guatemala's authoritarian leaders accepted Washington's political advice, and a measure of their obedience is that American marines never intervened.

United Fruit took part in Guatemala's political and economic affairs on a daily basis through the taxes it paid or evaded, the port it managed, and the president it supported or opposed. It represented America's interests and promoted the stability that marines often had to impose on unruly neighbors. Few Guatemalans recognized a distinction between the policies of the fruit company and those of the State Department; for all practical purposes,

United Fruit was the United States. Whatever the official policy of the U.S. government, whether the big stick of Theodore Roosevelt or the missionary diplomacy of Woodrow Wilson, both institutions pursued the same objective in Guatemala: a pro-American government that maintained social order and welcomed foreign investment. By the late 1920s, American trade and investment had surpassed that of Great Britain and Germany, thanks in large part to United Fruit. With economic leverage came enough power to enable the State Department to affect presidential politics by using diplomatic recognition as a tool to install or depose governments, as it did with Estrada Cabrera (1920), Herrera (1921), Orellana (1923), and Ubico (1930).[2]

Although United Fruit often boasted that it never called in the State Department or the marines to acquire or defend its interests, American diplomats intervened on behalf of the company on several occasions. At the request of UFCO and IRCA in 1914, President Wilson dispatched General George W. Davis on a special mission to resolve a dispute with Estrada Cabrera, who refused to process the land titles and mortgage registrations that IRCA and UFCO demanded. When Herrera annulled the Zacapa concession in May 1921, IRCA immediately requested and received the State Department's assistance in obtaining the contract's full reinstatement. In January 1929, UFCO deviated from its publicly avowed policy of not requesting diplomatic assistance when it faced seemingly insurmountable opposition to its Pacific port contract in the legislature. While some observers claim that the State Department limited its intervention to the resolution of minor claims disputes, American diplomacy supported the efforts of United Fruit and its allies in the Guatemalan government to suppress nationalistic opposition to its monopoly at several pivotal moments in the 1920s.[3]

Few observers have recognized the conflicts between the State Department and United Fruit, primarily because their interests generally coincided. As Walter LaFeber has pointed out, when private interests contradicted American foreign policy, the U.S. government usually prevented North American businessmen, including Minor Keith, from pursuing projects or policies that it opposed.[4] Until the 1930s the State Department and United Fruit essentially pursued similar objectives, but occasional displays of diplomatic indifference or hostility toward United Fruit foreshadowed more serious conflicts. In 1920, American Chargé d'Affaires Herbert S. Gould sympathized with Guatemalan efforts to renegotiate its contracts with IRCA because not even the Interstate Commerce Commission of the United States would tolerate IRCA's monopolistic practices. In 1922, minister Richard Southgate recommended the nationalization of the entire railroad network as a solution to the conflict over the Zacapa concession and infuriated both Keith and the State Department. The banana war between Cuyamel and United generated such anti-American sentiments throughout Central America in the late 1920s that the State Department privately attempted to mediate the dispute between the two companies.[5]

United Fruit may have symbolized Yankee imperialism, but it did not represent the State Department. It was a privately owned enterprise managed by a board of directors obligated to maximize profits for the shareholders; it had no responsibility for promoting the strategic interests of the United States, although its railroads were a matter of great concern to America's military planners. United kept diplomats at a fair distance because it opposed any interference in its internal affairs from either American or Guatemalan officials. United would have preferred to remain within its Caribbean enclaves, but its control of Guatemala's infrastructure necessarily involved it in larger political and economic issues.

In 1932, IRCA established a tariff policy that discriminated against American merchandise and favored European imports. When Puerto Barrios workers loaded imported merchandise on boxcars for delivery to Guatemala City, IRCA applied a tariff policy that differentiated products by point of origin; on goods imported from the United States, IRCA charged a higher rate per mile than on those originating in Europe.[6] In the opinion of high State Department officials, this practice violated Guatemalan law and contradicted the established foreign policy of the United States. For the first time, United Fruit faced a challenge from its home government, yet it resisted with the same determination that it had demonstrated in Guatemala, partly because the concessions it had acquired (and which the State Department occasionally defended) permitted the discriminatory rates that IRCA applied against American merchandise. To the great dismay of American diplomats, they realized that they had only slightly more power to regulate United Fruit's activities than the Guatemalan government. Zemurray's banana giant was a supranational organization that answered directly to no government.

The railroad established the new rates shortly after Franklin D. Roosevelt inaugurated the Good Neighbor policy toward Latin America. Zemurray considered Roosevelt a friend, supported the New Deal, and, at Roosevelt's request, served as an adviser to the board of economic warfare.[7] The rate policy IRCA followed, however, obstructed the execution of Roosevelt's Good Neighbor policy in Guatemala. Designed primarily to establish friendly relations with the Latin American countries on the basis of nonintervention, the Good Neighbor policy also promoted U.S. trade with Latin America through reciprocity agreements. In 1934, Congress approved the Reciprocal Trade Agreements Act that empowered the president to reduce existing U.S. tariffs up to 50 percent by means of bilateral agreements that did not require Senate approval. The State Department subsequently initiated bilateral negotiations with Guatemala and several other Latin American countries.[8]

The only previous reciprocity treaty with Guatemala lasted just three years (1891–1893), but U.S. trade with Guatemala increased nonetheless, primarily because Guatemala's two main exports, coffee and bananas, entered the American market duty-free without any reciprocity treaty. As a result, when Guatemala and the United States began negotiations on a new commercial treaty, the Americans had few tariff reductions to offer Guatemalan exports. Conversely, the Guatemalan government, whose revenues came in large part from import duties, could not grant any additional concessions to the United States without damaging its revenue base. In October 1935, after two years of negotiations over insignificant commodities, the two nations concluded a treaty more significant for the friendly relations it symbolized than for the duty reductions it contained. The United States accepted a binding agreement on duty-free entry of Guatemalan coffee, bananas, and chicle and accepted four minor duty-free products, including pineapples. In exchange the Guatemalan government agreed to reduce duties on fifteen commodities, most of them food products and manufactured goods.[9] While the United States failed to obtain the major tariff reductions it sought, the treaty nonetheless reflected the administration's desire to increase American exports to Guatemala.

Within one year American diplomats discovered that the United Fruit Company and the International Railways of Central America conspired to reduce American exports to Guatemala. In 1937 the American legation in Guatemala City received an inordinate amount of complaints about IRCA's freight rates, most of the protests coming from American, not Guatemalan, merchants. Subsequent investigations by the commercial attaché revealed that IRCA discriminated against merchandise imported from the United States, applying tariffs ranging from 50 to 1,650 percent higher than those applied to goods originating in Europe. For reasons that the legation could not yet understand, UFCO and IRCA were encouraging Guatemalans to purchase European products.[10]

The new rates increased the prices of American goods available to the Guatemalan consumer, thereby decreasing the competitiveness of American exporters. In 1937, for example, the Guatemalan government entertained bids for sixteen hundred tons of steel pipe for a new water works system. The order, potentially worth $200,000, nearly went to a European business because IRCA's tariffs raised the costs of American pipe to $11,400 more than the same item produced in Europe. Only after U.S. diplomats brought this case to the attention of IRCA did the railroad reduce its tariff enough for an American company to win the contract by a margin of less than $4,000. The firm would have lost the contract if IRCA had maintained the original rates.[11]

On practically all imports from the United States, IRCA charged higher rates than comparable imports of European origin. The company claimed that it applied the rate differential in order to equalize rates of through transportation to Guatemala City by either Puerto Barrios or San José. The State Department's economic adviser disputed this claim, stating that "a realistic view of this rate situation is that the railroad is charging what the traffic will bear without much or any reference to any such formula as that of east-west equalization. Puerto Barrios and San José are only mildly competitive. And since the railroad has a complete monopoly of transportation from the east coast to Guatemala City, it is able to charge whatever rates the traffic will bear."[12]

Since 1911, when IRCA instituted a prejudicial tariff schedule that diverted Guatemalan commerce from the Pacific to the Caribbean coast, United's corporate priorities had influenced the direction of Guatemalan commerce. It made no difference to United where Guatemalans purchased their goods, for its fleet of one hundred vessels dominated shipping from the eastern coast of Central America and would handle most of the country's commerce whether they imported from the United States or Europe. As United controlled the railroad network and virtually monopolized shipping from Puerto Barrios, it could modify rail or shipping rates at will, depending on how the board of directors decided to balance its far-flung interests. In the 1930s, the combined impact of a depressed banana market, hurricanes in Jamaica, currency restrictions in Germany, and quotas in France forced Elders and Fyffes, a wholly owned British subsidiary of United since 1913, to reduce the size of its fleet from thirty-six to twenty-one vessels. Under these circumstances, United would benefit by an increase in traffic that would otherwise not move to or from Europe if preferential rates were not made available.[13]

United altered IRCA's tariffs in accordance with its European competitors, maintaining a well-established tradition of cooperating with its rivals. The steamship companies that plied the Caribbean along with UFCO and Elders, primarily the Hamburg-American and the Royal Mail, regulated freight rates through conferences that minimized competition between the lines. United generally kept its rates in line with those of its competitors, knowing that Hamburg-American, which called at Puerto Barrios on its last stop before returning to Europe, could pick up a larger share of Guatemalan commerce if it engaged in a tariff war. Rather than compete with its rivals for diminishing freight, United collaborated with the European competitors. While it was not a member of the European Steamship Conference, United followed its lead and concluded one agreement with it whereby IRCA gave a 20 percent rebate on coffee shipments destined for Europe; it offered no similar inducements for coffee shipped to the United States. The rebate and IRCA's rate differentials formed part of United's strategy to increase Guatemalan trade with Europe.[14]

Unlike the State Department, United Fruit did not assume the responsibility for promoting exports of American manufacturers. United was a Boston-based corporation, with a majority of its shareholders residing in New England, but it engaged in business across national boundaries; it cultivated bananas in the Caribbean, marketed them in North America,

Europe, and parts of South America, and paid taxes to several governments. Since market forces, rather than geopolitical concerns, conditioned its trade and investment policies, United occasionally diverted Caribbean commerce to European markets.

The discriminatory rate policy in Guatemala coincided with United's effort to redirect the Jamaican banana trade to Europe, partly to provide Elders with a continuous supply of bananas. On December 31, 1936, United, Standard Fruit, and the Jamaica Banana Producers' Association, which collectively accounted for 95 percent of Jamaican banana exports, concluded a cartel agreement that remained in effect until 1941. By this agreement the cartel exported virtually all Jamaican bananas to the United Kingdom and Europe on Elders and Fyffes ships. As a result, Jamaican banana exports to the United States dropped from 1.2 million stems in 1936 to 38,000 stems in 1937.[15]

Given that United acquired its position in the Caribbean with the support and encouragement of the State Department, it is ironic that United eventually deployed its monopoly power against the political and economic interests of the United States. United's control of the best banana lands and the transportation facilities of the Caribbean enabled it to direct Caribbean commerce in accordance with private needs and market conditions that did not necessarily coincide with the State Department's interest in reserving trade and investment opportunities for American investors. At least in the banana trade, Boston, not Washington, determined trade and investment patterns. Figure 5 shows that in 1919, Honduras, Jamaica, and Panama ranked first, second, and third respectively in terms of total bananas exported to the United States. In 1951, Honduras still ranked first, but Ecuador and Costa Rica took over the second and third positions, while Jamaica did not even make the top ten. The disappearance of Jamaican bananas from the American market resulted not from a prohibitive U.S. tariff but from the Jamaican cartel's decision to market all of them in Europe. To replace the Jamaican bananas, United developed the export trade from new Ecuadorian plantations.[16]

Few Americans cared much about the origins of the bananas they ate, but the State Department was perturbed by a company that had sufficient power to obstruct America's foreign policy objectives. Roosevelt had committed the entire country to a Good Neighbor policy, and, through reciprocity treaties, the State Department hoped to establish friendly relations and expand trade with Latin America. United's discrimination against American trade presented a delicate situation to the State Department. Neither the State nor Commerce departments possessed the legal authority to regulate tariffs that IRCA charged for service within Guatemala. Although the rates obstructed foreign policy objectives, they did not violate American laws. How could the State Department hold IRCA and UFCO accountable for the partisan objectives of an American administration?

Figure 5. Origins of U.S. Banana Imports, 1919 and 1951

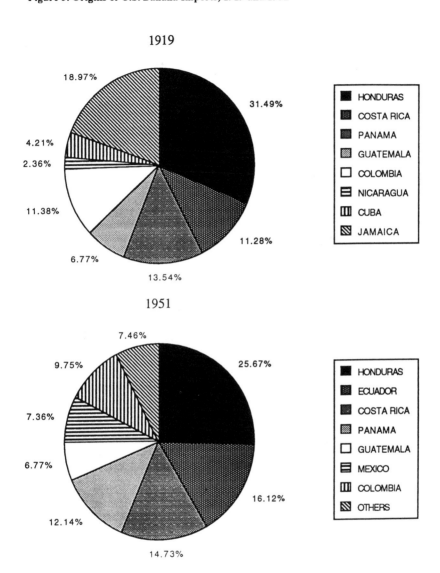

Source: U.S. Department of Justice, Anti-Trust Division, *United States v. United Fruit Co.*, Civil No. 4560, File 60-166-56, memorandum, Milton A. Kallis to Victor H. Kramer and W. Perry Epes, "Banana Investigation," December 20, 1952, 32–34.

The Guatemalan government had neither the will nor the authority to force a rate adjustment on the railroad. The concessions under which the railroad operated established only high maximum tariffs and gave the company exclusive management of its internal affairs. A railroad law of 1895 established some basic regulations that may have been applicable to IRCA, but the government had never invoked the law in any of its previous conflicts with the railroad. In this case the Ubico administration studied possible violations of the 1895 law, but, aside from some minor objections raised by the foreign minister, the government accepted IRCA's claims that the rates did not violate any of its clauses. The company claimed to be in full compliance with the letter and spirit of existing legislation, including one provision of the 1895 law that prohibited rates that favored any one nationality. Company officials argued that the new rates did not favor any country, although they neutralized the advantages that the U.S. exporter enjoyed solely because of geographical proximity. By adjusting the rates, the railroad claimed to promote competition based primarily on quality of merchandise.[17] The Ubico administration accepted this argument and never raised the issue again.

Since the State Department could not rely on Guatemalan support, it could either accept the rates as legal or improvise a legal challenge to the rates IRCA charged for service within another country. As the Good Neighbor policy was based on the principle of nonintervention, the range of options available to the State Department was limited by political concerns. If, by taking strong action against United Fruit, the State Department focused Latin American attention on the issue of U.S. investment and foreign policy, American credibility would suffer serious injury. Latin American nationalists often charged that foreign investors exploited their economies in the interests of their home countries. State Department efforts to bring IRCA's tariff policies in line with American policy could be used as evidence that the United States expected its companies to promote American interests rather than the interests of the host country.[18]

At the same time, the department recognized the political leverage it had over IRCA and UFCO, for both companies occasionally requested diplomatic assistance for their business in Latin America. The department's economic adviser suggested that "the prospect that this Government might be less energetic in supporting the companies than has been the disposition in the past may be regarded as an important means of increasing their amenability to this Department's desires in the inland freight matter." In the interest of maintaining cordial relations with its host government and promoting friendly relations between Guatemala and the United States, the adviser expected IRCA to adjust its tariffs, even if that meant lower profits. "After all, if we really wanted to be unpleasant about this, we could point out our serious doubts as to the benefits that some of the railroad's policies in Guatemala may be yielding to good relations between the two countries," the adviser concluded.[19]

Lacking jurisdiction in a politically sensitive case, the State Department still saw compelling reasons to move against United Fruit and its railroad subsidiary. The policies did not simply benefit Europe in general; they benefited Nazi Germany in particular, which initiated an impressive trade program in the hemisphere in the mid-1930s. In exchange for Central American exports the Nazis offered Aski-marks, currency or trade bonds that could be used only for the purchase of German goods, and this encouraged Central Americans to purchase their manufactured goods from Germany.[20] In the short term, German promotional efforts, the Aski-mark system, and IRCA's differential rate policies helped to increase Germany's share of the Guatemalan import business from 12.2 percent in 1932 to 32.4 percent in 1937, as shown in Figure 6.

Figure 6. Origins of Guatemalan Imports, 1932 and 1937 (As Percentage of Total Imports)

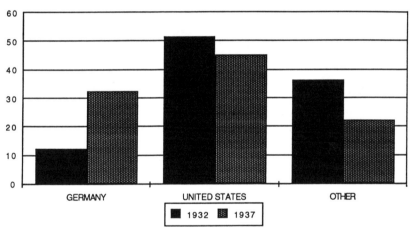

Source: U.S. Department of State, Record Group 59, Records of the Department of State Relating to Internal Affairs of Guatemala, 1930–1944, File 814.773/43, Commercial Attaché Howard Tewksbury to American minister, March 21, 1938, Appendix B.

The new rate policy did not significantly alter Guatemalan export patterns, although IRCA gave Germans additional advantages there as well. During World War I the United States replaced Germany as the largest consumer of Guatemalan exports, a position it held through the 1920s. Despite IRCA's 20 percent rebate on coffee shipments to Europe and the Germans' promotional efforts, Guatemalan exports to Germany declined while exports to the United States increased between 1932 and 1937. Because of trade surpluses in the early 1930s, the Guatemalans accumulated excessive Aski-marks and found alternative markets for their coffee in the United States, where they obtained cash for their products.[21] As a result, a majority of Guatemalan exports continued to flow into the United States, as shown in Figure 7.

Figure 7. Destination of Guatemalan Exports, 1932 and 1937 (As Percentage of Total Exports)

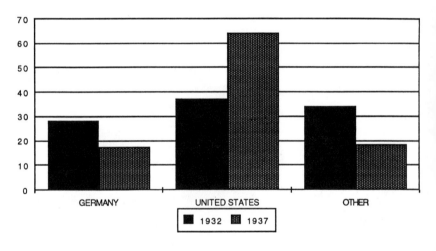

Source: U.S. Department of State, Record Group 59, Records of the Department of State Relating to Internal Affairs of Guatemala, 1930–1944, File 814.773/43, Commercial Attaché Howard Tewksbury to American minister, March 21, 1938, Appendix B.

Thus, the State Department wanted to increase American exports to Guatemala, while UFCO and IRCA's tariffs discouraged Guatemalans from buying American products. To exact more favorable rates from IRCA, the department first tried subtle persuasion. On December 28, 1937, six State Department officials discussed the case with Whitney Shepardson, vice president of IRCA, Allen Dulles, counsel for the railroad, and one United Fruit observer. Believing that American firms should promote American trade and investment, particularly in Guatemala, a country securely within the U.S. sphere of influence, the diplomats politely asked the companies to adjust the rates in favor of U.S. goods. Dulles and Shepardson declined, claiming that the rate differential equalized transportation rates from either Puerto Barrios or San José, thereby giving Guatemalans the option of importing through either port.[22]

Fay Allen Des Portes, the American minister to Guatemala, viewed IRCA's actions as an unpatriotic, politically motivated attack on Franklin D. Roosevelt and took stronger initiatives from Guatemala City. Breaking the traditional lines of communication, he appealed directly to the president in a lengthy memorandum dated December 23, 1937. Alarmed by the enormous increase in German exports to Guatemala, Roosevelt asked Sumner Welles, the architect of his Good Neighbor policy, to investigate the case and report back to him personally.[23]

In the meantime, Des Portes carried out his own investigations and pressured IRCA to adjust its policies as Washington dictated. Accustomed to giving instructions rather than receiving them from Washington, IRCA attacked what it perceived as the source of its immediate problem—the American minister. Charles Myers initiated a propaganda campaign to discredit Des Portes and have him removed from his post; he ordered all employees to withhold information from the legation.[24] Company officials had never tolerated Guatemalan interference in the management of the railroad, and they were not about to let American diplomats tell them how to run their business, either. The railroad's obstructionist attacks and foul play infuriated Des Portes, who unleashed his fury on Jack Armstrong, Myers's assistant. At a meeting in the U.S. legation, Des Portes asked Armstrong if he believed that the freight policies were consistent with Article 90 of the 1895 railroad law, which prohibited tariffs that gave one country advantages over another. If they were not, Des Portes asked him if the company "had enough influence with President Ubico to permit it to violate the law with impunity." Armstrong replied that "the company did not do business on the basis of violating the law with the acquiescence of the President."[25]

Few events happened in Ubico's Guatemala without the knowledge of the caudillo. A local IRCA official who deplored the company's discriminatory rate policy confessed to Des Portes that the only explanation for the policy was that German shippers were paying off Myers and the railroad.

Des Portes came to believe that IRCA deliberately assisted German trade with the encouragement of German coffee planters and Carlos Salazar, the minister of foreign relations. Suspecting Myers and Salazar of pro-Nazi sympathies, Des Portes described Myers as a self-proclaimed antagonist of Roosevelt's New Deal and speculated that he had taken it upon himself "to work against American interests in an effort to hurt the efforts of the trade agreements program."[26]

Some circumstantial evidence supports Des Portes's charges against Myers and Salazar. Whatever his political ideology, it would not have been out of character for Myers to provoke a confrontation with an opponent as formidable as the State Department. An excitable, aggressive man, he accepted a job with IRCA on the understanding that he would have a free hand to restructure the railroad's management to eliminate waste and inefficiencies. Even though his battle against intractable IRCA administrators wore down his physical and emotional strength, he took pleasure in defying authority. He did not accept the position of IRCA manager because he needed the money or because it was a good start up the career ladder; when he took the job he was already old and wealthy enough to retire comfortably on the income from his investments. According to George Bennett, UFCO manager, Myers was "not so much interested in the salary he receives, nor in the title given him, as in the personal satisfaction he might derive from doing a job that he likes and from doing it thoroughly and well."[27]

Salazar, a lawyer and a diplomat, had represented IRCA and Nottebohm Hermanos, a leading banking and coffee firm owned by Germans, before accepting his appointment to the cabinet in 1937. IRCA retained the legal services of his two sons after he became the foreign minister. While Grieb maintains that Salazar's previous ties exerted little influence on his policies, Otto Dorion, a prosperous Guatemalan businessmen, charged that Salazar drafted the decree expropriating German properties during World War II in such a way that it exempted Nottebohm, which claimed corporate citizenship of Liechtenstein.[28]

In any case, neither Myers nor Salazar could have conspired to promote Guatemalan trade with Germany without the support of the dictator, Jorge Ubico. While Ubico may not have identified with fascism, he extended the first diplomatic recognition of Francisco Franco in November 1936, and he personally admired Benito Mussolini, on whom he conferred the Order of the Quetzal in 1937. He considered Hitler a peasant, but he recognized the value of playing off Nazi Germany and the Roosevelt administration. While the caudillo could justify any pro-German commercial policy on the grounds that the diversification of the country's trading partners strengthened the economy, Ubico also had a personal stake in trading with Germany. Leon Guttman, a German resident in Guatemala, purchased coffee produced on Ubico's finca at two to three dollars above the market price and sold it in Germany. Ubico's ties to the German community, his admiration of fascist leaders, and his brutal repression of the labor movement convinced Des Portes that Ubico was reactionary to the point that he favored fascism, for he evidently had no great love of democratic principles or organizations.[29]

Myers, Salazar, and Ubico may have had personal political reasons for promoting trade with Germany, but the rates would not have been established without the express, advance permission of United Fruit. Since the early 1930s, United Fruit's traffic department had virtually dictated IRCA's tariff policies and even had represented IRCA at steamship conferences.[30] One of Des Portes's investigators uncovered evidence that the coffee rebate scheme was "in accordance with an agreement between the railroad company and steamship companies operating between Puerto Barrios and Europe [Elders and Fyffes]." As for the higher rates assessed goods exported from the United States, the officer explained: "The American owned steamship companies agreed on certain set rates on different articles shipped from the United States to Central American countries; that these rates are much higher than steamship rates on the same articles from Europe, resulting in the purchase of European articles in many instances where U.S. made products were formerly purchased."[31]

After six months of confidential discussions, the State Department adopted a more aggressive attitude toward IRCA, which gave no indication that its position had softened. In May 1938, Welles prepared to demand Whitney Shepardson's immediate compliance with the State Department. Although his advisers cautioned him that the State Department did not have the authority to act as an "extra-territorial Interstate Commerce Commission," Welles could not tolerate the un-American behavior of two prestigious companies that deliberately sabotaged the spirit if not the letter of the recently concluded reciprocity treaty between the United States and Guatemala. Welles criticized IRCA for creating unwarranted restrictions on American exports to Guatemala; its rate differentials eliminated the cost advantages that U.S. manufacturers enjoyed because of their proximity to Central America. Should the company refuse to modify its policies, Welles implied that the department would not provide any assistance to it in the event that Guatemala prosecuted the railroad for violating Article 90 of the 1895 railroad law.[32]

While Shepardson tried to argue that his company assisted Guatemalan efforts to develop European markets for their products, Welles exposed the hypocrisy of the company's self-proclaimed benevolence. The rate policies served United's interest in boosting its profits; the Guatemalan government may have acquiesced in the scheme, but it did not request IRCA's assistance in promoting trade with Germany. In fact, Ubico rebuffed German efforts to negotiate a reciprocity treaty for fear of alienating the Roosevelt administration. The issue was IRCA's tariffs, not Guatemala's commercial policy. Welles warned Shepardson that his department could no longer support a private company that ignored American foreign policy and obstructed

Guatemala's economic development. If IRCA failed to adjust its policies to the satisfaction of the department, Welles threatened to expose the State Department's serious reservations about an American company that arbitrarily directed the course of Guatemala's foreign trade in defiance of both the American and Guatemalan governments.[33]

There is no evidence that Shepardson ever received this strongly worded letter, but his company acted as if it finally realized that the State Department expected immediate action. Shepardson could not have afforded to call Welles's bluff, for a public condemnation of IRCA's business practices by the State Department would have validated the positions of its critics. When Marcial Prem blasted Minor Keith's corrupt and stifling business practices in 1921 and the Puerto Barrios strikers condemned IRCA's monopoly power in 1923, the State Department defended IRCA. If Prem and the strikers had received an unequivocal endorsement of their demands from the chief Latin American policymaker of the United States, the Guatemalan government would have found it difficult to suppress the challenges.

On June 9, Myers reiterated his company's right to maintain the tariffs and still denied that it discriminated against American goods, but the department's consistent opposition to the policies eventually forced IRCA to compromise. On July 1 it repeated its demand that IRCA eliminate the discriminatory tariffs, reciting the rationale that because of geographical proximity, American exporters should enjoy considerable advantages over their European competitors.[34] That same day, IRCA issued an amended tariff structure that eliminated some of the discriminatory rates. In almost every case, the new preferential or equitable rates came in items of secondary importance to U.S. commerce. Freight rates for cotton textiles, machinery, iron and steel, and chemicals—items in which competition between the United States and Germany was intense—still gave the Europeans preference. On cotton textiles, IRCA charged $1.15 per one hundred pounds of the American product and only $0.95 per one hundred pounds of European fabric. The discriminatory rates explain the fact that Germany supplied nearly 60 percent of the cotton textiles imported by Guatemala in 1937. Recognizing that the new rates were only a 50 percent improvement over the old ones, Des Portes maintained his demand for at least the equalization of freight rates between Puerto Barrios and Guatemala City.[35]

Had it not been for World War II the conflict between UFCO and the State Department could have gone on indefinitely. The department's dissatisfaction with IRCA's uncooperative attitude is partly reflected in its favorable view of the construction of an automobile highway between Puerto Barrios and Guatemala City. By January 1939 one half of the road had been completed, but a financial shortfall of $200,000 put the entire project on hold.[36] If the highway were completed, trucks could divert some of the freight currently handled by IRCA, thereby providing IRCA with the kind of competition that might force it to adjust its rates. Ironically, when this highway became a pet project of Guatemalan revolutionaries in the 1950s, former United Fruit and IRCA lawyers Allen and John Foster Dulles directed the Central Intelligence Agency and the State Department. As Eisenhower's point men on Guatemala, they considered the highway evidence of the Guatemalan's anti-American and anticapitalist attitude.[37]

Germany's invasion of Poland in August 1939 suspended but did not resolve the IRCA problem for the State Department. With Europe at war, United Fruit shipments to Europe dropped from an average of seven to eight per week to only one per week in October 1939. After the United States entered the war, the War Department requisitioned thousands of merchant vessels for use in supplying the Allied war effort; of the 113 ships UFCO provided, the Axis powers sank 42 of them. Guatemalan banana exports dropped from 8.2 million stems in 1940 to 7.1 million stems in 1941, forcing United to terminate all expansion work then under way.[38]

World War II presented United Fruit with an opportunity to improve relations between it and the State Department, for their mutual survival depended upon effective collaboration. United required government assistance for the stabilization of the American banana market, and in the interest of maintaining stable economies at home and throughout Latin America, the government worked closely with it and other foreign enterprises. The State Department recognized the danger that severe cuts in production and exports presented for the political and economic stability of the Caribbean region, an area of unquestioned strategic importance to the war effort. To stabilize the banana business, the War Production Board met quarterly with representatives of United Fruit and Standard Fruit to allocate shipping space between them. At times the board established quotas as low as 50 percent of prewar needs, and the result was a reduction in U.S. banana imports to the lowest levels since 1899, but the banana companies survived the war.[39]

The prospect of labor unrest in the banana regions also concerned the State Department, for it was determined to maintain a solid, pro-Allied ring of friendly regimes in the Caribbean. It encouraged the banana companies to retain as many workers as possible in Guatemala and Honduras, but without shipping the companies could not afford to keep the plantations in full production. Even though the Tiquisate division abandoned ten thousand acres in 1942, no labor problems resulted, for most of the workers returned to their homes in the highland where they could still obtain temporary employment during the coffee season. The Bananera division kept its plantations producing, but Welles was prepared to offer financial aid for a road construction project in the Petén in the event that UFCO were forced to abandoned its Caribbean division and dismiss thousands of workers.[40]

The exigencies of war reminded the State Department that United Fruit shared its interest in maintaining pro-American regimes in power throughout the region. It also provided material support for the war effort beyond the ships requisitioned for service. As Japanese conquests in the Pacific eliminated or reduced American supplies of rubber, quinine, abaca, palm oils, and twenty other tropical products, the U.S. government encouraged private industry to develop alternative sources of supply in the Caribbean. Under contract with the American government, United Fruit planted some new crops on an experimental basis in Guatemala and five other countries, but it had no intention of operating these plantations on a permanent basis.[41]

Hence, just a few years after flirting with the commercial policies of Nazi Germany, IRCA and UFCO restored friendly relations with the American government. The two companies never yielded much ground to the State Department, but the war eliminated the main point of contention between them and the diplomats. The State Department diplomats had been concerned only about commercial traffic to and from Guatemala; it was not preoccupied with the impact of IRCA's monopolistic practices on Guatemala's economic development. World War II essentially erased the memory of a time when the United States questioned the propriety of an American corporation dictating Guatemala's commercial policy.

During the war, United Fruit's agents skillfully manipulated public opinion and politics to serve their private economic interests. As if it demanded political compensation for its services to the war effort, United Fruit requested government support for its efforts to conceal the true extent of its power. In 1938, Sumner Welles was prepared to disclose embarrassing opinions about the company, but with the world at war, the revelation of United's control of IRCA would arouse anti-Americanism and weaken support for the war effort in Latin America. In 1943, Arthur Nicholson, United's treasurer, asked the Securities and Exchange Commission (SEC) not to reveal the amount of IRCA stock that UFCO controlled (256,000 shares), fearing it would provide ammunition to "agitators" who could cause unforeseeable trouble and impede the war effort.[42]

The SEC acceded to the request, and with the acquiescence of other American agencies, thereby assisted the company's efforts to maximize profits and suppress its critics. As Nicholson explained to the SEC, the disclosure of United's stockholdings in IRCA would create a series of problems for both companies: "Such confusion of the companies in the public mind would spell ruin for the railroad company in Guatemala, as it would prepare the way for demands for higher wages, lower freight and passenger rates, extension of lines, heavy judgments in damage cases, etc., because it would be considered that the United Fruit Company was the same as the Railway Company and could afford all these things."[43]

United Fruit used the Nazi threat to detract attention from the real issue of its monopolization of Guatemalan bananas, railroads, and ports. It is significant that the State Department, not the Guatemalan government, opposed the manner in which UFCO and IRCA arbitrarily directed Guatemala's commercial policy. Ubico refused to take issue with the discriminatory tariffs because he, and a string of authoritarian rulers before him, placed the company's priorities ahead of those of the country. Guatemala's ruling elite had tolerated United's monopolistic practices for decades, and the State Department either ignored or tolerated the policies until they contradicted America's foreign economic policy.

The ease with which UFCO redirected Guatemalan trade to European markets revealed the company's extraordinary power and the peculiar characteristics of Guatemala's political and economic system. United had built and defended its empire with the approval and encouragement of two main dictators, Manuel Estrada Cabrera and Jorge Ubico. Over the years it constructed two formidable enclaves that were carefully insulated from outside interference, either by the American or Guatemalan governments. Neither government possessed sufficient regulatory power, and only one of them demonstrated the willingness to restrain the business practices of IRCA or UFCO before 1944. Despite direct pressure from the State Department, the fruit company continued the discriminatory rate policy until 1945, when IRCA could no longer afford to maintain it.[44]

United Fruit and IRCA operated beyond the regulatory arms of either the Guatemalan or American government for over forty years. Officials within both governments occasionally expressed dissatisfaction with the companies, but they never accumulated the political strength required to bring them under effective control. During the Liberal period of Guatemalan history, a succession of authoritarian and corrupt chief executives provided UFCO and IRCA with the concessions they needed and political repression they occasionally required to maintain their privileges. It would take a popular revolution to unseat the dictators who did the bidding of the fruit company first and served the economic interests of their country second.

Notes

1. Cited in Munro, *Intervention and Dollar Diplomacy*, 116.

2. LaFeber, *Inevitable Revolutions*, 60–62; on U.S. policy toward Guatemala and Central America see Lester D. Langley, *The United States and the Caribbean in the Twentieth Century* (Athens: University of Georgia Press, 1980); Dinwoodie, "Expedient Diplomacy."

3. Arthur Geissler to State, January 31, 1929, SD 814.1561/14; Gleijeses, *Shattered Hope*, 90; Grieb, *Guatemalan Caudillo*, 182.

4. LaFeber, *Inevitable Revolutions*, 80.

5. Herbert S. Gould to State, December 28, 1920, SD 814.00/517; Richard Southgate to State, May 5, 1922, SD 814.77/113; memorandum of conversation, Francis White and Joseph Montgomery, April 8, 1929, SD 815.6156/34 1/2.

6. Sumner Welles (undersecretary of state) to President Franklin D. Roosevelt, January 18, 1938, enclosure, Fay Allen Des Portes (minister to Guatemala) to Roosevelt, December 23, 1937, SD 814.773/32.

7. Kobler, "Sam the Banana Man," 84.

8. Irwin F. Gellman, *Good Neighbor Diplomacy: U.S. Policies in Latin America, 1933–1945* (Baltimore: Johns Hopkins Press, 1979), 48; Kenneth Grieb, "Negotiating a Reciprocal Trade Agreement with an Underdeveloped Country: Guatemala as a Case Study, *Prologue* 5 (Spring 1973): 23–29.

9. Grieb, "Negotiating a Reciprocal Trade Agreement," 27–29; Dick Steward, *Trade and Hemisphere: The Good Neighbor Policy and Reciprocal Trade* (Colombia: University of Missouri Press, 1975), 211.

10. White (adviser on international economic affairs), "Some Notes on the International Railways of Central America Case," SD 814.773/24.

11. Welles to Roosevelt, January 18, 1938, SD 814.773/32.

12. White, "Notes on the IRCA Case," SD 814.773/24.

13. Davies, *Fyffes and the Banana*, 160–61; White, "Notes on the IRCA Case," SD 814.773/24.

14. Kepner and Soothill, *Banana Empire*, 179–85; memorandum of conversation, Charles Myers and Drew, June 8, 1938, SD 814.773/51; naval attache's report, March 22, 1938, SD 814.773/47; Welles to Roosevelt, January 18, 1938, enclosure, Des Portes to Roosevelt, December 23, 1937, SD 814.773/32; White, "Notes on the IRCA Case," SD 814.773/24.

15. Milton A. Kallis to Victor H. Kramer and W. Perry Epes, December 20, 1952, 9–11, DOJ, File 60-166-6; Davies, *Fyffes and the Banana*, 147–49.

16. Davies, *Fyffes and the Banana*, 147–49; Vincent Blaise D'Antoni, "A Case Study and Critique of the United Fruit Company and the Consent Decree" (DBA diss., Washington University, 1965).

17. Des Portes to State, March 4, 1938, enclosure no. 1, SD 814.773/38; Des Portes to State, April 2, 1938, SD 814.773/46.

18. Welles to Whitney Shepardson, [May 1938], memorandum from the adviser on International Economic Affairs, SD 814.773/40.

19. White, "Notes on the IRCA Case," SD 814.773/24.

20. Bulmer-Thomas, *Political Economy*, 78.

21. Welles to Shepardson, [May 1938], memorandum, SD 814.773/40; Grieb, *Guatemalan Caudillo*, 148; Bulmer-Thomas, *Political Economy*, 79.

22. Memorandum on International Railways of Central America, December 28, 1937, SD 814.773/28.

23. Des Portes to Roosevelt, December 23, 1937, SD 814.773/32; Welles to Roosevelt, January 18, 1933.

24. Welles to Roosevelt, January 18, 1932, SD 814.773/32.

25. Memorandum of telephone conversation, February 4, 1938, SD 814.773/34.

26. Des Portes to State, April 2, 1938, SD 814.773/46.

27. George Bennett (manager, UFCO) to George P. Chittenden, July 14, 1931, DOJ, Series 537, IRCA-85 [PX 145].

28. Des Portes, memorandum of telephone conversation, February 4, 1938, SD 814.773/34; Grieb, *Guatemalan Caudillo*, 27; Sidney E. O'Donoghue (U.S. embassy in Mexico) to John W. Carrigan (State Department), SD 814.00/1-12545.

29. Grieb, *Guatemalan Caudillo*, 248–51; report of the military attaché, January 20, 1938, SD 814.00MID/15; Des Portes to State, March 15, 1938, SD 814.00B/30; Des Portes to State, February 3, 1937, SD 814.504/35.

30. Memorandum, May 29, 1930, DOJ, Series 537, IRCA-76.

31. Intelligence Division, Office of Chief of Naval Operations, Navy Department, attache's report, March 22, 1938, SD 814.773/47.

32. Welles to Shepardson, SD 814.773/40.

33. Ibid.

34. Duggan to Myers, July 1, 1938, SD 814.773/50.

35. Des Portes to Duggan, July 28, 1938, SD 814.773/53; Des Portes to State, August 8, 1938, SD 814.773/54.

36. Walter H. McKinney (chargé d'affaires ad interim) to State, January 13, 1939, SD 814.773/56.

37. Immerman, *CIA in Guatemala*, 124.

38. Des Portes to State, October 25, 1939, SD 814.6156/19; Dunn, "Situation of the Banana Industry," May 4, 1942, SD 814.6156/24; Wilson, *Empire in Green and Gold*, 288.

39. Karnes, *Tropical Enterprise*, 208–9; Wilson, *Empire in Green and Gold*, 288.

40. Welles to American legation, September 1, 1942, SD 814.154/134A; Drew to State, September 20, 1942, SD 814.154/135; J. M. Cabot to Bonsal, November 19, 1942, SD 814.6156; Dunn, "Situation of the Banana Industry," May 4, 1942, SD 814.6156/24.

41. Wilson, *Empire in Green and Gold*, 295.

42. Arthur Nicholson to Purcell, January 23, 1943, DOJ, File 60-166-56, Series 537, IRCA-142.

43. Nicholson to Jerome N. Frank, February 3, 1941, DOJ, File 60-166-56, Series 537, IRCA-34.

44. Thomas Bradshaw to John L. Simpson, October 8, 1946, DOJ, File 60-166-56, Series 537, IRCA-154 [PX 257].

Epilogue

General Jorge Ubico resigned on July 1, 1944. For the last two weeks of June, students, teachers, workers, women, and middle-class professionals had demonstrated their opposition to his dictatorial policies. The old dictator fought at first and then decided that he had had enough. He left power in the hands of a military triumvirate, from which General Federico Ponce Vaídes emerged as the leading candidate for dictator. On October 20, 1944, young military officers deposed General Ponce in a lightning-quick coup. Generals Ubico and Ponce fled the country, and the seventy-three-year rule of the Liberal party came to an end.[1]

For decades, if not centuries, the Guatemalan elite sat on a revolutionary powder keg. From a society in which a majority of people were ill fed, underemployed, illiterate, and politically repressed, a revolutionary movement could have sprung at virtually any moment. Without the periodic deployment of military force, the generals, *finqueros*, and foreign capitalists could not have maintained a political economic system that promoted the interests of a minority at the expense of the majority.

Only the most intransigent and insensitive decision makers did not recognize a pressing need for change. Liberal policies had produced tangible, almost impressive material results, primarily in infrastructure. Yet the expansion of coffee and banana exports that those developments facilitated did not benefit the majority of Guatemalans. That fact was evident even in the U.S. government, which was certainly not known for its sensitivity to Guatemala's repressed majority. In 1941 the Office of Strategic Services (OSS, the predecessor of the CIA) explained the heart of the matter: "The benefits of coffee and banana production, the main source of wealth, are realized by foreigners and a small group of ladinos."[2]

The gross inequities of the Guatemalan system became a concern for U.S. policymakers in the 1940s because they, unlike Generals Ubico and Ponce, worried that the interests of the majority could not be ignored much longer. The majority of Guatemalans lived in conditions that the OSS characterized as "extraordinarily low, lower than a number of comparable areas in the American tropics." In 1941, 80 percent of Guatemalans could neither read nor write, and only 5 percent of school-age children were enrolled in school. According to the OSS analysts, the sources of Guatemalan insecurity were a "primitive, impoverished Indian population ruled by an absolute dictator, a national economy largely dependent on two export crops, coffee and bananas, and a general agricultural backwardness which leaves four fifths of the land totally uncultivated."[3]

The modernization that the Liberal elite had been promoting reached only a fraction of the people. After seven decades of economic growth, only a small wealthy class enjoyed a decent standard of living. Life for the majority of the people was characterized by poor housing, dietary deficiencies, inadequate sanitation, and substandard medical care. As described by an OSS analyst in 1943, the average Guatemalan lived in an unhealthy environment: "Dwellings are usually one room adobe or mud and stick huts with thatch or tile roofs, dirt floors and no windows or screens. The walls and roofs harbor vermin and noxious insects. Sanitary facilities are completely lacking and the water supply is often polluted and insufficient."[4]

The most repressed people of Guatemalan society, however, did not lead the revolution of 1944. The revolution sprang from the urban middle and lower classes, people who owed their positions to opportunities created by a modernization process that required professors, teachers, bureaucrats, military officers, lawyers, hotel managers, small businessmen, doctors, and bankers. These people drove the anti-Ubico movement and pushed for a series of reforms designed to open the political structure and spread the benefits of modernization to a larger sector of society.[5]

While the workers played only a minor role in the events leading to Ubico's resignation, the proletariat mobilized quickly and led the attack on United Fruit's monopoly. The resignation of Ubico left the political apparatus intact and did no damage to United Fruit's empire. From early July to October 1944, railroad and plantation workers, acting locally and spontaneously at first, began to transform a political reform movement into a revolutionary front that aimed at the destruction of United Fruit's monopoly.

By July 8, IRCA workers had formed Guatemala's first true labor union, the Sindicato de Acción y Mejoramiento Ferrocarrilero (SAMF, Syndicate for Action and Betterment of Railway Workers).[6] Shortly thereafter, plantation workers at Bananera and Tiquisate petitioned United for better working conditions and recognition of their new labor unions. Although they were some of the highest paid workers in Guatemala, they had been hurt by an inflationary spiral that had reduced their standard of living. On July 7, workers in the Bananera Divisions petitioned for wage increases on the grounds that the prices of basic necessities had risen 150 percent, and because the overthrow of General Ubico had opened a new era of "liberty and progress," the workers felt that they had the right to demand higher wages. The workers had made a similar request in October 1943, but they withdrew it at the request of the government, only to have their demands ignored. This time, the workers threatened to strike on July 10 if UFCO did not meet their demands.[7]

As far as General Ponce and United Fruit were concerned, Guatemala had not yet entered a new era. They initially balked at the workers' demands for a 75 to 100 percent wage increase because they feared that it would contribute to inflation. Management therefore offered only 10 to 15 percent increases, and the workers accepted. Inspired by their colleagues in Bananera, the Tiquisate workers struck on July 24. To protect United Fruit personnel and property, the government sent in troops and brought both sides to the bargaining table. The labor settlement of August 9 represented another minor victory for labor. While wages were increased only 15 percent, for the first time United recognized the eight-hour workday and promised not to take punitive actions against the strike leaders.[8]

The Tiquisate strike was accompanied by a more serious dispute between railroad workers and IRCA management. On July 15, SAMF petitioned IRCA president Jack Armstrong for a salary increase, compliance with all labor laws, better medical service, pensions, overtime, and paid vacations. The workers set an August 5 deadline for Armstrong's response and threatened to shut down the railroad. When the response came on August 4, it was totally unsatisfactory, but the government convinced the workers to postpone the strike.[9]

IRCA's problems continued a month longer, partly because the labor controversy became tied up with larger political issues. The middle-class reformists lent their support to the workers and gave them a power and credibility that helped them extract concessions from a company that had grown accustomed to ignoring worker demands. On August 17, Armstrong offered only a 15 percent wage increase, claiming that his company was nearly bankrupt. As for the other demands, he reminded the workers that they enjoyed better working conditions that any other laborers in Guatemala.[10]

Armstrong's reactionary position came under attack from the Frente Popular Libertador (FPL), one of the reformist political parties that emerged following Ubico's resignation. The FPL presented statistics to refute Armstrong's claim that the company could not afford to accede to the wage demands. It took particular exception to the company's wage scale, which gave foreign managers six hundred to two thousand quetzales per month, while no Guatemalan made more than three hundred quetzales per month. This foreign firm, the FPL argued, was organized and directed by persons who were a discredit to their nationality.[11]

Never before had a political party represented and promoted the interests of the working class. The Conservatives had used the workers in 1920 to wrest control of the government from Manuel Estrada Cabrera and the Liberals, but they discarded them once Herrera had assumed the presidency.

The FPL sympathized with the demands of the workers and promoted a political agenda that included labor legislation and the suppression of monopolies.[12] In an alliance between the workers and middle-class reformists lay the greatest potential for the destruction of the Liberal state and United Fruit's empire.

The immediate objective of the reformists was the removal of the militaristic leaders who served United Fruit, because Ubico's resignation had not eliminated the clique of generals eager to replace him. General Ponce, believing himself a fitting heir to Ubico, was attempting to repress the democratic movement and build another corrupt dictatorship. In fact, his clique may have exploited the IRCA labor dispute for its own sordid purposes. Ponce's minister of finance, Manuel Melgar, suggested that the dispute could be fixed by the "use of a little money," but Armstrong refused to settle the controversy by bribing him. Ambassador Boaz Long also heard credible reports that General Ponce was prolonging the dispute in order to create social disturbances that might justify the establishment of a new dictatorship.[13]

Skeptical of the government's willingness to support his company, Armstrong accepted the decision of a commission that Ponce appointed to resolve the labor dispute. While an agreement of September 7 split the difference between the wages demanded by the workers and Armstrong's offer, the commission supported the company on all other issues. The workers did not win the eight-hour workday, sick leave, vacation time, or better medical service. The agreement contained one clause by which management affirmed what the agreement was not—a collective contract; Armstrong held firm to the company's long-standing policy of not recognizing the workers' right to strike or bargain collectively. It was only a tentative step forward for the workers.[14]

As long as the generals held onto power, the workers could not expect any more from the government. Ponce and the political-military apparatus had to be destroyed before the workers and the reformists could begin the attack on United Fruit's monopoly. Over the course of the next month, it became clear that Ponce could only be removed by force. While the military units commanded by Major Francisco Arana and Captain Jacobo Arbenz led the assault against General Ponce on the morning of October 20, civilian units composed of students and workers also took up arms and engaged the defenders of the old order. By one account the rebellious military units distributed about five thousand arms to civilians and deployed the civil brigades as police units, some of which actually participated in combat.[15]

The revolution of October 20 was no ordinary military rebellion. It was a broadly based popular movement in which civilians, both men and women, fought for more than just the removal of General Ponce and the clique he served. They intended to revolutionize society, and thousands of people risked their lives for a more democratic and just country. When the firing stopped, the rule of the Liberal party was over. The struggle that pitted nationalistic Guatemalans against the United Fruit Company and the U.S. government, however, was just beginning. A new day had dawned in Guatemala, and United could no longer count on the support of a repressive government.

From 1944 to 1954 one revolutionary junta and two democratically elected presidents severed the ties between the government and the foreign monopolies. President Juan José Arévalo (1945–1950) passed a comprehensive labor code that guaranteed workers the right to organize, strike, and bargain collectively. For supporting labor, establishing a social security system, and interfering with the company's internal affairs, Arévalo earned the enmity of United Fruit. With United's cozy ties to the government definitively broken, its rivals recognized an opportunity to compete for a share of the banana business. In 1948, Standard Fruit incorporated a subsidiary in Guatemala to purchase bananas from independent planters, and it was soon exporting one hundred thousand stems per month from Puerto Barrios.[16]

President Jacobo Arbenz (1951–1954) intensified the attack on United's power with the full support of the labor organizations and the Communist party. To encourage competition with UFCO and IRCA, Arbenz accelerated construction of a highway to the Atlantic and initiated work on a new Caribbean port. To the applause of workers, labor organizers, and radical revolutionaries, he expropriated over four hundred thousand acres of uncultivated United Fruit land in 1953. He took from the company that which it had acquired from corrupt dictators. United Fruit responded by unleashing a furious propaganda assault against Arbenz and supporting the counterrevolutionary movement organized by the Central Intelligence Agency. Arbenz resigned on June 27, and Colonel Carlos Castillo Armas, a favorite of the CIA and United Fruit, assumed the presidency two weeks later.[17]

On July 2 the DOJ filed suit against United Fruit, claiming that it had stifled competition and controlled banana prices in violation of the Sherman Antitrust Act. The DOJ asked the court to dissolve or divorce from United Fruit some or all of eleven wholly owned subsidiary corporations, including the Compañía Agrícola de Guatemala.[18] The department was prepared to file the suit in June 1953, but at the request of John Foster Dulles, secretary of state and former UFCO lawyer, the National Security Council postponed the suit for fear of validating the charges leveled against it by the Arbenz administration.[19]

The installation of Castillo Armas restored United Fruit's friendly relations with the Guatemalan government, but for reasons of national security and domestic economic welfare, the United States could no longer afford to have its policies closely identified with UFCO. There is no doubt that influential members of the Eisenhower administration had intimate relations with United. Allen Dulles, director of the CIA, was a former counsel to IRCA and a UFCO shareholder; General Robert Cutler, special assistant to the president for national security affairs, was a former president of Boston's Old Colony Trust Company and a former UFCO director; Thomas Corcoran was a paid consultant to UFCO at the same time he worked for the CIA. Yet because so many Latin Americans believed that American foreign policy served the interests of United Fruit, John Foster Dulles supported the antitrust suit in June 1954 on the grounds that the formal disassociation of the government from United Fruit would have a positive impact on U.S. relations with Latin America.[20] The elimination of Arbenz and the perceived Communist threat ironically removed the only remaining reason for the Eisenhower administration to conceal its opposition to United Fruit's monopolistic practices.

Hence, the DOJ initiated the process that broke United Fruit's monopoly on Guatemala's railroad network and the banana business. The DOJ never won a conviction in court, and United maintained its innocence to the end, for in 1958 the parties settled the dispute through a consent decree that implied no admission of guilt on the part of UFCO. At the same time, the decree specifically prohibited United from entering into any agreements by which it restricted the production, transportation, or sale of bananas. The decree compelled United to divest of its holdings in IRCA and form an independent banana company with the capacity of importing nine million stems annually. Although United was slow to comply with the many conditions of the consent decree, it sold its interest in IRCA, and the Guatemalan government purchased the line in 1968. Del Monte purchased what remained of United's highly productive banana properties in 1972.[21]

While the U.S. government terminated United Fruit's monopoly, it also had provided timely assistance to it. American diplomatic intervention helped United repress occasional challenges to its authority, and U.S. policy always supported regimes that welcomed and protected American investment. United Fruit could not have built its empire without the acquiescence of a corrupt cadre of caudillos who were more interested in personal aggrandizement than in national development. These people sanctioned United's monopoly, authorized its concessions, repressed labor, and silenced opposition to it in the press and legislature. While the State Department may have encouraged the Guatemalan elite to adopt pro-American policies, it did not dictate the terms under which United Fruit conducted business in Guatemala. Through discreet negotiations that usually involved either bribery or extortion, United Fruit obtained its properties and concessions from the Guatemalan government, not from the State Department.

We should not concern ourselves with the question of who committed the more serious offense, the person who offered or the person who accepted illicit payoffs. High-ranking officers of the United Fruit Company—

Minor Keith, Victor Cutter, and Samuel Zemurray—and high-ranking officers of the Guatemalan government—Manuel Estrada Cabrera, Lázaro Chacón and Jorge Ubico—are equally responsible for the repression and injustices that existed in Guatemala. United Fruit by no means created the poverty and exploitation that existed in the villages and the fincas, where the Guatemalan elite reigned supreme. The American capitalists and their collaborators in the government, however, must be held accountable for a monopolistic system that deprived Guatemalans of resources that could have been diverted toward a more broadly based national development program.

From 1904 until 1944 the United Fruit Company and its affiliate, the International Railways of Central America, controlled Guatemala's railroad, ports, and banana industry. It paid few taxes and low wages while it exported profits and paid dividends to New England shareholders. United Fruit answered to no regulatory body, and caudillos abdicated their responsibilities for personal gain. When young students and officers overthrew the Liberal party in October 1944, they dared to fight for the principle that their government should respond to and promote the political and economic interests of those it governed. Although the 1944 revolution failed, United Fruit and the Liberal dictatorships have been defeated, and opposition to exploitation by American enterprise and corrupt governments still shapes contemporary political struggles.

Notes

1. For the history of the revolutionary movement see Grieb, *Guatemalan Caudillo*, 265–80; Immerman, *CIA in Guatemala*, 37–43.
2. "Current Factors of Insecurity in Guatemala," November 12, 1941, O.S.S./State Department Intelligence and Research Reports, vol. 14, *Latin America: 1941–1961* (hereafter cited as OSS Reports).
3. Ibid.
4. "Survey of Guatemala," July 19, 1943, OSS Reports.
5. Jaime Diaz Rozzotto, *El carácter de la revolución guatemalteca* (México: Ediciones Revista "Horizonte," 1958), 35; Susanne Jonas, *The Battle for Guatemala: Rebels, Death Squads, and U.S. Power* (Boulder: Westview Press, 1991), 23; Mario Monteforte Toledo, *La revolución en Guatemala* (Guatemala: Editorial Universitaria, 1975), 11; Rene Poitevín, *El proceso de industrialización en Guatemala* (San José: Editorial Universitaria Centroamericana, 1977), 143–50.
6. Bush, *Organized Labor*, pt. 3, 2.
7. Boaz Long (ambassador to Guatemala) to State, SD 814.504/7-1444; *Nuestro Diario*, July 19, 1944.
8. Long to State, SD 814.504/7-1544; Long to State, SD 814.504/7-2544; Long to State, SD 814.504/8-1144.

9. Long to State, SD 814.504/8-444; "Pronto será resuelto el problema ferrocarrillero," *El Libertador*, August 12, 1944.

10. "La Empresa Ferrocarrillera será responsable de la huelga," *El Libertador*, August 21, 1944.

11. "Otros casos de explotación por la Ferrocarrilera," *El Libertador*, August 12, 1944; "Cinicas declaraciones de J. P. Armstrong," *El Libertador*, August 18, 1944.

12. "Ideario del Frente Popular Libertador," *El Libertador*, July 23, 1944.

13. Long to State, SD 814.504/9-444; Long to State, SD 814.504/9-2644.

14. Long to State, SD 814.504/9-1444.

15. William C. Affeld (chargé d'affaires ad interim) to State, October 24, 1944, enclosure 3, Victor R. Rose (assistant military attaché), "Revolution of 20 October 1944," October 23, 1944, SD 814.00/10-2444.

16. Karnes, *Tropical Enterprise*, 270–71. On the revolutionary period there are a number of excellent works, particularly Gleijeses, *Shattered Hope*, and Immerman, *CIA in Guatemala*.

17. Gleijeses, *Shattered Hope*, 149–70; Immerman, *CIA in Guatemala*, 161–86; Schlesinger and Kinzer, *Bitter Fruit*, 65–97.

18. "Antitrust Suit is Faced by UFC," *Times Picayune* (New Orleans), July 3, 1954; D'Antoni, "A Case Study of United Fruit," 1–26.

19. "Effect on National Security Interests in Latin America of Possible Anti-Trust Proceedings," June 1, 1953, *FRUS, 1952–1954*, 4: 191–96;

20. Mosley, *Dulles*, 347; Immerman, *CIA in Guatemala*, 124–25; "Memorandum of Discussion at the 202d Meeting of the National Security Council on Thursday, June 17, 1954," *FRUS, 1952–1954*, 4: 224–26.

21. D'Antoni, "A Case Study of United Fruit," 29–35; Jonas and Tobis, *Guatemala*, 131.

Bibliography

U.S. Department of State records constitute a primary source of documentation for this study of United Fruit in Guatemala. While historians have generally extracted only political and diplomatic data from the State Department records, the political files form only a small part of the total documentary record. In addition to reports on political affairs from the U.S. minister, the files contain analyses by military, economic, and commercial attachés. American officials promoted and defended U.S. economic interests, and businessmen routinely sought the advice and protection of their legation, particularly when threatened by hostile hosts. As a result, the State Department records contain valuable documents on the operations of American businesses in Latin America.

The original State Department files are housed in the National Archives in Washington, DC, and are divided into two principal groups: Record Group 59, General Records of the Department of State (known as the Decimal File); and Record Group 84, Diplomatic and Consular Post Records. Since many of the post records are reproduced in the Decimal File, the researcher should begin with this group of documents. Prior to 1906 the State Department simply filed despatches and reports as they arrived in Washington, making it difficult for subsequent scholars to access documentation. Between 1906 and 1910 the State Department used a numerical file system that proved to be completely unmanageable. Beginning in 1910 it adopted a classification system in which countries and topics are assigned a number. The decimal file system, as it is called, has worked well for both diplomats and scholars. The 814.00 file deals with general political conditions in Guatemala; 814.20, military affairs; 814.50, economic affairs; 814.60, agriculture and industry; and 814.77, railroads.

There are further topical subdivisions, and the records for 1910–1929 are indexed. However, from 1910 on, all records can be accessed by the file number only. Hence, in all references to Record Group 59 in this study, I have cited the decimal file number, date, and author. With the decimal file number the documents can be easily accessed in the National Archives or in one of several microfilm series.

A large portion of the State Department records from the 1820s to the 1950s has been microfilmed and distributed to many U.S. libraries. Researchers should utilize the microfilm records before visiting the National Archives, since the archivists will direct all researchers to the microfilm if it is available. The following microfilm series were consulted during the course of this study:

U.S. Department of State. Despatches from U.S. Consuls in Guatemala, 1824–1906.

————. Despatches from U.S. Ministers to Central America, 1824–1906.

————. Notes from Central American Legations in the United States, 1823–1906.

————. Records of the Department of State Relating to Internal Affairs of Central America, 1910–1929. (File 813.00)

————. Records of the Department of State Relating to Internal Affairs of Guatemala, 1910–1929. (File 814.00)

————. Records of the Department of State Relating to Internal Affairs of Guatemala, 1930–1944. (File 814.00)

————. Records of the Department of State Relating to Internal Affairs of Guatemala, 1945–1949. (File 814.00)

————. Records of the Department of State Relating to Internal Affairs of Honduras, 1910–1929. (File 815.00)

Items dealing specifically with inter-American relations are found in the 700 file. Information on the Guatemalan-Honduran boundary dispute, in which United Fruit played a pivotal role, is filed under 714.15. These records have been microfilmed in twenty-six reels and are easily accessible by an index:

U.S. Department of State. Records of the Department of State Relating to Political Relations between Guatemala and Other States, 1910–1929.

Unfortunately, only a small portion of Record Group 84 has been microfilmed, and the records are generally more difficult to access in the National Archives. This record group holds documents accumulated by diplomatic and consular posts around the world. Not all of these documents were transmitted to the State Department, so the post records contain valuable information unavailable elsewhere. For this study the records of the Guatemala City legation and consulate were the most important, since the various consulates transmitted most of their reports and documentation to this post. Some of the records are ostensibly classified according to the decimal file system, but the records of subconsular officials are filed consecutively in bound volumes without an index. Access to Record Group 84 seems imposing at first, but the archivists will guide the researcher through a series that contains useful information. The following post records have been cited in this study:

U.S. National Archives. Diplomatic Branch. Record Group 84, Foreign Service Post Records, Washington, DC.
Diplomatic Post Records, Guatemala City, 1912–1935
Consular Post Records
Guatemala City Consulate, 1912–1935
Livingston Consulate, 1882–1920
Puerto Barrios Consulate, 1914–1934

One can only wish that more Guatemalan government documents would be released and cataloged. The Archivo General de Centro América (AGCA) contains the records of the Ministerio de Fomento, which handled negotiations with foreign companies, analyzed proposed concessions, and theoretically monitored the activities of United Fruit. Unfortunately, very few post-1900 Ministerio de Fomento documents are available, and those that are accessible have not been cataloged. The AGCA has the personal papers of Manuel Estrada Cabrera, but they are not yet indexed, and they apparently contain few documents of any value. Of greater use to this study was the index to the Ministerio de Fomento documents, which is available upon request at the AGCA. The *legajos* are not always subdivided by *expediente*, so precise citations to these documents are sometimes impossible. The following *legajos* were consulted:

Ministerio de Fomento. Signatura B129

22170	Miscellaneous Projects
22171–22178	Ferrocarril de Los Altos
22179	Ferrocarril Occidental
22180–22181	Ferrocarril Central
22182	Ferrocarril Iztapa
22183	Ferrocarril del Norte
22184	Ferrocarril Occidental
22185–22187	Ferrocarril Ocós
22188	Ferrocarril Verapaz
22189–22190	Ferrocarril Zacapa-Frontera
22191–22027	Ferrocarriles Internacionales de Centro América
22091–22092	Cía. Frutera

Another important documentary collection is the records of the Pacific Improvement Company, a subsidiary of Collis P. Huntington's

U.S. Southern Pacific Railroad, which owned the strategically important Guatemala Central Railroad from 1884 to 1912. These documents were donated to Stanford University and contain the only known records of a U.S. corporation with holdings in Guatemala. The Guatemala Central Railroad Company documents form a significant portion of the total collection. Included in the records are balance sheets, contracts, concessions, and miscellaneous correspondence. The documents are available at:

Stanford University Libraries. Department of Special Collections and University Archives. Pacific Improvement Company Records, JL 1 and JL 17.

The primary documents utilized in this study are those of the Department of Justice (DOJ), and they provided the most valuable insights. Investigators in the Anti-Trust Division of the DOJ subpoenaed thousands of documents from the United Fruit Company and other sources and, based on an examination of evidence submitted by United, the DOJ filed an antitrust suit against the company in 1954. Some of the materials accumulated in the course of the investigation have been released under the Freedom of Information Act, while many others may remain classified under a court order. These documents include some materials normally available only in a corporate archive, including minutes of the board of directors meetings, correspondence between Boston and division headquarters, private contracts, and policies toward independent planters and rival companies. DOJ documents have been cited in the text by file number (60-166-56), series number, author, date, and, where applicable, a brief title. The documents are available through:

U.S. Department of Justice. Anti-Trust Division. *United States v. United Fruit Co.* Civil No. 4560. File 60-166-56.

Published Government Reports and Documents

Bourne, Kenneth, and D. Cameron Watt, eds. and comps. *British Documents on Foreign Affairs. Reports and Papers from the Foreign Office Confidential Print, Part II, Series D, Latin America, 1914–1939*. Bethesda, MD: University Publications of America, 1990.
Comisión Técnica de demarcación de la frontera entre Honduras y Guatemala. *Informe detallado de la Comisión Técnica de Demarcación de la frontera entre Honduras y Guatemala*. Washington: W. F. Roberts Company, 1937.

Great Britain. Board of Trade. Department of Overseas Trade. *Report on the Economic and Financial Conditions in Guatemala*. 1906, 1922–1937.

Guatemala. Asamblea Legislativa. *Diario de las Sesiones de la Asamblea Legislativa de la República de Guatemala*. Guatemala, 1930.

Guatemala. Secretaría de Agricultura. *Apertura de un Puerto Moderno en el Pacífico: Memorandum del Señor Ministro de Agricultura al Señor Presidente de la Comisión Extraordinaria de Fomento de la Asamblea Nacional Legislativa*. Guatemala, 1930.

Guatemala. Secretaría de Guerra. *Memoria de la Secretaría de Guerra, Año 1924*. Guatemala, 1924.

Guatemala-Honduras Boundary Arbitration. *The Case of Guatemala Submitted to the Arbitral Tribunal Composed of: The Hon. Charles Evans Hughes, Chief Justice of the United States of America; Hon. Luis Casto Ureña, from Costa Rica; Hon. Emilio Bello Codesido, from Chile. Under Treaty of July 16, 1930*. Washington, 1932.

Guatemala Railway Company. *Annual Report of the Guatemala Railway Company, 1911*. New York, 1911.

International Railways of Central America. *Annual Report, 1920*. New York, 1920.

———. *International Railways of Central America, Concessions, Contracts and Decrees, 1877–1912*. Boston: Press of George H. Ellis Company, 1913.

United Fruit Company. *Annual Report*. 1899/1900–1960.

U.S. Congress. House. Committee on the Merchant Marine and Fisheries. *Proceedings of the Committee on the Merchant Marine and Fisheries in the Investigation of Shipping Combinations under House Resolution 587*. 62 Cong., 2d sess., 1913.

———. Senate. Committee on Interstate Commerce. *United Fruit Company, Hearing before a Subcommittee of the Committee on Interstate Commerce, United States Senate . . . on Resolution S. No. 139, submitted by Mr. Johnston, directing the Dept. of Commerce and Labor to Make an Investigation into the Character and Operation of the United Fruit Company*. 60th Cong., 1st sess., 1908.

U.S. Department of State. Bureau of Foreign and Domestic Commerce. *Consular Reports*. Vols. 1–75 (1880–1903).

———. *Papers Relating to the Foreign Relations of the United States*. 1917, 1919, 1928.

———. *Review of the World's Commerce, 1899*.

U.S. OSS/State Department Intelligence and Research Reports, Vol. XIV. *Latin America: 1941–1961*. Washington: University Publications of America Microfilm Project.

Books

Adams, Frederick Upham. *Conquest of the Tropics: The Story of the Creative Enterprises Conducted by the United Fruit Company.* Garden City, NY: Doubleday, Page & Company, 1914.

Aguilar Peralta, J. Humberto. *Vida y muerte de una dictadura: el drama político de Guatemala.* México: Linotipográfica Nieto's, 1944.

Arévalo Martínez, Rafael. *¡Ecce Pericles! Historia de la tiranía de Manuel Estrada Cabrera.* 2 vols. 2d ed., Costa Rica: Editorial Universitaria Centroamericana, 1971.

———. *Ubico.* Guatemala: Tipografía Nacional, 1984.

Asturias, Miguel Angel. *The Eyes of the Interred.* Translated by Gregory Rabassa. New York: Delacorte Press, 1973.

———. *The Green Pope.* Translated by Gregory Rabassa. New York: Delacorte Press, 1971.

———. *Strong Wind.* Translated by Gregory Rabassa. New York: Delacorte Press, 1968.

Bauer Paiz, Alfonso. *Como opera el capital yanqui en Centroamérica: el caso de Guatemala.* México: Editora Ibero-Mexicana, 1956.

Beals, Carleton. *Banana Gold.* Philadelphia: J. B. Lippincott Company, 1932.

Beaver, Patrick. *Yes! We Have Some; The Story of Elders & Fyffes.* Welwyn Garden City, Hertfordshire, England: Broadwater Press, 1976.

Bitter, Friedrich Wilhelm. *Die wirtschaftliche eroberung Mittelamerikas durch den bananen-trust.* Hamburg: G. Westerman, 1921.

Bourgois, Philippe. *Ethnicity at Work: Divided Labor on a Central American Banana Plantation.* Baltimore: Johns Hopkins University Press, 1989.

Bryce-Laporte, Roy Simon, with Trevor Purcell. "A Lesser-known Chapter of the African Diaspora: West Indians in Costa Rica, Central America." In *Global Dimensions of the African Diaspora*, edited by Joseph Harris, 219–39. Washington: Howard University Press, 1982.

Bulmer-Thomas, Victor. *The Political Economy of Central America since 1920.* Cambridge: Cambridge University Press, 1987.

Bush, Archer C. *Organized Labor in Guatemala, 1944–1949: A Case Study of an Adolescent Labor Movement in an Underdeveloped Country.* Hamilton, NY: Colgate University, 1950.

Butchelder, Charles Foster. *Tropic Gold: The Story of the Banana Pioneer, Captain Lorenzo Dow Baker.* Boston: W. D. Bradstreet, 1951.

Cambranes, Julio Castellano. *Coffee and Peasants in Guatemala: The Origins of the Modern Plantation Economy in Guatemala, 1853–1897.* Stockholm: Institute for Latin American Studies, 1985.

―――. *El Imperialismo Alemán en Guatemala: el Tratado de Comercio de 1887.* Guatemala: Universidad de San Carlos, Instituto de Investigaciones Económicas y Sociales, 1977.

Cardoso, Ciro F. S., and Héctor Pérez Brignoli. *Centro América y la economía occidental, 1530–1930.* San José: Editorial Universidad de Costa Rica, 1977.

Cardoso, Fernando Henrique, and Enzo Falleto. *Dependency and Development in Latin America.* Translated by Marjory Mattingly Urquidi. Berkeley: University of California Press, 1979.

Casey Gaspar, Jeffrey. *Limón: 1880–1940; un estudio de la industria bananera en Costa Rica.* San José: Editorial Costa Rica, 1979.

Clayton, Lawrence. *Grace: W. R. Grace & Co., The Formative Years, 1850–1930.* Ottawa, IL: Jameson Books, 1985.

Coatsworth, John. *Growth Against Development: The Economic Impact of Railroads in Porfirian Mexico.* DeKalb: Northern Illinois University Press, 1981.

Conniff, Michael. *Black Labor on a White Canal: Panama, 1904–1981.* Pittsburgh: University of Pittsburgh Press, 1985.

Crowther, Samuel. *The Romance and Rise of the Tropics.* Garden City, NY: Doubleday & Doran, 1929.

Cutter, Victor M. *Trade Relations with Latin America.* Boston: United Fruit Company, 1929.

Davies, Peter. *Fyffes and the Banana: A Centenary History, 1898–1988.* London: The Athlone Press, 1990.

De León Aragón, Oscar. *Los contratos de la United Fruit Company y las compañías muelleras en Guatemala.* Guatemala: Ministerio de Educación Pública, 1950.

Deutsch, Hermann Bacher. *The Incredible Yanqui: The Career of Lee Christmas.* New York: Longmans, Green and Company, 1931.

Diaz Rozzotto, Jaime. *El carácter de la revolución guatemalteca.* México: Ediciones Revista "Horizonte," 1958.

Drake, Paul W. *The Money Doctor in the Andes: The Kemmerer Missions, 1923–1933.* Durham: Duke University Press, 1989.

―――, ed. *Money Doctors, Foreign Debts, and Economic Reforms in Latin America from the 1890s to the Present.* Wilmington, DE: Scholarly Resources, 1993.

Dunkerley, James. *Power in the Isthmus: A Political History of Modern Central America.* London: Verso, 1988.

Galich, Manuel. *Guatemala.* Havana: Casa de las Américas, 1968.

García Laguardia, Jorge Mario. *La reforma liberal en Guatemala: vida política y orden constitucional.* Guatemala: Editorial Universitaria, Universidad de San Carlos de Guatemala, 1985.

Gellman, Irwin F. *Good Neighbor Diplomacy: U.S. Policies in Latin America, 1933–1945*. Baltimore: Johns Hopkins University Press, 1979.

Gleijeses, Piero. *Shattered Hope: The Guatemalan Revolution and the United States, 1944–1954*. Princeton: Princeton University Press, 1991.

González, Nancie L. Solien. *Black Carib Household Structure: A Study of Migration and Modernization*. Seattle: University of Washington Press, 1969.

González Dávison, Fernando. *El régimen liberal en Guatemala (1871–1944)*. Guatemala: Editorial Universitaria, Universidad de San Carlos de Guatemala, 1987.

Gould, Charles A. *The Last Titan: Percival Farquhar, American Entrepreneur in Latin America*. Stanford: Institute of Hispanic American and Luso-Brazilian Studies, Bolívar House, Stanford University, 1964.

Grieb, Kenneth J. *Guatemalan Caudillo: The Regime of Jorge Ubico, Guatemala, 1931–1944*. Athens: Ohio University Press, 1979.

Griffith, William J. *Empires in the Wilderness: Foreign Colonization and Development in Guatemala, 1834–1844*. Chapel Hill: University of North Carolina Press, 1965.

Handy, Jim. *Gift of the Devil: A History of Guatemala*. Boston: South End Press, 1984.

Hatch, John Keith. *Minor C. Keith: Pioneer of the American Tropics*. N.p., 1963.

Herrera Soto, Roberto, and Rafael Romero Castañeda. *La zona bananera del Magdalena*. Bogotá: Instituto Caro y Cuervo, 1979.

Herrick, Thomas. *Desarrollo económico y político de Guatemala durante el período de Justo Rufino Barrios (1871–1885)*. Translated by Rafael Piedra-Santa Arandi. Guatemala: Editorial Universitaria Centroamericana, 1974.

Immerman, Richard H. *The CIA in Guatemala: The Foreign Policy of Intervention*. Austin: University of Texas Press, 1982.

International Bank for Reconstruction and Development. *The Economic Development of Guatemala; Report of a Mission Sponsored by the International Bank for Reconstruction and Development, in Collaboration with the Government of Guatemala*. Baltimore: Johns Hopkins University Press, 1951.

Ireland, Gordon. *Boundaries, Possessions, and Conflicts in Central and North America and the Caribbean*. 2d ed. New York: Octagon Books, 1971.

Jonas, Susanne. *The Battle for Guatemala: Rebels, Death Squads, and U.S. Power*. Boulder, CO: Westview Press, 1991.

Jonas, Susanne, and David Tobis, eds. *Guatemala*. Berkeley: North American Congress on Latin America, 1974.

Jones, Chester Lloyd. *Guatemala: Past and Present*. 1940. Reprint. New York: Russell & Russell, 1966.

Josephson, Matthew. *The Robber Barons*. 1934. Reprint. New York: Harcourt Brace Jovanovich, 1962.

Karnes, Thomas. *The Failure of Union: Central America, 1824–1975*. Tempe: Arizona State University, Center for Latin American Studies, 1976.

———. *Tropical Enterprise: The Standard Fruit and Steamship Company in Latin America*. Baton Rouge: Louisiana State University Press, 1978.

Kemble, John Haskell. *The Panama Route, 1848–1869*. Berkeley and Los Angeles: University of California Press, 1943.

Kendrick, J. W. *A Report upon International Railways of Central America, Located in the Republics of Guatemala and Salvador*. Chicago: N.p., 1921.

Kepner, Charles David. *Social Aspects of the Banana Industry*. 1936. Reprint. New York: AMC Press, 1967.

Kepner, Charles David, and Jay H. Soothill. *The Banana Empire: A Case Study of Economic Imperialism*. 1935. Reprint. New York: Russell & Russell, 1963.

Krehm, William. *Democracies and Tyrannies of the Caribbean*. Westport, CT: Lawrence Hill & Company, 1984.

LaFeber, Walter. *Inevitable Revolutions: The United States in Central America*. New York: W. W. Norton, 1983.

Langley, Lester D. *The United States and the Caribbean in the Twentieth Century*. Athens: University of Georgia Press, 1980.

Lewis, Oscar. *The Big Four: The Story of Huntington, Stanford, Hopkins, and Crocker, and of the Building of the Central Pacific*. 1938. Reprint. New York: Alfred A. Knopf, 1966.

Long, Rodney W. *Railways of Central America and the West Indies*. Washington: U.S. Department of Commerce, Bureau of Foreign and Domestic Commerce, Trade Promotion Series, no. 5, 1925.

López Larrave, Mario. *Breve historia del movimiento sindical guatemalteco*. Guatemala: Editorial Universitaria, 1976.

Macleod, Murdo. *Spanish Central America: A Socio-Economic History, 1520–1720*. Berkeley: University of California Press, 1973.

McBeth, B. S. *Juan Vicente Gómez and the Oil Companies in Venezuela, 1908–1935*. Cambridge: Cambridge University Press, 1983.

McCann, Thomas P. *An American Company: The Tragedy of United Fruit*. New York: Crown Publishers, 1976.

McCreery, David. *Development and State in Reforma Guatemala, 1871–1885*. Athens: Ohio University Center for International Studies, 1983.

McNeely, John H. *The Railways of Mexico: A Study in Nationalization*. El Paso: Texas Western College, Southwestern Studies, Monograph no. 5, 1964.

Marroquín Rojas, Clemente. *La Bomba, historia del primer atentado contra Estrada Cabrera*. Guatemala: Tipografía Nacional, 1967.

————. *Los cadetes, historia del segundo atentado contra Estrada Cabrera*. Guatemala: Tipografía Sánchez y de Guise, 1930.

May, Stacy, and Galo Plaza. *The United Fruit Company in Latin America*. New York: National Planning Association, 1958.

Monteforte Toledo, Mario. *La revolución en Guatemala*. Guatemala: Editorial Universitaria, 1975.

Moreno S., Rubén. *Ecuador, economía y política en el último siglo*. Quito: Facultad de Ciencias Económicas, 1984.

Morris, James A. *Honduras: Caudillo Politics and Military Rulers*. Boulder: Westview Press, 1984.

Mosley, Leonard. *Dulles: A Biography of Eleanor, Allen, and John Foster Dulles and Their Family Network*. New York: The Dial Press, 1978.

Munro, Dana G. *The Five Republics of Central America*. New York: Oxford University Press, 1918.

————. *Intervention and Dollar Diplomacy in the Caribbean, 1900–1921*. Princeton: Princeton University Press, 1964.

————. *The United States and the Caribbean Republics, 1921–1933*. Princeton: Princeton University Press, 1974.

Obando Sánchez, Antonio. *Memorias: la historia del movimiento obrero*. Guatemala: Editorial Universitaria, 1978.

Peckenham, Nancy, and Annie Street, eds. *Honduras: Portrait of a Captive Nation*. New York: Praeger, 1985.

Perez-Brignoli, Hector. *A Brief History of Central America*. Translated by Ricardo B. Sawrey A. and Susana Stettri de Sawrey. Berkeley and Los Angeles: University of California Press, 1989.

Poitevín, Rene. *El proceso de industrialización en Guatemala*. San José: Editorial Universitaria Centroamericana, 1977.

Posas, Mario, and Rafael del Cid. *La construcción del sector público y del estado nacional de Honduras, 1876–1979*. San José: Editorial Universitaria Centroamericana, 1981.

Pruessen, Ronald W. *John Foster Dulles: The Road to Power*. New York: The Free Press, 1982.

Reynolds, Philip Keep. *The Banana: Its History, Cultivation and Place Among Staple Foods*. Boston: Houghton Mifflin, 1927.

Rodríguez Beteta, Virgilio. *No es guerra de hermanos sino de bananos; como evite la guerra en Centroamérica en 1928*. Guatemala: Universidad de San Carlos, 1969.

Ross, Delmer G. *Visionaries and Swindlers: The Development of Railways of Honduras*. Mobile: Institute for Research in Latin America, 1975.

Sáenz, Alfredo. *La situación bananera en los países del Caribe*. San José: Imprenta Borrasé, 1928.

Salazar, Carlos. *Memoria de los servicios prestados a la nación, 1908–1944*. 2d. ed. Guatemala: Grupo Literario Editorial, 1987.

Sands, William F. *Our Jungle Diplomacy*. Chapel Hill: University of North Carolina Press, 1944.

Schlesinger, Stephen, and Stephen Kinzer. *Bitter Fruit: The Untold Story of the American Coup in Guatemala*. New York: Doubleday, 1982.

Schneider, Ronald. *Communism in Guatemala, 1944–1954*. New York: Praeger, 1959.

Schoonover, Thomas. *The United States in Central America, 1860–1911*: *Episodes of Social Imperialism and Imperial Rivalry in the World System*. Durham: Duke University Press, 1991.

Sealy, Theodore. *Jamaica's Banana Industry: A History of the Banana Industry with Particular Reference to the Part Played by the Jamaica Banana Producers Association, Ltd*. Kingston: The Association, 1984.

Solórzano Fernández, Valentín. *Evolución Económica de Guatemala*. 4th ed. Guatemala: Ministerio de Educación, Editorial José de Piñeda Ibarra, 1977.

Steward, Dick. *Trade and Hemisphere: The Good Neighbor Policy and Reciprocal Trade*. Columbia: University of Missouri Press, 1975.

Stewart, Watt. *Keith and Costa Rica: A Biographical Study of Minor C. Keith*. Albuquerque: University of New Mexico Press, 1964.

Toriello, Guillermo. *Tras la cortina de banano*. México: Fondo de Cultura Económica, 1976.

Torres-Rivas, Edelberto. *Interpretación del desarrollo social centroamericano; procesos y estructuras de una sociedad dependiente*. 2d ed. San José: EDUCA, 1971.

Vaughan, Walter. *The Life and Work of Sir William Van Horne*. New York: The Century Company, 1920.

White, Judith. *Historia de una ignominia: la United Fruit Co. en Colombia*. Bogotá: Editorial Presencia, 1978.

Wilson, Charles Morrow. *Empire in Green and Gold: The Story of the American Banana Trade*. 1947. Reprint. New York: Greenwood Publishers, 1968.

Wilson, Hugh. *The Education of a Diplomat*. London: Longmans, Green and Company, 1938.

Woodward, Ralph Lee, Jr. *Central America: A Nation Divided*. 2d. ed. New York: Oxford University Press, 1985.

———. *Class Privilege and Economic Development: The Consulado de Comercio of Guatemala, 1793–1871*. Chapel Hill: University of North Carolina Press, 1966.

Wortman, Miles. *Government and Society in Central America, 1680–1840*. New York: Columbia University Press, 1982.

Wyld Ospina, Carlos. *El autócrata: ensayo político social*. Guatemala: Tipografía Sánchez & De Guise, 1929.

Young, John P. *Central American Currency and Finance*. Princeton: Princeton University Press, 1925.

Zanetti, Oscar, ed. *United Fruit Company: un caso del dominio imperialista en Cuba*. Habana: Editorial de Ciencias Sociales, 1976.

Articles

Arrivillaga, Alfonso, and Alfredo Gómez. "Antecedentes históricos, movilizaciones sociales y reivindicaciones étnicas en la Costa Atlántica de Guatemala." *Estudios Sociales Centroamericanos* 48 (1988): 35–47.

Baker, George W., Jr. "The Woodrow Wilson Administration and Guatemalan Relations." *The Historian* 27:2 (1965): 155–69.

Birdseye, Sidney H. "The Guatemala-Honduras Boundary Survey." *Bulletin of the Pan American Union* 69:9 (September 1935): 700–711.

Brown, Stanley. "United Fruit's Shotgun Marriage." *Fortune* 79 (April 1969): 132–34.

Calvert, Peter. "The Last Occasion on which Britain Used Coercion to Settle a Dispute with a Non-Colonial Territory in the Caribbean: Guatemala and the Powers, 1909–1913." *Inter-American Economic Affairs* 25:3 (1971): 57–75.

Cutter, Victor M. "Caribbean Tropics in Commercial Transition." *Economic Geography* 2:4 (October 1926): 494–507.

Dawson, Frank Griffith. "Labor Legislation and Social Integration in Guatemala: 1871–1944." *The American Journal of Comparative Law* 14 (1965–66): 124–42.

Dinwoodie, David Hepburn. "Dollar Diplomacy in Light of the Guatemalan Loan Project, 1909–1913." *The Americas* 26:3 (1970): 237–53.

"Empire Builder." *The Nation* July 3, 1929, 5.

Figueroa Ibarra, Carlos. "Contenido de clase y participación obrera en el movimiento antidictatorial de 1920." *Política y Sociedad* 4 (July–December 1977): 5–51.

———. "La insurrección armada de 1920 en Guatemala." *Política y Sociedad* [Guatemala] 8 (July–December 1979): 91–142.

Ghidinelli, Azzo. "Aspectos Económicos de la Cultura de los Caribes Negros del Municipio de Livingston." *Guatemala Indígena* 7:4 (1972): 71–152.

Grieb, Kenneth J. "Negotiating a Reciprocal Trade Agreement with an Underdeveloped Country: Guatemala as a Case Study." *Prologue* 5 (Spring 1973): 23–29.

Jerez, César. "La United Fruit Company en Guatemala." *Estudios Centroamericanos* [San Salvador] 26:269 (1971): 117–28.

Kemmerer, Donald L., and Bruce R. Dalgaard. "Inflation, Intrigue, and Monetary Reform in Guatemala, 1919–1926." *The Historian* 46:1 (1983): 21–38.

Kit, Wade. "The Fall of Guatemalan Dictator, Manuel Estrada Cabrera: U.S. Pressure or National Opposition." *Canadian Journal of Latin American and Caribbean Studies* 15:29 (1990): 105–28.

Kobler, John. "Sam the Banana Man." *Life* 30:8 (February 19, 1951): 83–84.

Laínez, Vilma, and Victor Meza. "El enclave bananero en la historia de Honduras." *Anuario de Estudios Centroamericanos* 1 (1974): 187–225.

LeGrand, Catherine. "Colombian Transformations: Peasants and the Wage Labourers in the Santa Marta Banana Zone." *Journal of Peasant Studies* 11:4 (1984): 178–200.

Lewis, Colin M. "The Financing of Railway Development in Latin America, 1850–1914." *Ibero-Amerikanisches Archiv* 9:3–4 (1983): 255–78.

McCreery, David. "Coffee and Class: The Structure of Development in Liberal Guatemala." *Hispanic American Historical Review* 56:3 (August 1976): 438–60.

———."Debt Servitude in Rural Guatemala, 1876–1936." *Hispanic American Historical Review* 63:4 (1983): 735–59.

———. "An Odious Feudalism: Mandamiento Labor and Commercial Agriculture in Guatemala, 1858–1920." *Latin American Perspectives* 13:1 (1986): 99–117.

Mosk, Sanford A. "The Coffee Economy of Guatemala, 1850–1918: Development and Signs of Instability." *Inter-American Economic Affairs* 4 (1955): 6–20.

Neruda, Pablo. "The United Fruit Co." *Monthly Review* 18:4 (September 1966): 32–33.

Palmer, Jesse T. "The Banana in the Caribbean Trade." *Economic Geography* 8:3 (July 1932): 262–73.

Parsons, James J. "Bananas in Ecuador: A New Chapter in the History of Tropical Agriculture." *Economic Geography* 33 (1957): 201–16.

Penney, William T. "Notas y comentarios sobre acontecimientos y experiencias vividos durante mis viajes por México y Centroamérica." *Mesoamérica* 16 (1988): 361–77.

Platt, Raye R. "The Guatemala-Honduras Boundary Dispute." *Foreign Affairs*: 7:2 (January 1929): 323–26.

Pringle, Henry F. "A Jonah Who Swallowed the Whale." *American Magazine* 116 (September 1933): 45.

Rippy, J. Fred. "Relations of the United States and Guatemala during the Epoch of Justo Rufino Barrios." *Hispanic American Historical Review* 22:4 (1942): 595–605.

Ross, Delmer G. "The Construction of the Interoceanic Railroad of Guatemala." *The Americas* 33:3 (January 1977): 430–56.

Schoonover, Thomas and Ebba. "Statistics for an Understanding of Foreign Intrusions into Central America from the 1820s to 1930." *Anuario de Estudios Centroamericanos* 15:1 (1989): 93–117.

Segreda Sagot, Gilda, and Jorge Arriaga. "El proceso histórico en la formación urbana guatemalteca (1773–1944)." *Anuario de Estudios Centroamericanos* 7 (1981): 43–69.

Seidel, Robert N. "American Reformers Abroad: The Kemmerer Missions in South America, 1923–1931." *Journal of Economic History* 32:2 (June 1972): 520–45.

Smith, Carol A. "El desarrollo de la primacía urbana, la dependencia en la exportación, y la formación de clases en Guatemala." *Mesoamérica* 8 (1984): 195–278.

Solow, Herbert. "The Ripe Problems of United Fruit." *Fortune* 59 (March 1959): 97–99.

Taracena Arriola, Arturo. "La Confederación Obrera de Centro América (COCA): 1921–1928." *Anuario de Estudios Centroamericanos* 10 (1984): 81–93.

———. "Presencia anarquista en Guatemala entre 1920 y 1932." *Mesoamérica* 15 (1988): 1–23.

———. "El primer Partido Comunista de Guatemala (1922–1932); Diez años de una historia olvidada." *Anuario de Estudios Centroamericanos* 15:1 (1989): 49–63.

Tisdell, E. F. "Guatemalan Railroad Construction." *Bulletin of the Pan American Union*, 32 (February 1911): 270–76.

"United Fruit." *Fortune* 7:3 (March 1933): 24–38.

Wagner, Regina. "Actividades empresariales de los alemanes en Guatemala, 1850–1920." *Mesoamérica* 13 (June 1987): 87–123.

Warner, Patrick. "Garifuna Genesis: The Sad Story of a Displaced People." *African Commentary* 2:3 (March 1990): 26–28.

Whitfield, Stephen J. "Strange Fruit: The Career of Samuel Zemurray." *American Jewish History* 73 (March 1984): 307–23.

Woodward, Ralph Lee, Jr. "The Historiography of Modern Central America since 1960." *Hispanic American Historical Review* 67:3 (1987): 461–96.

———. "Pensamiento científico y desarrollo económico en Centroamérica, 1860–1920." *Revista del pensamiento Centroamericano* 36 (1981): 73–86.

Unpublished Documents

Anderson, Wayne Foster. "The Development of Export Transportation in Liberal Guatemala, 1871–1920." Ph.D. dissertation, Tulane University, 1985.

Bartlett, Wilson Randolph. "Lorenzo Dow Baker and the Development of the Banana Trade between Jamaica and the U.S., 1881–1890." Ph.D. dissertation, American University, 1977.

Beck, Warren Albert. "American Policy in Guatemala, 1839–1900." Ph.D. dissertation, Ohio State University, 1958.

Berger, Susan Ann. "State and Agrarian Development: Guatemala (1931–1978)." Ph.D. dissertation, Columbia University, 1986.

Chomsky, Aviva. "Plantation Society, Land and Labor on Costa Rica's Atlantic coast, 1870–1940." Ph.D. dissertation, University of California, Berkeley, 1990.

D'Antoni, Vincent Blaise. "A Case Study and Critique of the United Fruit Company and the Consent Decree." DBA dissertation, Washington University, 1965.

Dinwoodie, David Hepburn. "Expedient Diplomacy: The United States and Guatemala, 1898–1920." Ph.D. dissertation, University of Colorado, Boulder, 1966.

Dosal, Paul. "Dependency, Revolution, and Industrial Development in Guatemala, 1821–1986." Ph.D. dissertation, Tulane University, 1987.

Jackson, Henry Franklin. "The Technological Development of Central America, 1823–1913." Ph.D. dissertation, University of Chicago, 1948.

LaBarge, Richard Allan. "A Study of United Fruit Company Operations in Isthmian America, 1946–1956." Ph.D. dissertation, Duke University, 1960.

McCreery, David. "Developmental Aspects of the Construction of the Guatemala Northern Railroad: The First Attempt, 1879 to 1885." M.A. thesis, Tulane University, 1969.

McKibbin, Davidson B. "Percival Farquhar: American Promoter in Latin America, 1900–1914." Ph.D. dissertation, University of Chicago, 1950.

Nañez Falcón, Guillermo. "Erwin Paul Dieseldorf, German Entrepreneur in the Alta Verapaz of Guatemala, 1889–1937." Ph.D. dissertation, Tulane University, 1970.

Palmer, Steven Paul. "A Liberal Discipline: Inventing Nations in Guatemala and Costa Rica, 1870–1900." Ph.D. dissertation, Columbia University, 1990.

Pitti, Joseph A. "Jorge Ubico and Guatemalan Politics in the 1920s." Ph.D. dissertation, University of New Mexico, 1975.

Rendon, Mary Catherine. "Manuel Estrada Cabrera: Guatemalan President, 1898–1920." Ph.D. dissertation, Oxford University, 1987.

Ross, Delmer G. "The Construction of the Railroads of Central America." Ph.D. dissertation, University of California, Santa Barbara, 1970.

Ruddick, Girard B. "A Study in Monopoly: The United Fruit Company." M.A. thesis, Duke University, 1929.

Williams, John L. "The Rise of the Banana Industry and Its Influence on Caribbean Countries." M.A. thesis, Clark University, 1925.

Index

Latin American Silhouettes
Studies in History and Culture

William H. Beezley and
Judith Ewell
Editors

_____

Volumes Published

William H. Beezley and Judith Ewell, eds., *The Human Tradition in Latin America: The Twentieth Century* (1987). Cloth ISBN 0-8420-2283-X Paper ISBN 0-8420-2284-8

Judith Ewell and William H. Beezley, eds., *The Human Tradition in Latin America: The Nineteenth Century* (1989). Cloth ISBN 0-8420-2331-3 Paper ISBN 0-8420-2332-1

David G. LaFrance, *The Mexican Revolution in Puebla, 1908–1913: The Maderista Movement and the Failure of Liberal Reform* (1989). ISBN 0-8420-2293-7

Mark A. Burkholder, *Politics of a Colonial Career: José Baquíjano and the Audiencia of Lima*, 2d ed. (1990). Cloth ISBN 0-8420-2353-4 Paper ISBN 0-8420-2352-6

Kenneth M. Coleman and George C. Herring, eds. (with Foreword by Daniel Oduber), *Understanding the Central American Crisis: Sources of Conflict, U.S. Policy, and Options for Peace* (1991). Cloth ISBN 0-8420-2382-8   Paper ISBN 0-8420-2383-6

Carlos B. Gil, ed., *Hope and Frustration: Interviews with Leaders of Mexico's Political Opposition* (1992). Cloth ISBN 0-8420-2395-X Paper ISBN 0-8420-2396-8

Charles Bergquist, Ricardo Peñaranda, and Gonzalo Sánchez, eds., *Violence in Colombia: The Contemporary Crisis in Historical Perspective* (1992). Cloth ISBN 0-8420-2369-0 Paper ISBN 0-8420-2376-3

Heidi Zogbaum, *B. Traven: A Vision of Mexico* (1992). ISBN 0-8420-2392-5

Jaime E. Rodríguez O., ed., *Patterns of Contention in Mexican History* (1992). ISBN 0-8420-2399-2

Louis A. Pérez, Jr., ed., *Slaves, Sugar, and Colonial Society: Travel Accounts of Cuba, 1801–1899* (1992). Cloth ISBN 0-8420-2354-2 Paper ISBN 0-8420-2415-8

Peter Blanchard, *Slavery and Abolition in Early Republican Peru* (1992). Cloth ISBN 0-8420-2400-X Paper ISBN 0-8420-2429-8

Paul J. Vanderwood, *Disorder and Progress: Bandits, Police, and Mexican Development*. Revised and Enlarged Edition (1992). Cloth ISBN 0-8420-2438-7 Paper ISBN 0-8420-2439-5

Sandra McGee Deutsch and Ronald H. Dolkart, eds., *The Argentine Right: Its History and Intellectual Origins, 1910 to the Present* (1993). Cloth ISBN 0-8420-2418-2 Paper ISBN 0-8420-2419-0

Jaime E. Rodríguez O., ed., *The Evolution of the Mexican Political System* (1993). ISBN 0-8420-2448-4

Steve Ellner, *Organized Labor in Venezuela, 1958–1991: Behavior and Concerns in a Democratic Setting* (1993). ISBN 0-8420-2443-3

Paul J. Dosal, *Doing Business with the Dictators: A Political History of United Fruit in Guatemala, 1899–1944* (1993). ISBN 0-8420-2475-1

Marquis James, *Merchant Adventurer: The Story of W. R. Grace* (1993). ISBN 0-8420-2444-1

John C. Chasteen and Joseph S. Tulchin, eds., *Problems in Modern Latin American History: A Reader* (1993). Cloth ISBN 0-8420-2327-5 Paper ISBN 0-8420-2328-3